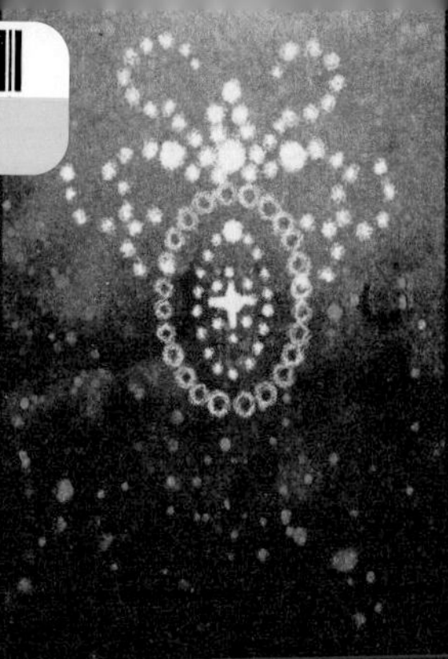

While traveling, I met a driver. I promised I'd use his name in one of my stories... It was a casual comment, not very serious.

I never came up with a character that fit the name, so I didn't get a chance to use it, even after several years. In the final chapter of this volume, however, I finally kept my promise.

It was a ridiculously tiny promise made in a foreign land. But it kept bugging me.

There are too many promises that can't be kept or will never be carried out. Leaving a promise unfulfilled gets under my skin.

Again, today, I find myself making a promise.

—Hiroyuki Asada, 2010

Hiroyuki Asada made his debut in *Monthly Shonen Jump* in 1986. He's best known for his basketball manga *I'll*. He's a contributor to artist Range Murata's quarterly manga anthology *Robot*. *Tegami Bachi: Letter Bee* is his most recent series.

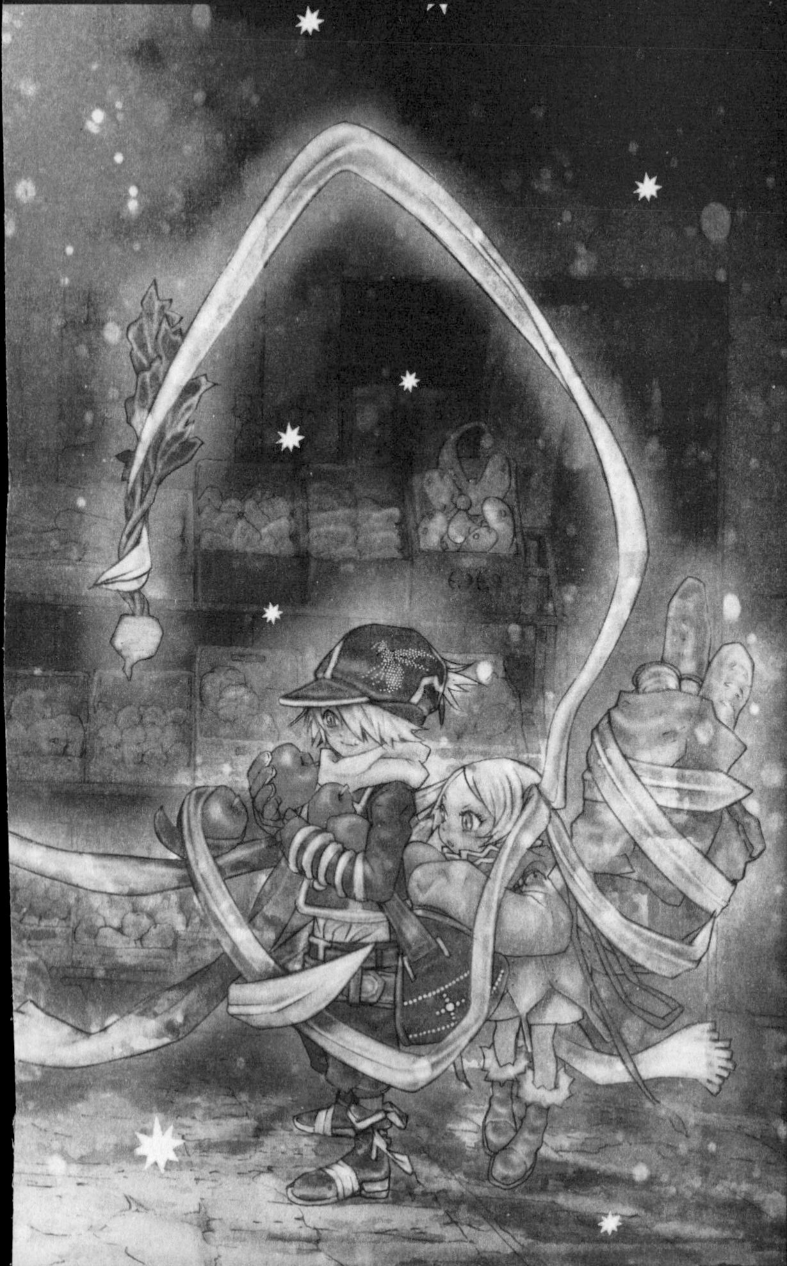

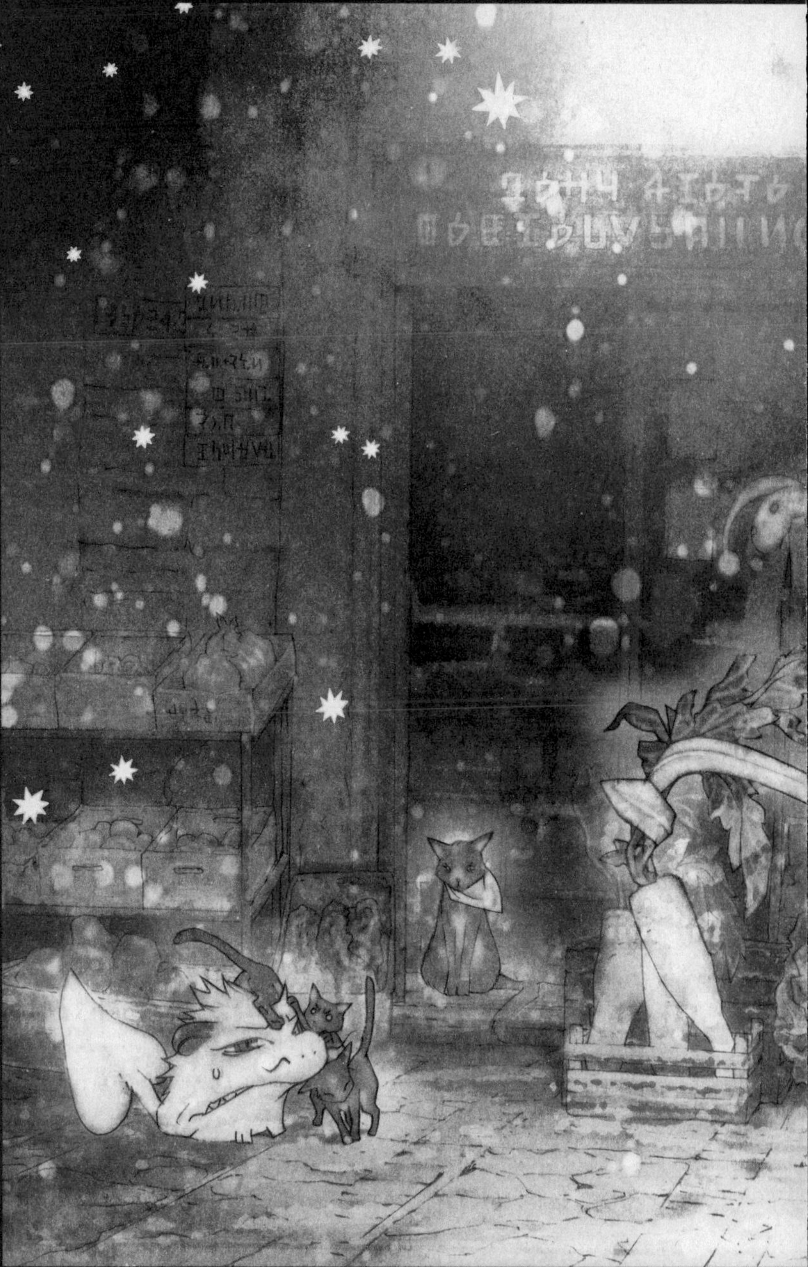

# Tegami Bachi
## LETTER · BEE

Volume 9

SHONEN JUMP Manga Edition

Story and Art by Hiroyuki Asada

English Adaptation/Rich Amtower
Translation/JN Productions
Touch-up & Lettering/Annaliese Christman
Design/Amy Martin
Editor/Shaenon K. Garrity

TEGAMIBACHI © 2006 by Hiroyuki Asada. All rights reserved.
First published in Japan in 2006 by SHUEISHA Inc., Tokyo. English
translation rights arranged by SHUEISHA Inc.

Printed in the U.S.A.

Published by VIZ Media, LLC
P.O. Box 77010
San Francisco, CA 94107

10 9 8 7 6 5 4 3 2 1
First printing, May 2012

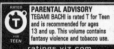

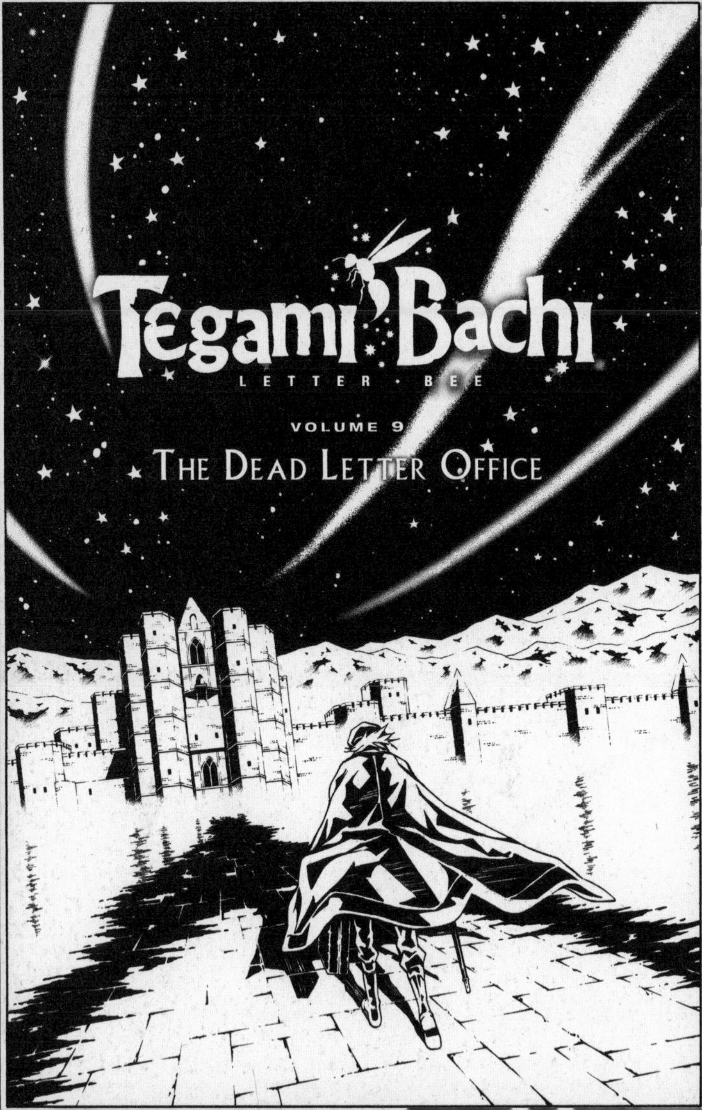
Tegami Bachi
LETTER BEE
VOLUME 9
THE DEAD LETTER OFFICE

This is a country known as Amberground, where night never ends.

Its capital, Akatsuki, is illuminated by a man-made sun. The farther one strays from the capital, the weaker the light. The Yuusari region is cast in twilight; the Yodaka region survives only on pale moonlight.

Letter Bee Gauche Suede and young Lag Seeing meet in the Yodaka region— a postal worker and the "letter" he must deliver. In their short time together, they form a fast friendship, but when the journey ends, each departs down his own path. Gauche longs to become Head Bee, while Lag himself wants to be a Letter Bee, like Gauche.

In time, Lag becomes a Letter Bee. He learns that Gauche has lost his *heart* and become a marauder named Noir, working for the rebel organization Reverse. Lag's only hope for saving Gauche is a Shindan called Letter Bullet, which may awaken his lost memories.

In the town of Lament, Lag discovers that the local convent is a front for a Reverse base and infiltrates it disguised as a girl. He overhears a plot to use human sacrifices to summon a Gaichuu to attack the capital. When Sunny, a girl from the convent, loses her *heart* to the Gaichuu, Lag is consumed with rage and enveloped in a strange glow. He shoots his Letter Bullet into Gauche, who loses consciousness...

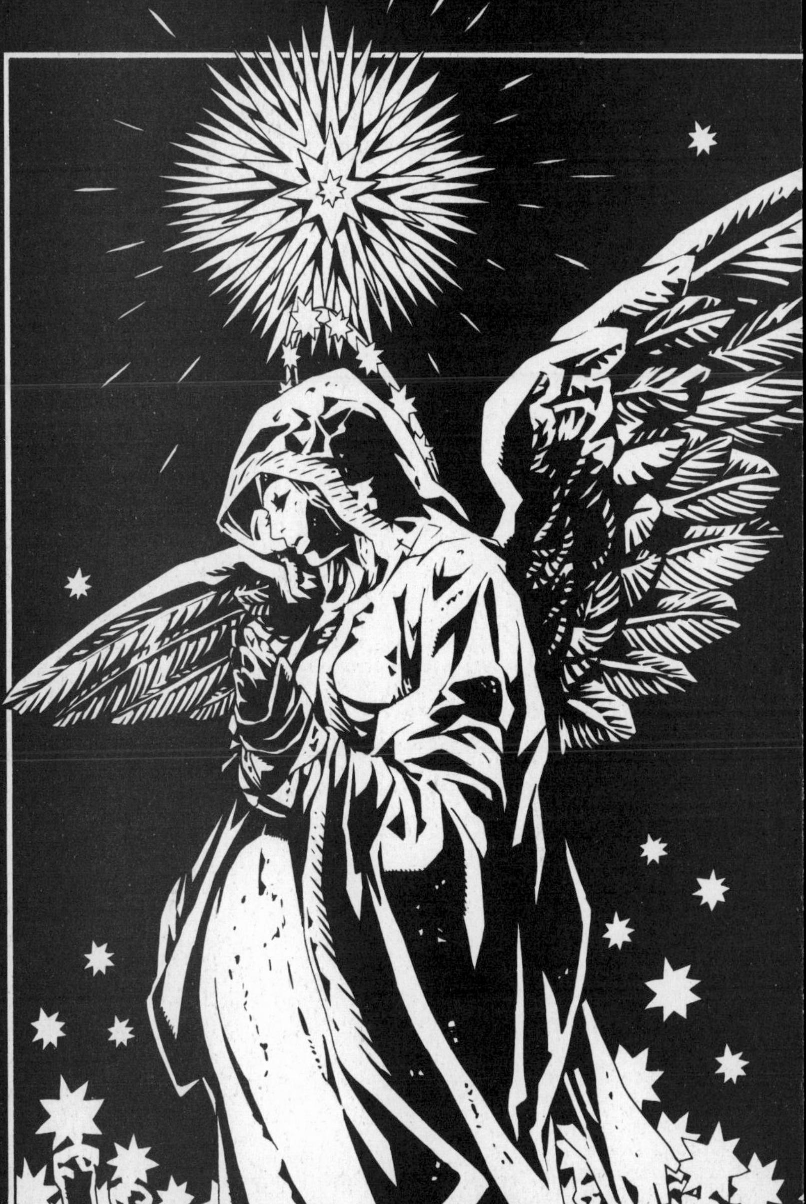

# LIST OF CHARACTERS

**ARGO LLOYD**
Beehive Director

**ARIA LINK**
Beehive Assistant
Director

**LAG SEEING**
Letter Bee

**DR. THUNDERLAND, JR.**
Member of the AG
Biological Science
Advisory Board,
Third Division and
Head doctor at the
Beehive

**CONNOR KLUFF**
Letter Bee

**STEAK**
Niche's...
live bait?

**NICHE**
Lag's
Dingo

**GUS**
Connor's Dingo

**ZAZIE**
Letter Bee

**WASIOLKA**
Zazie's Dingo

**JIGGY PEPPER**
Express Delivery
Letter Bee

**HARRY**
Jiggy's Dingo

**MOC SULLIVAN**
Letter Bee

**THE MAN WHO COULD
NOT BECOME SPIRIT**
The ringleader of
Reverse

# Tegami Bachi
### LETTER · BEE

**VOLUME 9**
## THE DEAD LETTER OFFICE

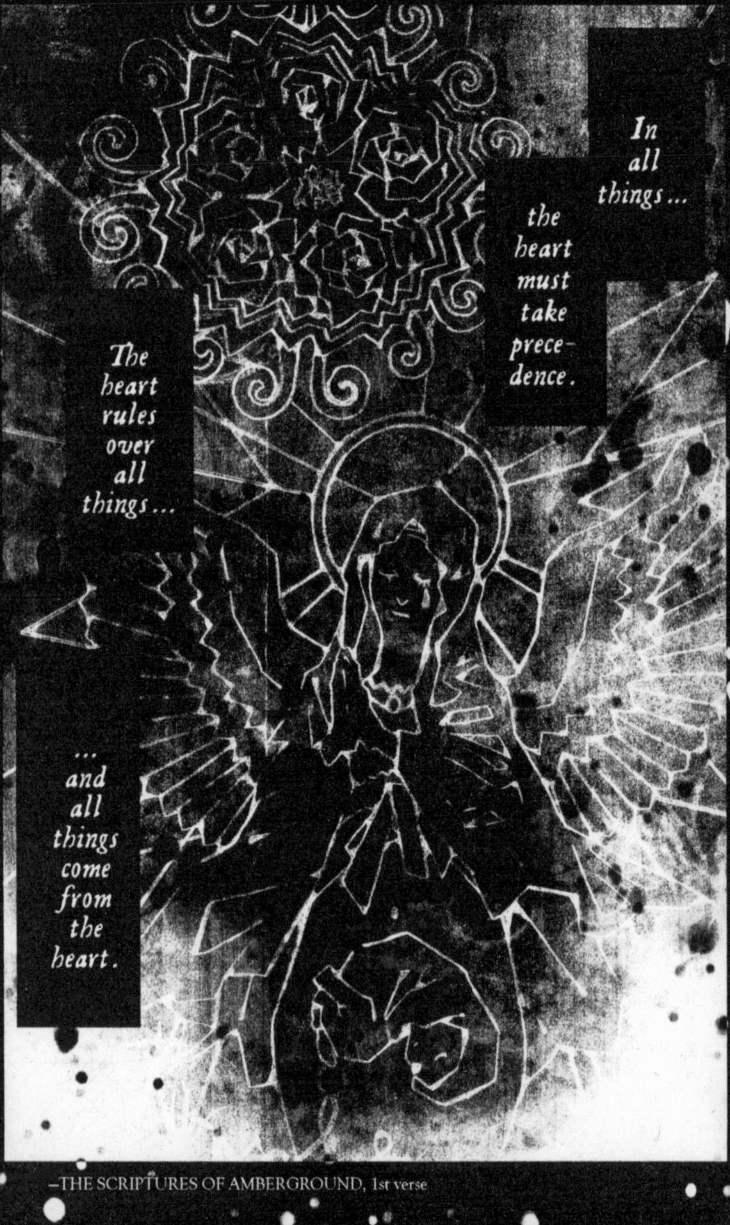
In all things...
the heart must take precedence.
The heart rules over all things...
...and all things come from the heart.

–THE SCRIPTURES OF AMBERGROUND, 1st verse

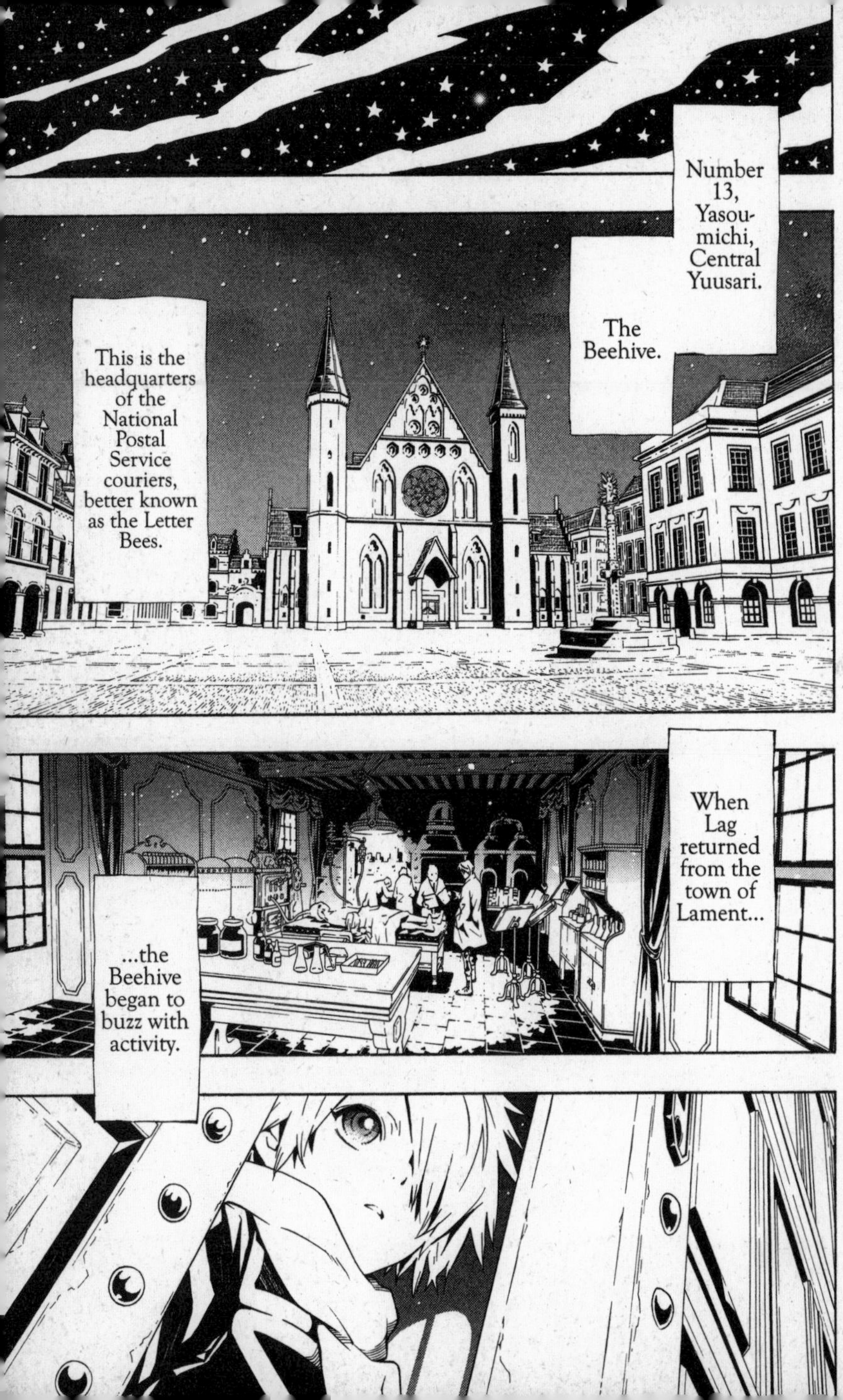
Number 13, Yasou-michi, Central Yuusari.
The Beehive.
This is the headquarters of the National Postal Service couriers, better known as the Letter Bees.
When Lag returned from the town of Lament...
...the Beehive began to buzz with activity.

# Chapter 31: Back to the Beehive

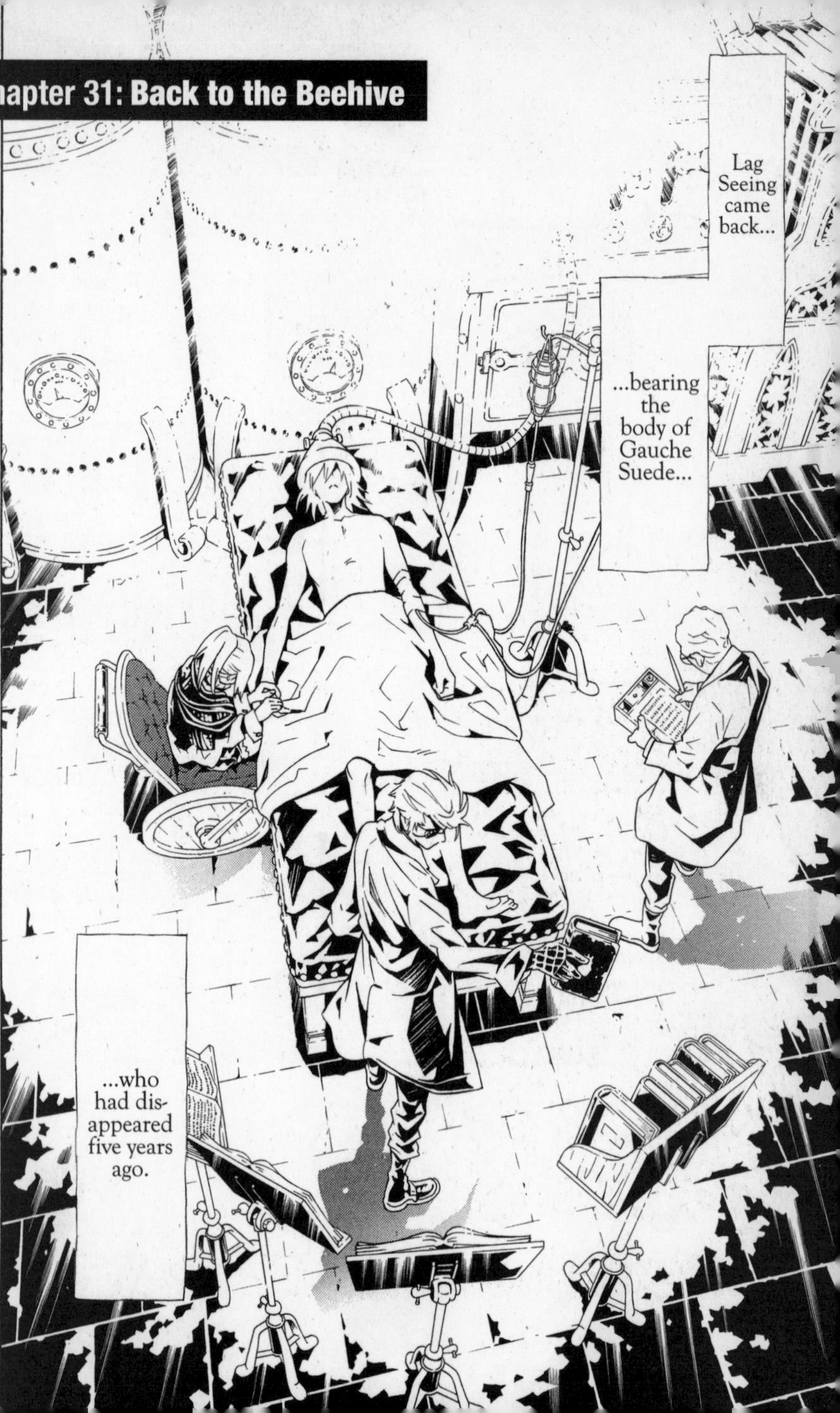
Lag Seeing came back...
...bearing the body of Gauche Suede...
...who had disappeared five years ago.

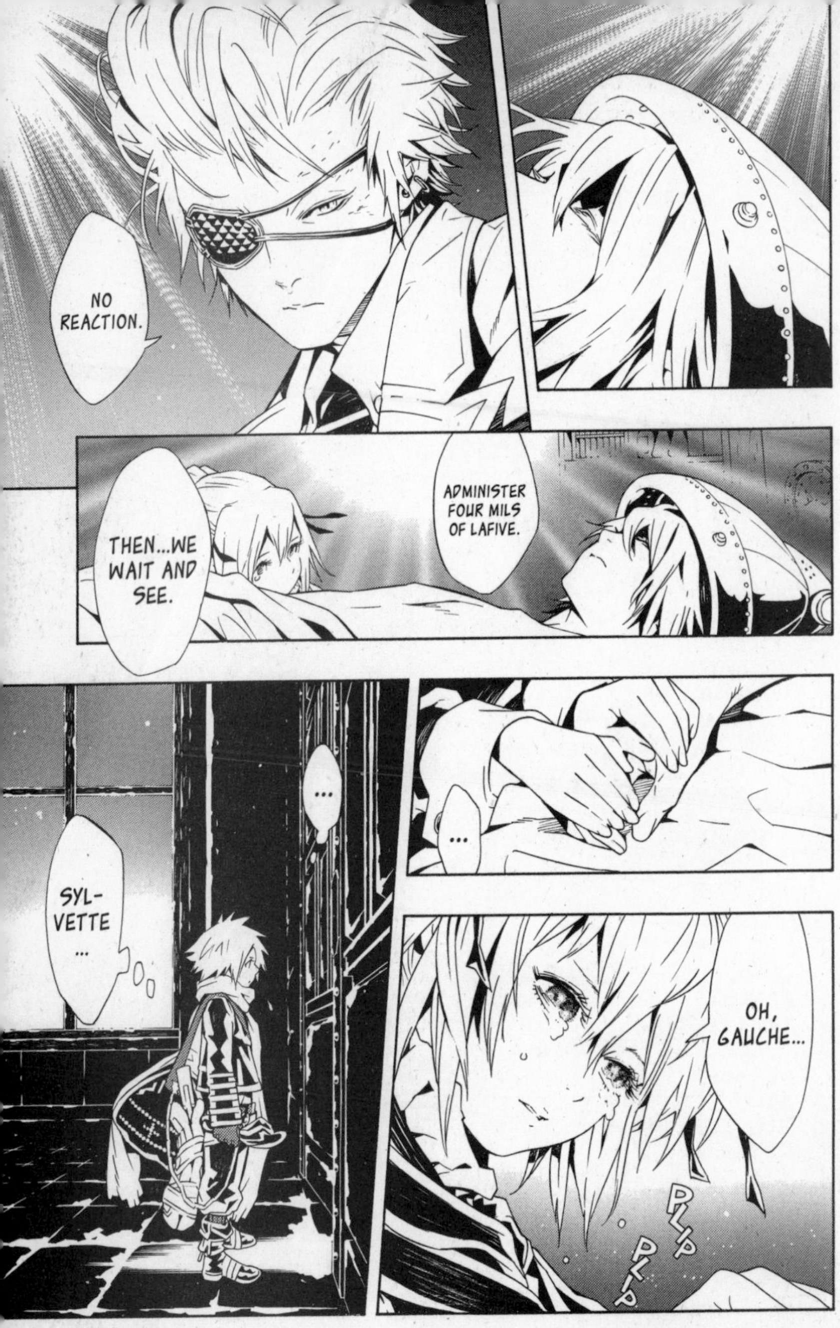
NO REACTION.
ADMINISTER FOUR MILS OF LAFIVE.
THEN...WE WAIT AND SEE.
...
OH, GAUCHE...
PLIP
PLIP
...
SYL-VETTE ...

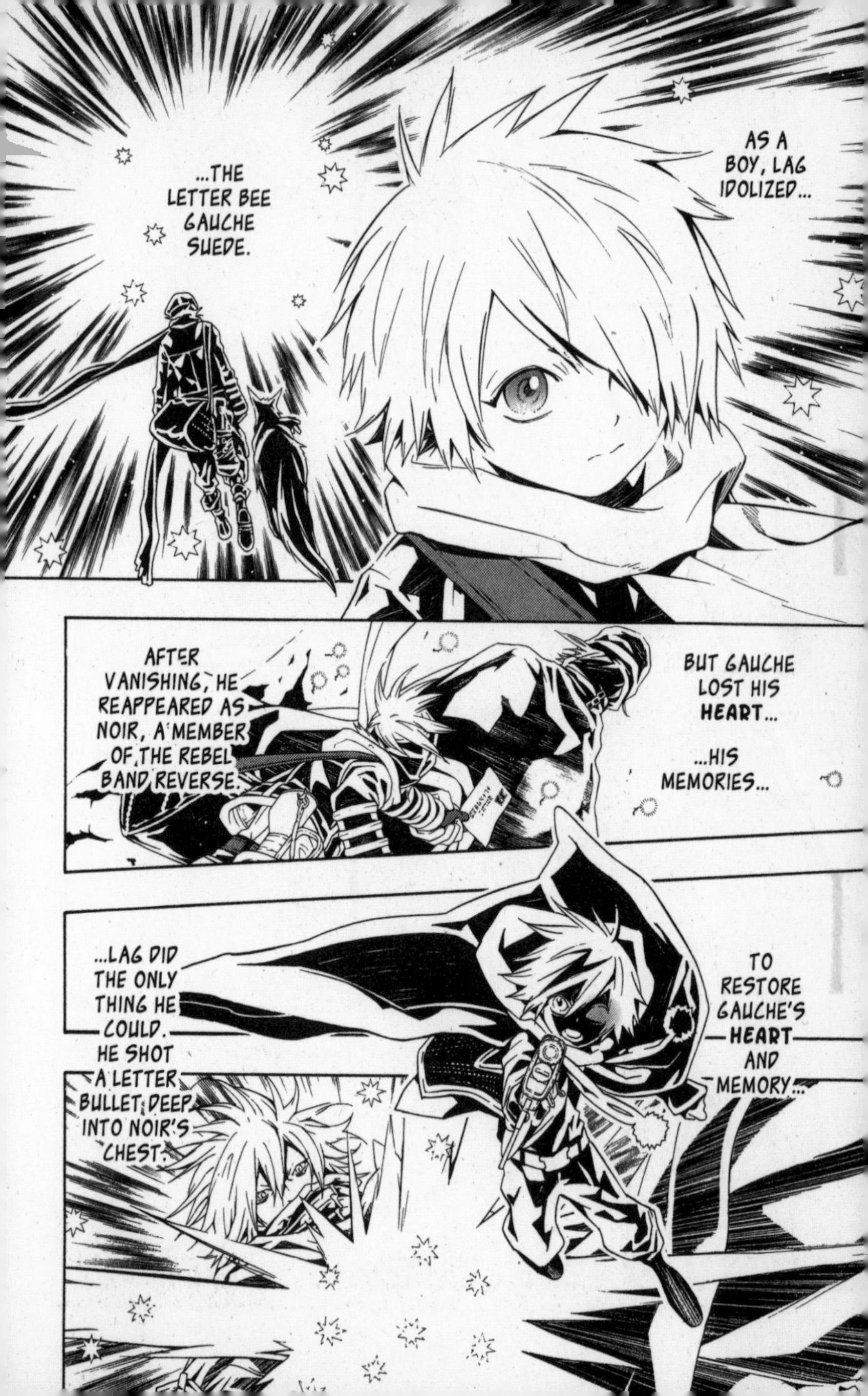
AS A BOY, LAG IDOLIZED...
...THE LETTER BEE GAUCHE SUEDE.
BUT GAUCHE LOST HIS HEART...
...HIS MEMORIES...
AFTER VANISHING, HE REAPPEARED AS NOIR, A MEMBER OF THE REBEL BAND REVERSE.
TO RESTORE GAUCHE'S HEART AND MEMORY...
...LAG DID THE ONLY THING HE COULD. HE SHOT A LETTER BULLET DEEP INTO NOIR'S CHEST.

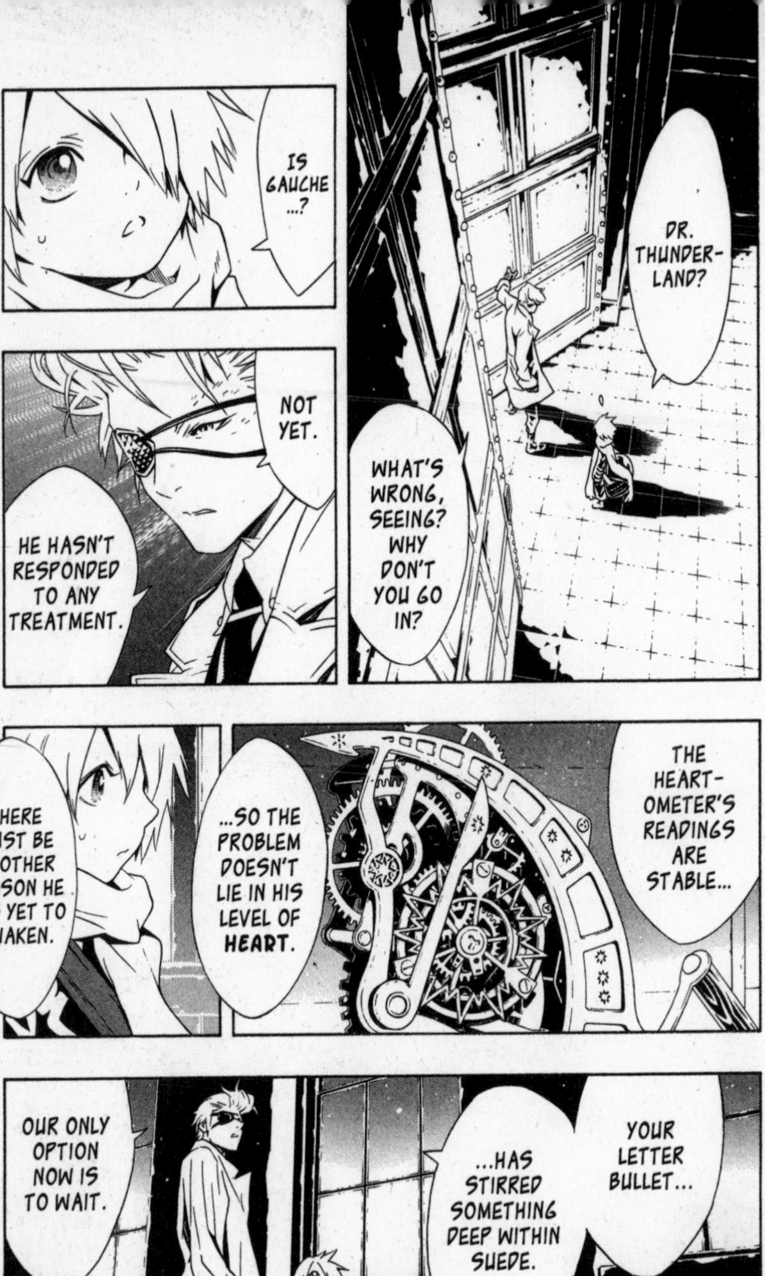
DR. THUNDER-LAND?
WHAT'S WRONG, SEEING? WHY DON'T YOU GO IN?
IS GAUCHE ...?
NOT YET.
HE HASN'T RESPONDED TO ANY TREATMENT.
THE HEART-OMETER'S READINGS ARE STABLE...
...SO THE PROBLEM DOESN'T LIE IN HIS LEVEL OF **HEART**.
THERE MUST BE ANOTHER REASON HE HAS YET TO AWAKEN.
YOUR LETTER BULLET...
...HAS STIRRED SOMETHING DEEP WITHIN SUEDE.
OUR ONLY OPTION NOW IS TO WAIT.

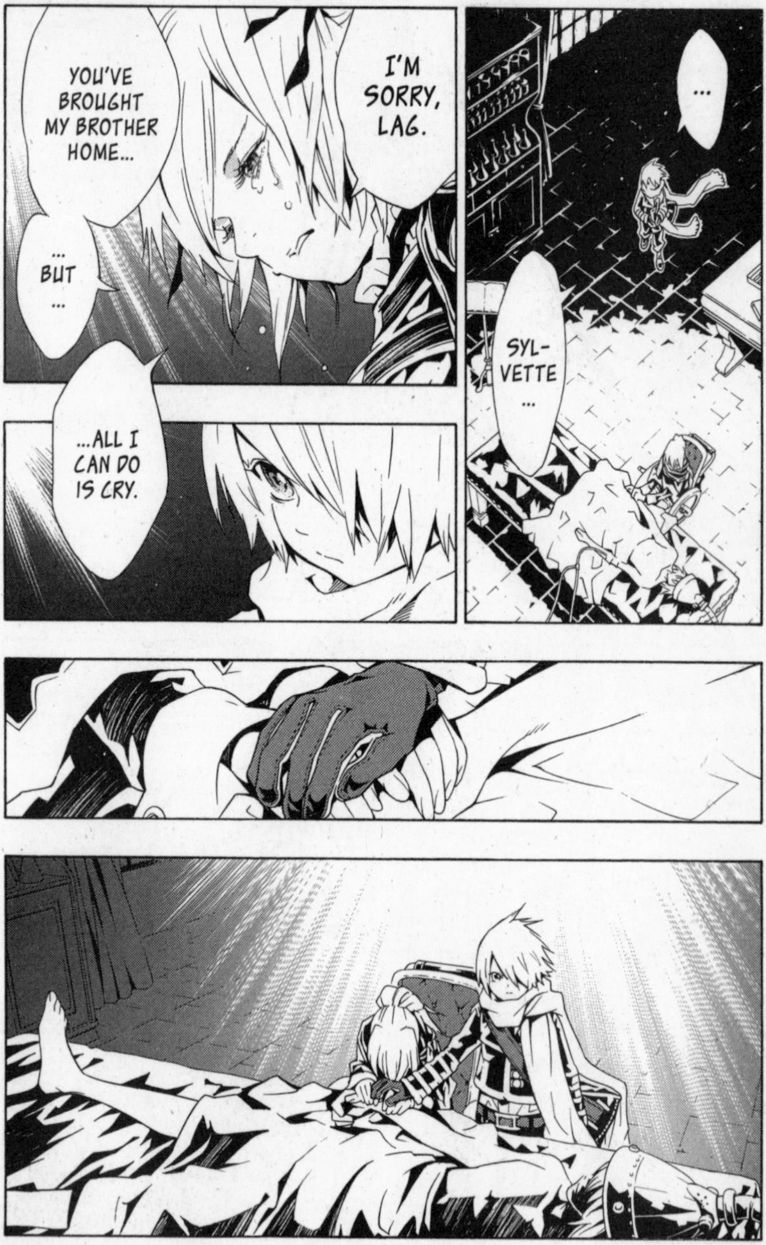
...
SYL-VETTE ...
I'M SORRY, LAG.
YOU'VE BROUGHT MY BROTHER HOME...
... BUT ...
...ALL I CAN DO IS CRY.

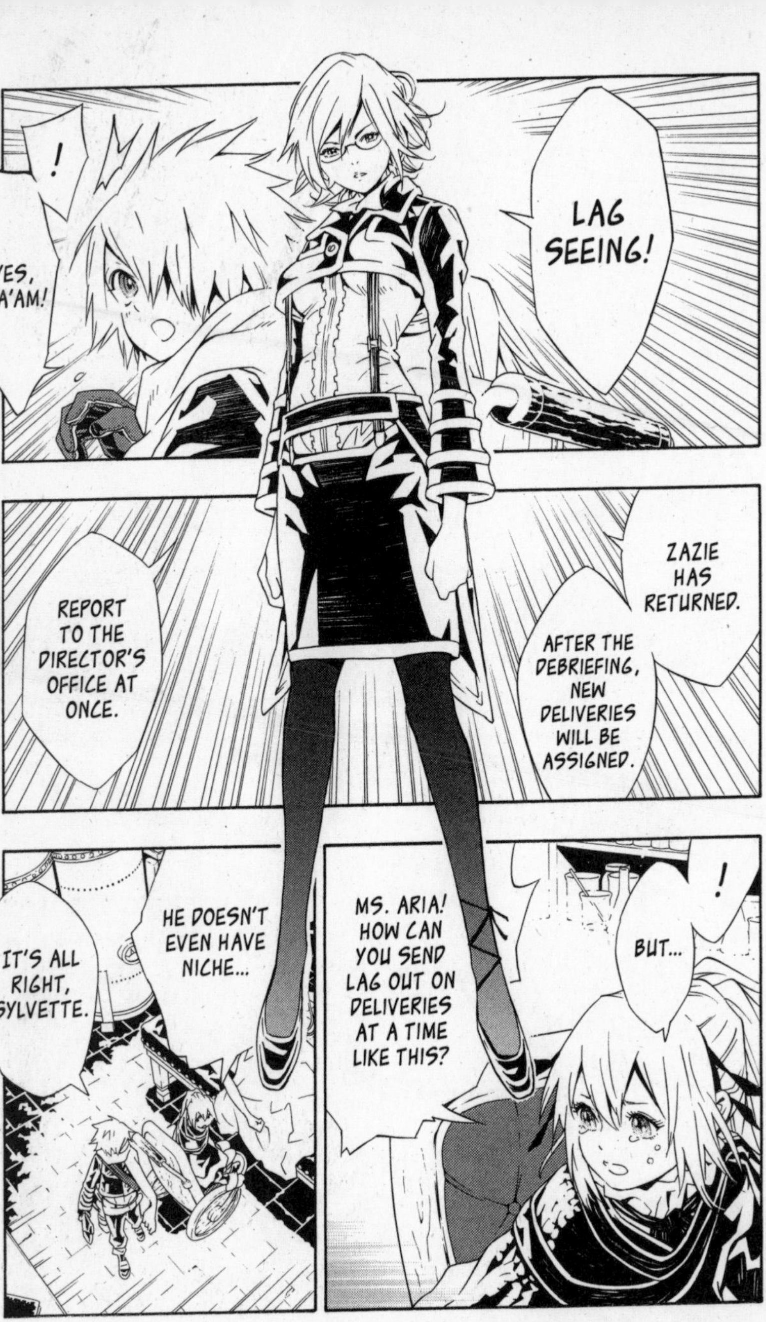
LAG SEEING!
!
YES, MA'AM!
ZAZIE HAS RETURNED.
AFTER THE DEBRIEFING, NEW DELIVERIES WILL BE ASSIGNED.
REPORT TO THE DIRECTOR'S OFFICE AT ONCE.
MS. ARIA! HOW CAN YOU SEND LAG OUT ON DELIVERIES AT A TIME LIKE THIS?
HE DOESN'T EVEN HAVE NICHE...
IT'S ALL RIGHT, SYLVETTE.
!
BUT...

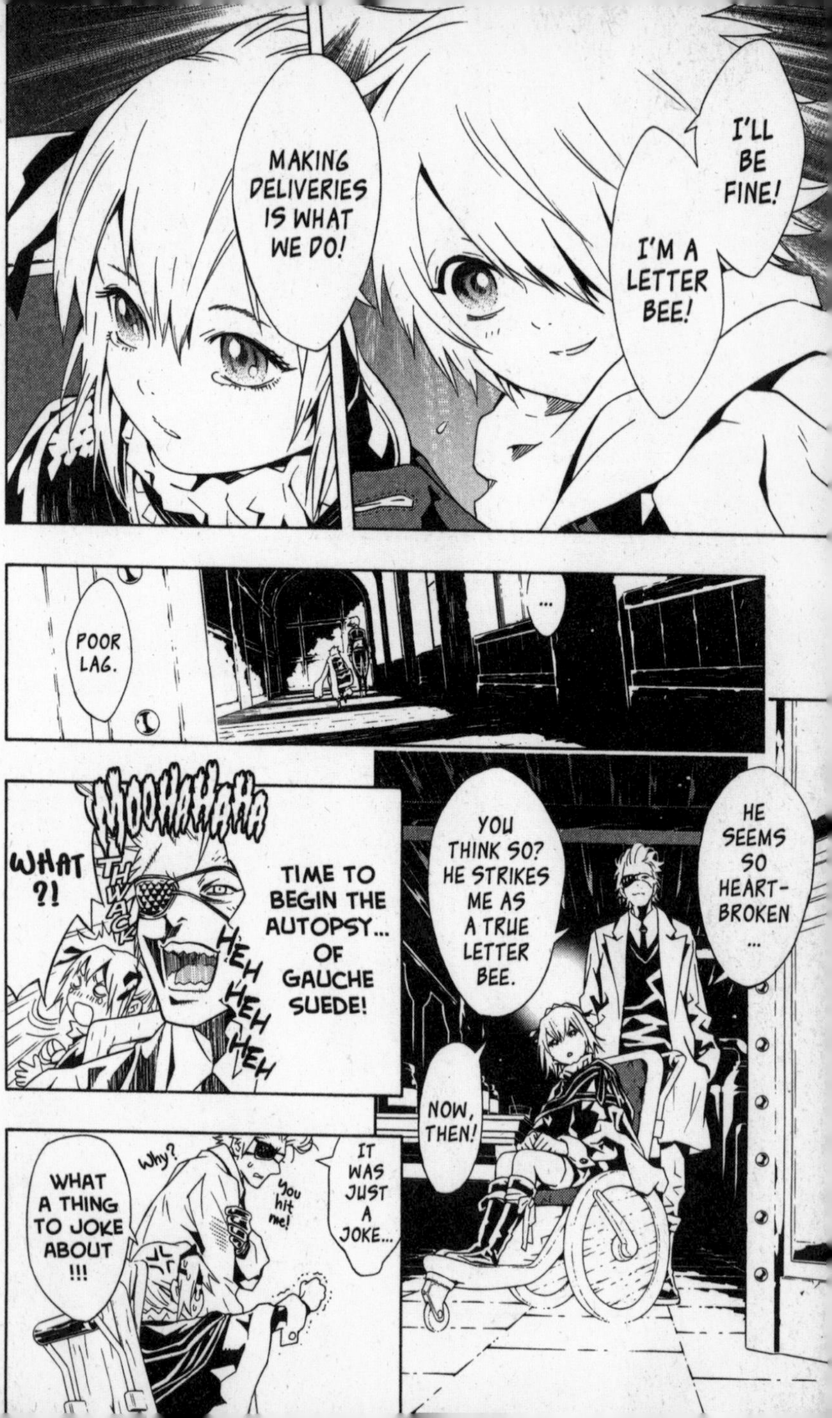
I'LL BE FINE!
I'M A LETTER BEE!
MAKING DELIVERIES IS WHAT WE DO!
...
POOR LAG.
HE SEEMS SO HEART-BROKEN...
YOU THINK SO? HE STRIKES ME AS A TRUE LETTER BEE.
NOW, THEN!
TIME TO BEGIN THE AUTOPSY... OF GAUCHE SUEDE!
MOOHAHAHA
HEH HEH HEH HEH
THWACK
WHAT ?!
IT WAS JUST A JOKE...
Why?
You hit me!
WHAT A THING TO JOKE ABOUT !!!

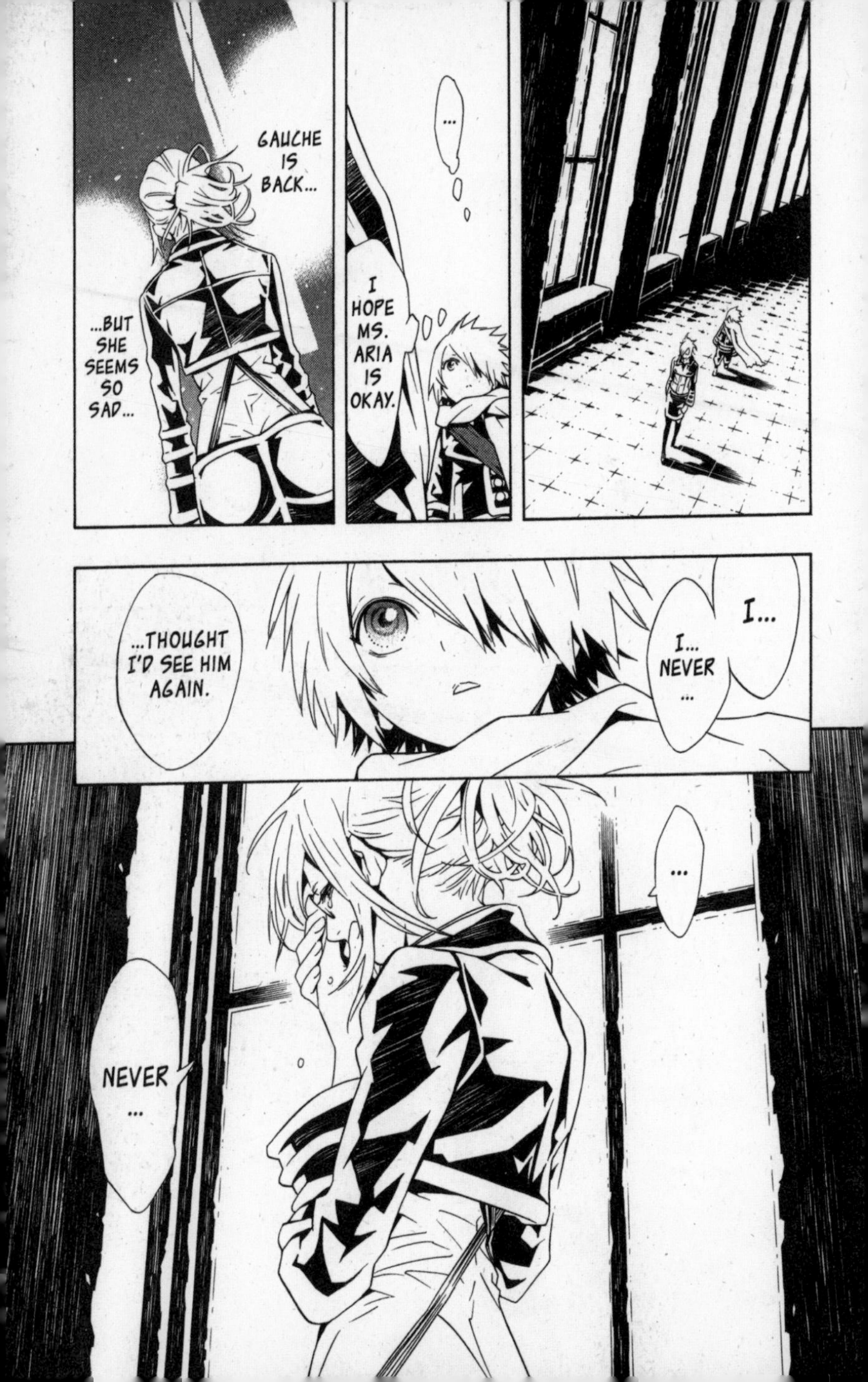
...
I HOPE MS. ARIA IS OKAY.
GAUCHE IS BACK...
...BUT SHE SEEMS SO SAD...
I...
I... NEVER ...
...THOUGHT I'D SEE HIM AGAIN.
...
NEVER ...

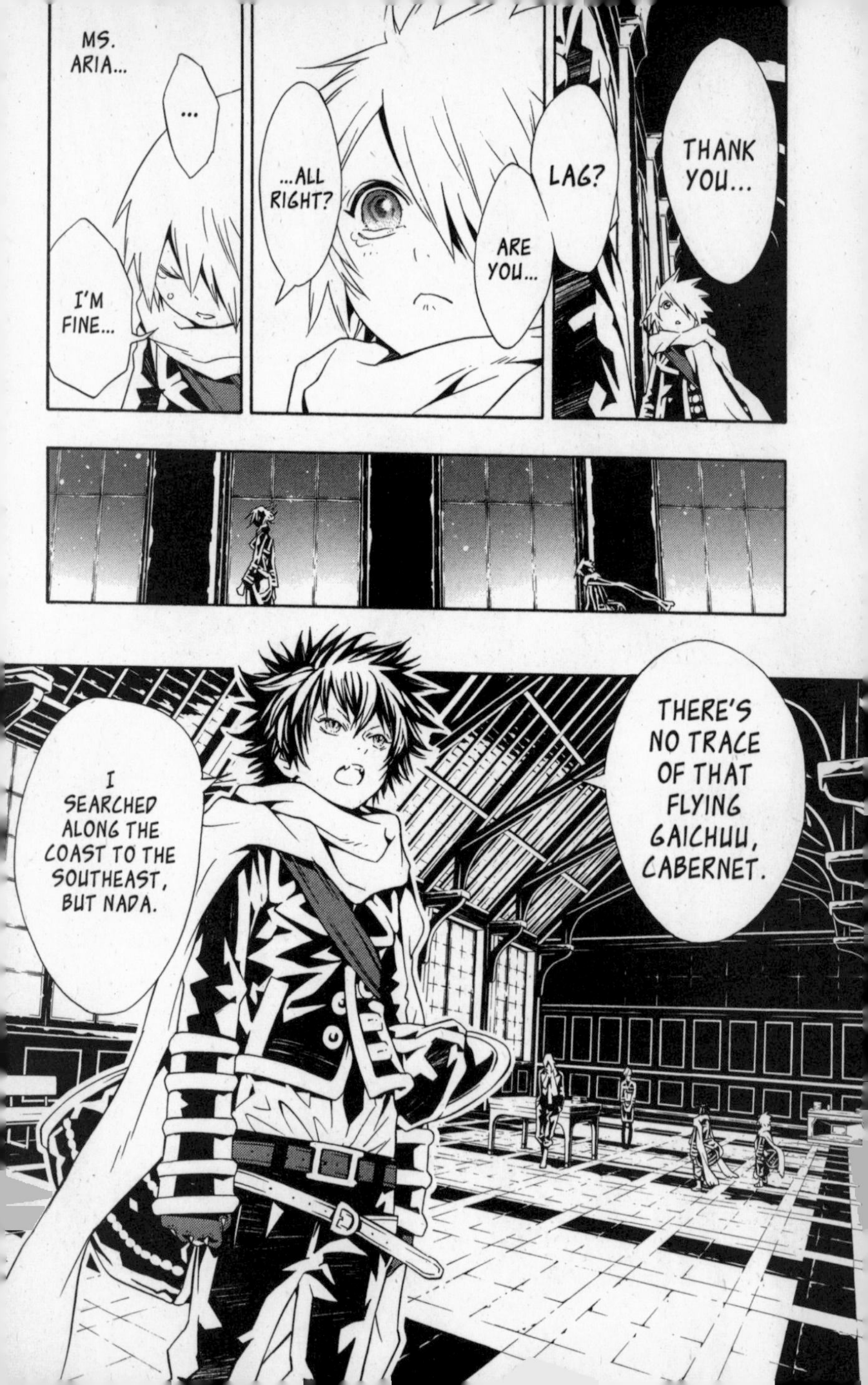
THANK YOU...
LAG?
ARE YOU...
...ALL RIGHT?
MS. ARIA...
...
I'M FINE...
THERE'S NO TRACE OF THAT FLYING GAICHUU, CABERNET.
I SEARCHED ALONG THE COAST TO THE SOUTHEAST, BUT NADA.

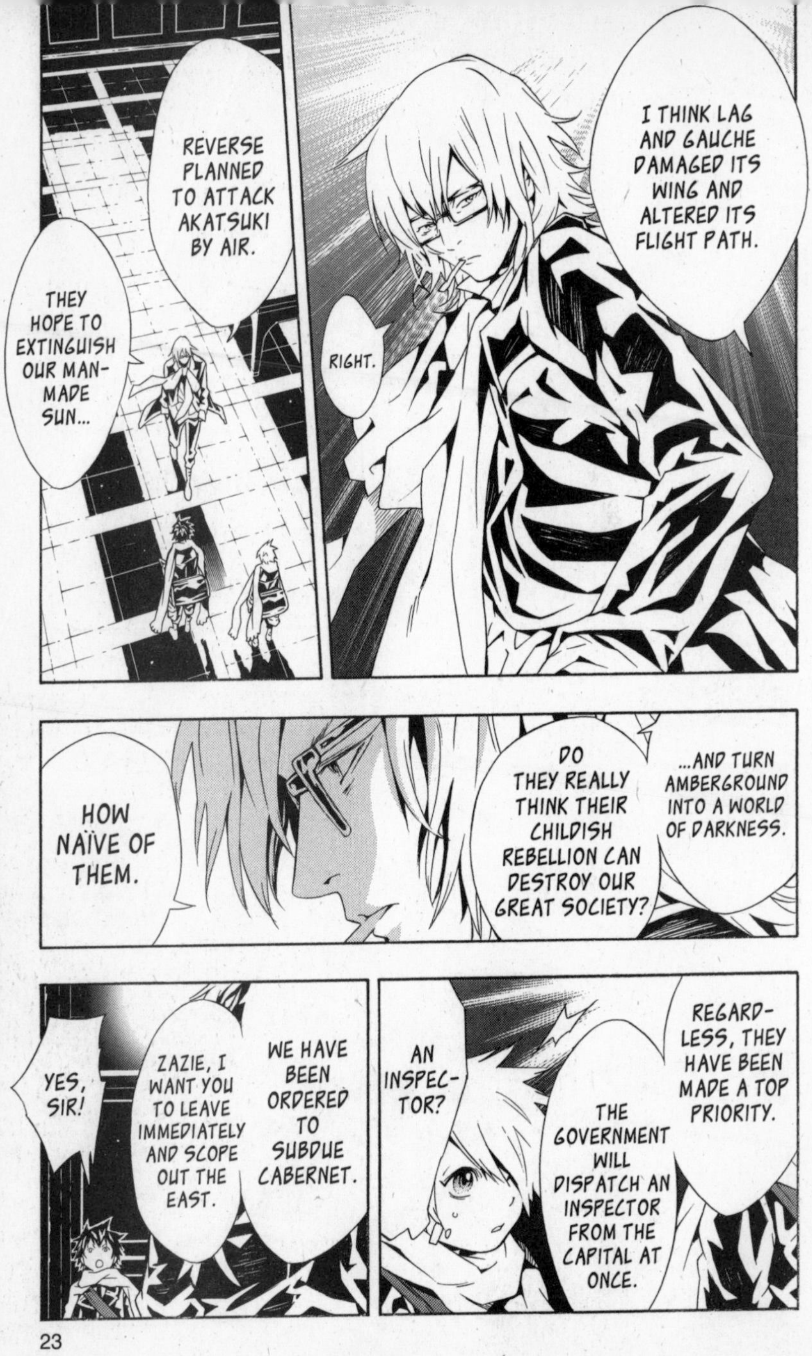
I THINK LAG AND GAUCHE DAMAGED ITS WING AND ALTERED ITS FLIGHT PATH.
RIGHT.
REVERSE PLANNED TO ATTACK AKATSUKI BY AIR.
THEY HOPE TO EXTINGUISH OUR MAN-MADE SUN...
...AND TURN AMBERGROUND INTO A WORLD OF DARKNESS.
DO THEY REALLY THINK THEIR CHILDISH REBELLION CAN DESTROY OUR GREAT SOCIETY?
HOW NAÏVE OF THEM.
REGARDLESS, THEY HAVE BEEN MADE A TOP PRIORITY.
THE GOVERNMENT WILL DISPATCH AN INSPECTOR FROM THE CAPITAL AT ONCE.
AN INSPECTOR?
WE HAVE BEEN ORDERED TO SUBDUE CABERNET.
ZAZIE, I WANT YOU TO LEAVE IMMEDIATELY AND SCOPE OUT THE EAST.
YES, SIR!

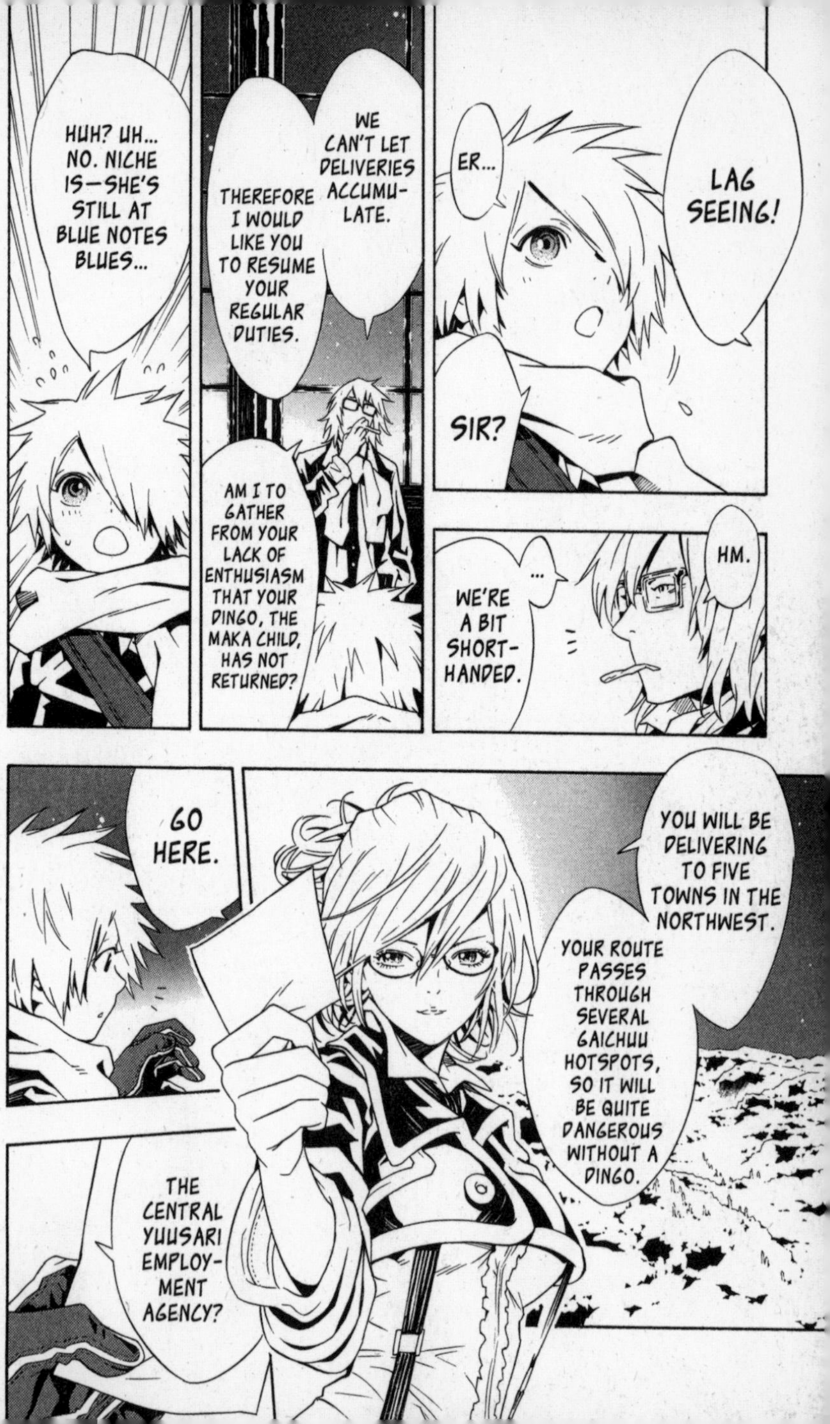
LAG SEEING!
ER...
SIR?
HM.
...
WE'RE A BIT SHORT-HANDED.
WE CAN'T LET DELIVERIES ACCUMU-LATE.
THEREFORE I WOULD LIKE YOU TO RESUME YOUR REGULAR DUTIES.
AM I TO GATHER FROM YOUR LACK OF ENTHUSIASM THAT YOUR DINGO, THE MAKA CHILD, HAS NOT RETURNED?
HUH? UH... NO. NICHE IS—SHE'S STILL AT BLUE NOTES BLUES...
YOU WILL BE DELIVERING TO FIVE TOWNS IN THE NORTHWEST.
YOUR ROUTE PASSES THROUGH SEVERAL GAICHUU HOTSPOTS, SO IT WILL BE QUITE DANGEROUS WITHOUT A DINGO.
GO HERE.
THE CENTRAL YUUSARI EMPLOY-MENT AGENCY?

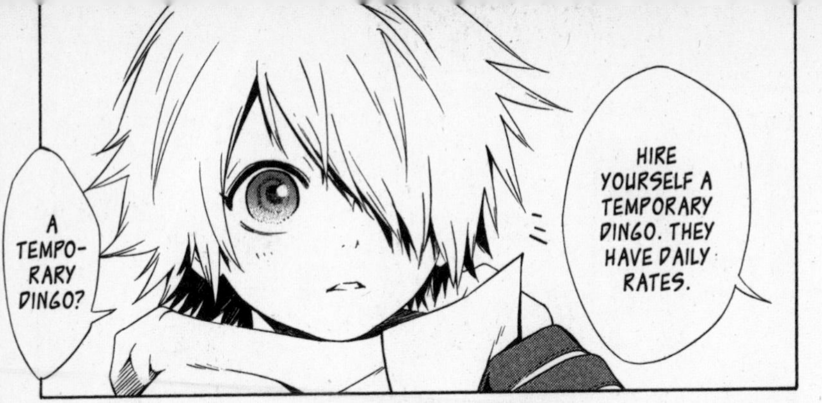
HIRE YOURSELF A TEMPORARY DINGO. THEY HAVE DAILY RATES.
A TEMPO-RARY DINGO?

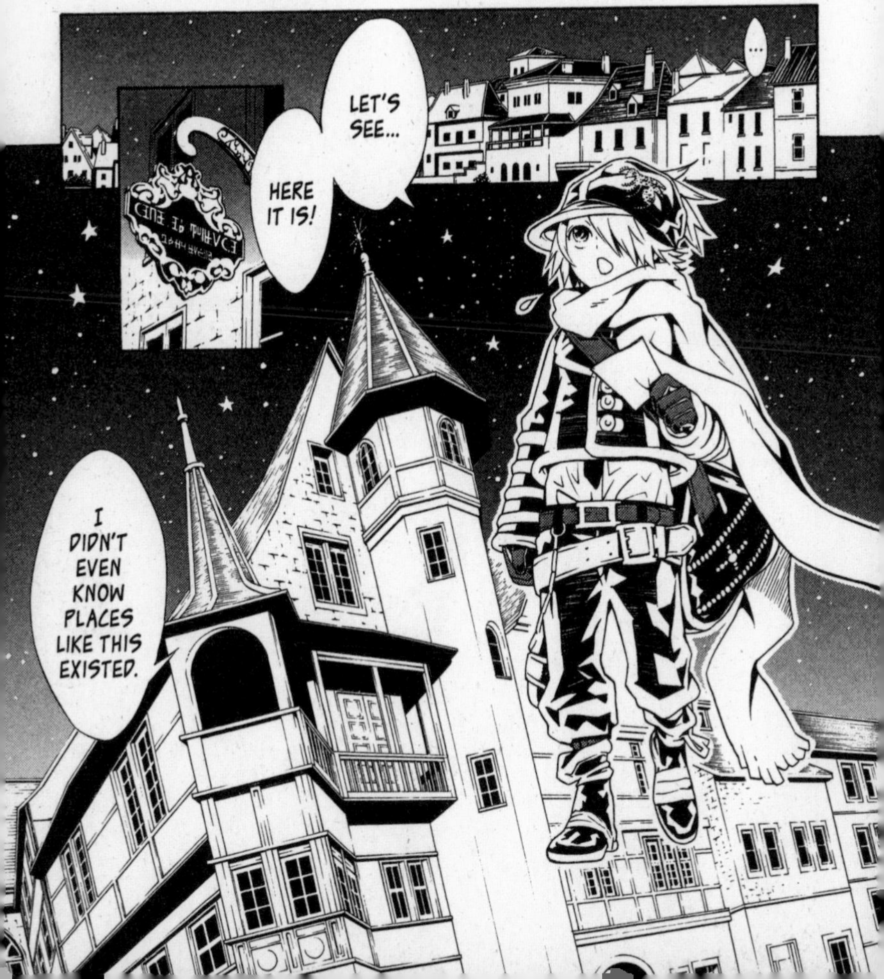
...
LET'S SEE...
HERE IT IS!
I DIDN'T EVEN KNOW PLACES LIKE THIS EXISTED.

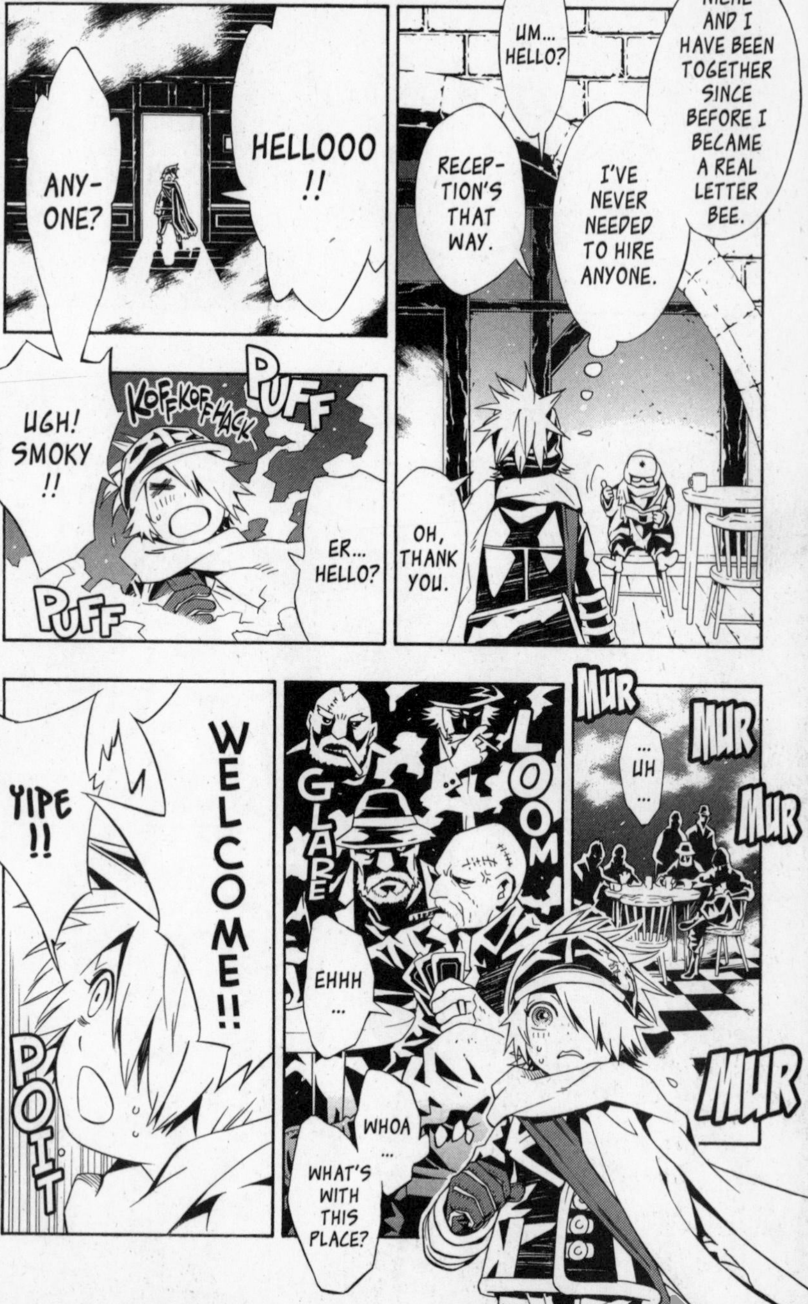
NICHE AND I HAVE BEEN TOGETHER SINCE BEFORE I BECAME A REAL LETTER BEE.
UM... HELLO?
I'VE NEVER NEEDED TO HIRE ANYONE.
RECEP-TION'S THAT WAY.
OH, THANK YOU.
HELLOOO!!
ANY-ONE?
PUFF
KOFF KOFF HACK
UGH! SMOKY!!
ER... HELLO?
PUFF
MUR
MUR
...UH...
MUR
MUR
LOOM
GLARE
EHHH...
WHOA...
WHAT'S WITH THIS PLACE?
WELLCOME!!
YIPE!!
POIT

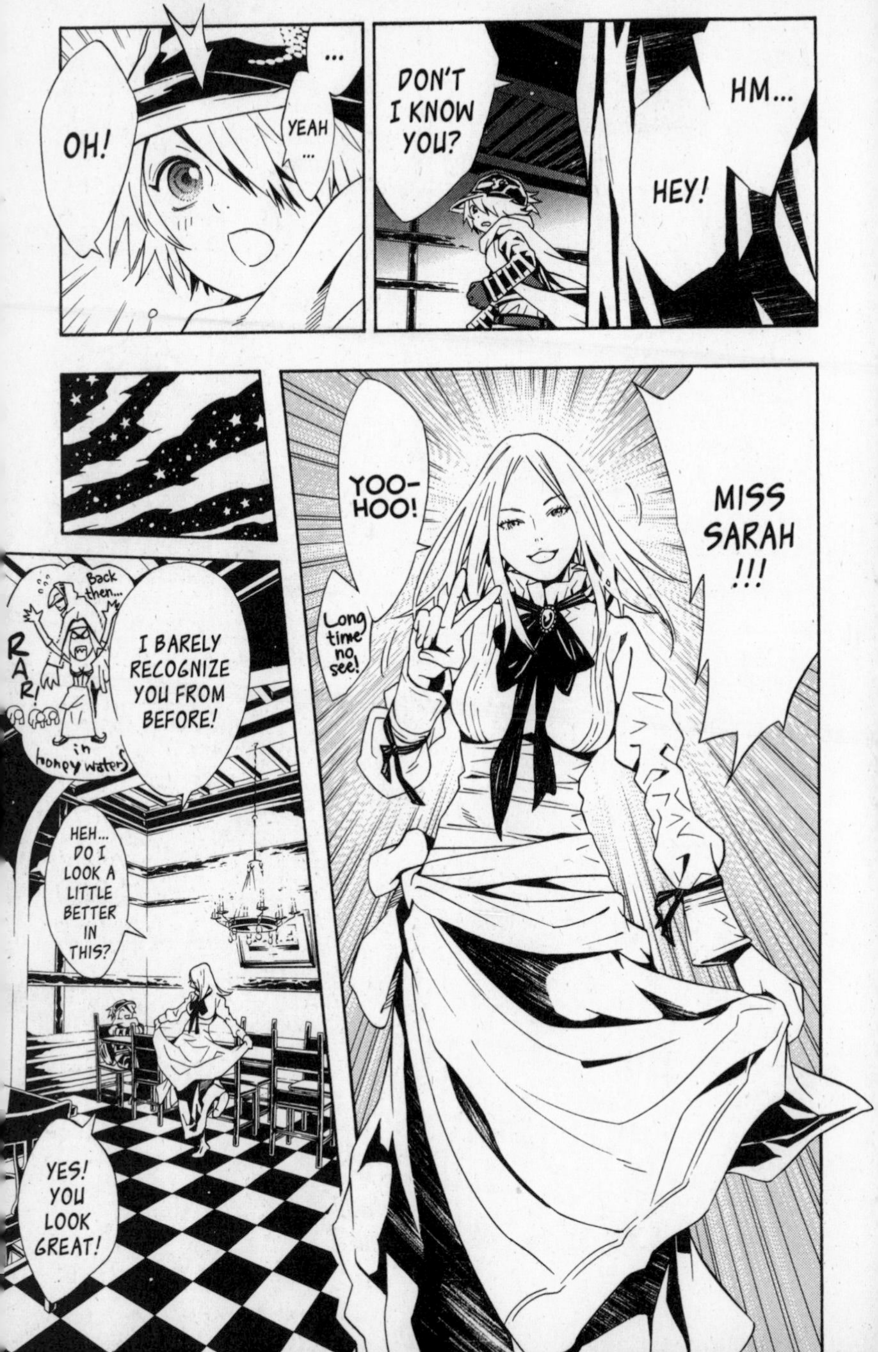
HM...
HEY!
DON'T I KNOW YOU?
...
YEAH ...
OH!
MISS SARAH !!!
YOO-HOO!
Long time no see!
I BARELY RECOGNIZE YOU FROM BEFORE!
Back then...
RAR!
in honey waters
HEH... DO I LOOK A LITTLE BETTER IN THIS?
YES! YOU LOOK GREAT!

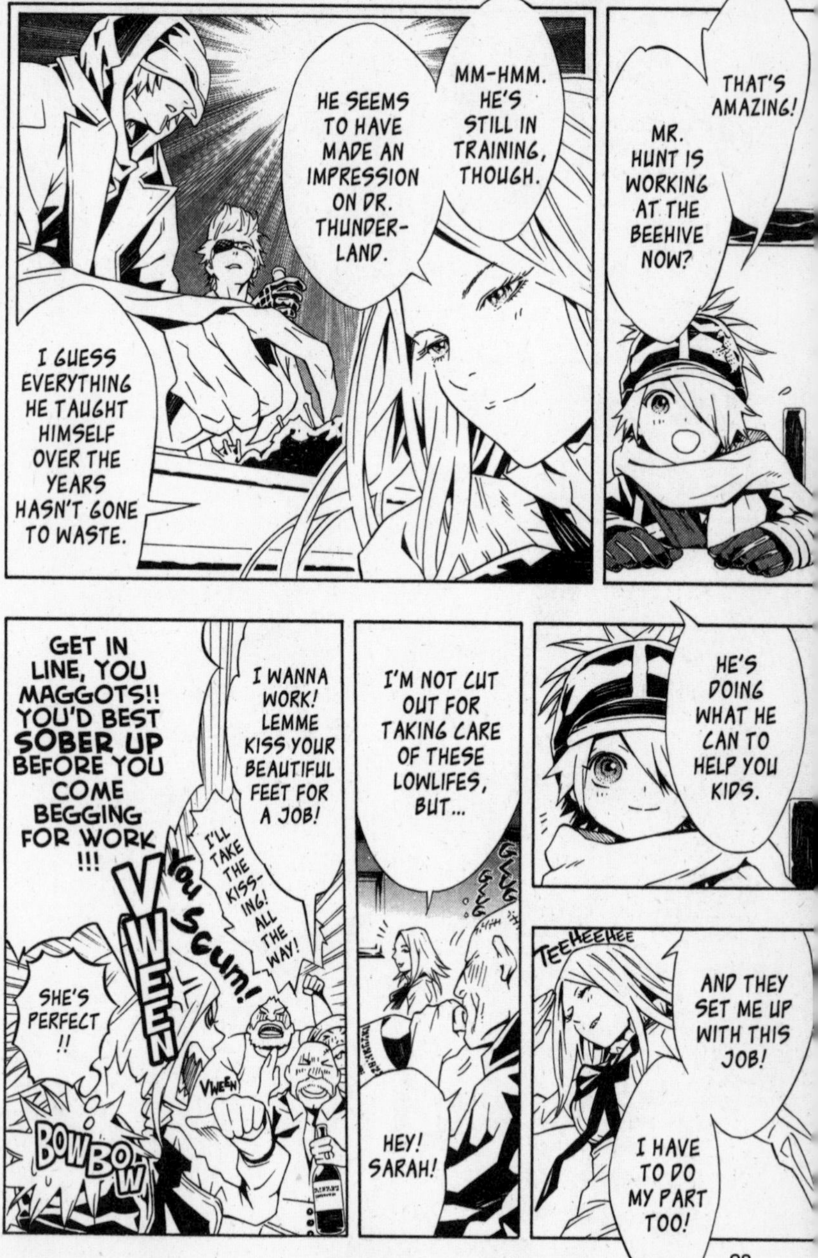
THAT'S AMAZING!
MR. HUNT IS WORKING AT THE BEEHIVE NOW?
MM-HMM. HE'S STILL IN TRAINING, THOUGH.
HE SEEMS TO HAVE MADE AN IMPRESSION ON DR. THUNDER-LAND.
I GUESS EVERYTHING HE TAUGHT HIMSELF OVER THE YEARS HASN'T GONE TO WASTE.
HE'S DOING WHAT HE CAN TO HELP YOU KIDS.
TEEHEEHEE
AND THEY SET ME UP WITH THIS JOB!
I HAVE TO DO MY PART TOO!
I'M NOT CUT OUT FOR TAKING CARE OF THESE LOWLIFES, BUT...
GLUG GLUG
HEY! SARAH!
I WANNA WORK! LEMME KISS YOUR BEAUTIFUL FEET FOR A JOB!
GET IN LINE, YOU MAGGOTS!! YOU'D BEST SOBER UP BEFORE YOU COME BEGGING FOR WORK!!!
I'LL TAKE THE KISS-ING! ALL THE WAY!
YOU SCUM!
VWEEN
SHE'S PERFECT!!
VWEEN
BOWBOWOW

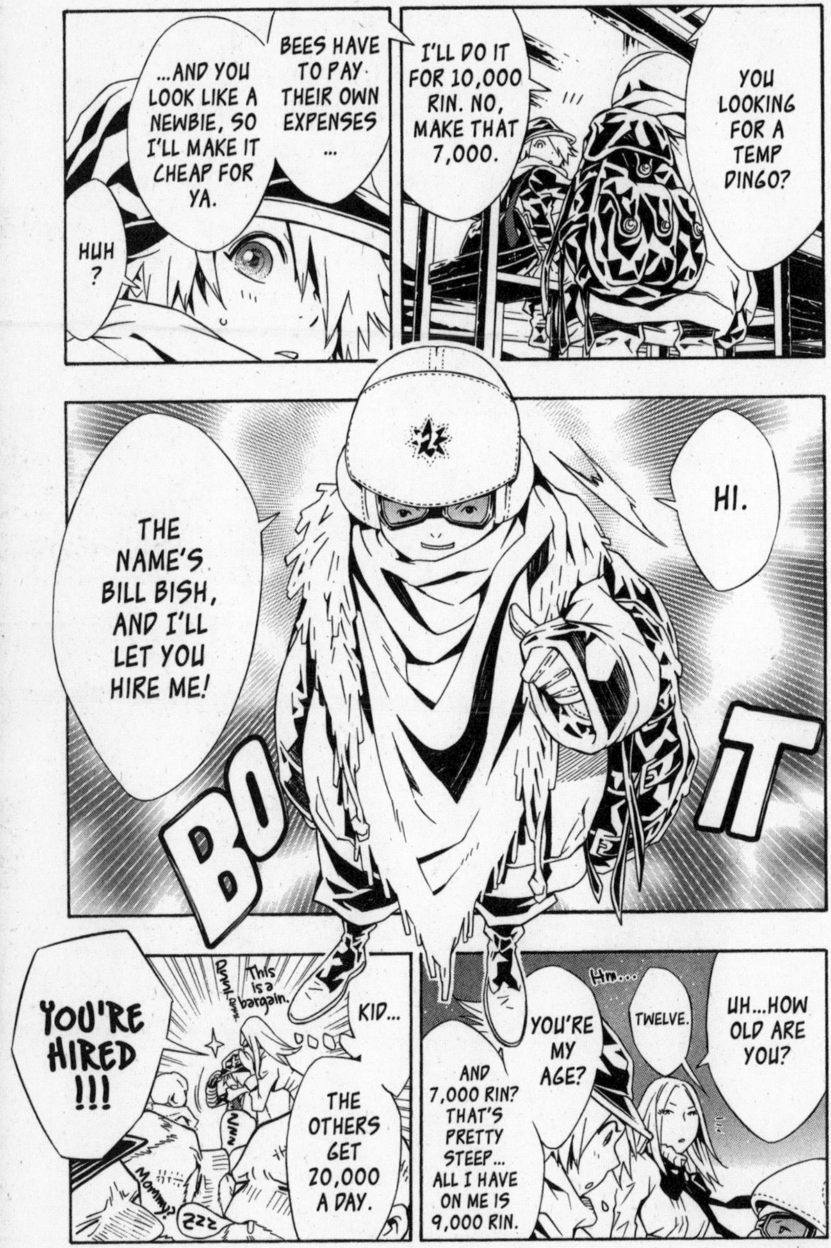

YOU LOOKING FOR A TEMP DINGO?
I'LL DO IT FOR 10,000 RIN. NO, MAKE THAT 7,000.
BEES HAVE TO PAY THEIR OWN EXPENSES ...
...AND YOU LOOK LIKE A NEWBIE, SO I'LL MAKE IT CHEAP FOR YA.
HUH?
HI.
THE NAME'S BILL BISH, AND I'LL LET YOU HIRE ME!
BOIT
UH...HOW OLD ARE YOU?
TWELVE.
Hm...
YOU'RE MY AGE?
AND 7,000 RIN? THAT'S PRETTY STEEP... ALL I HAVE ON ME IS 9,000 RIN.
KID...
THE OTHERS GET 20,000 A DAY.
This is a bargain.
YOU'RE HIRED!!!
Mommy!
ZZZ

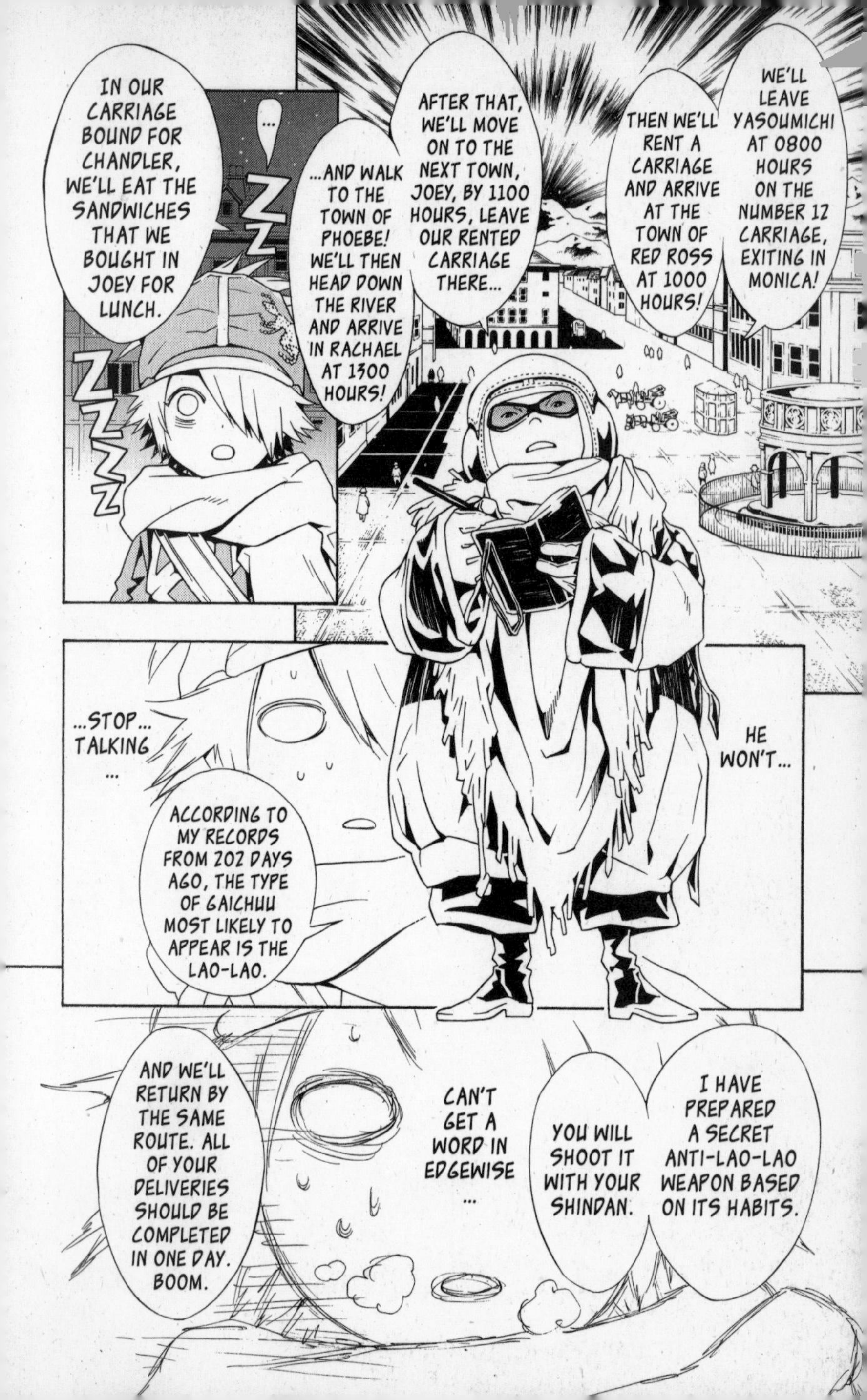
WE'LL LEAVE YASOUMICHI AT 0800 HOURS ON THE NUMBER 12 CARRIAGE, EXITING IN MONICA!
THEN WE'LL RENT A CARRIAGE AND ARRIVE AT THE TOWN OF RED ROSS AT 1000 HOURS!
AFTER THAT, WE'LL MOVE ON TO THE NEXT TOWN, JOEY, BY 1100 HOURS, LEAVE OUR RENTED CARRIAGE THERE...
...AND WALK TO THE TOWN OF PHOEBE! WE'LL THEN HEAD DOWN THE RIVER AND ARRIVE IN RACHAEL AT 1300 HOURS!
...
IN OUR CARRIAGE BOUND FOR CHANDLER, WE'LL EAT THE SANDWICHES THAT WE BOUGHT IN JOEY FOR LUNCH.
ZZZ
ZZZZZ
HE WON'T...
ACCORDING TO MY RECORDS FROM 202 DAYS AGO, THE TYPE OF GAICHUU MOST LIKELY TO APPEAR IS THE LAO-LAO.
...STOP... TALKING ...
I HAVE PREPARED A SECRET ANTI-LAO-LAO WEAPON BASED ON ITS HABITS.
YOU WILL SHOOT IT WITH YOUR SHINDAN.
CAN'T GET A WORD IN EDGEWISE ...
AND WE'LL RETURN BY THE SAME ROUTE. ALL OF YOUR DELIVERIES SHOULD BE COMPLETED IN ONE DAY. BOOM.

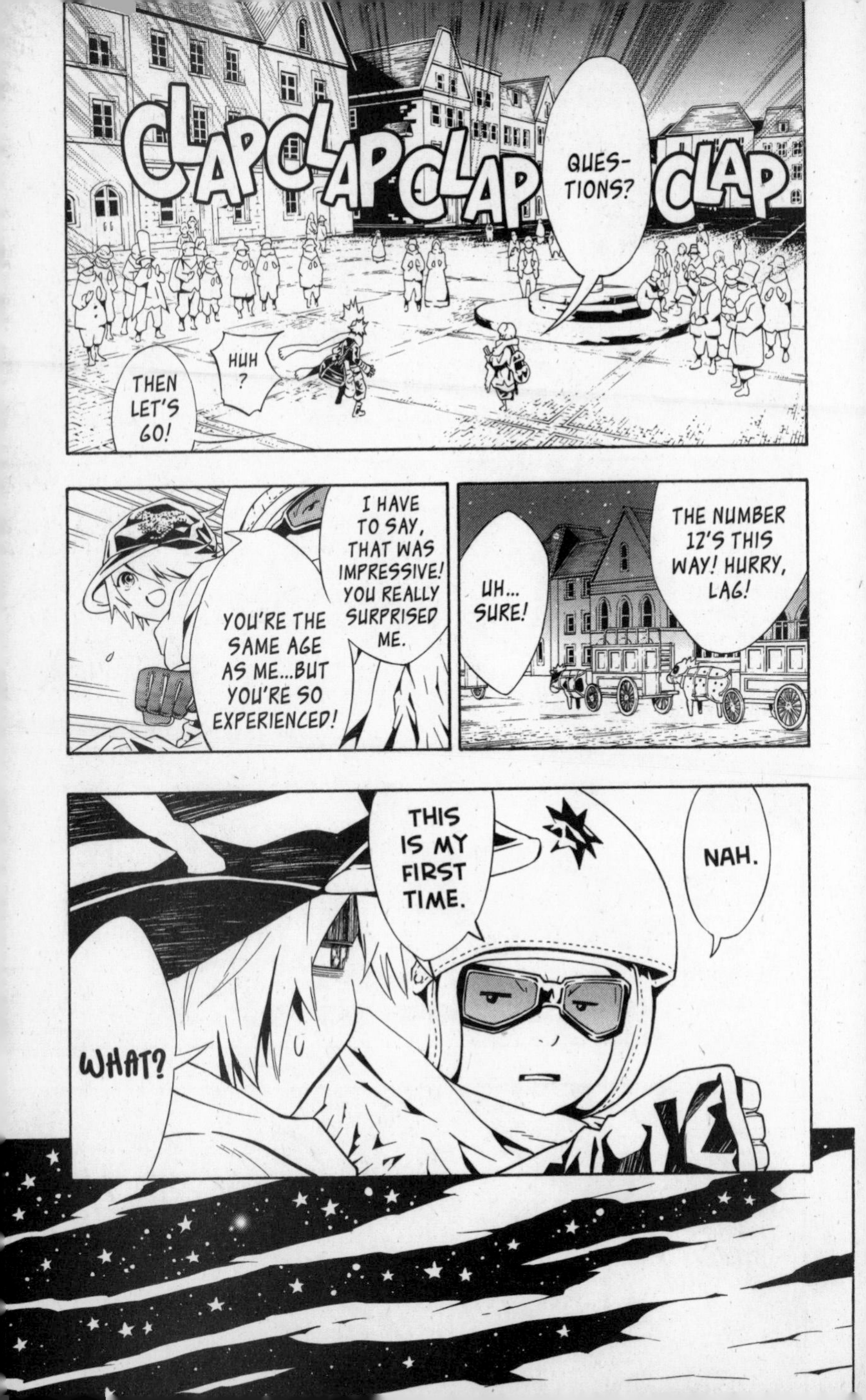
CLAP CLAP CLAP CLAP
QUESTIONS?
HUH?
THEN LET'S GO!
THE NUMBER 12'S THIS WAY! HURRY, LAG!
UH... SURE!
I HAVE TO SAY, THAT WAS IMPRESSIVE! YOU REALLY SURPRISED ME.
YOU'RE THE SAME AGE AS ME...BUT YOU'RE SO EXPERIENCED!
NAH.
THIS IS MY FIRST TIME.
WHAT?

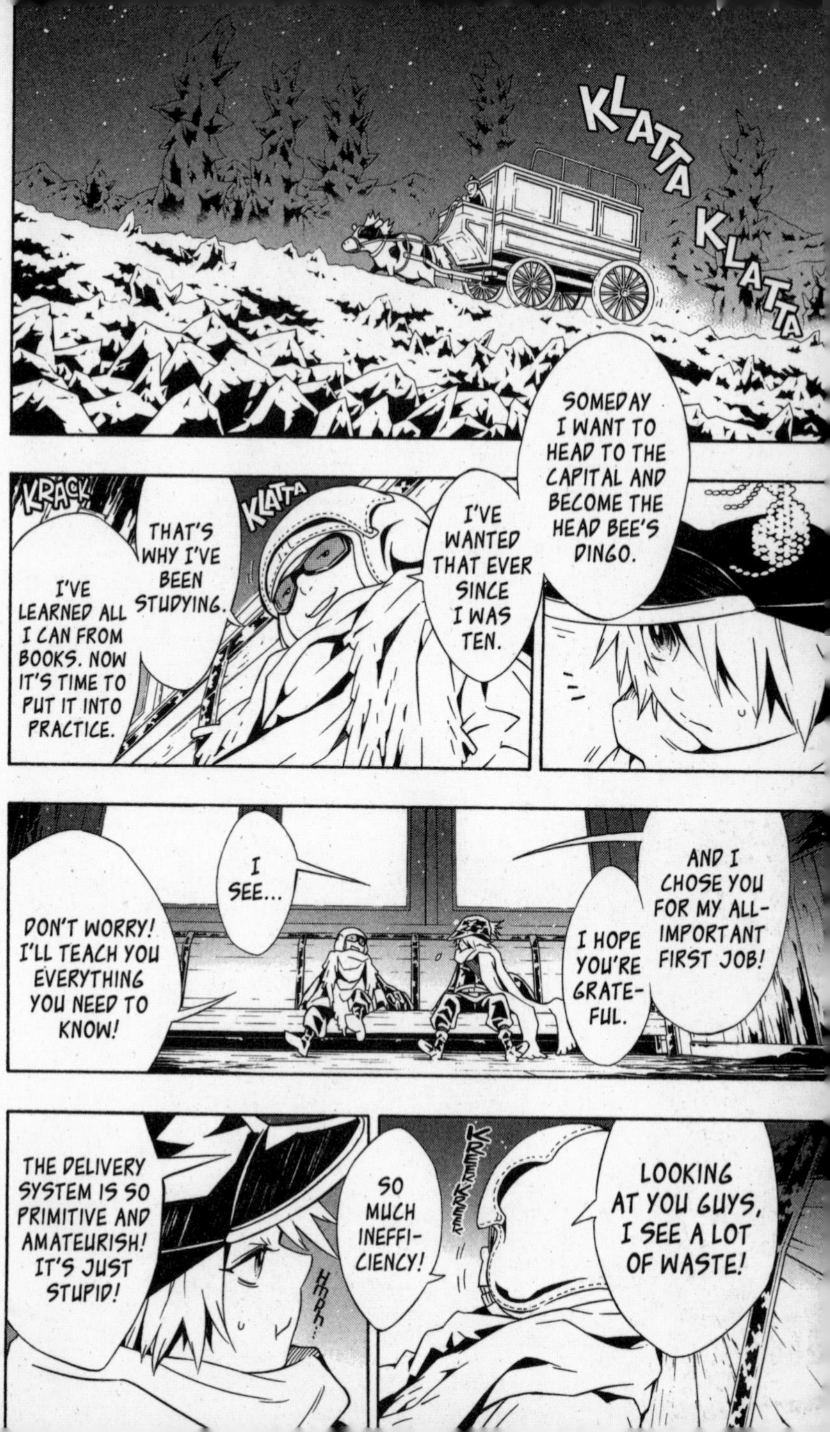
KLATTA
KLATTA
KLATTA
SOMEDAY I WANT TO HEAD TO THE CAPITAL AND BECOME THE HEAD BEE'S DINGO.
I'VE WANTED THAT EVER SINCE I WAS TEN.
KLATTA
THAT'S WHY I'VE BEEN STUDYING.
KRACK
I'VE LEARNED ALL I CAN FROM BOOKS. NOW IT'S TIME TO PUT IT INTO PRACTICE.
AND I CHOSE YOU FOR MY ALL-IMPORTANT FIRST JOB!
I HOPE YOU'RE GRATEFUL.
I SEE...
DON'T WORRY! I'LL TEACH YOU EVERYTHING YOU NEED TO KNOW!
LOOKING AT YOU GUYS, I SEE A LOT OF WASTE!
KREEK KREEK
SO MUCH INEFFI-CIENCY!
Hmph...
THE DELIVERY SYSTEM IS SO PRIMITIVE AND AMATEURISH! IT'S JUST STUPID!

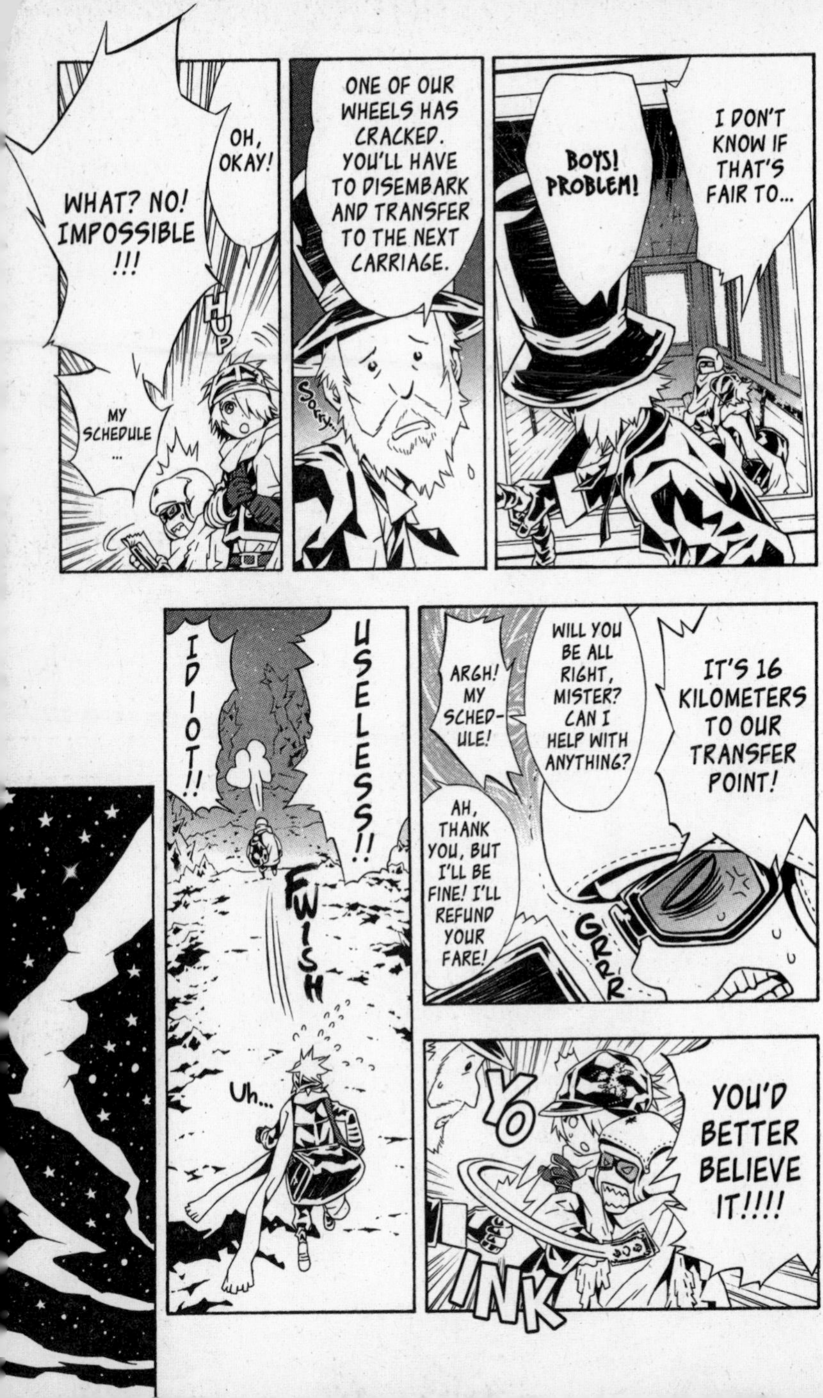
I DON'T KNOW IF THAT'S FAIR TO...
BOYS! PROBLEM!
ONE OF OUR WHEELS HAS CRACKED. YOU'LL HAVE TO DISEMBARK AND TRANSFER TO THE NEXT CARRIAGE.
Sorry...
OH, OKAY!
HUP
WHAT? NO! IMPOSSIBLE!!!
MY SCHEDULE...
IT'S 16 KILOMETERS TO OUR TRANSFER POINT!
WILL YOU BE ALL RIGHT, MISTER? CAN I HELP WITH ANYTHING?
ARGH! MY SCHED-ULE!
GRRR
AH, THANK YOU, BUT I'LL BE FINE! I'LL REFUND YOUR FARE!
YOU'D BETTER BELIEVE IT!!!!
YO
INK
USELESS!!
IDIOT!!
FWISH
Uh...

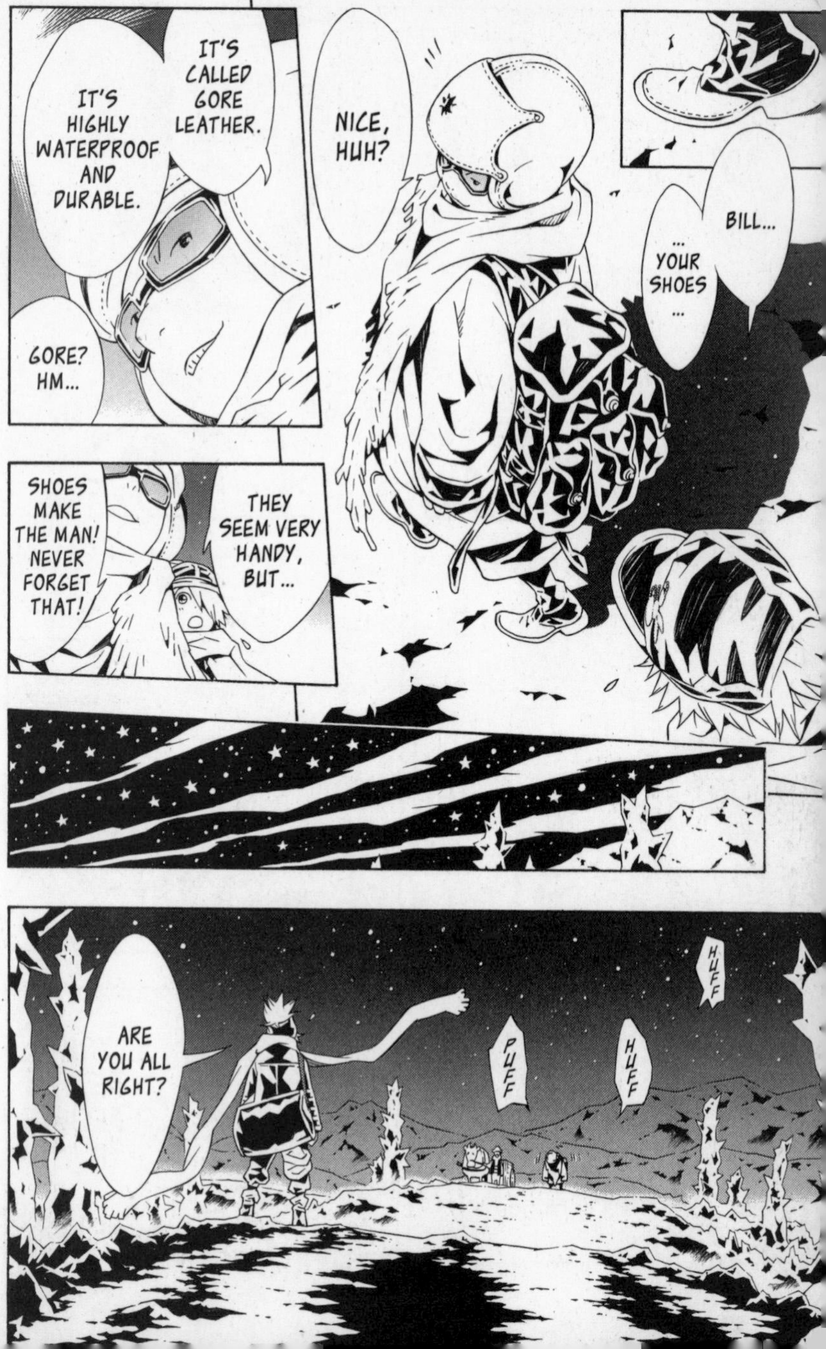
BILL...
...YOUR SHOES...
NICE, HUH?
IT'S CALLED GORE LEATHER.
IT'S HIGHLY WATERPROOF AND DURABLE.
GORE? HM...
THEY SEEM VERY HANDY, BUT...
SHOES MAKE THE MAN! NEVER FORGET THAT!
HUFF
HUFF
PUFF
ARE YOU ALL RIGHT?

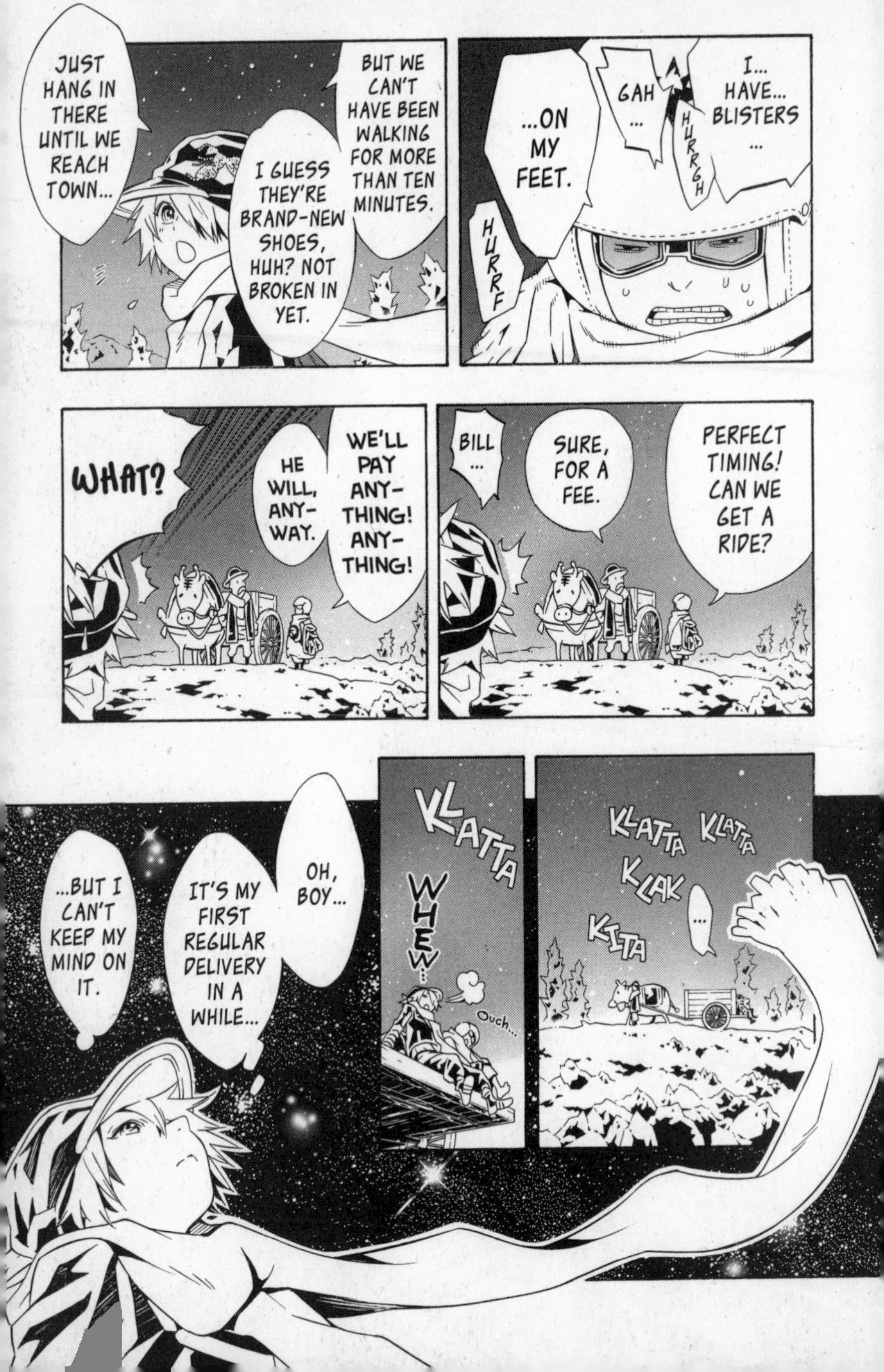
I... HAVE... BLISTERS...
GAH...
HURRGH
...ON MY FEET.
HURRF
BUT WE CAN'T HAVE BEEN WALKING FOR MORE THAN TEN MINUTES.
I GUESS THEY'RE BRAND-NEW SHOES, HUH? NOT BROKEN IN YET.
JUST HANG IN THERE UNTIL WE REACH TOWN...
PERFECT TIMING! CAN WE GET A RIDE?
SURE, FOR A FEE.
BILL...
WE'LL PAY ANY-THING! ANY-THING!
HE WILL, ANY-WAY.
WHAT?
KLATTA KLATTA
KLAK
KLITA
...
KLATTA
WHEW...
Ouch...
OH, BOY...
IT'S MY FIRST REGULAR DELIVERY IN A WHILE...
...BUT I CAN'T KEEP MY MIND ON IT.

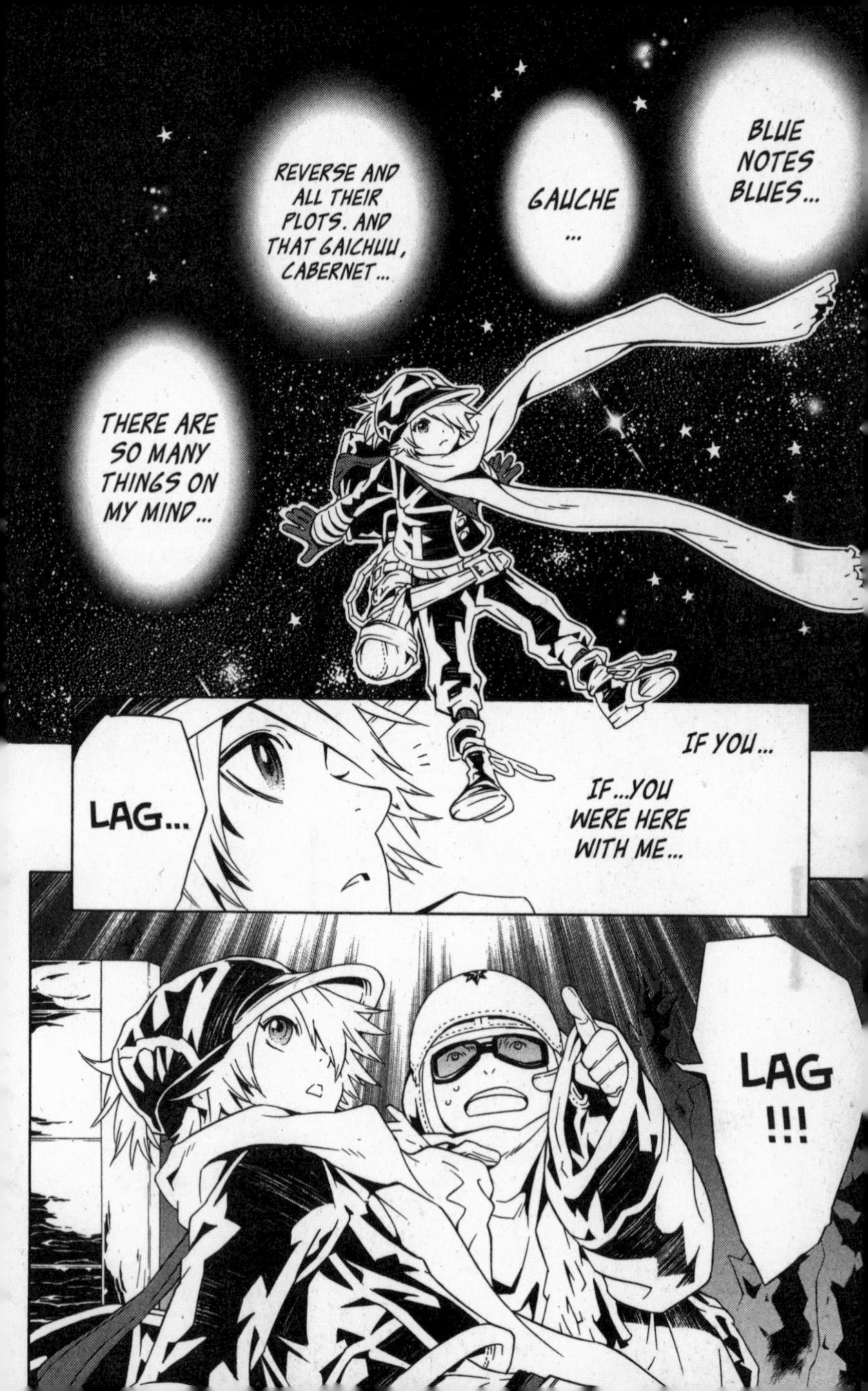
BLUE NOTES BLUES...
GAUCHE ...
REVERSE AND ALL THEIR PLOTS. AND THAT GAICHUU, CABERNET...
THERE ARE SO MANY THINGS ON MY MIND...
IF YOU...
IF...YOU WERE HERE WITH ME...
LAG...
LAG !!!

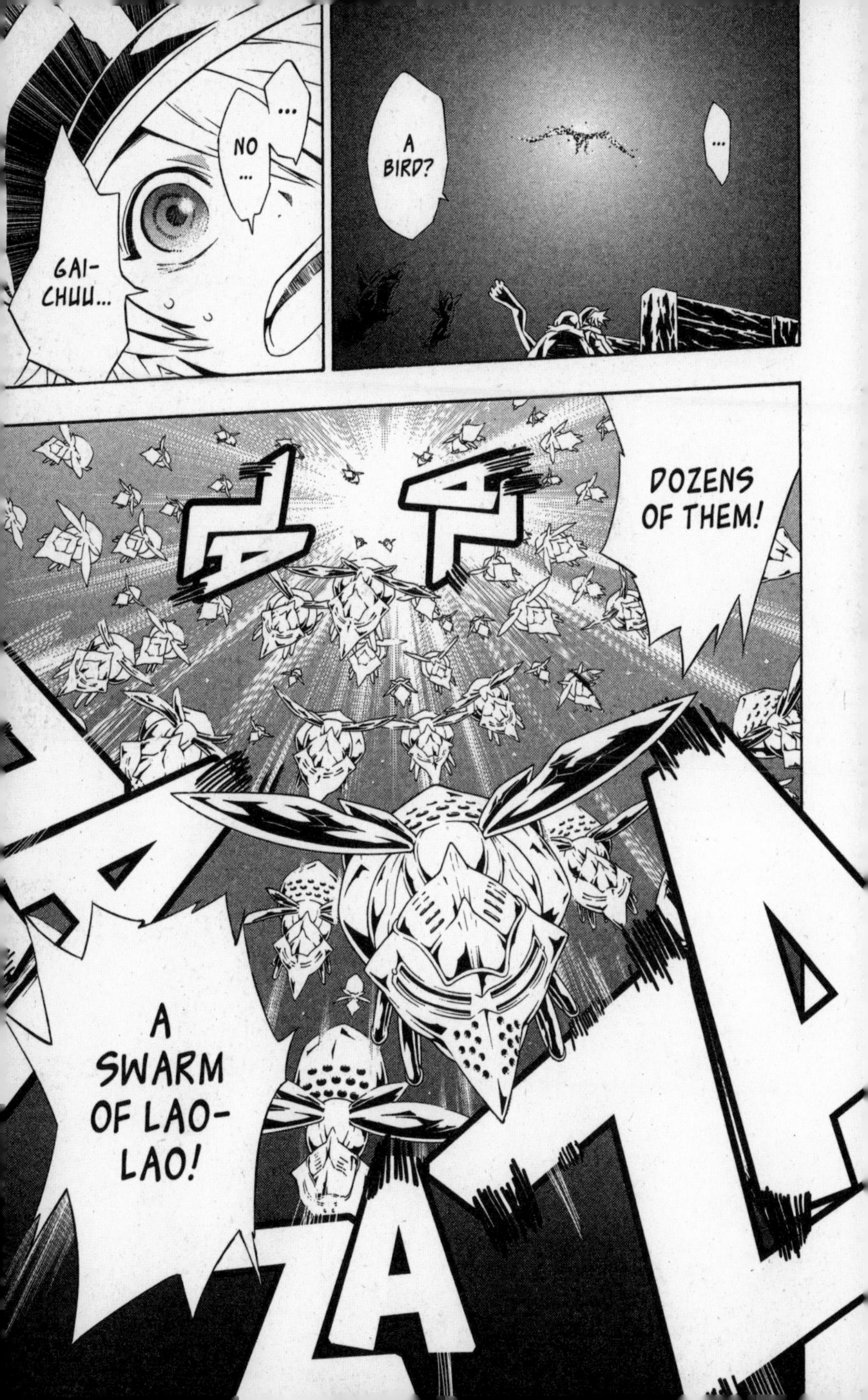
...
A BIRD?
... NO ...
GAI-CHUU...
DOZENS OF THEM!
A SWARM OF LAO-LAO!

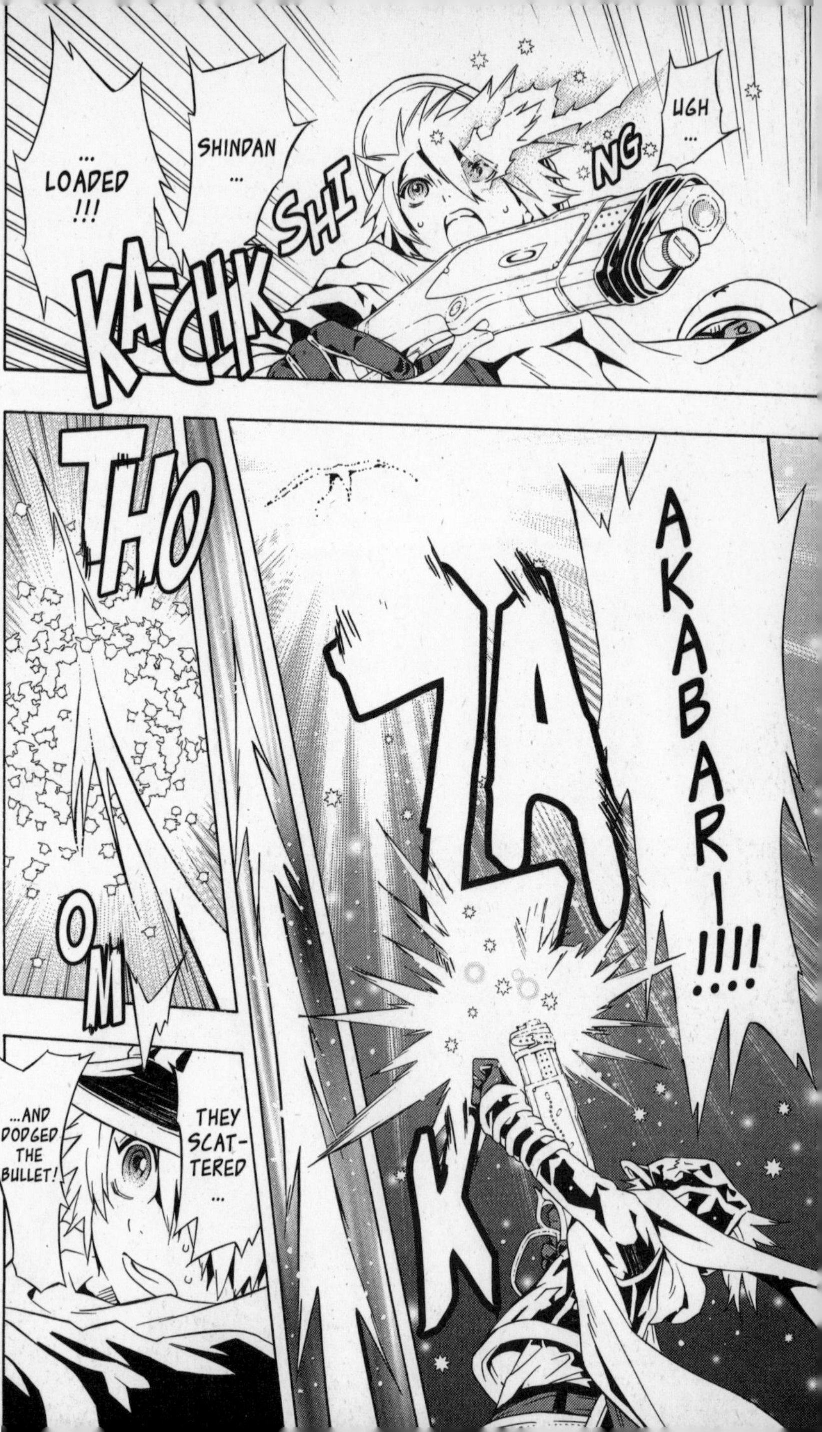
UGH ...
SHING
SHINDAN ...
... LOADED !!!
KA-CHK
AKABARI!!!!!
ZAK
THOOM
THEY SCATTERED ...
...AND DODGED THE BULLET!

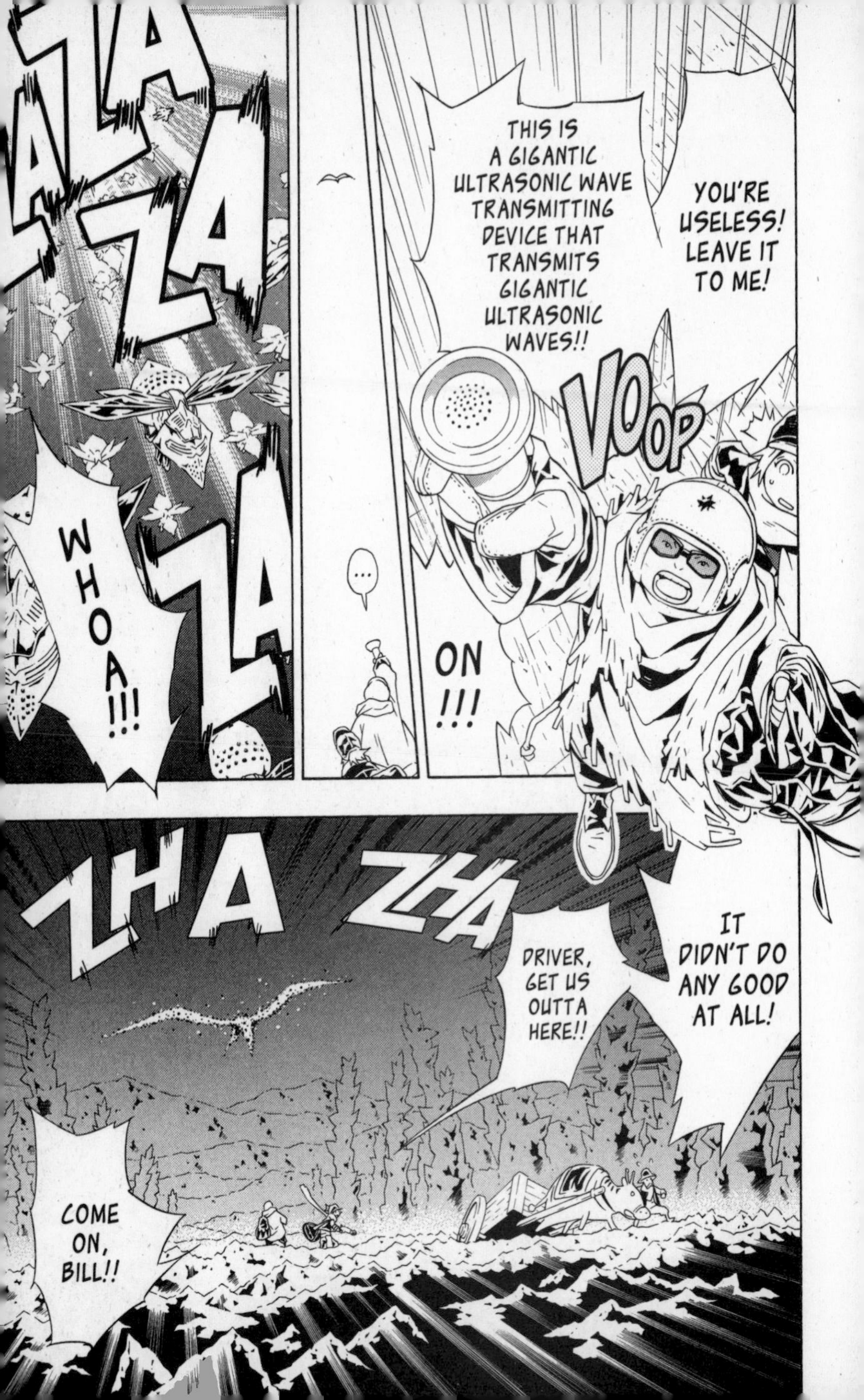
YOU'RE USELESS! LEAVE IT TO ME!
THIS IS A GIGANTIC ULTRASONIC WAVE TRANSMITTING DEVICE THAT TRANSMITS GIGANTIC ULTRASONIC WAVES!!
VOOP
ON!!!
...
ZAZAZA
WHOA!!!
IT DIDN'T DO ANY GOOD AT ALL!
DRIVER, GET US OUTTA HERE!!
ZHA ZHA
COME ON, BILL!!

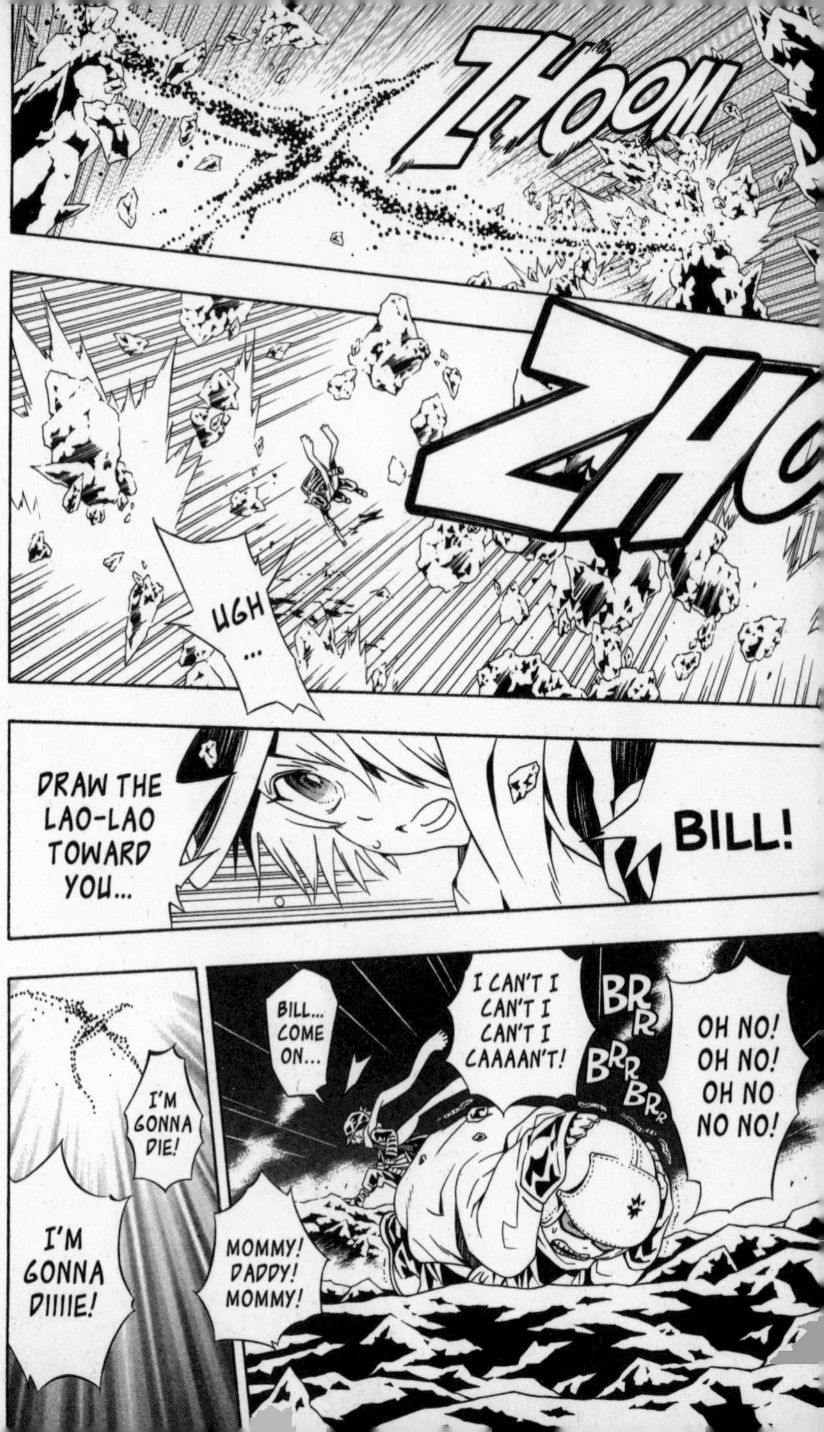
ZHOOM
ZHO
UGH...
BILL!
DRAW THE LAO-LAO TOWARD YOU...
OH NO! OH NO! OH NO NO NO!
BRR BRRRBRR
I CAN'T I CAN'T I CAN'T I CAAAAN'T!
BILL... COME ON...
MOMMY! DADDY! MOMMY!
I'M GONNA DIE!
I'M GONNA DIIIIE!

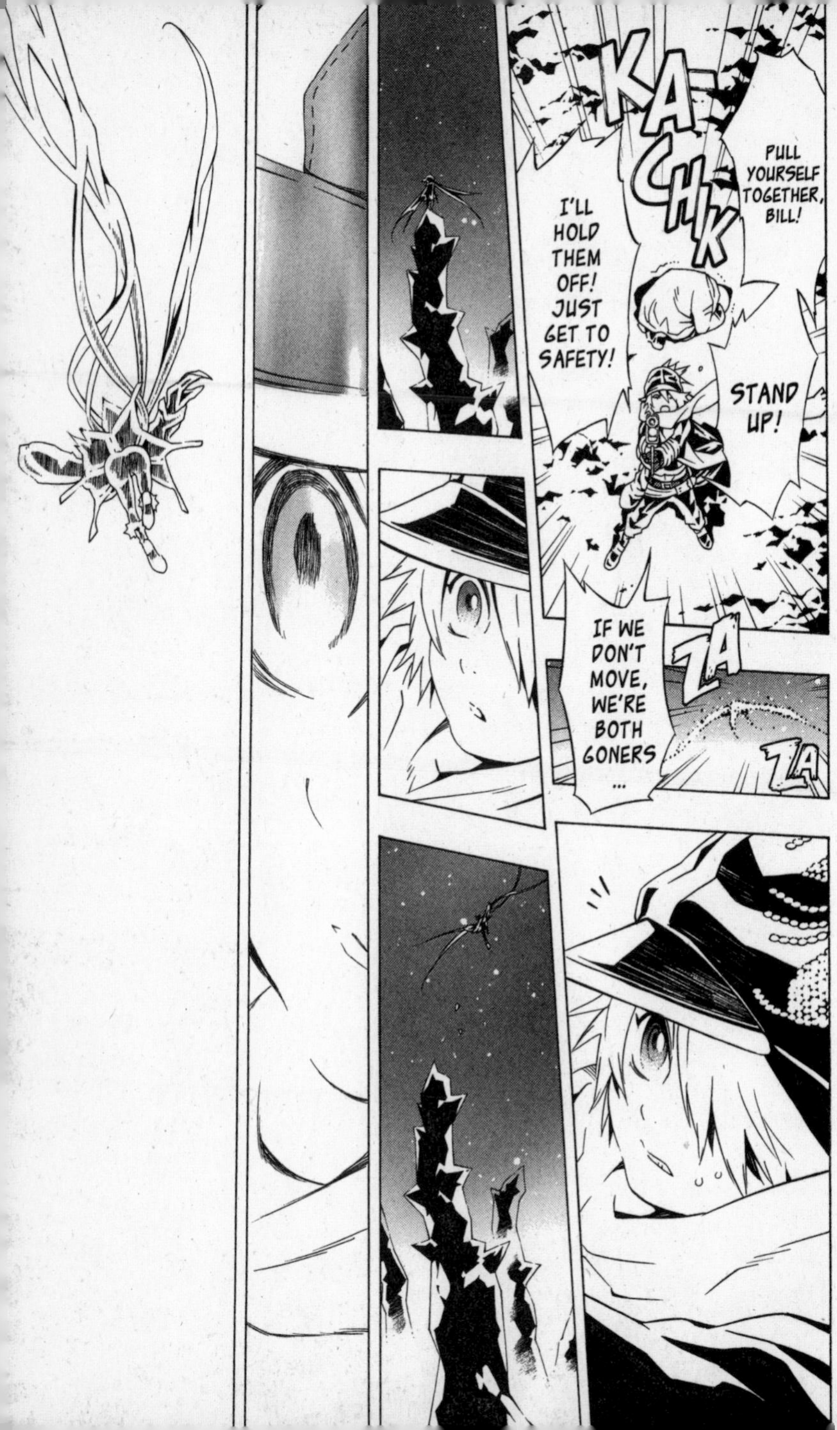
KA-CHIK
PULL YOURSELF TOGETHER, BILL!
I'LL HOLD THEM OFF! JUST GET TO SAFETY!
STAND UP!
IF WE DON'T MOVE, WE'RE BOTH GONERS...
ZA
ZA

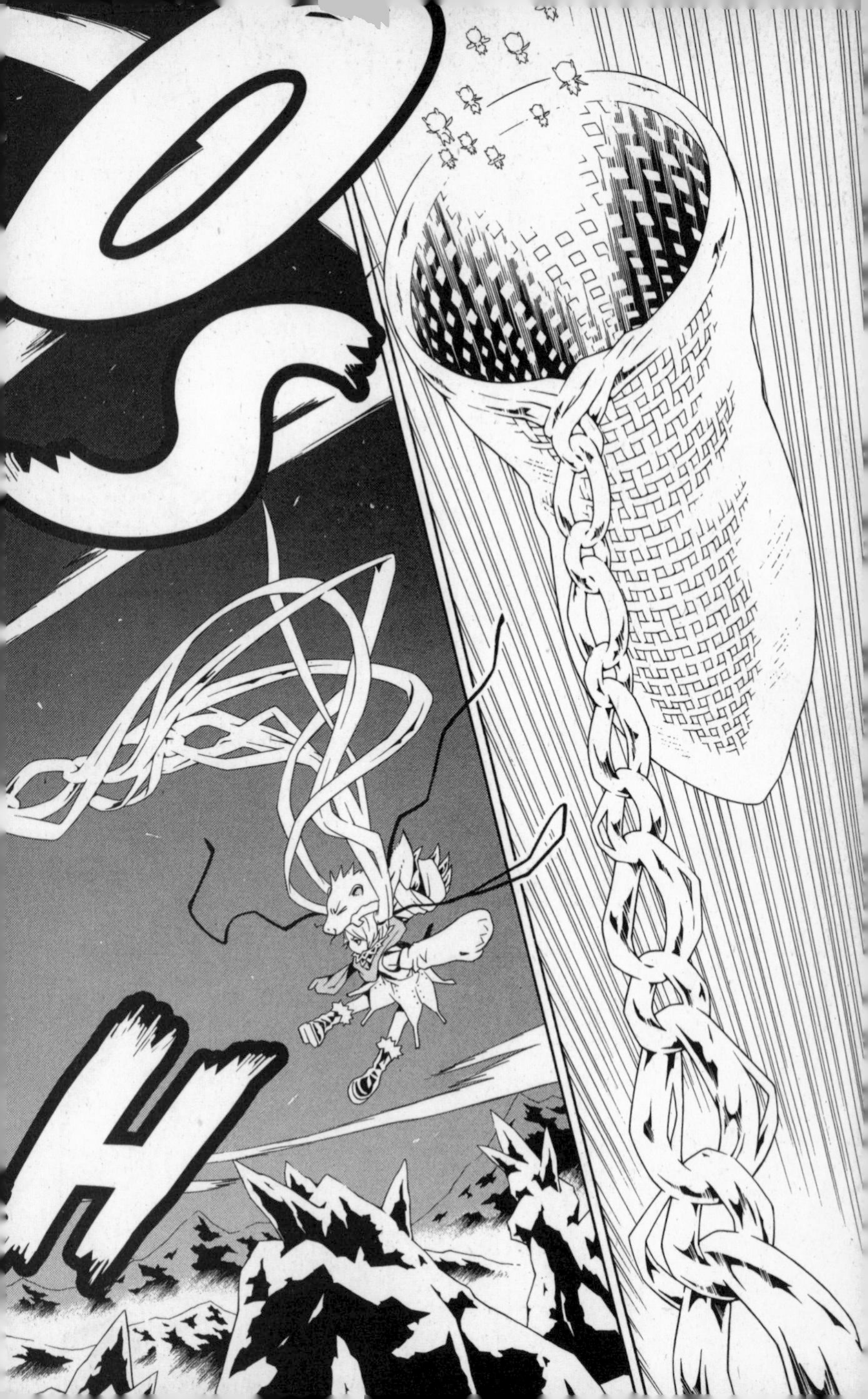
OSH

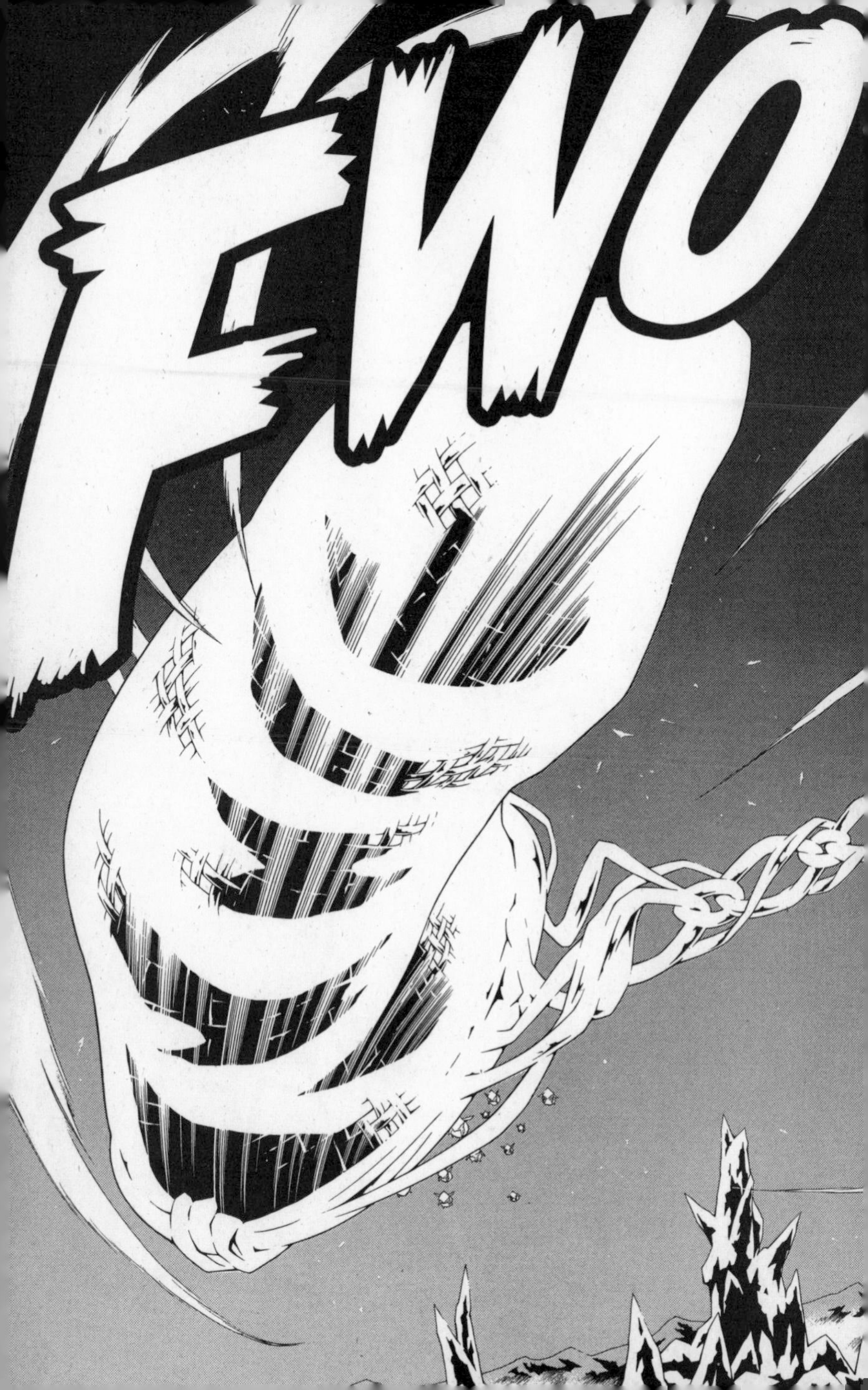
FWO

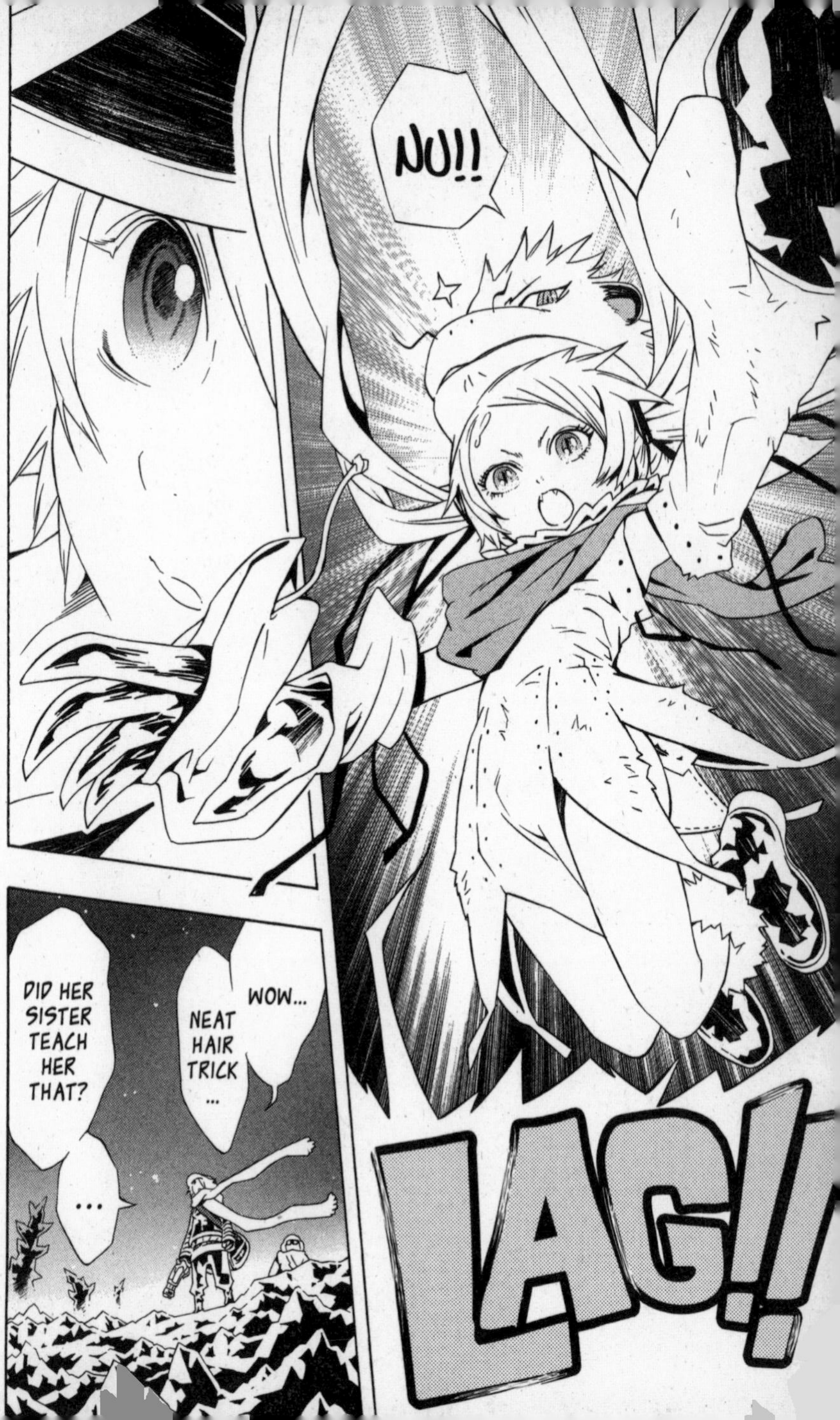
NU!!
LAG!!
WOW... NEAT HAIR TRICK ...
DID HER SISTER TEACH HER THAT?
...

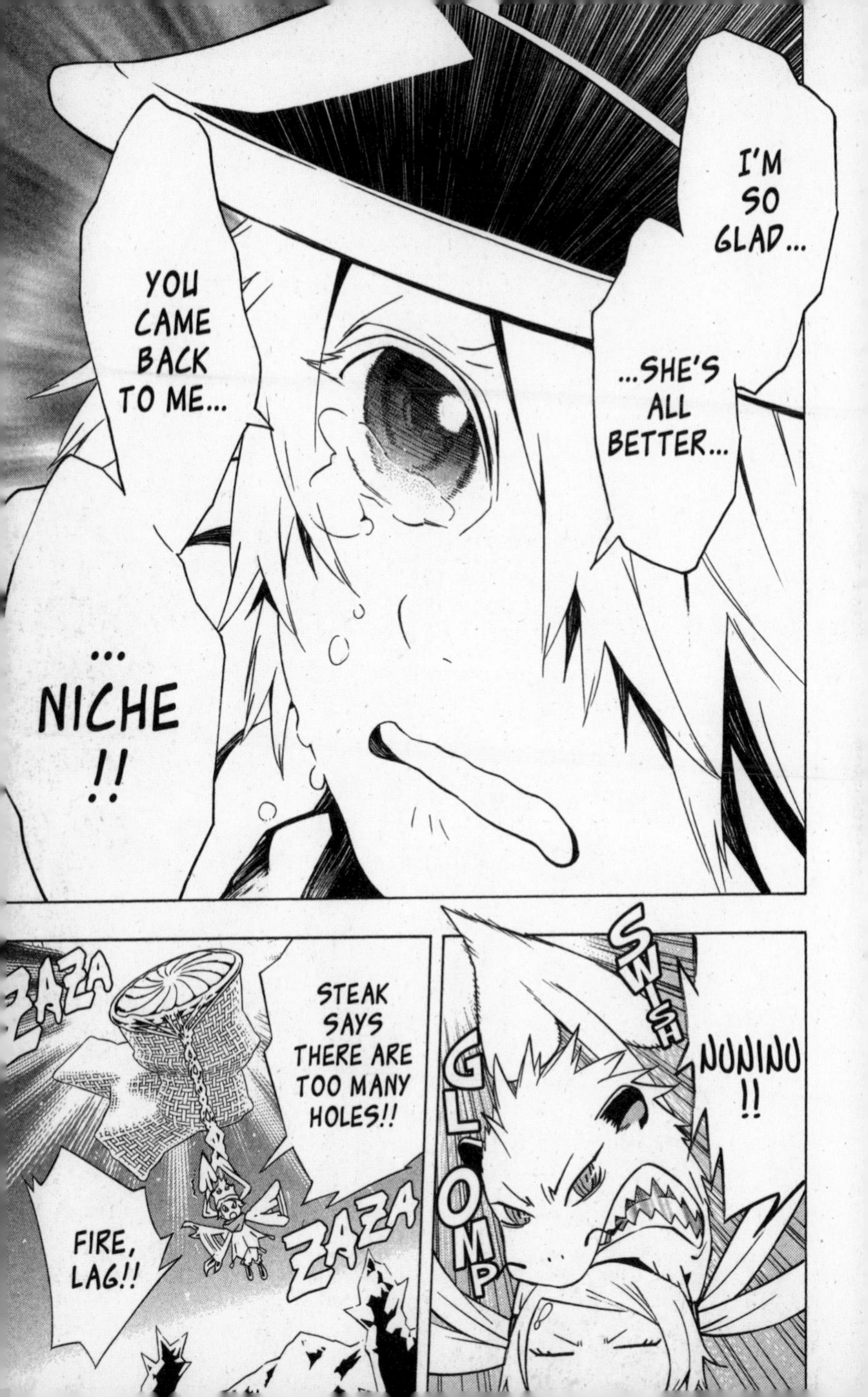
I'M SO GLAD...
...SHE'S ALL BETTER...
YOU CAME BACK TO ME...
...NICHE!!
SWISH
NUNINU!!
GLOMP
STEAK SAYS THERE ARE TOO MANY HOLES!!
ZAZA
FIRE, LAG!!
ZAZA

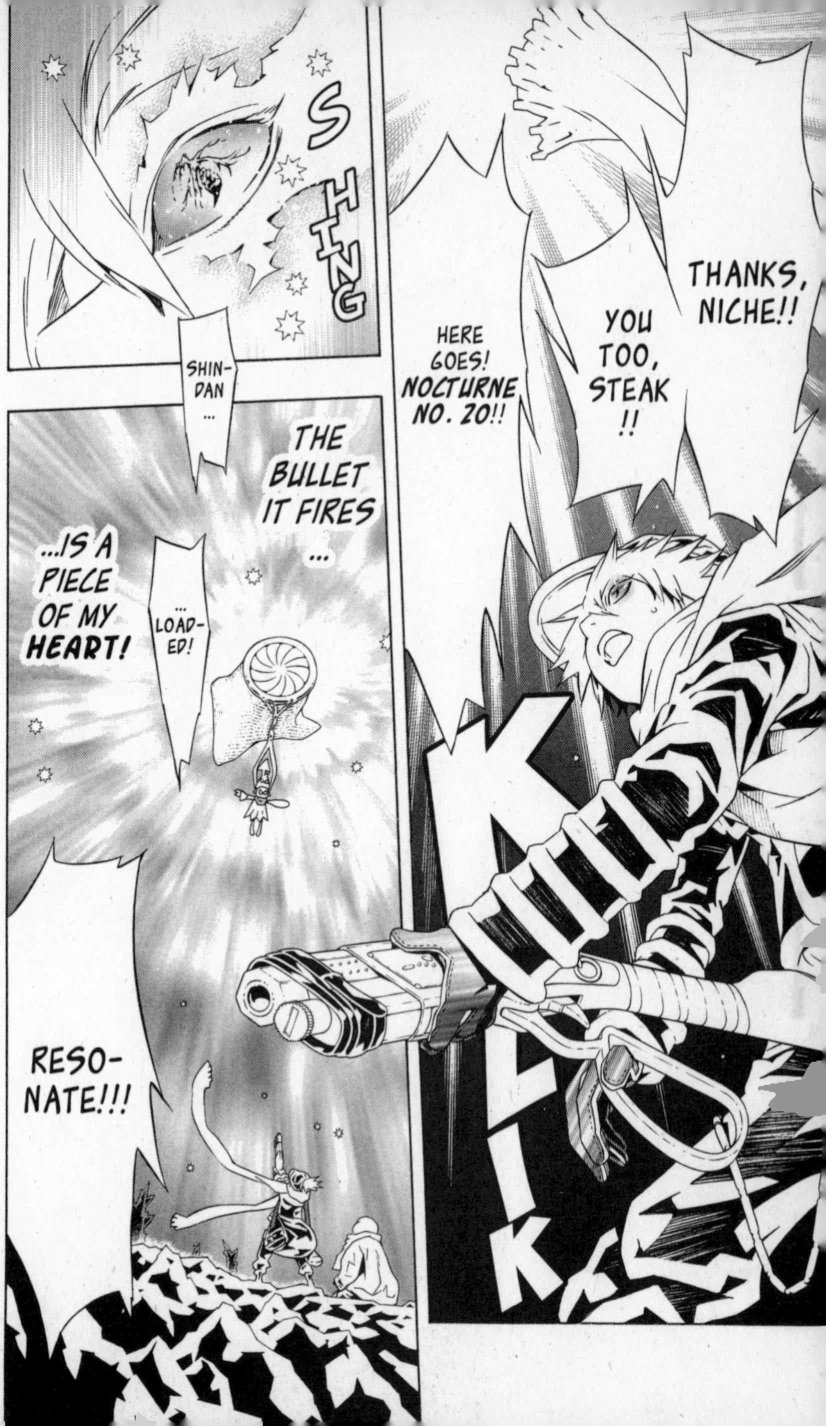
THANKS, NICHE!!
YOU TOO, STEAK!!
HERE GOES! NOCTURNE NO. 20!!
KLIK
SHING
SHIN-DAN...
THE BULLET IT FIRES...
...LOADED!
...IS A PIECE OF MY HEART!
RESONATE!!!

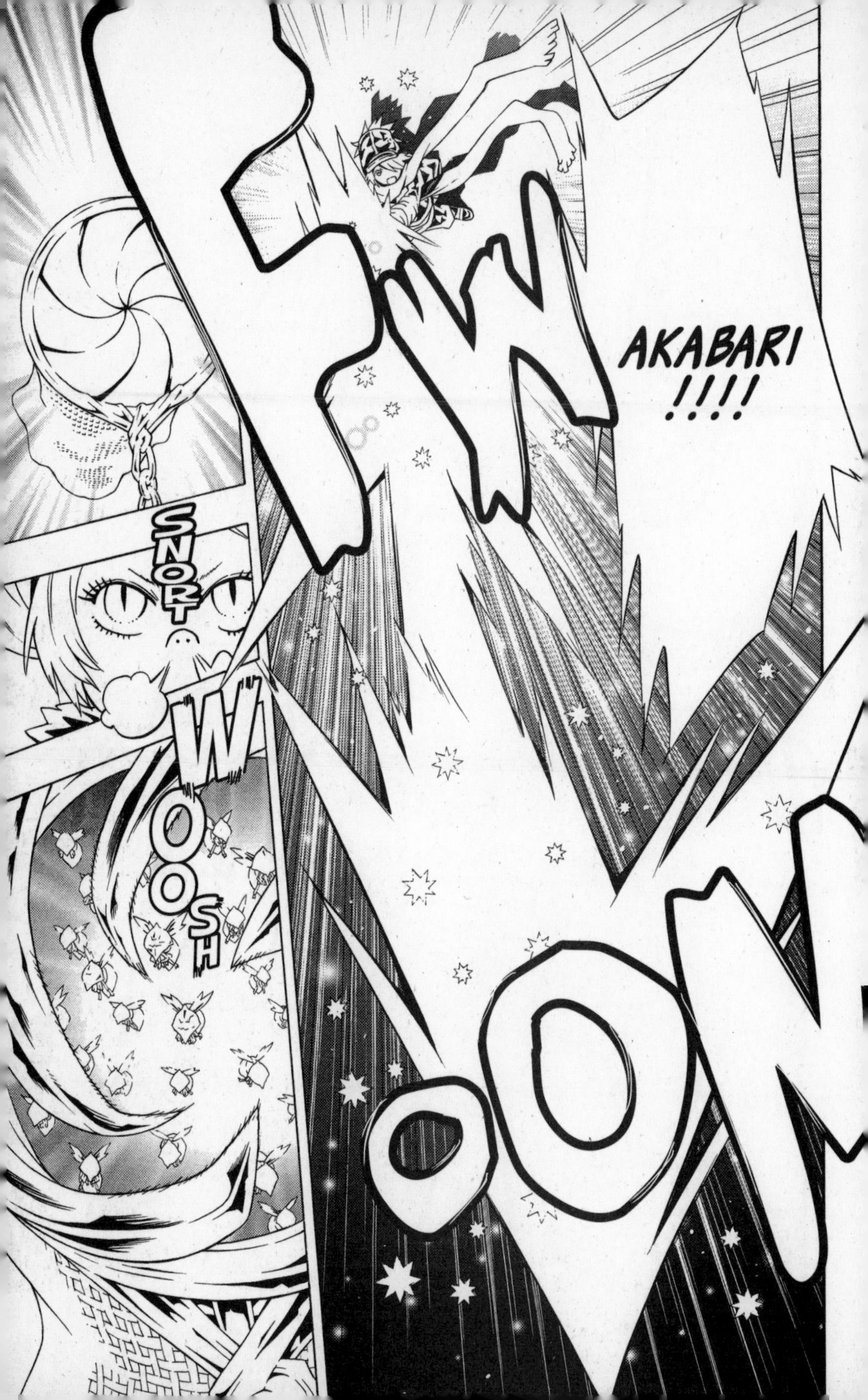
AKABARI
!!!!
SNORT
WHOOSH

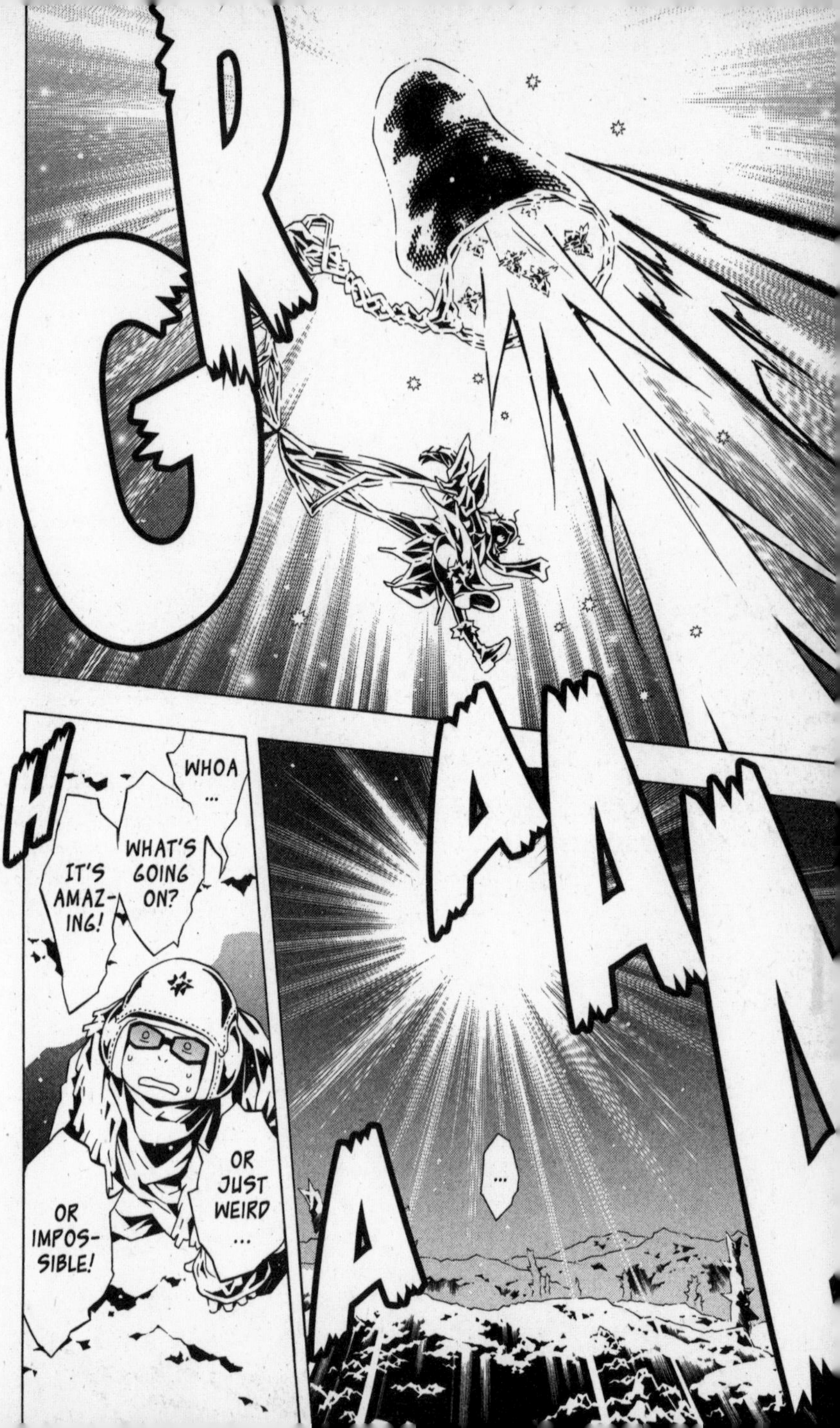
GRAAAAH
...
WHOA ...
WHAT'S GOING ON?
IT'S AMAZ-ING!
OR JUST WEIRD ...
OR IMPOS-SIBLE!

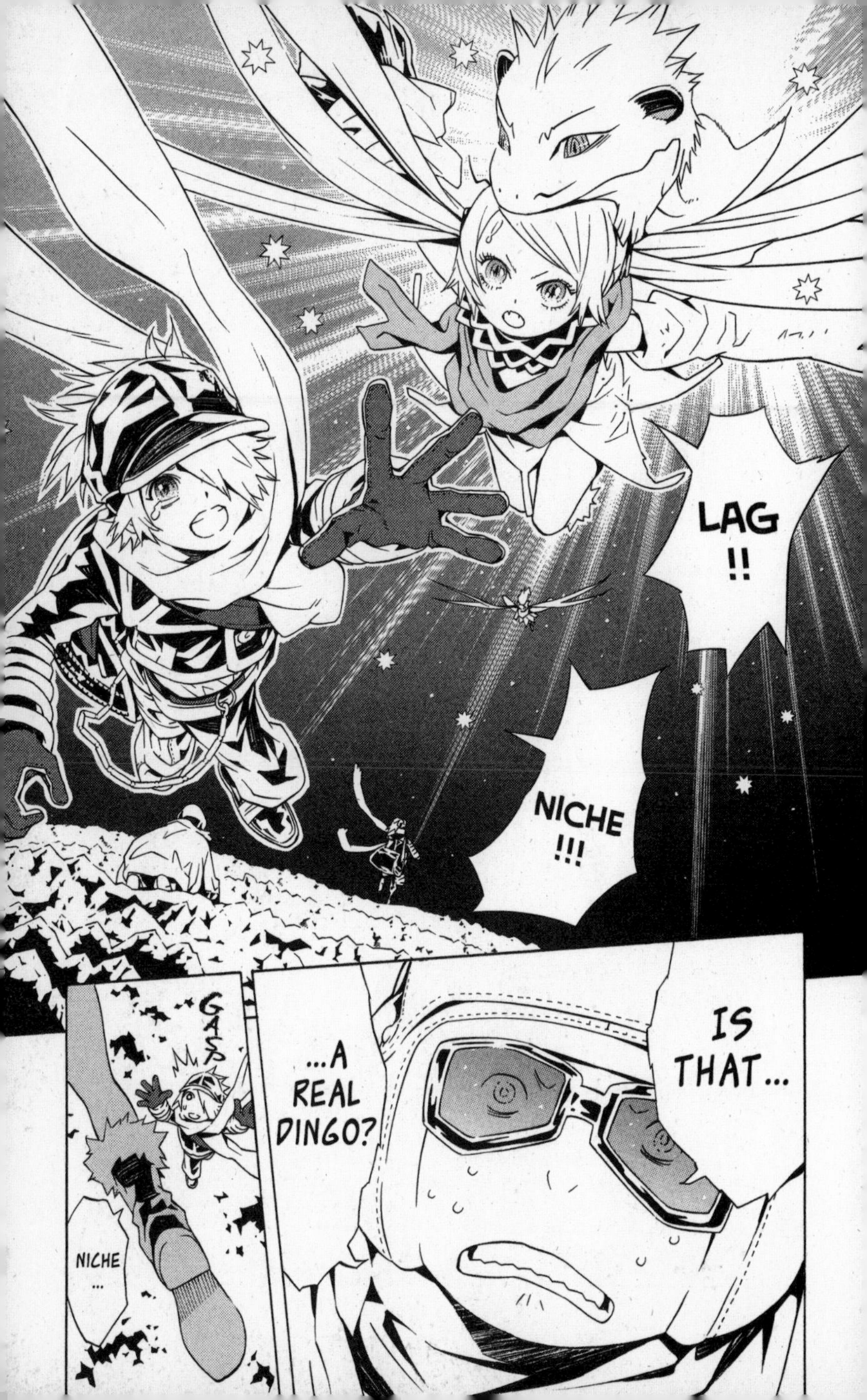
LAG !!
NICHE !!!
IS THAT...
...A REAL DINGO?
GASP
NICHE ...

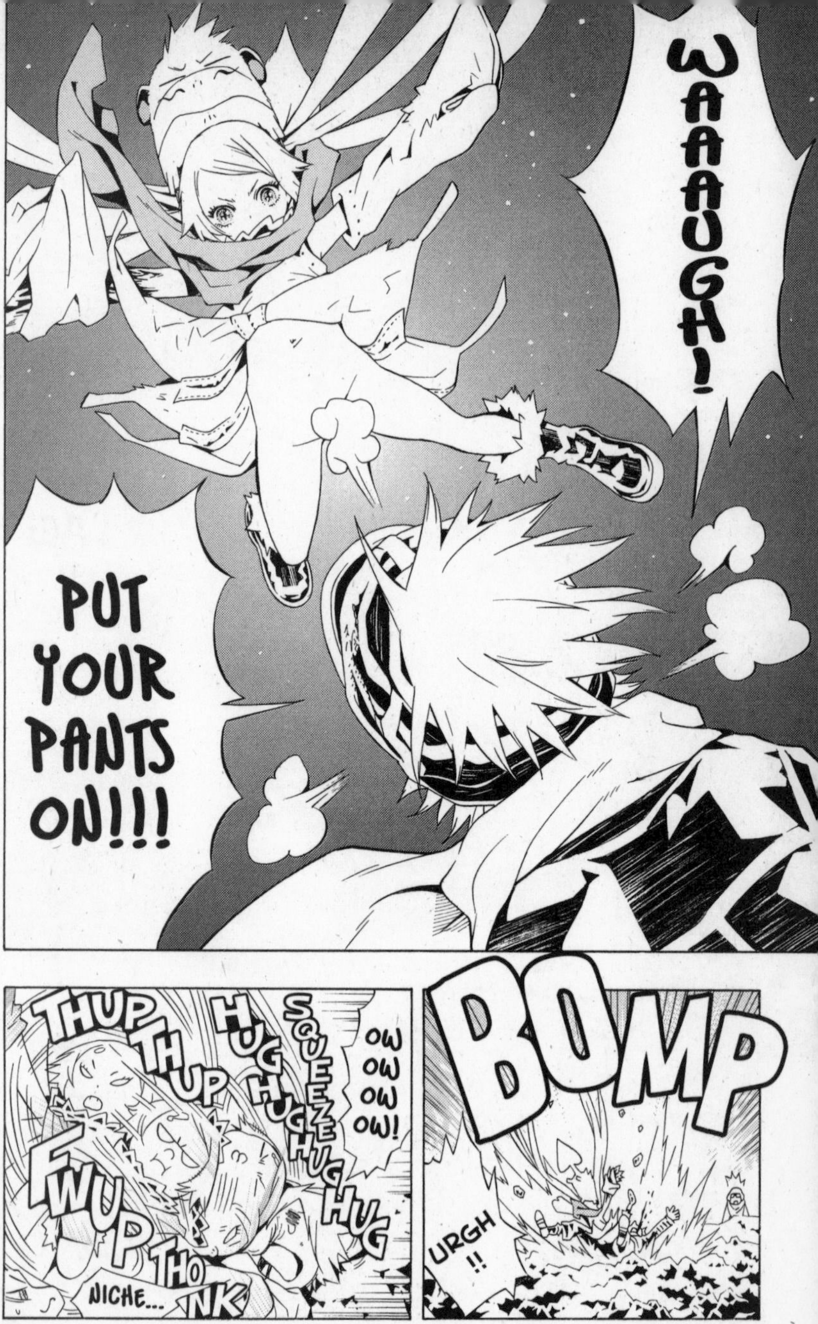
WAAAAUGH!
PUT YOUR PANTS ON!!!
BOMP
URGH!!
OW OW OW OW!
SQUEEZE
HUG HUG HUG HUG
THUP THUP
FWUP
THONK
NICHE...

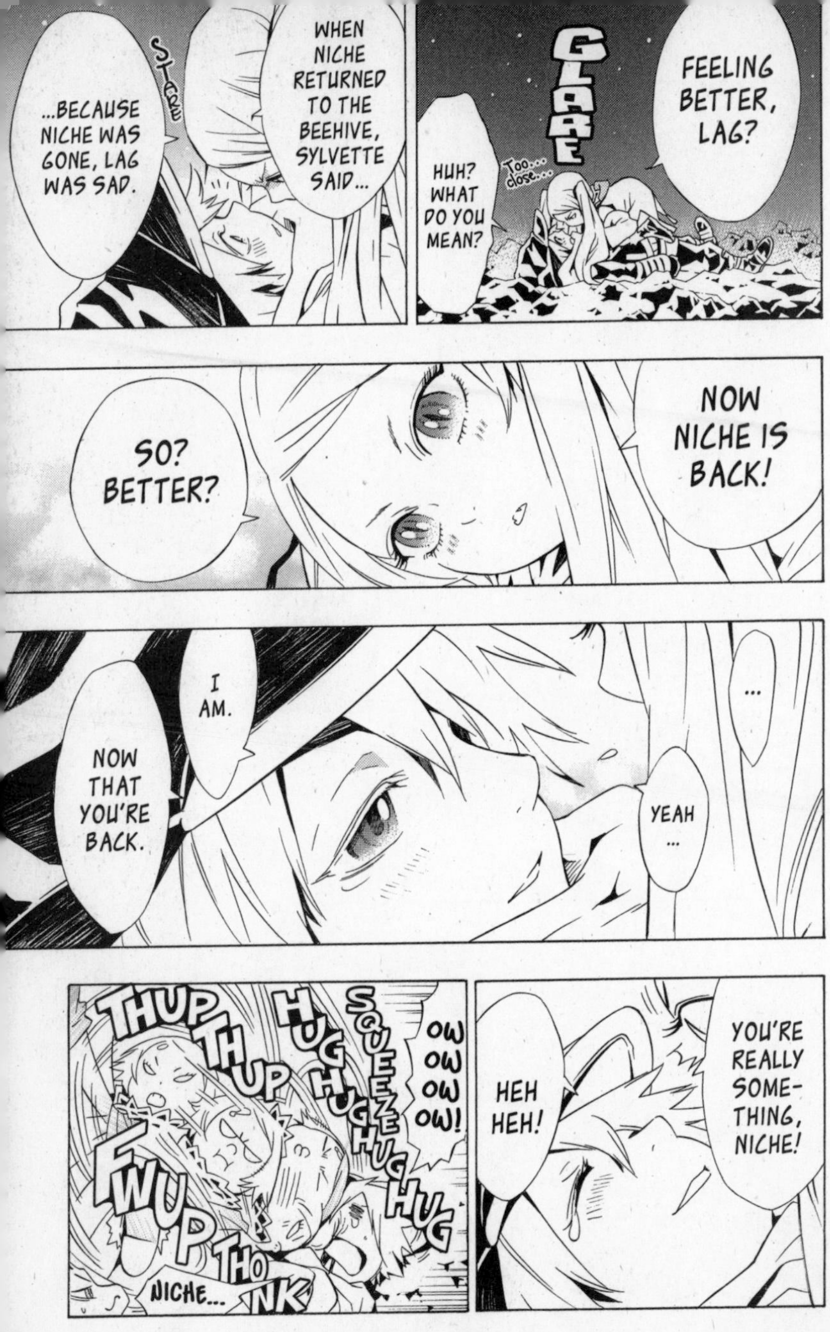
GLARE
FEELING BETTER, LAG?
Too... close...
HUH? WHAT DO YOU MEAN?
WHEN NICHE RETURNED TO THE BEEHIVE, SYLVETTE SAID...
STARE
...BECAUSE NICHE WAS GONE, LAG WAS SAD.
NOW NICHE IS BACK!
SO? BETTER?
...
YEAH ...
I AM.
NOW THAT YOU'RE BACK.
YOU'RE REALLY SOME-THING, NICHE!
HEH HEH!
OW OW OW OW!
SQUEEZE
HUG HUG HUG HUG
THUP THUP
FWUP
THONK
NICHE...

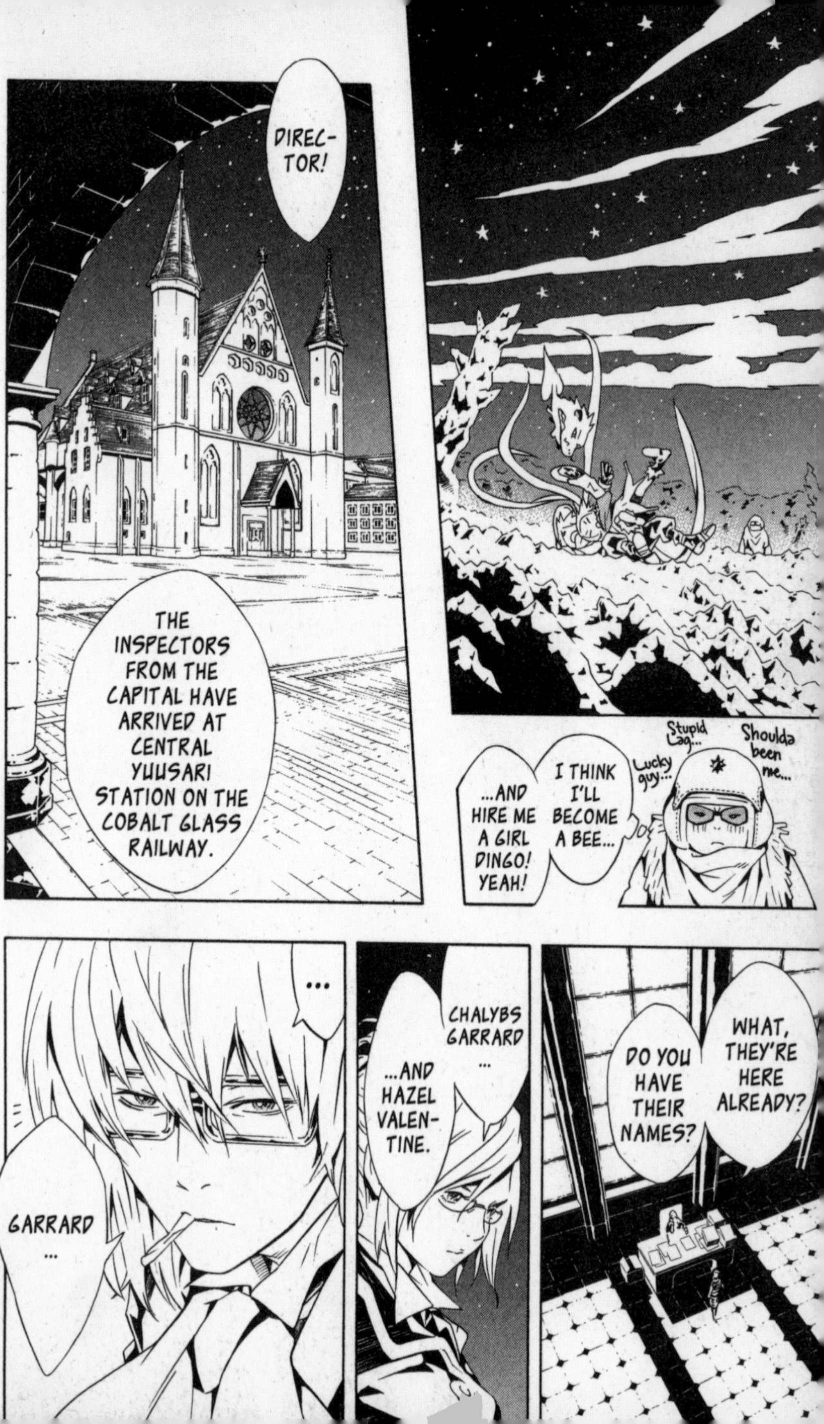
Shoulda been me...
Stupid Lag...
Lucky guy...
I THINK I'LL BECOME A BEE...
...AND HIRE ME A GIRL DINGO! YEAH!
DIREC-TOR!
THE INSPECTORS FROM THE CAPITAL HAVE ARRIVED AT CENTRAL YUUSARI STATION ON THE COBALT GLASS RAILWAY.
WHAT, THEY'RE HERE ALREADY?
DO YOU HAVE THEIR NAMES?
CHALYBS GARRARD...
...AND HAZEL VALEN-TINE.
...
GARRARD...

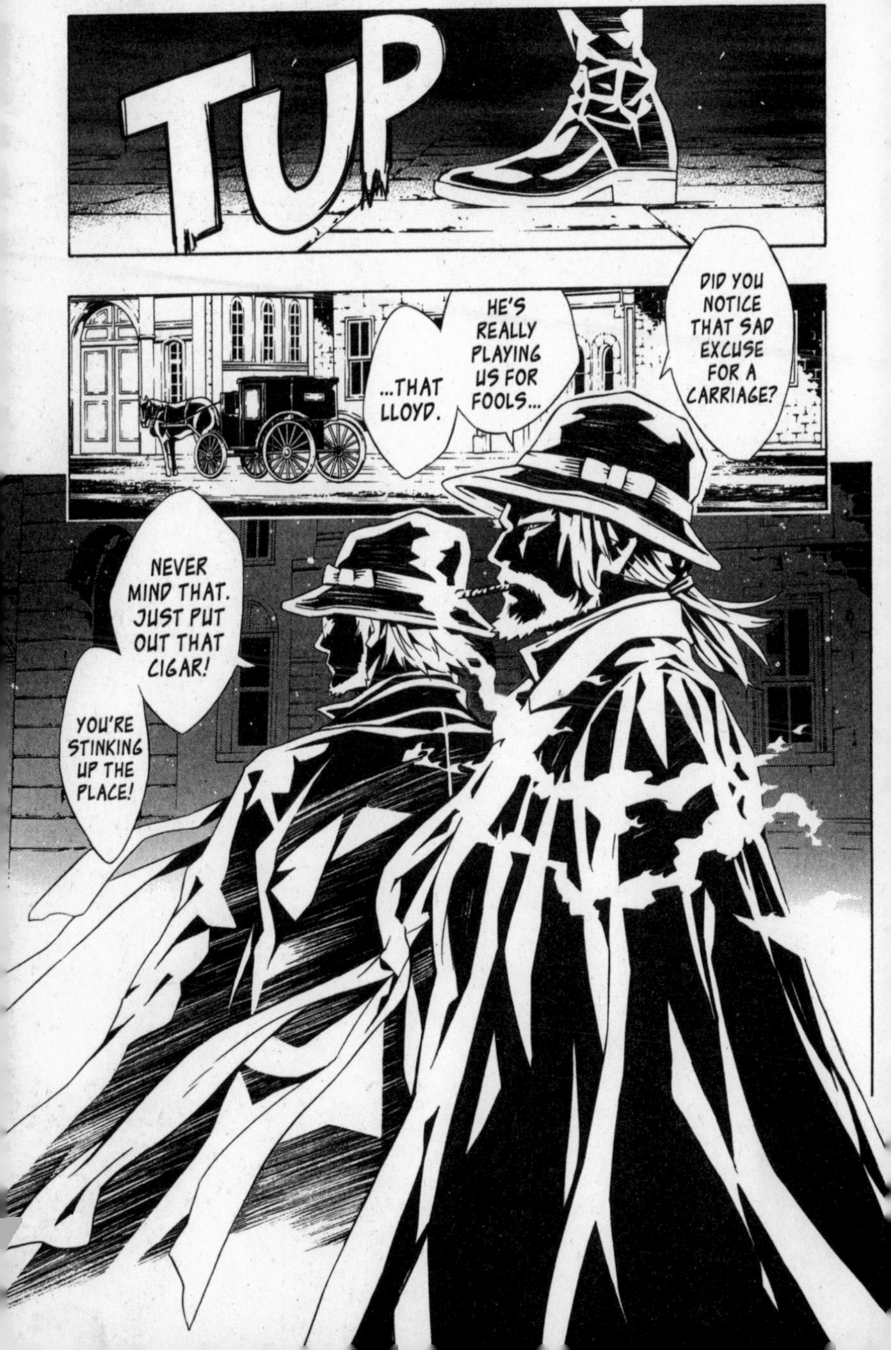
TUP
DID YOU NOTICE THAT SAD EXCUSE FOR A CARRIAGE?
HE'S REALLY PLAYING US FOR FOOLS...
...THAT LLOYD.
NEVER MIND THAT. JUST PUT OUT THAT CIGAR!
YOU'RE STINKING UP THE PLACE!

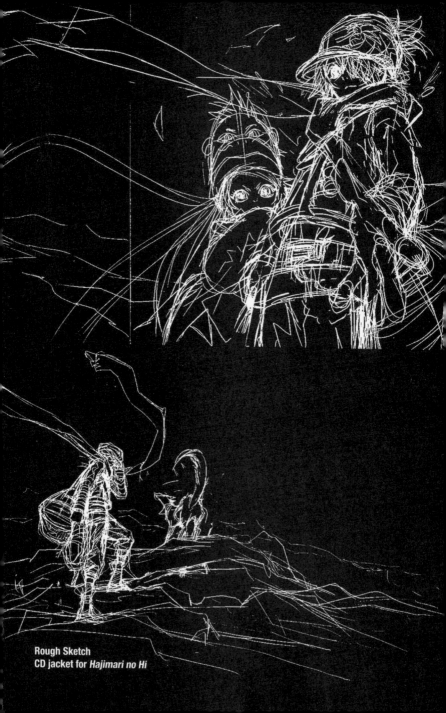

Rough Sketch
CD jacket for *Hajimari no Hi*

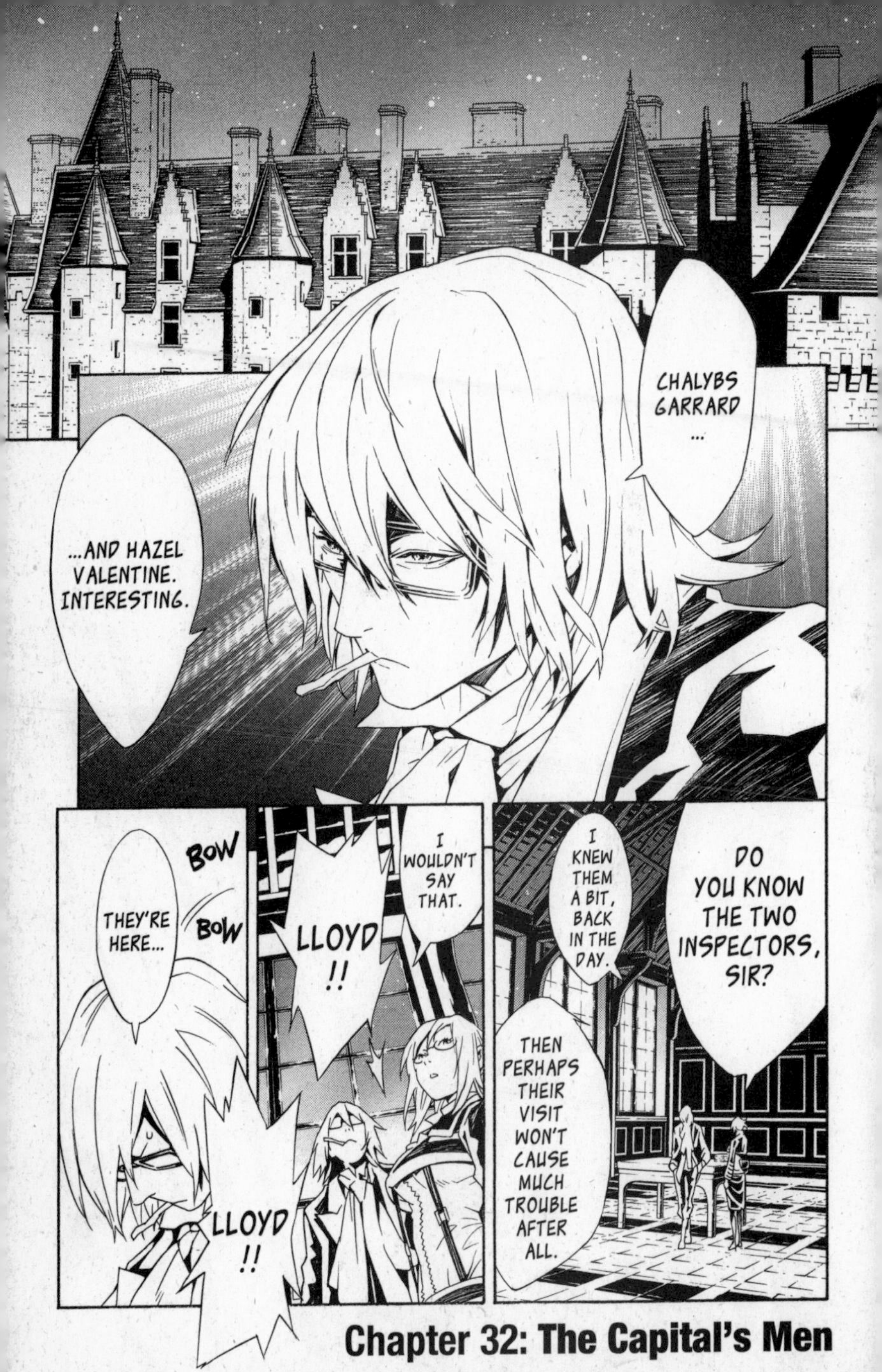
CHALYBS GARRARD ...
...AND HAZEL VALENTINE. INTERESTING.
DO YOU KNOW THE TWO INSPECTORS, SIR?
I KNEW THEM A BIT, BACK IN THE DAY.
THEN PERHAPS THEIR VISIT WON'T CAUSE MUCH TROUBLE AFTER ALL.
I WOULDN'T SAY THAT.
LLOYD !!
BOW
BOW
THEY'RE HERE...
LLOYD !!

## Chapter 32: The Capital's Men

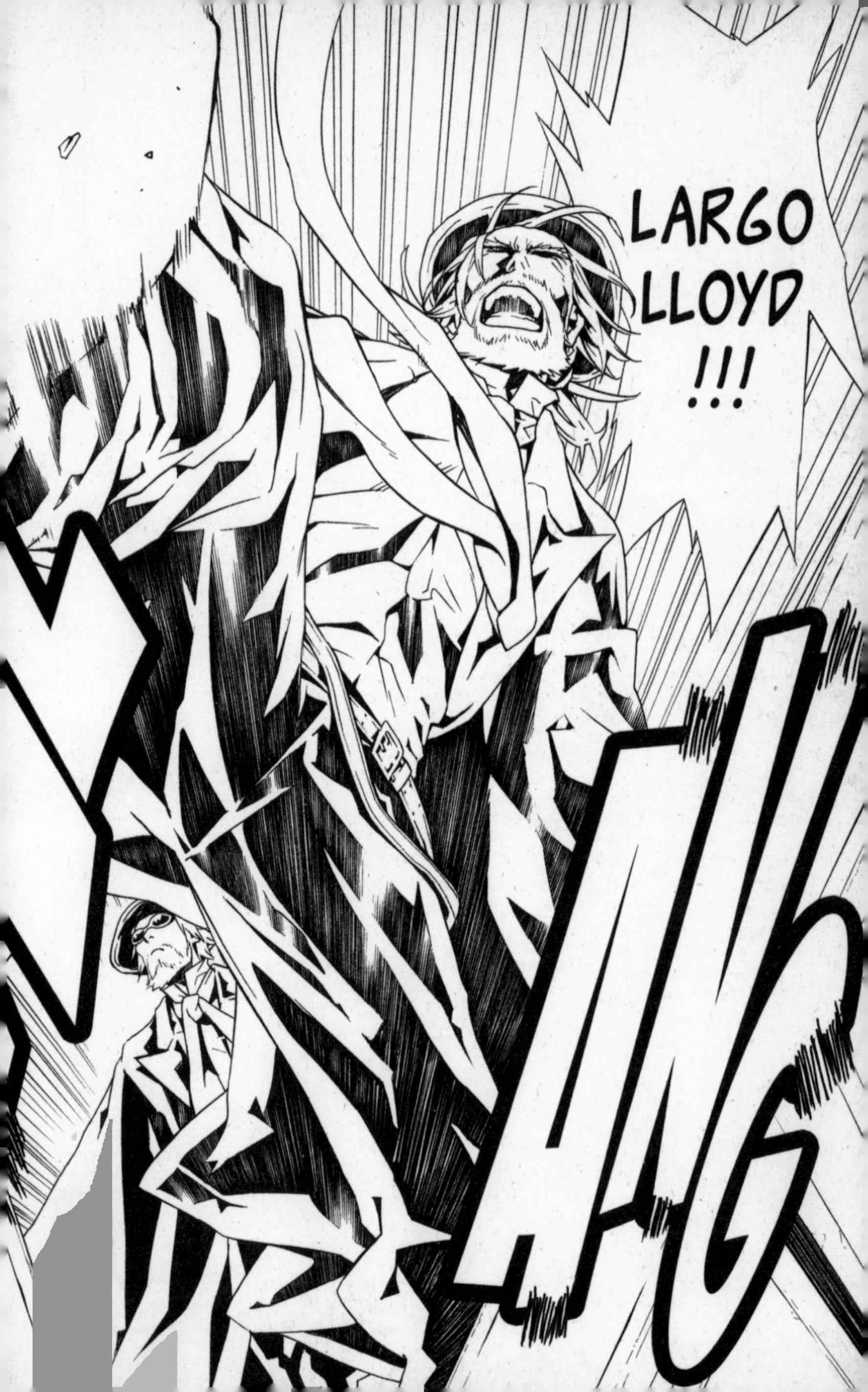
LARGO LLOYD !!!

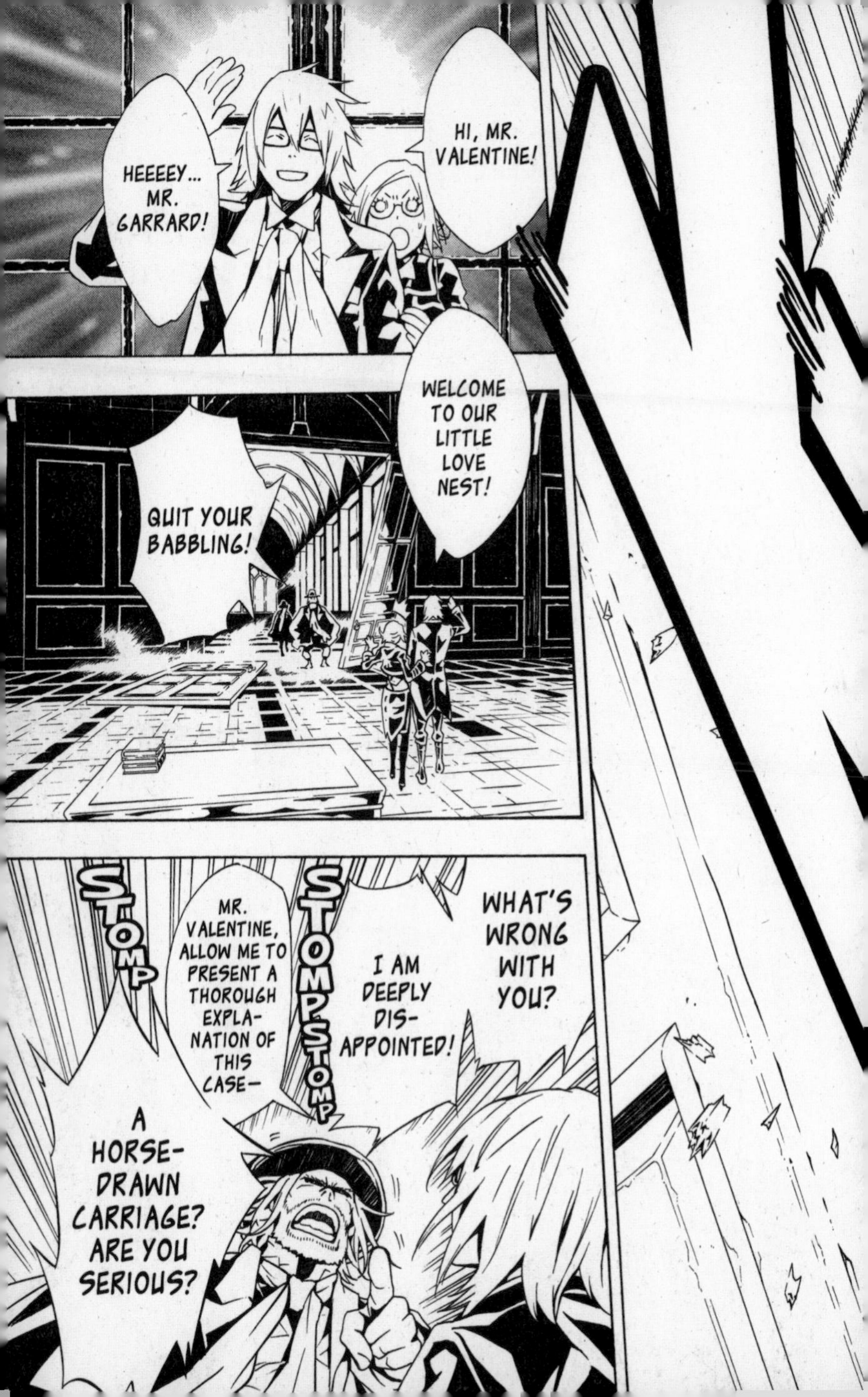
HI, MR. VALENTINE!
HEEEEY... MR. GARRARD!
WELCOME TO OUR LITTLE LOVE NEST!
QUIT YOUR BABBLING!
WHAT'S WRONG WITH YOU?
I AM DEEPLY DIS-APPOINTED!
STOMPSTOMP
MR. VALENTINE, ALLOW ME TO PRESENT A THOROUGH EXPLA-NATION OF THIS CASE—
STOMP
A HORSE-DRAWN CARRIAGE? ARE YOU SERIOUS?

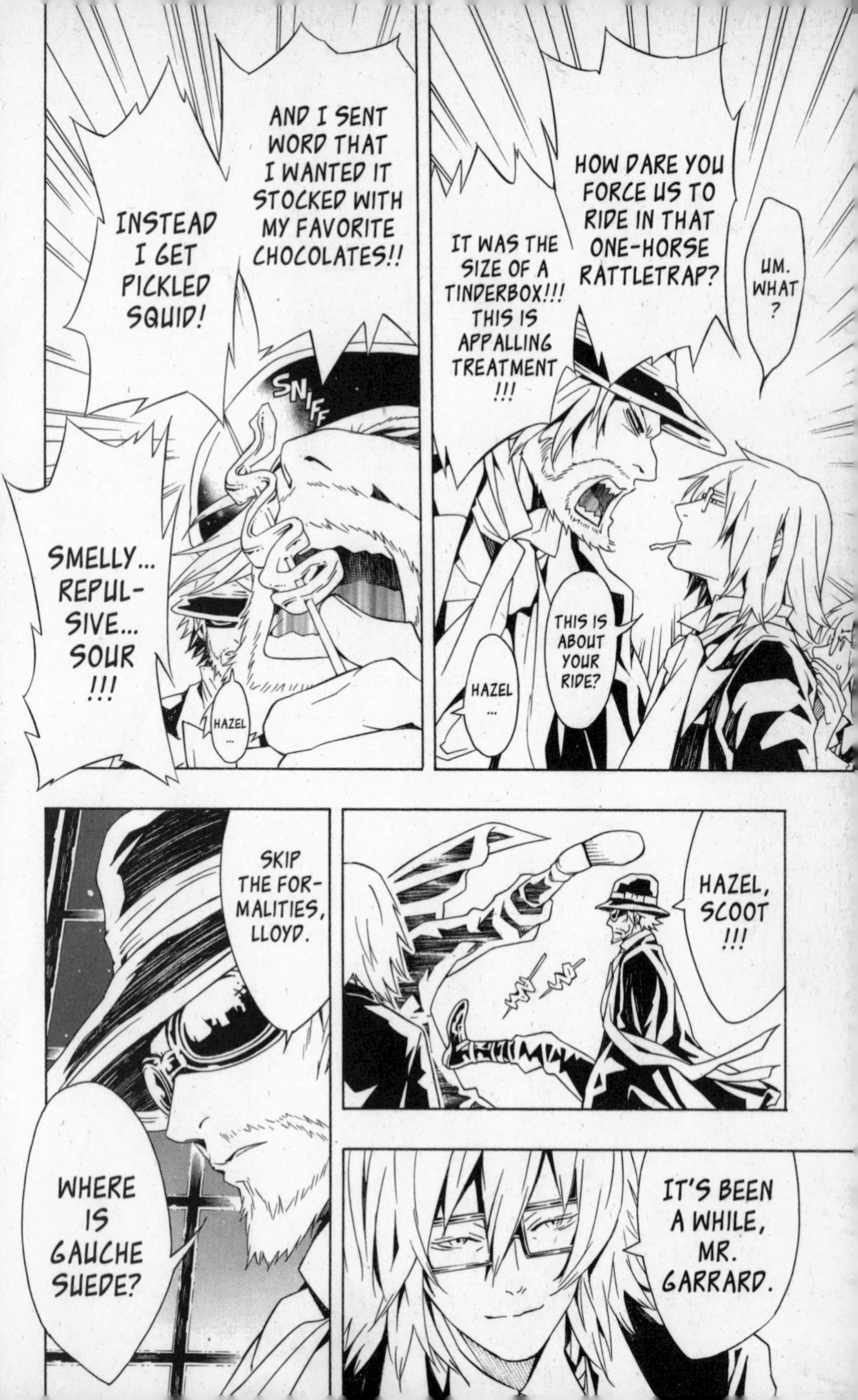
UM. WHAT?
HOW DARE YOU FORCE US TO RIDE IN THAT ONE-HORSE RATTLETRAP?
IT WAS THE SIZE OF A TINDERBOX!!! THIS IS APPALLING TREATMENT!!!
THIS IS ABOUT YOUR RIDE?
HAZEL...
AND I SENT WORD THAT I WANTED IT STOCKED WITH MY FAVORITE CHOCOLATES!!
INSTEAD I GET PICKLED SQUID!
SNIFF
SMELLY... REPULSIVE... SOUR!!!
HAZEL...
HAZEL, SCOOT!!!
IT'S BEEN A WHILE, MR. GARRARD.
SKIP THE FORMALITIES, LLOYD.
WHERE IS GAUCHE SUEDE?

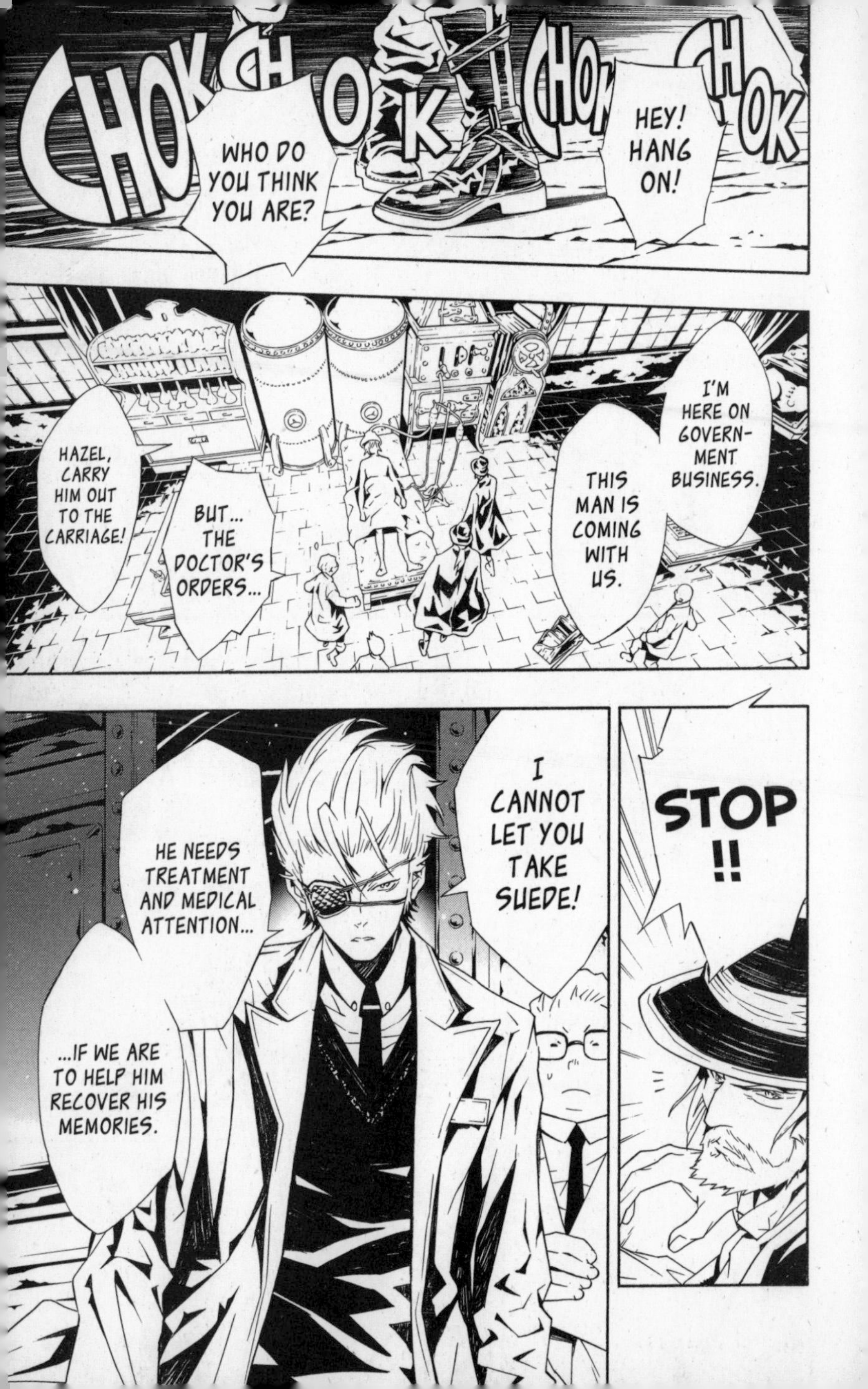
CHOK
HEY! HANG ON!
CHOK
CHOK
WHO DO YOU THINK YOU ARE?
CHOK
I'M HERE ON GOVERNMENT BUSINESS.
THIS MAN IS COMING WITH US.
BUT... THE DOCTOR'S ORDERS...
HAZEL, CARRY HIM OUT TO THE CARRIAGE!
STOP!!
I CANNOT LET YOU TAKE SUEDE!
HE NEEDS TREATMENT AND MEDICAL ATTENTION...
...IF WE ARE TO HELP HIM RECOVER HIS MEMORIES.

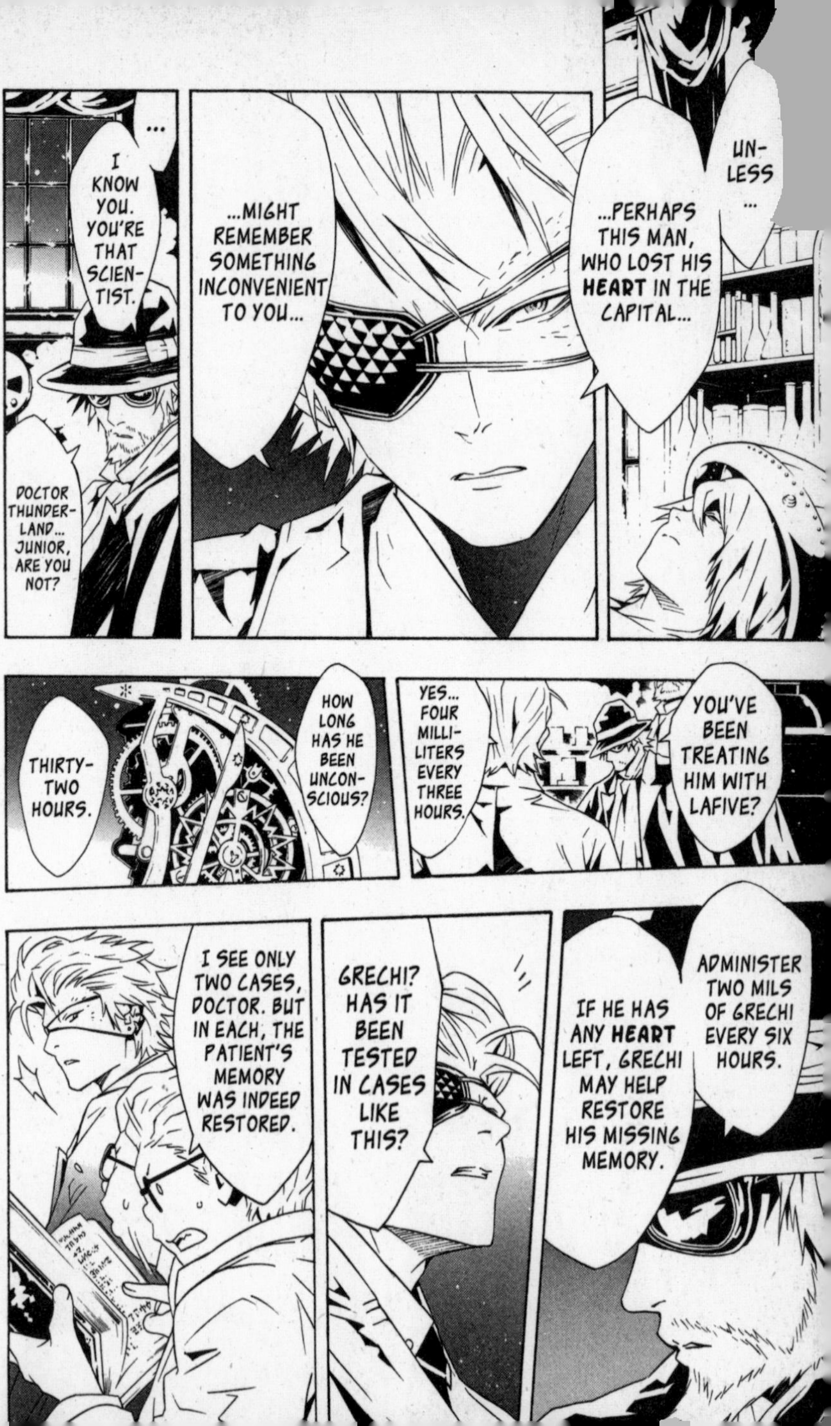
UNLESS...
...PERHAPS THIS MAN, WHO LOST HIS **HEART** IN THE CAPITAL...
...MIGHT REMEMBER SOMETHING INCONVENIENT TO YOU...
...
I KNOW YOU. YOU'RE THAT SCIENTIST.
DOCTOR THUNDERLAND... JUNIOR, ARE YOU NOT?
YOU'VE BEEN TREATING HIM WITH LAFIVE?
YES... FOUR MILLILITERS EVERY THREE HOURS.
HOW LONG HAS HE BEEN UNCONSCIOUS?
THIRTY-TWO HOURS.
ADMINISTER TWO MILS OF GRECHI EVERY SIX HOURS.
IF HE HAS ANY **HEART** LEFT, GRECHI MAY HELP RESTORE HIS MISSING MEMORY.
GRECHI? HAS IT BEEN TESTED IN CASES LIKE THIS?
I SEE ONLY TWO CASES, DOCTOR. BUT IN EACH, THE PATIENT'S MEMORY WAS INDEED RESTORED.

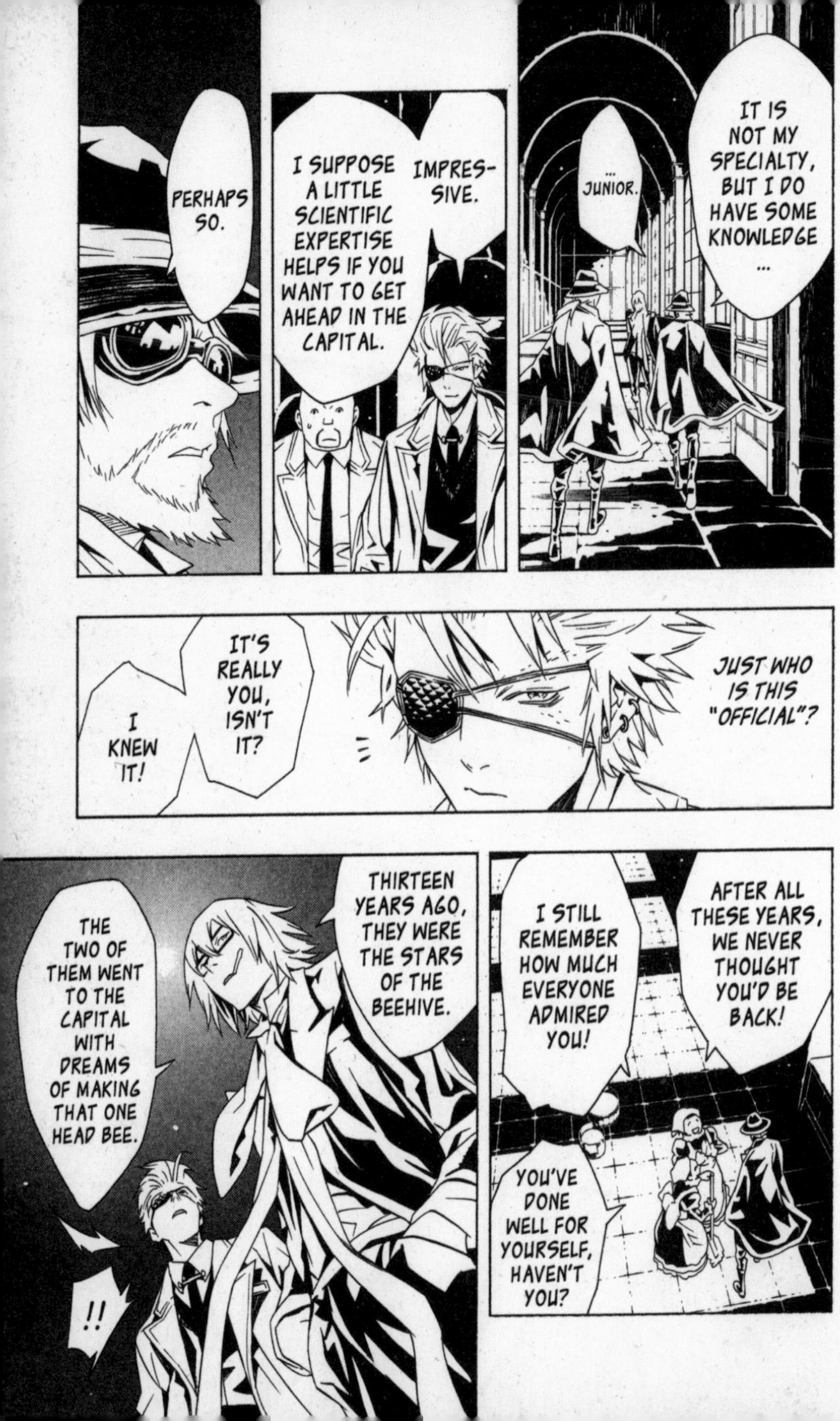
IT IS NOT MY SPECIALTY, BUT I DO HAVE SOME KNOWLEDGE ...
... JUNIOR.
IMPRES-SIVE.
I SUPPOSE A LITTLE SCIENTIFIC EXPERTISE HELPS IF YOU WANT TO GET AHEAD IN THE CAPITAL.
PERHAPS SO.
JUST WHO IS THIS "OFFICIAL"?
IT'S REALLY YOU, ISN'T IT?
I KNEW IT!
AFTER ALL THESE YEARS, WE NEVER THOUGHT YOU'D BE BACK!
I STILL REMEMBER HOW MUCH EVERYONE ADMIRED YOU!
YOU'VE DONE WELL FOR YOURSELF, HAVEN'T YOU?
THIRTEEN YEARS AGO, THEY WERE THE STARS OF THE BEEHIVE.
THE TWO OF THEM WENT TO THE CAPITAL WITH DREAMS OF MAKING THAT ONE HEAD BEE.
!!

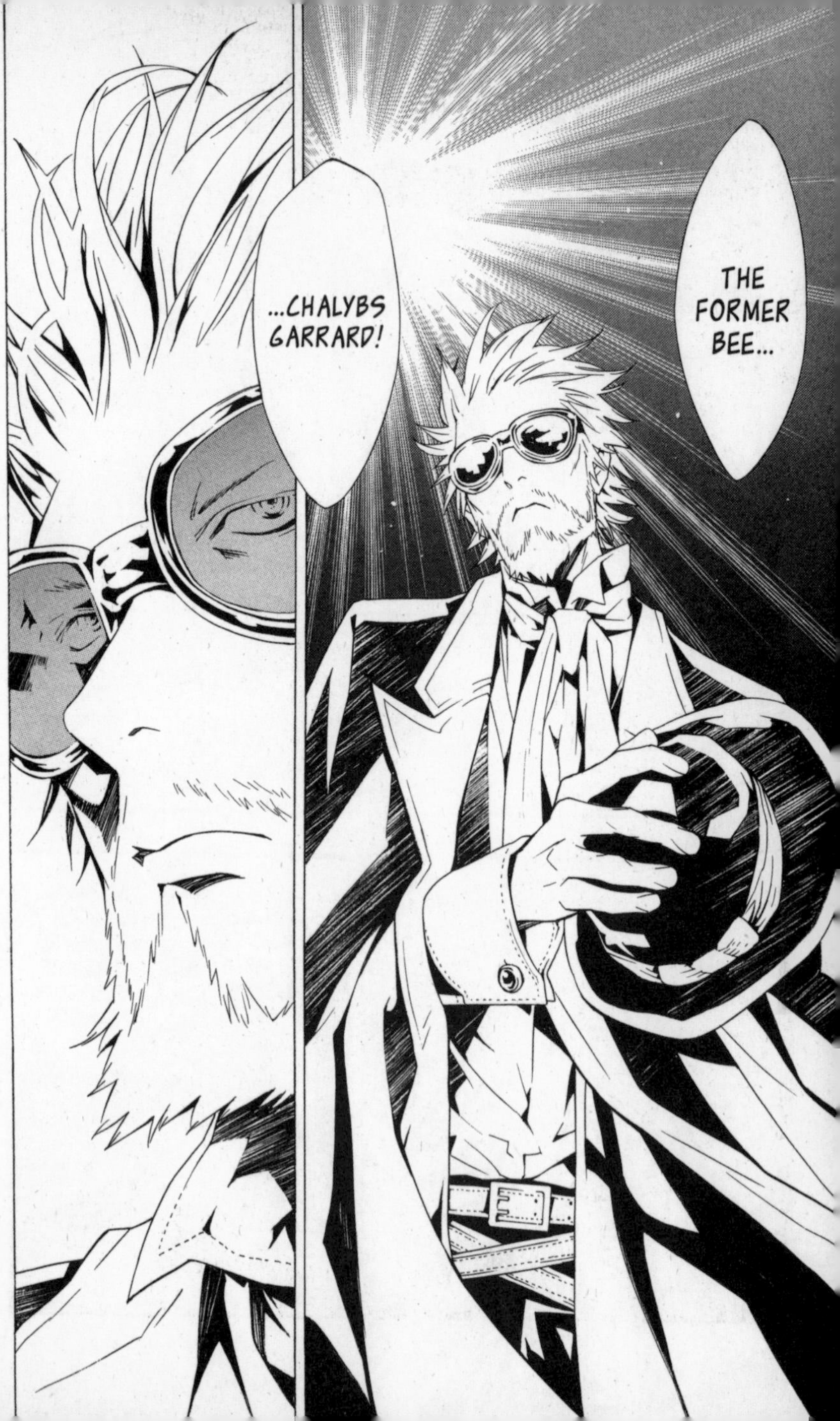
THE FORMER BEE...
...CHALYBS GARRARD!

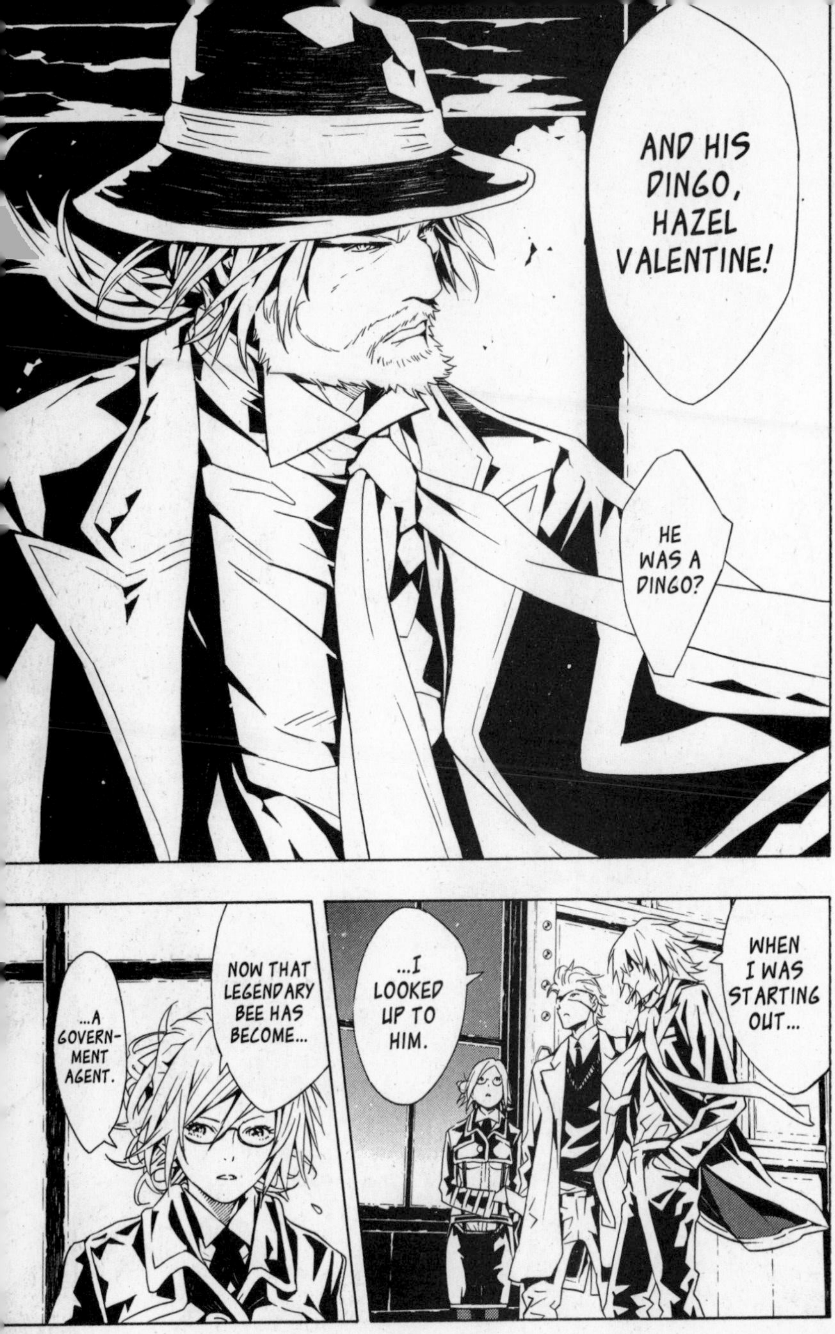
AND HIS DINGO, HAZEL VALENTINE!
HE WAS A DINGO?
WHEN I WAS STARTING OUT...
...I LOOKED UP TO HIM.
NOW THAT LEGENDARY BEE HAS BECOME...
...A GOVERNMENT AGENT.

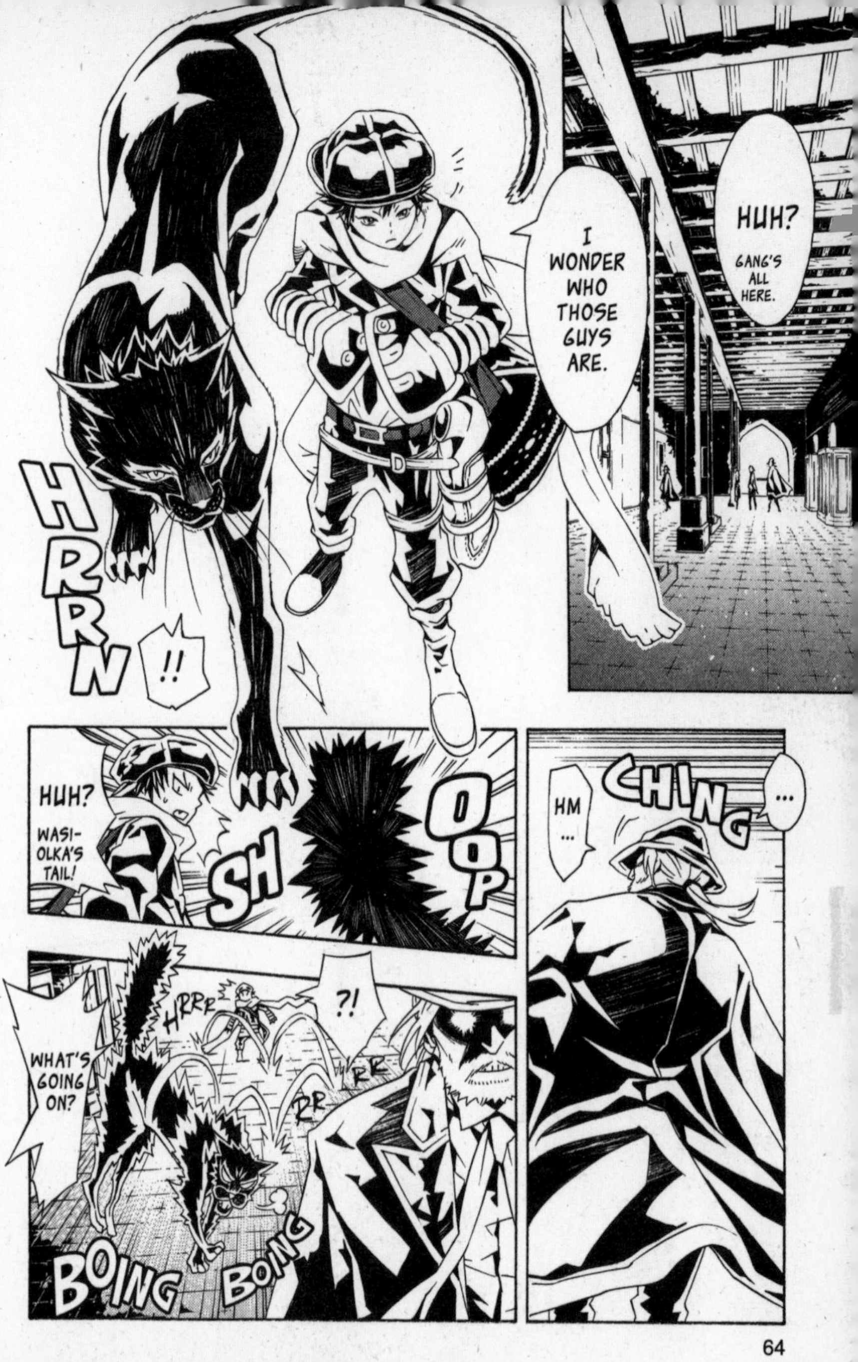
HUH?
GANG'S ALL HERE.
I WONDER WHO THOSE GUYS ARE.
HRRRN
!!
HM...
CHING
...
HUH?
WASI-OLKA'S TAIL!
SHOOP
?!
HRRR
RR
RR
WHAT'S GOING ON?
BOING BOING

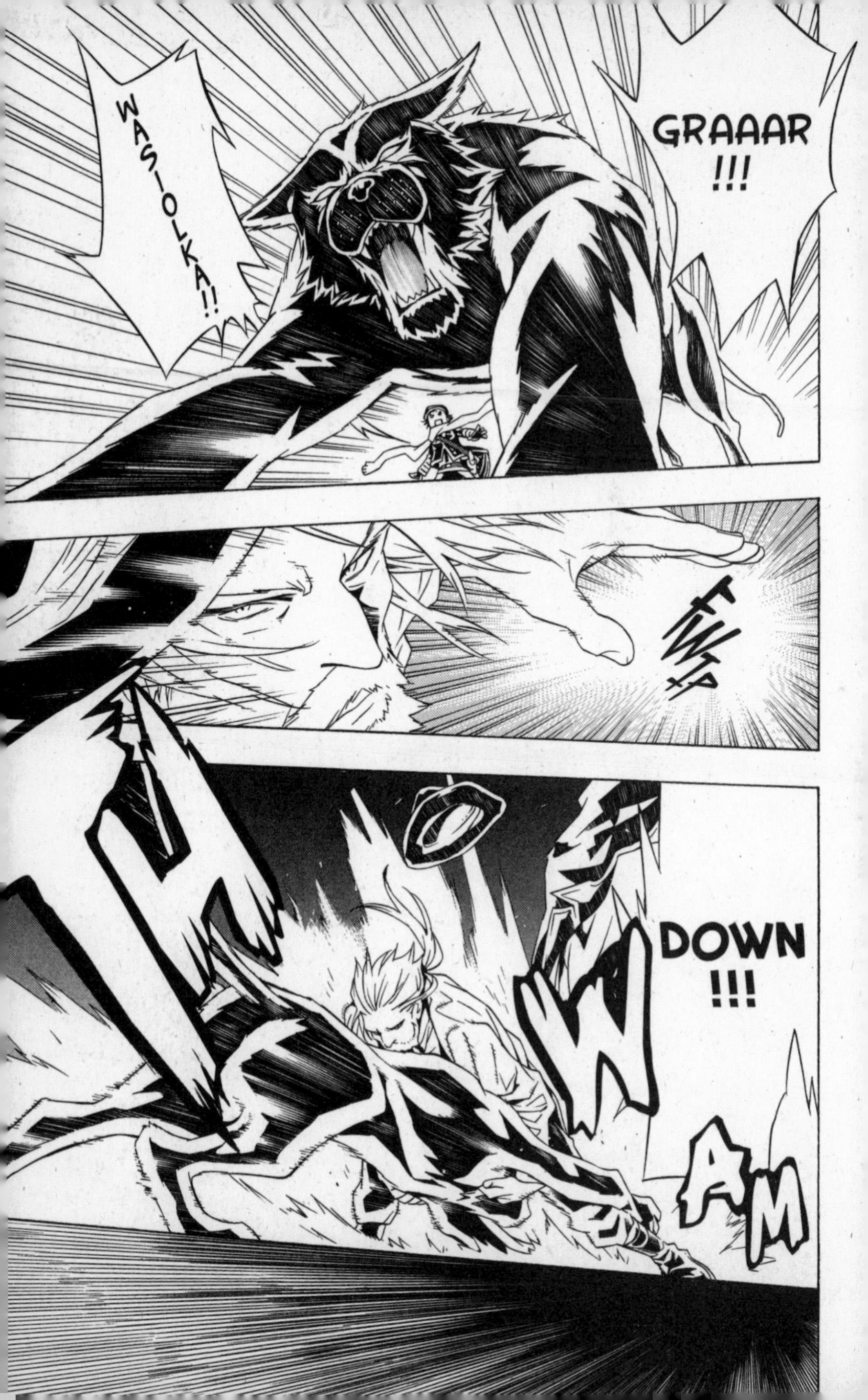
GRAAAR !!!
WASIOLKA!!
FWIP
DOWN !!!

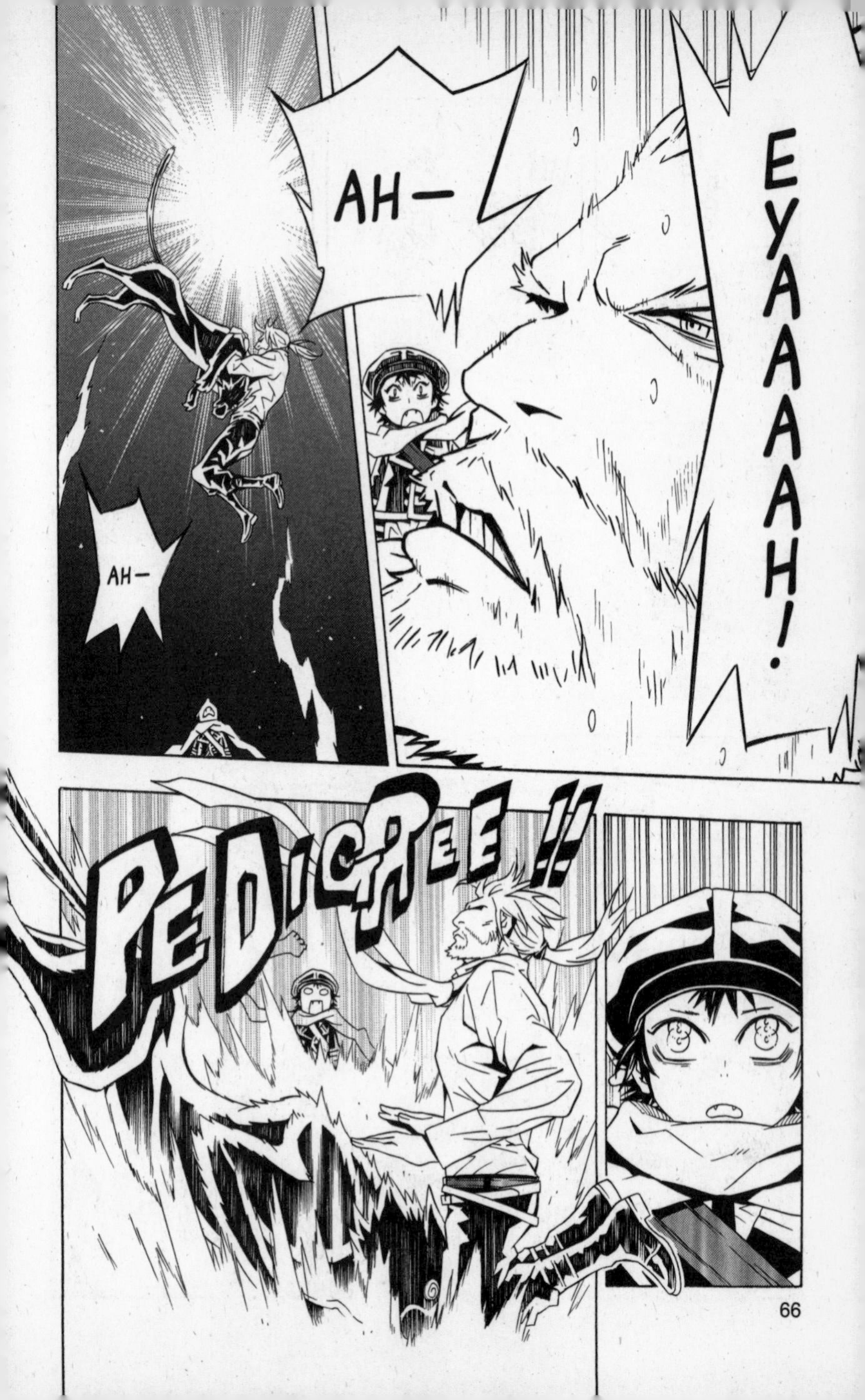
AH—
EYAAAAH!
AH—
PEDIGREE!!

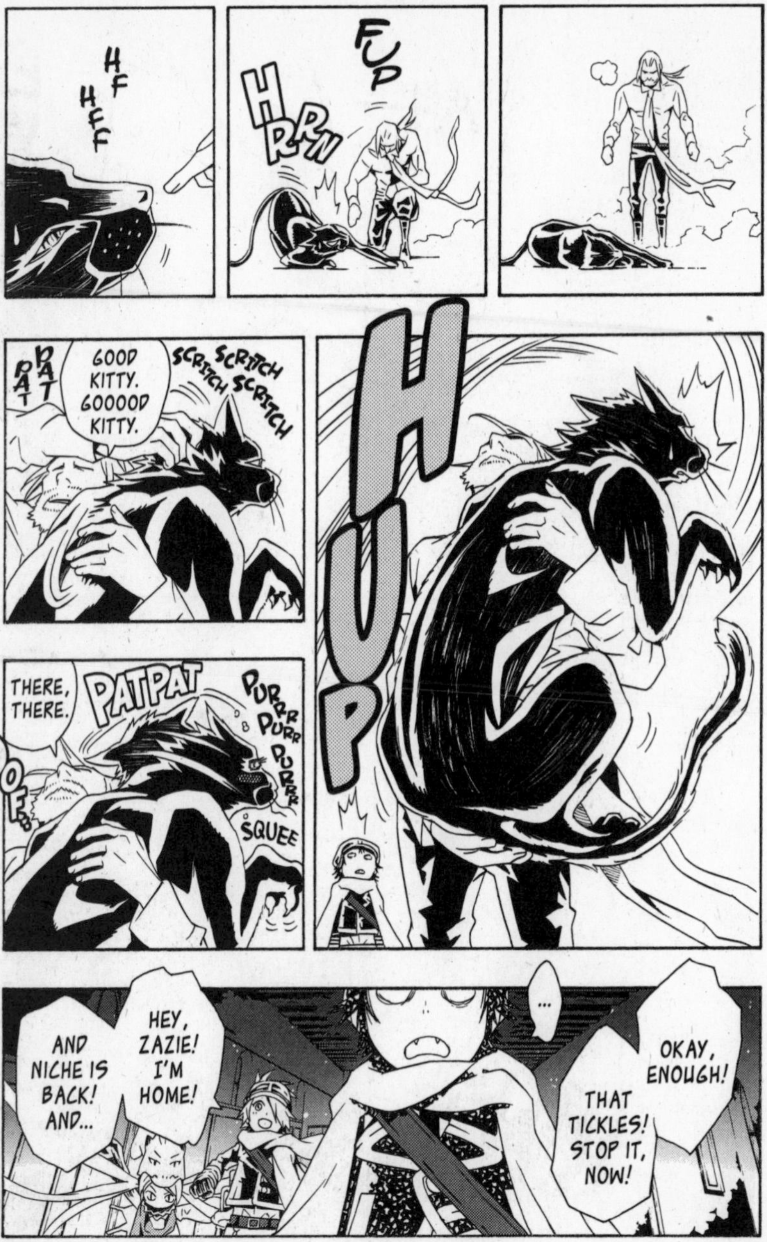
FUP
HRRN
HF
HFF
HUP
SCRITCH SCRITCH
SCRITCH SCRITCH
GOOD KITTY. GOOOOD KITTY.
PAT PAT
PURRR PURRR PURRR
SQUEE
PATPAT
THERE, THERE.
OOF
...
OKAY, ENOUGH!
THAT TICKLES! STOP IT, NOW!
HEY, ZAZIE! I'M HOME!
AND NICHE IS BACK! AND...

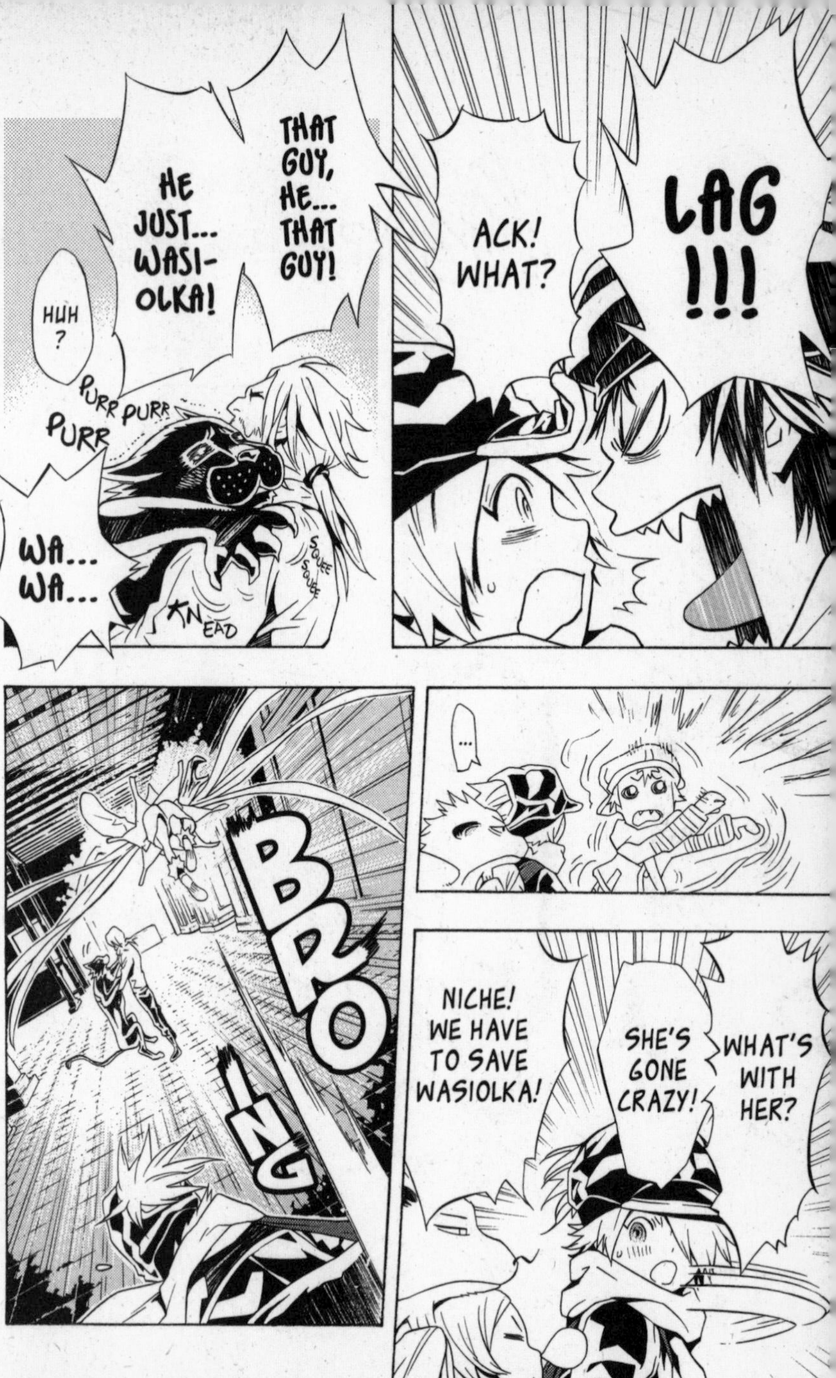
LAG!!!
ACK! WHAT?
THAT GUY, HE... THAT GUY!
HE JUST... WASI-OLKA!
HUH?
PURR PURR
PURR
WA... WA...
SQUEE SQUEE
KNEAD
...
WHAT'S WITH HER?
SHE'S GONE CRAZY!
NICHE! WE HAVE TO SAVE WASIOLKA!
BROING

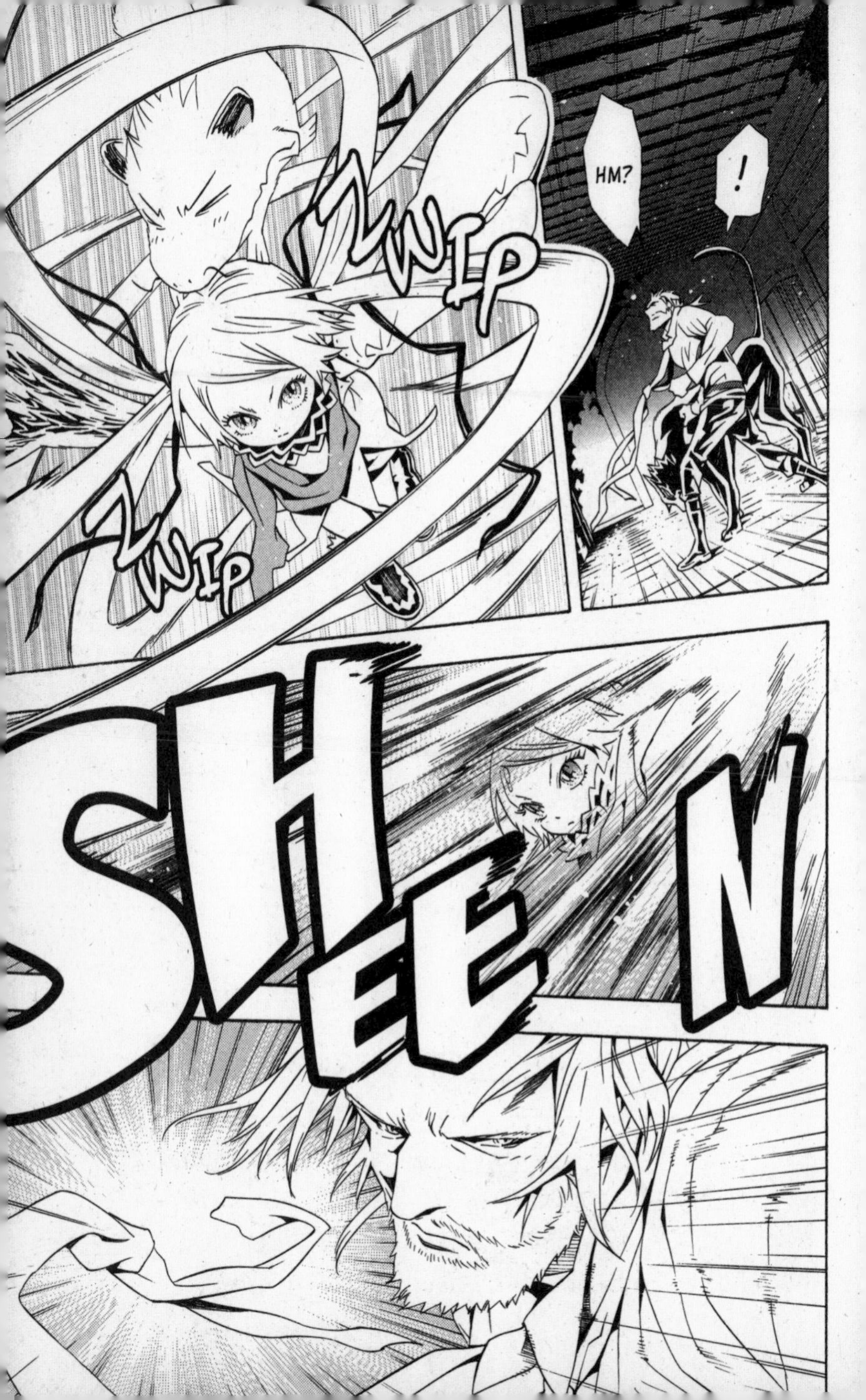
!
HM?
ZWIP
ZWIP
SHIEEN

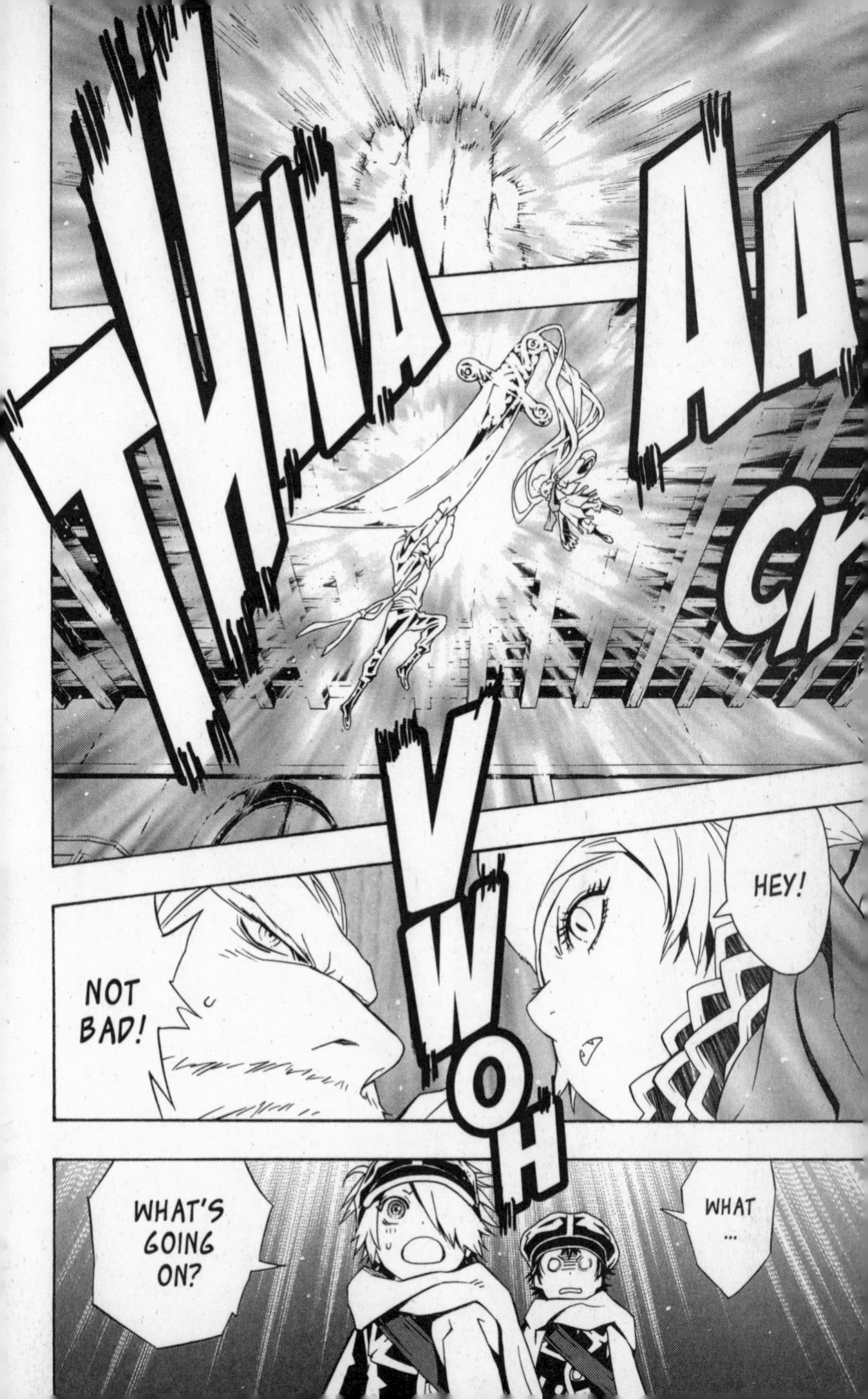
THWAAACK
VWOOH
HEY!
NOT BAD!
WHAT ...
WHAT'S GOING ON?

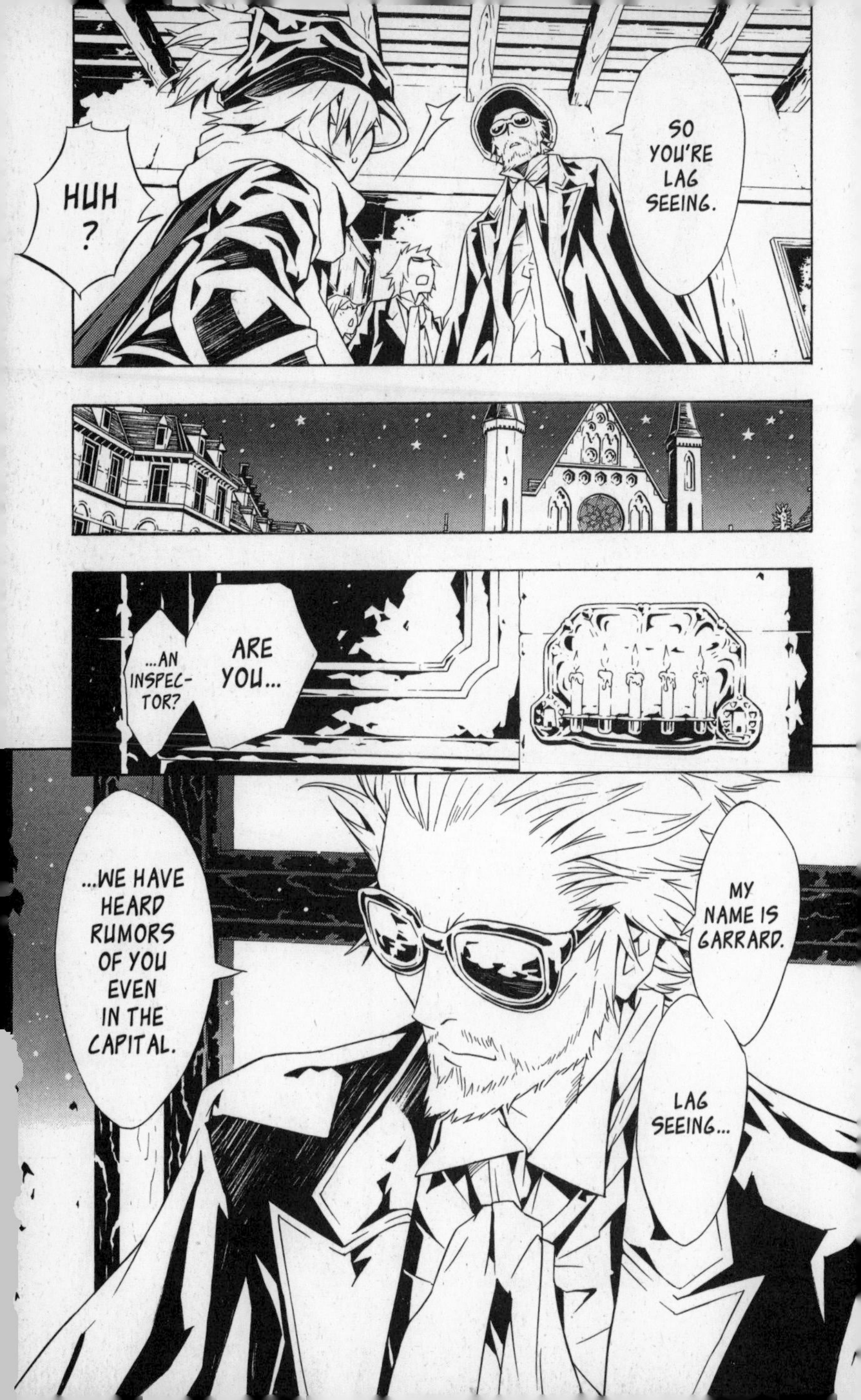
SO YOU'RE LAG SEEING.
HUH ?
ARE YOU...
...AN INSPECTOR?
MY NAME IS GARRARD.
LAG SEEING...
...WE HAVE HEARD RUMORS OF YOU EVEN IN THE CAPITAL.

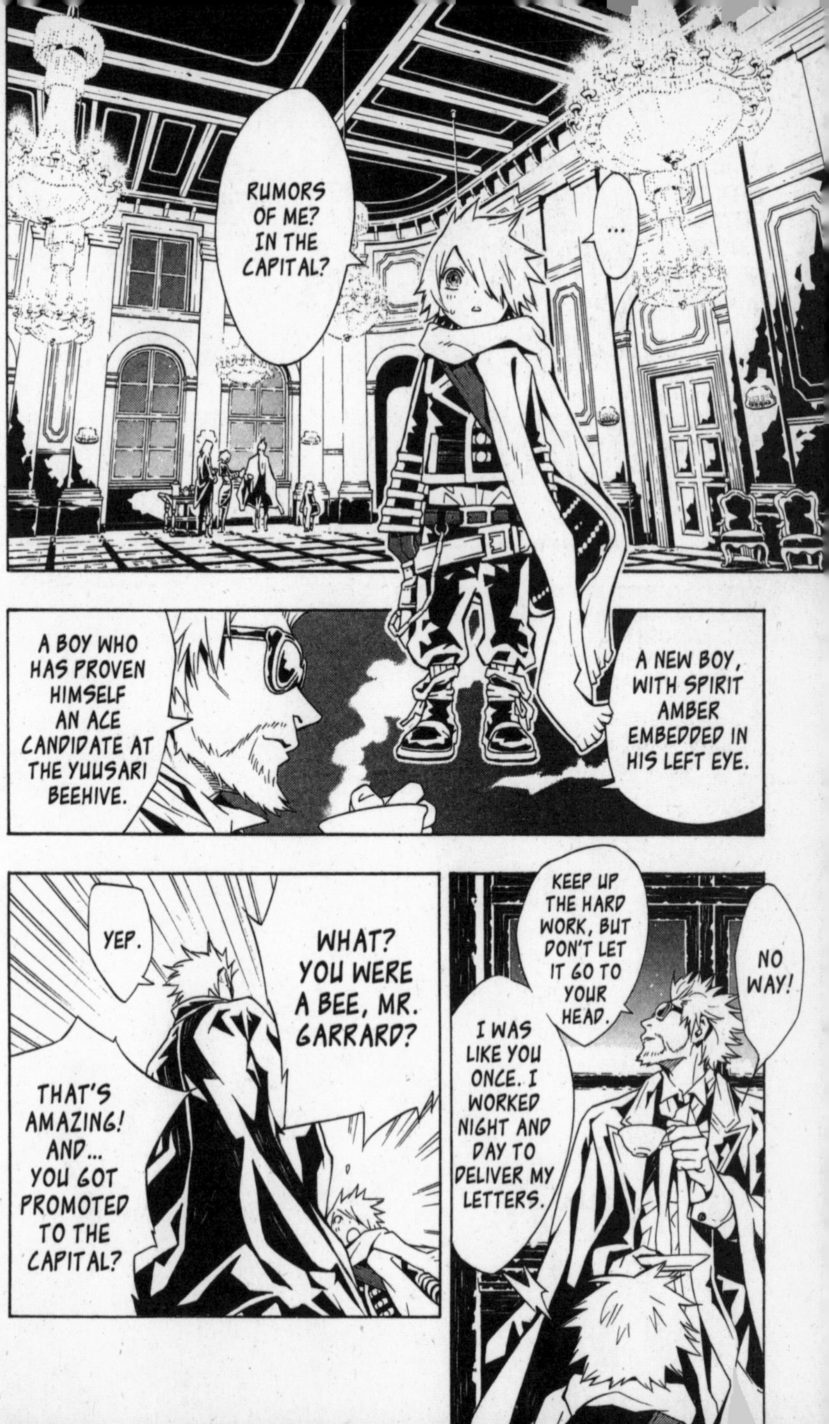
...
RUMORS OF ME? IN THE CAPITAL?
A NEW BOY, WITH SPIRIT AMBER EMBEDDED IN HIS LEFT EYE.
A BOY WHO HAS PROVEN HIMSELF AN ACE CANDIDATE AT THE YUUSARI BEEHIVE.
NO WAY!
KEEP UP THE HARD WORK, BUT DON'T LET IT GO TO YOUR HEAD.
I WAS LIKE YOU ONCE. I WORKED NIGHT AND DAY TO DELIVER MY LETTERS.
WHAT? YOU WERE A BEE, MR. GARRARD?
YEP.
THAT'S AMAZING! AND... YOU GOT PROMOTED TO THE CAPITAL?

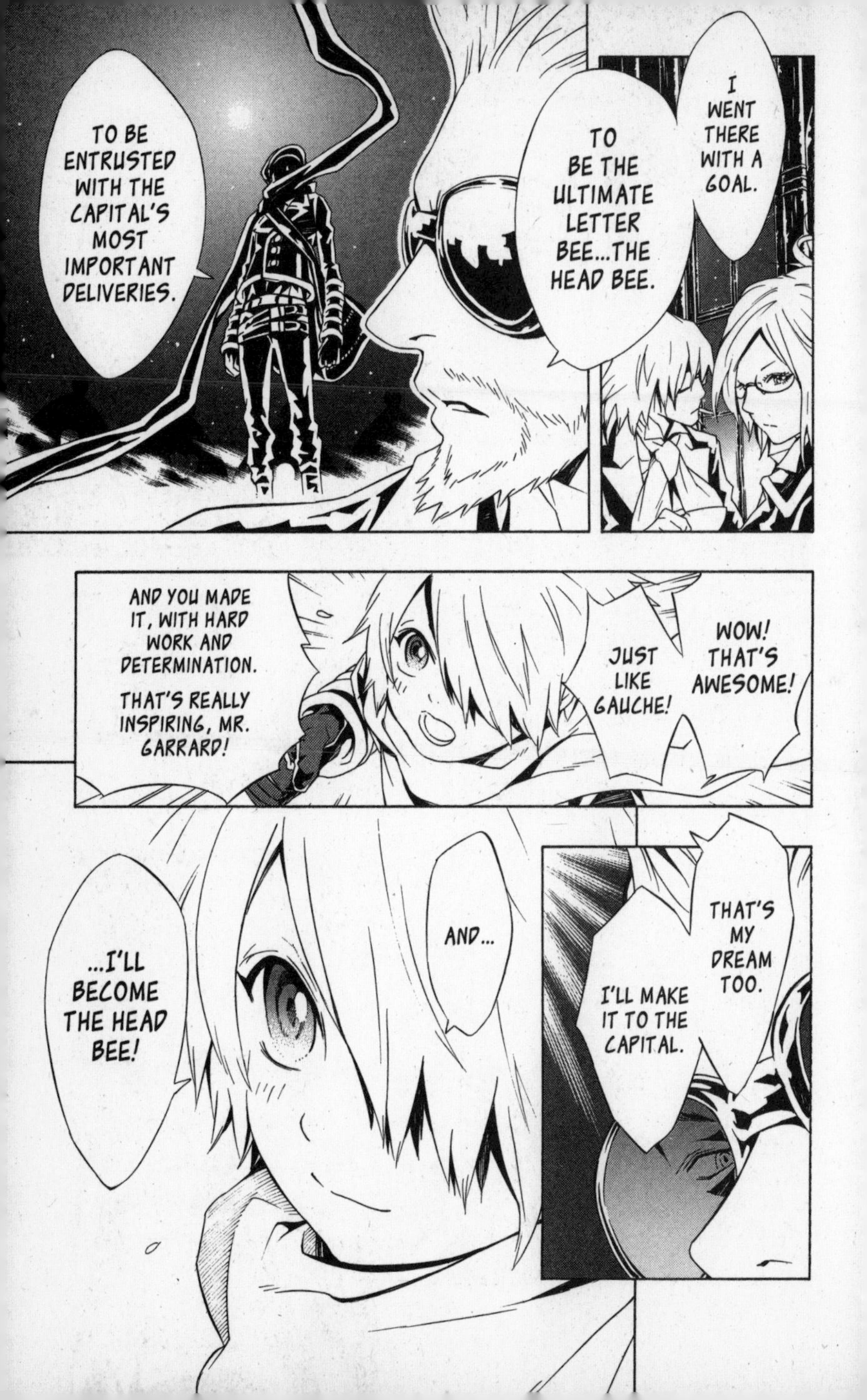
I WENT THERE WITH A GOAL.
TO BE THE ULTIMATE LETTER BEE...THE HEAD BEE.
TO BE ENTRUSTED WITH THE CAPITAL'S MOST IMPORTANT DELIVERIES.
WOW! THAT'S AWESOME!
JUST LIKE GAUCHE!
AND YOU MADE IT, WITH HARD WORK AND DETERMINATION.
THAT'S REALLY INSPIRING, MR. GARRARD!
THAT'S MY DREAM TOO.
I'LL MAKE IT TO THE CAPITAL.
AND...
...I'LL BECOME THE HEAD BEE!

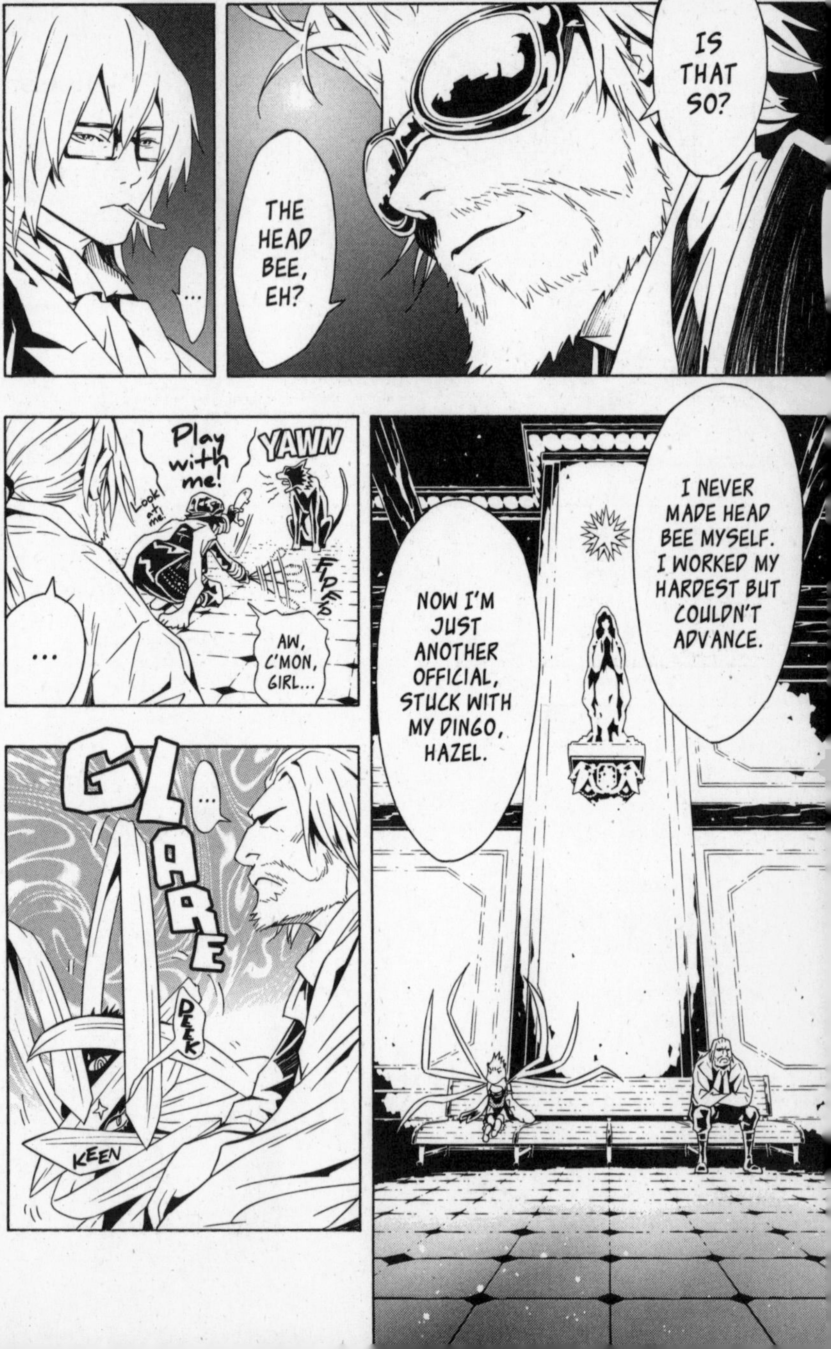
IS THAT SO?
THE HEAD BEE, EH?
...
I NEVER MADE HEAD BEE MYSELF. I WORKED MY HARDEST BUT COULDN'T ADVANCE.
NOW I'M JUST ANOTHER OFFICIAL, STUCK WITH MY DINGO, HAZEL.
YAWN
Play with me!
Look at me!
FIDFID
AW, C'MON, GIRL...
...
GLARE
...
PEEK
KEEN

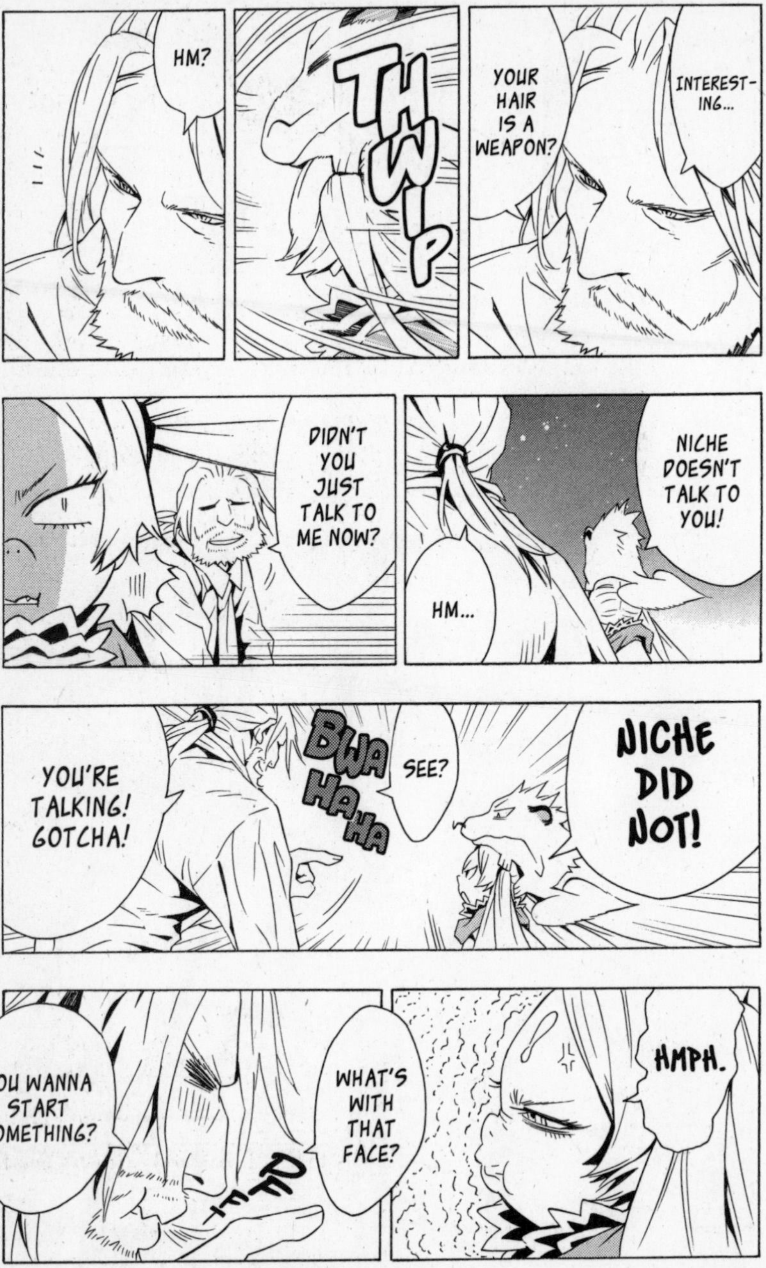
INTERESTING...
YOUR HAIR IS A WEAPON?
THWIP
HM?
NICHE DOESN'T TALK TO YOU!
HM...
DIDN'T YOU JUST TALK TO ME NOW?
NICHE DID NOT!
SEE?
BWAHAHA
YOU'RE TALKING! GOTCHA!
HMPH.
WHAT'S WITH THAT FACE?
PFFT
YOU WANNA START SOMETHING?

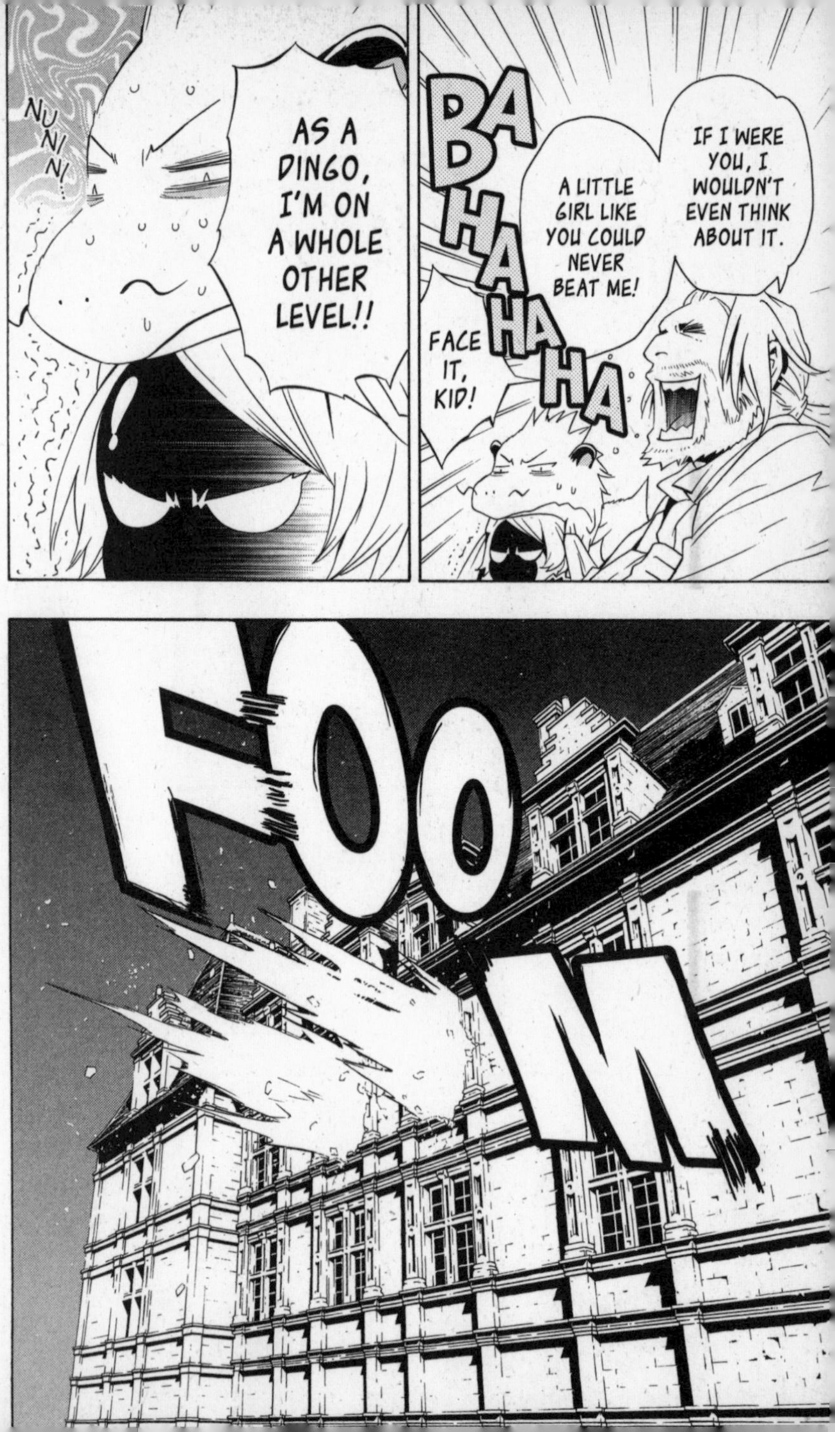
IF I WERE YOU, I WOULDN'T EVEN THINK ABOUT IT.
A LITTLE GIRL LIKE YOU COULD NEVER BEAT ME!
BAHAHAHAHA
FACE IT, KID!
AS A DINGO, I'M ON A WHOLE OTHER LEVEL!!
NU NI NI...
FOOM

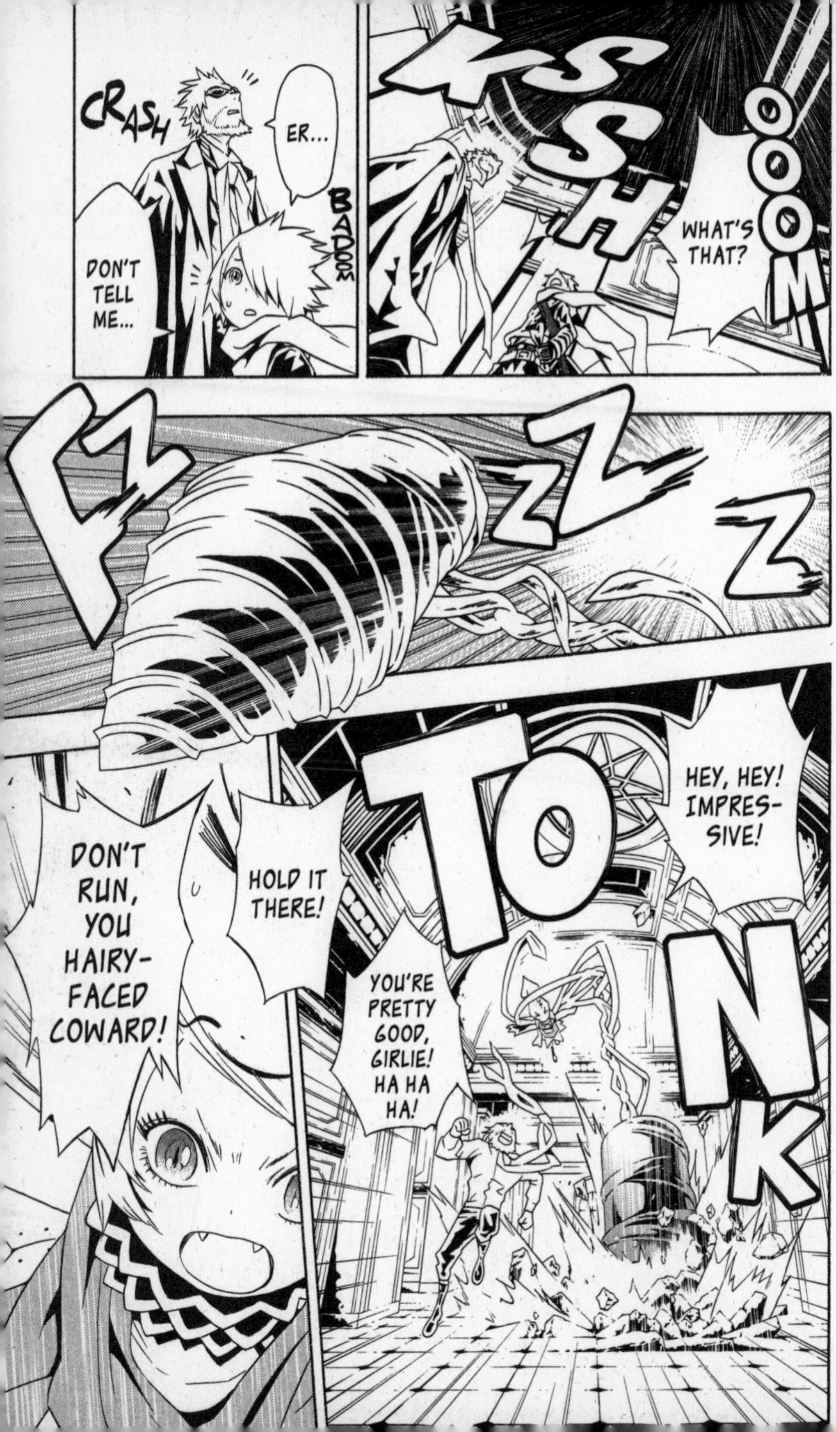
KSSH
OOOOM
WHAT'S THAT?
CRASH
ER...
BADOOM
DON'T TELL ME...
FZZZZ
HEY, HEY! IMPRES-SIVE!
TONK
YOU'RE PRETTY GOOD, GIRLIE! HA HA HA!
HOLD IT THERE!
DON'T RUN, YOU HAIRY-FACED COWARD!

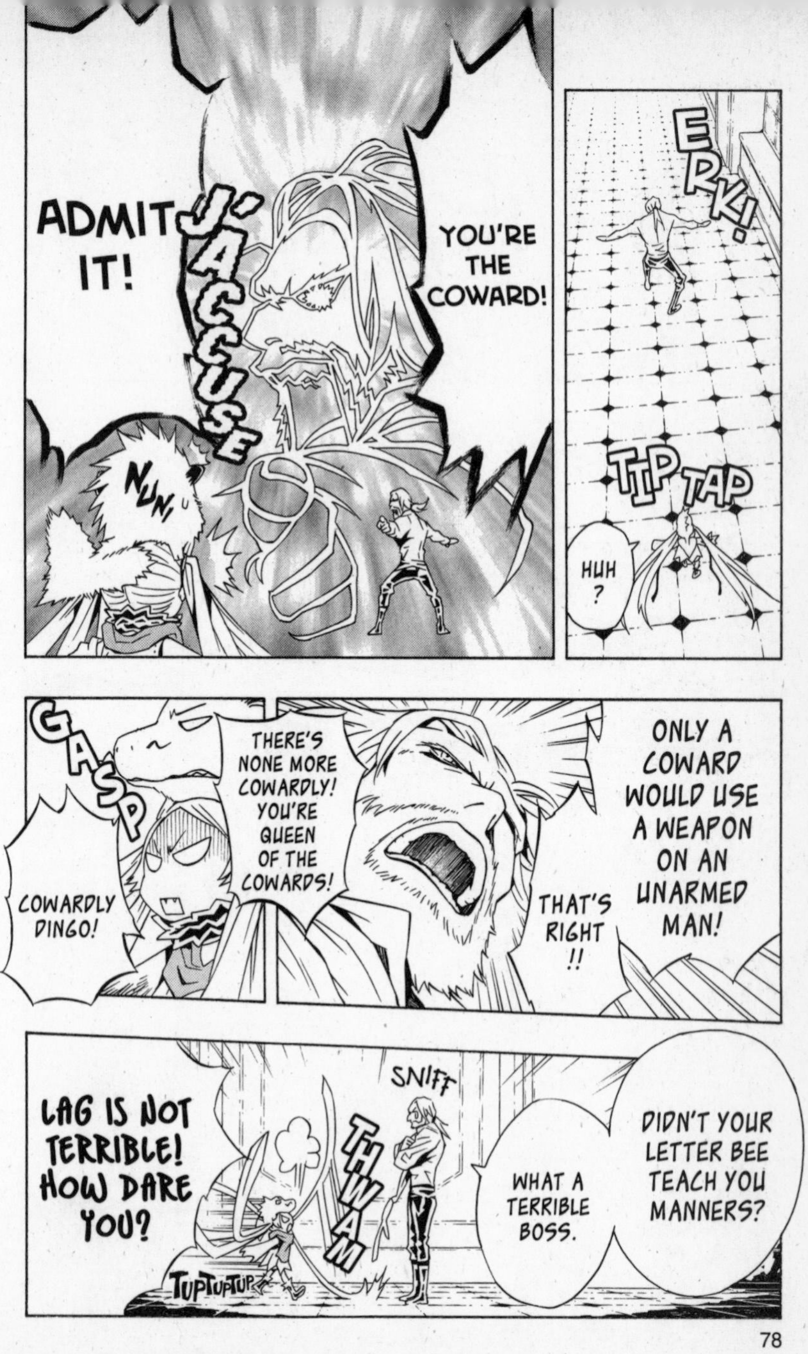
ERK!
TIP TAP
HUH?
YOU'RE THE COWARD!
J'ACCUSE
ADMIT IT!
NUNI
ONLY A COWARD WOULD USE A WEAPON ON AN UNARMED MAN!
THAT'S RIGHT!!
THERE'S NONE MORE COWARDLY! YOU'RE QUEEN OF THE COWARDS!
GASP
COWARDLY DINGO!
DIDN'T YOUR LETTER BEE TEACH YOU MANNERS?
WHAT A TERRIBLE BOSS.
SNIFF
THWAM
LAG IS NOT TERRIBLE! HOW DARE YOU?
TUPTUPTUP

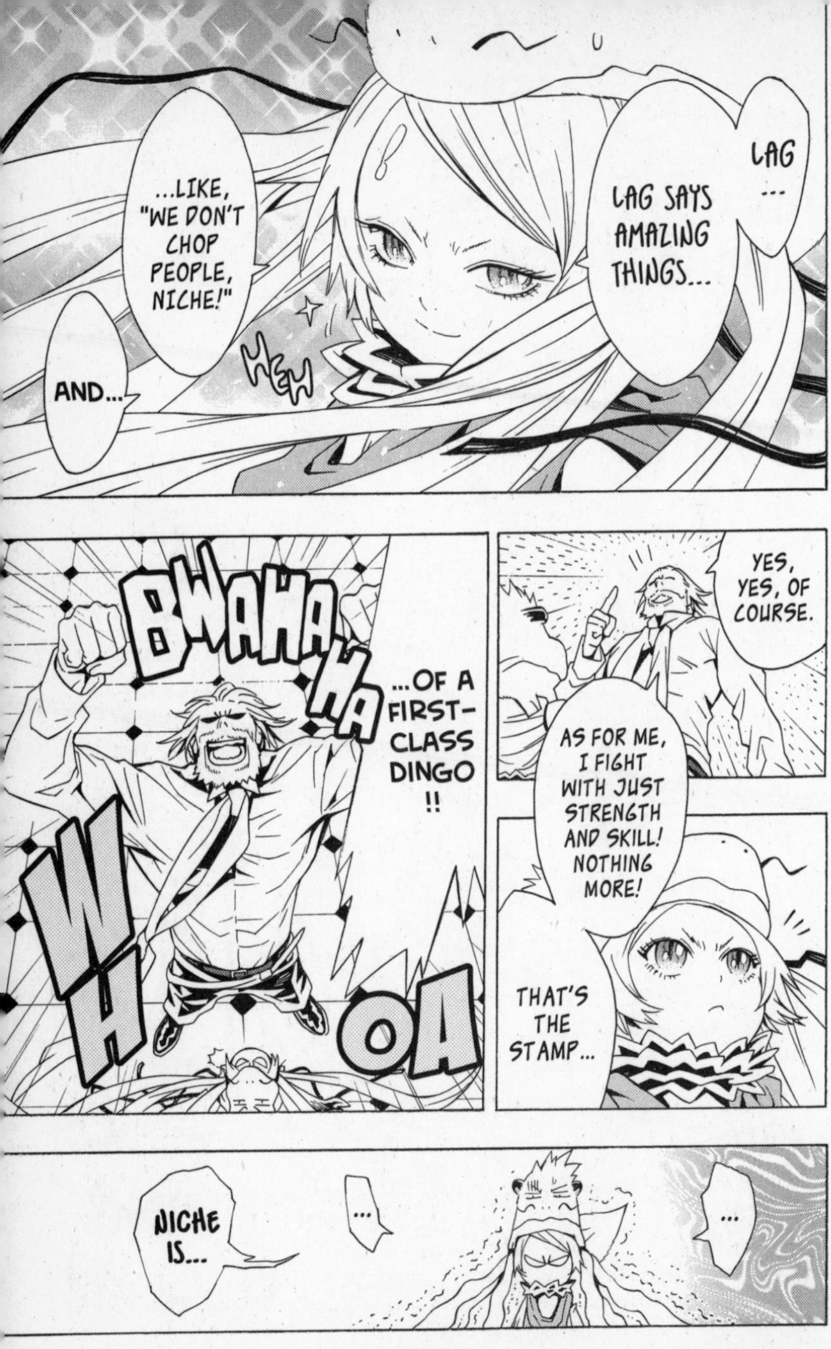
LAG ...
LAG SAYS AMAZING THINGS...
...LIKE, "WE DON'T CHOP PEOPLE, NICHE!"
AND...
HEH
YES, YES, OF COURSE.
AS FOR ME, I FIGHT WITH JUST STRENGTH AND SKILL! NOTHING MORE!
THAT'S THE STAMP...
...OF A FIRST-CLASS DINGO !!
BWAHAHAHA
WHOA
...
...
NICHE IS...

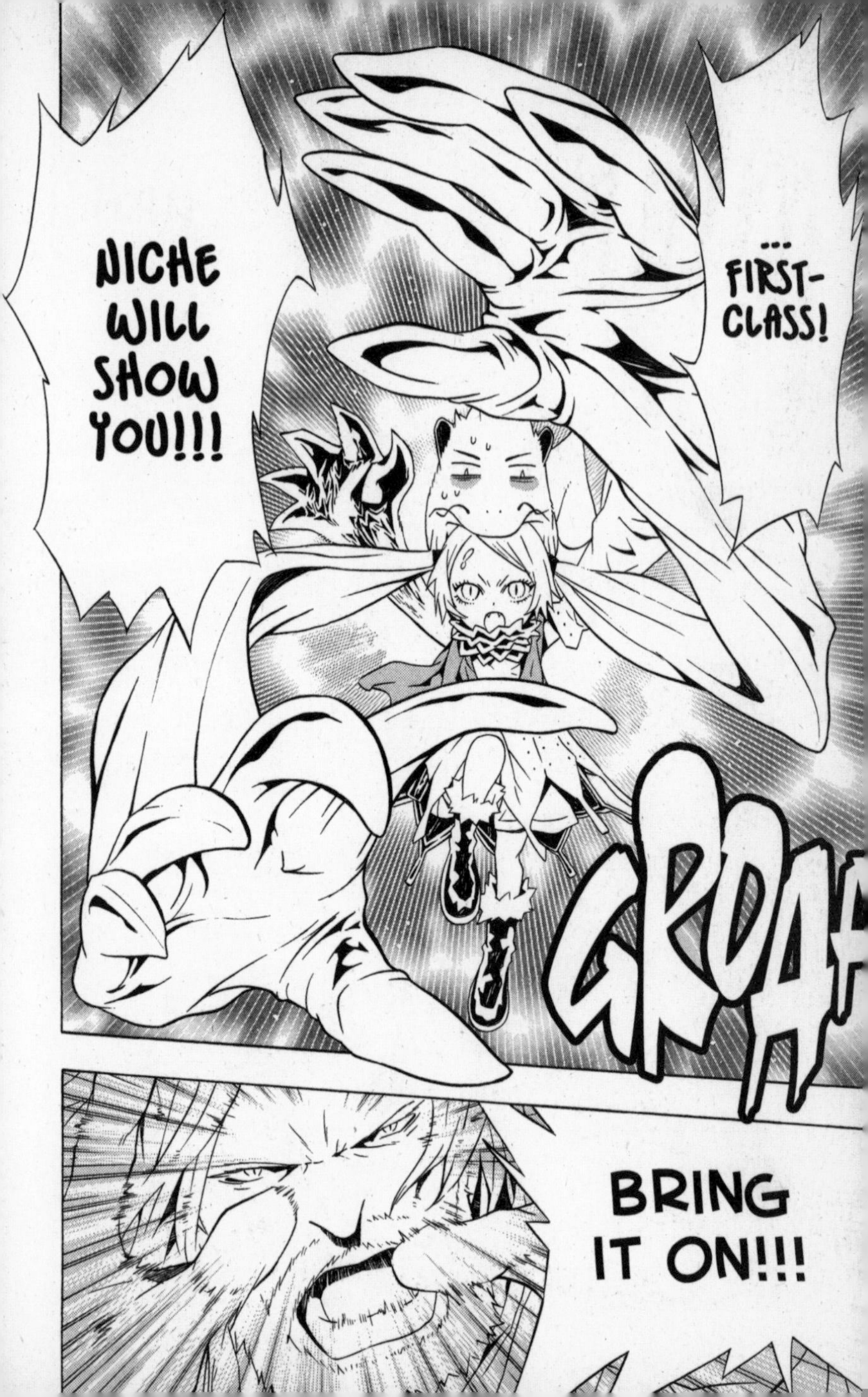
...FIRST-CLASS!
NICHE WILL SHOW YOU!!!
GROA
BRING IT ON!!!

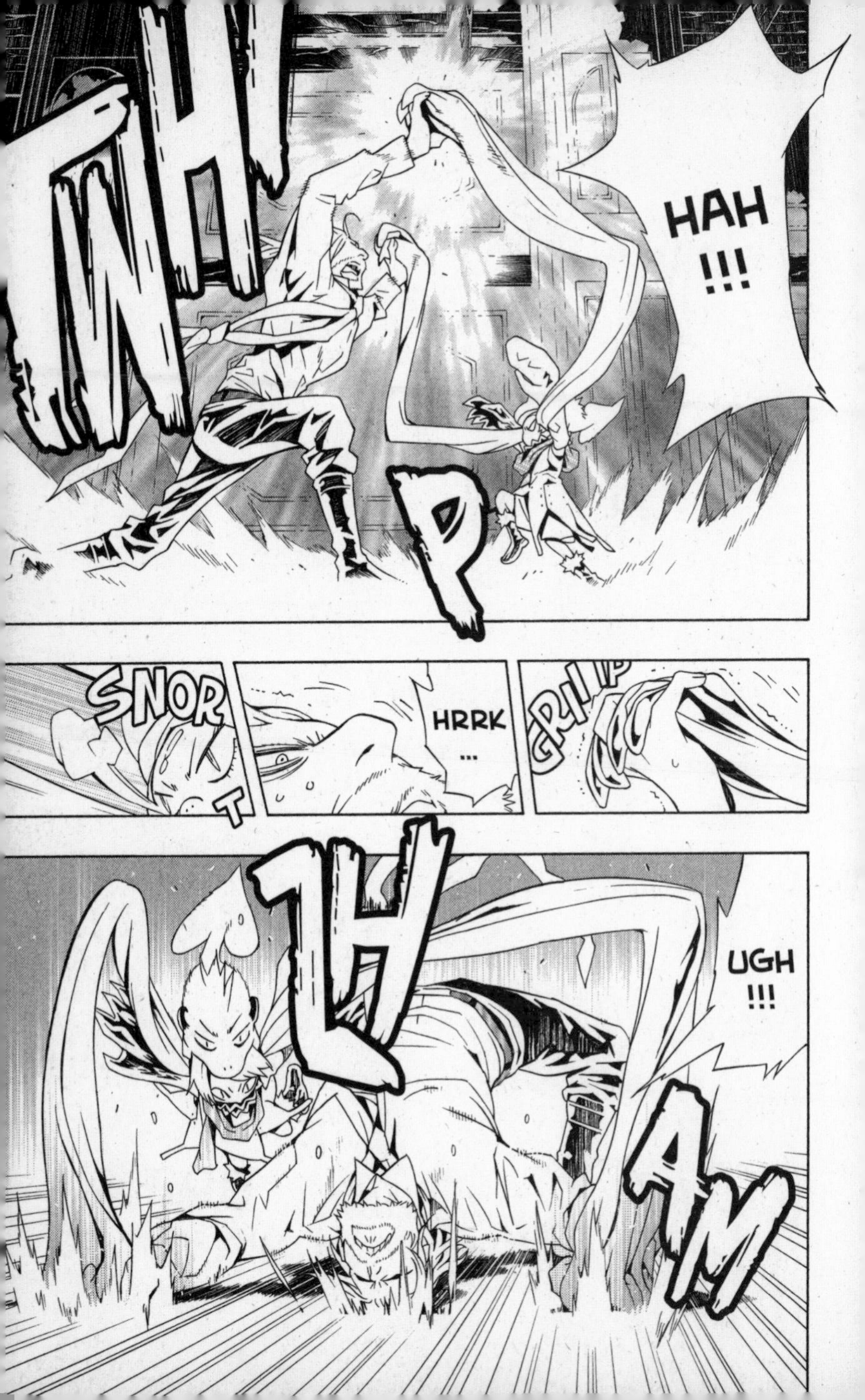

HAH !!!
GRIIIP
HRRK ...
SNORT
UGH !!!

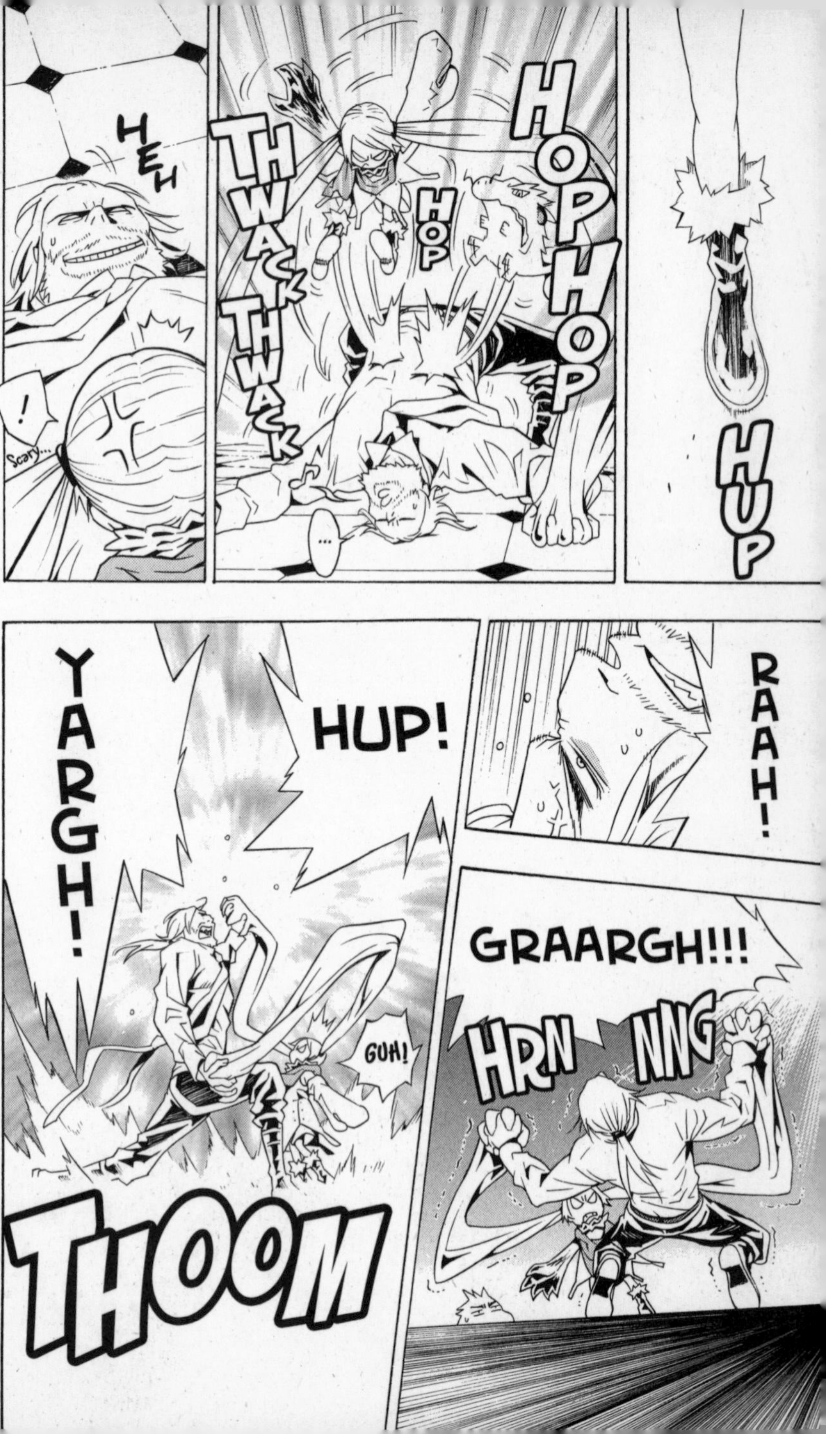
HUP
HOP HOP HOP
HOP
THWACK THWACK
...
HEH
!
Scary...
RAAH!
GRAARGH!!!
HRN NNG
HUP!
YARGH!
GUH!
THOOM

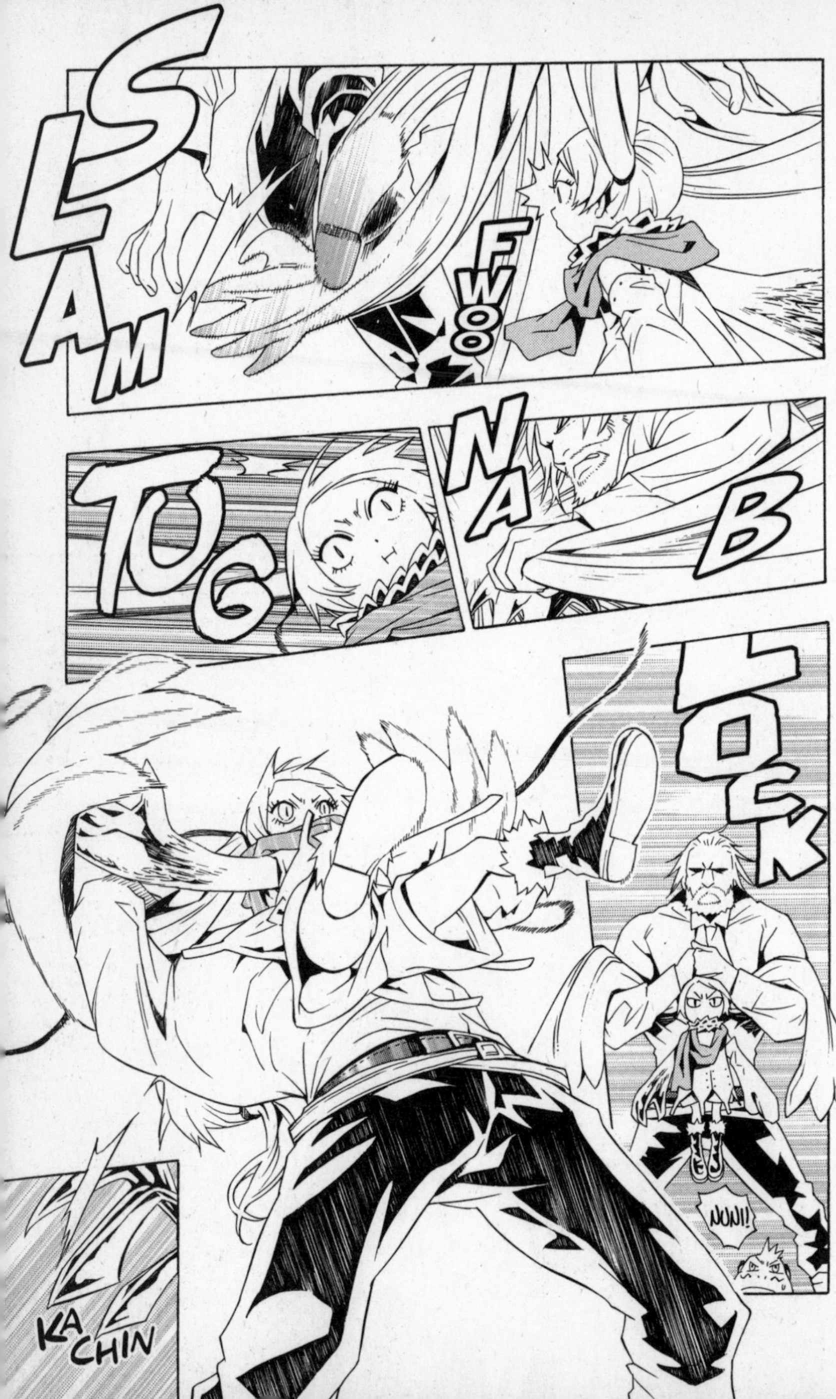
FWOO
SLAM
NAB
TUG
LOCK
NUNI!
KA CHIN

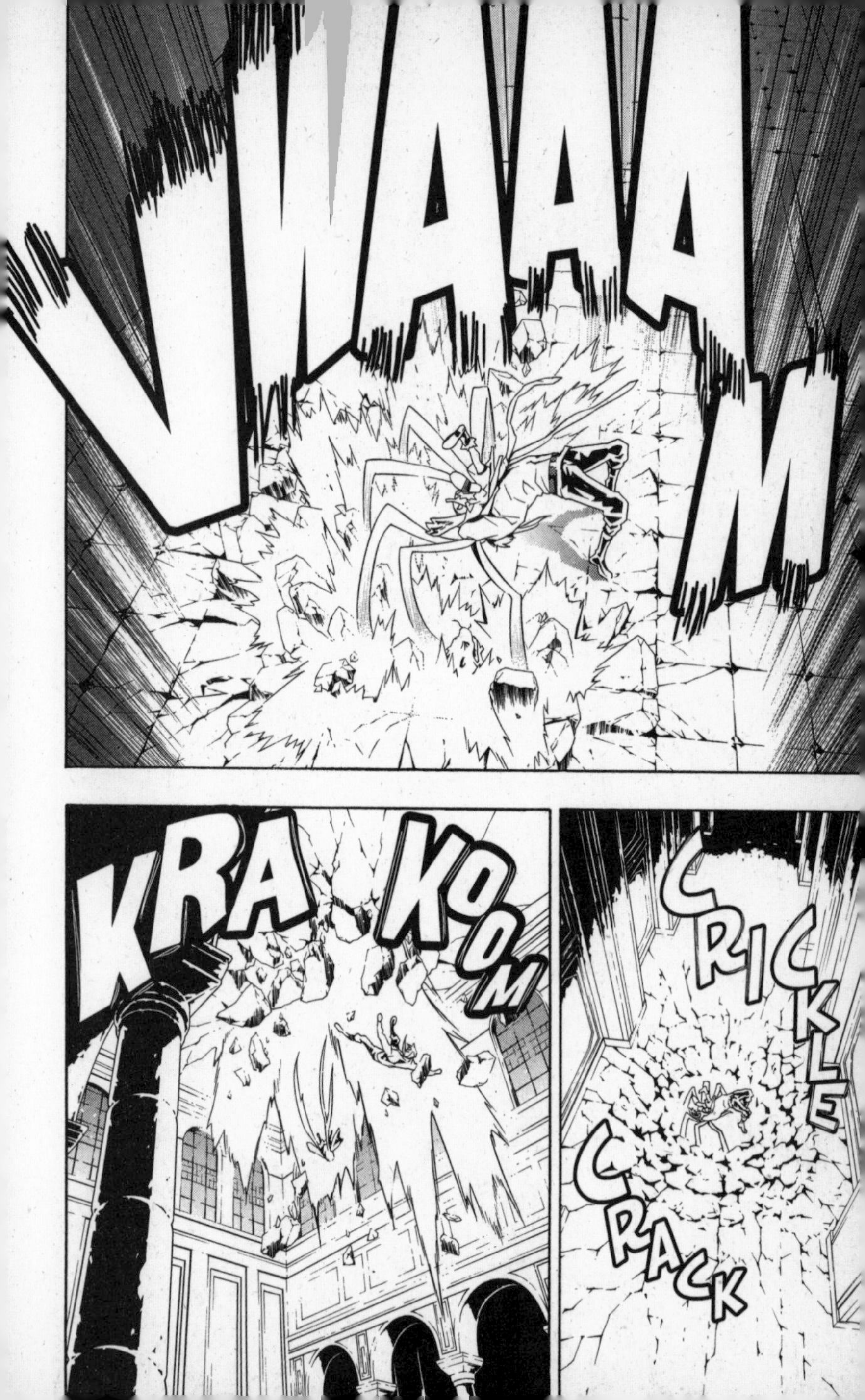
VWAAM
CRICKLE
CRACK
KRAKOOM

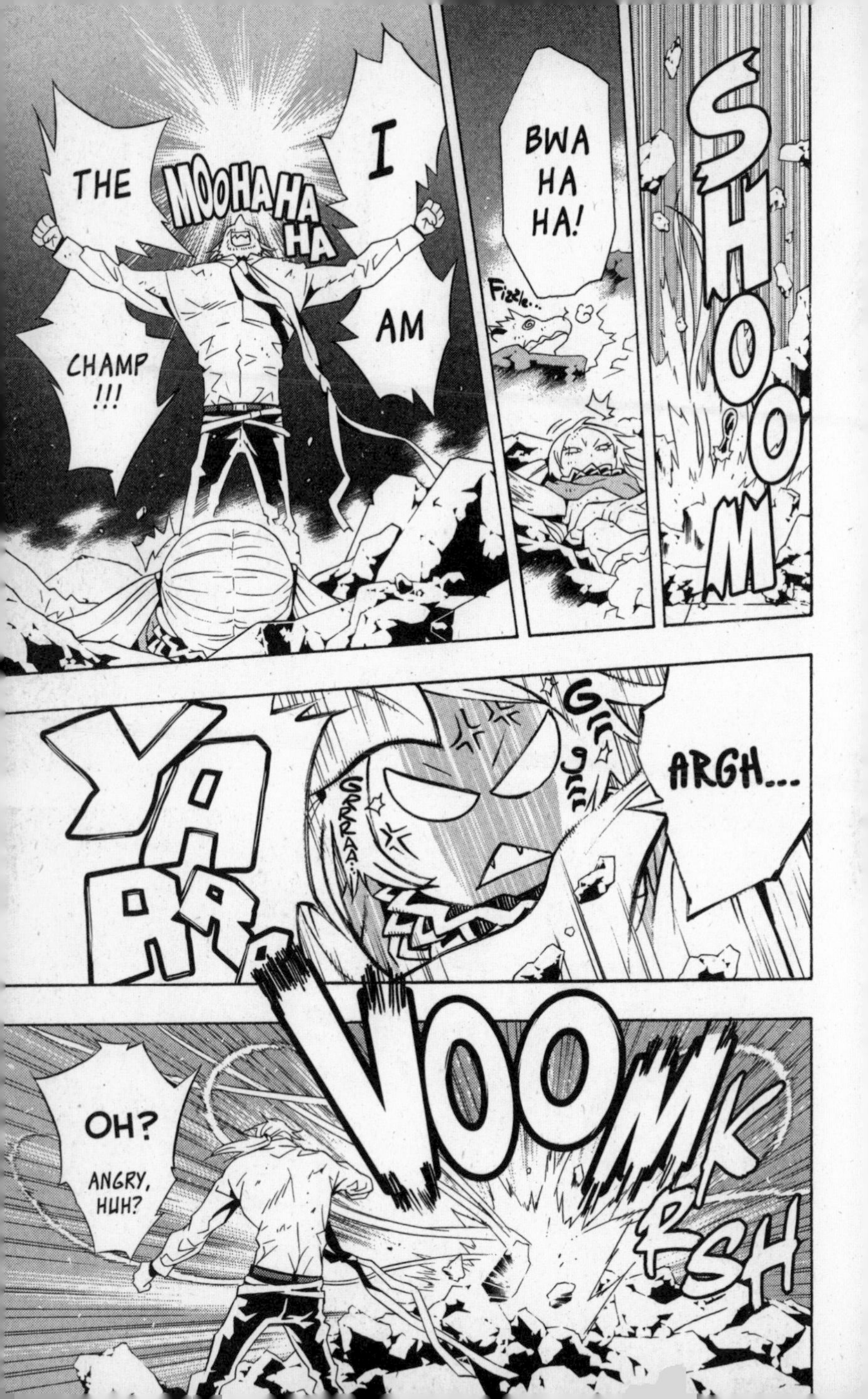
SHOOOM
BWA HA HA!
Fizzle...
I
AM
THE
CHAMP!!!
MOOHAHAHA HA
ARGH...
Grrr...
GRRRAA...
YARR
VOOM
KRSH
OH?
ANGRY, HUH?

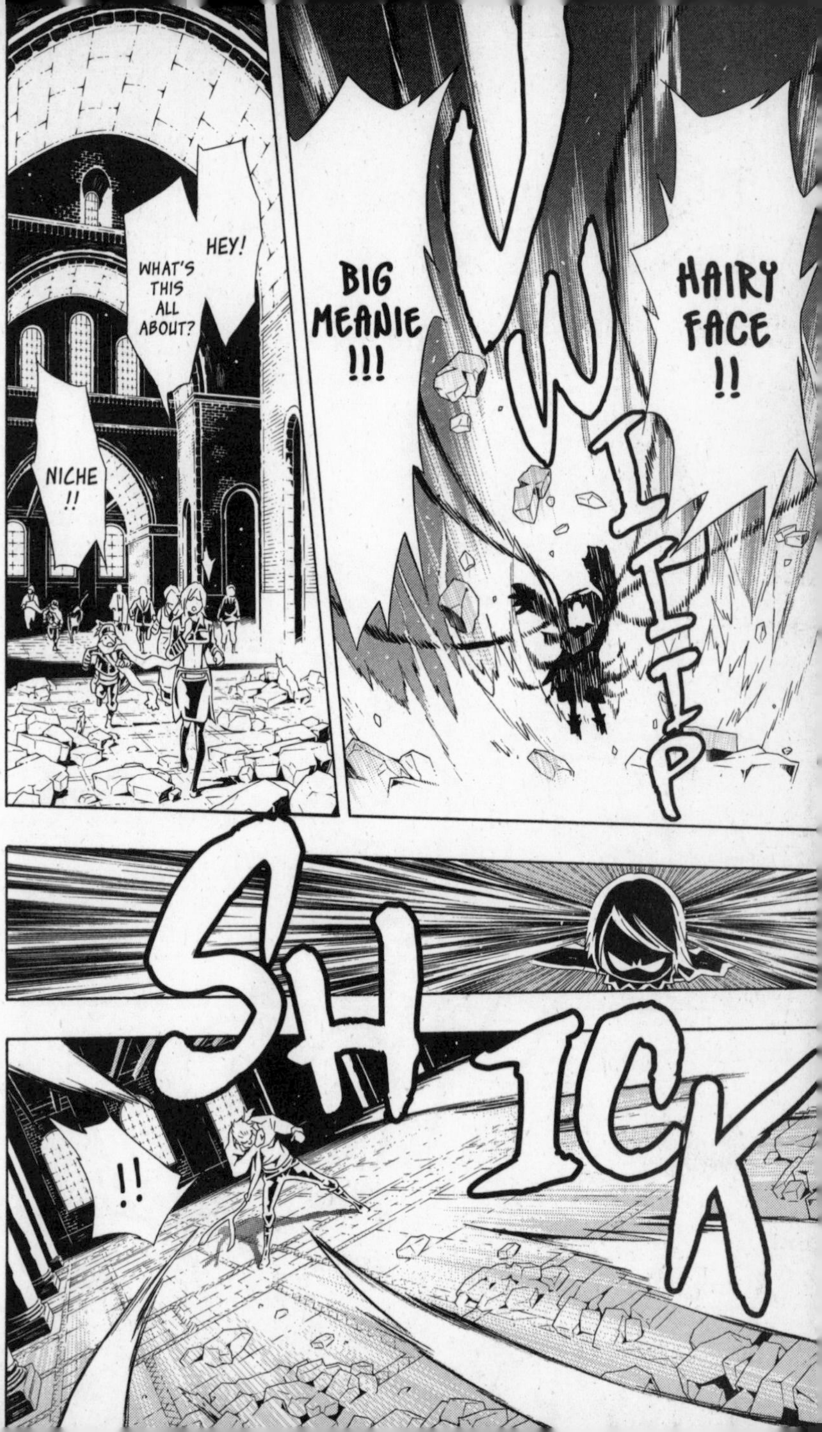
HAIRY FACE!!
WHIIIP
BIG MEANIE!!!
HEY!
WHAT'S THIS ALL ABOUT?
NICHE!!
SHICK
!!

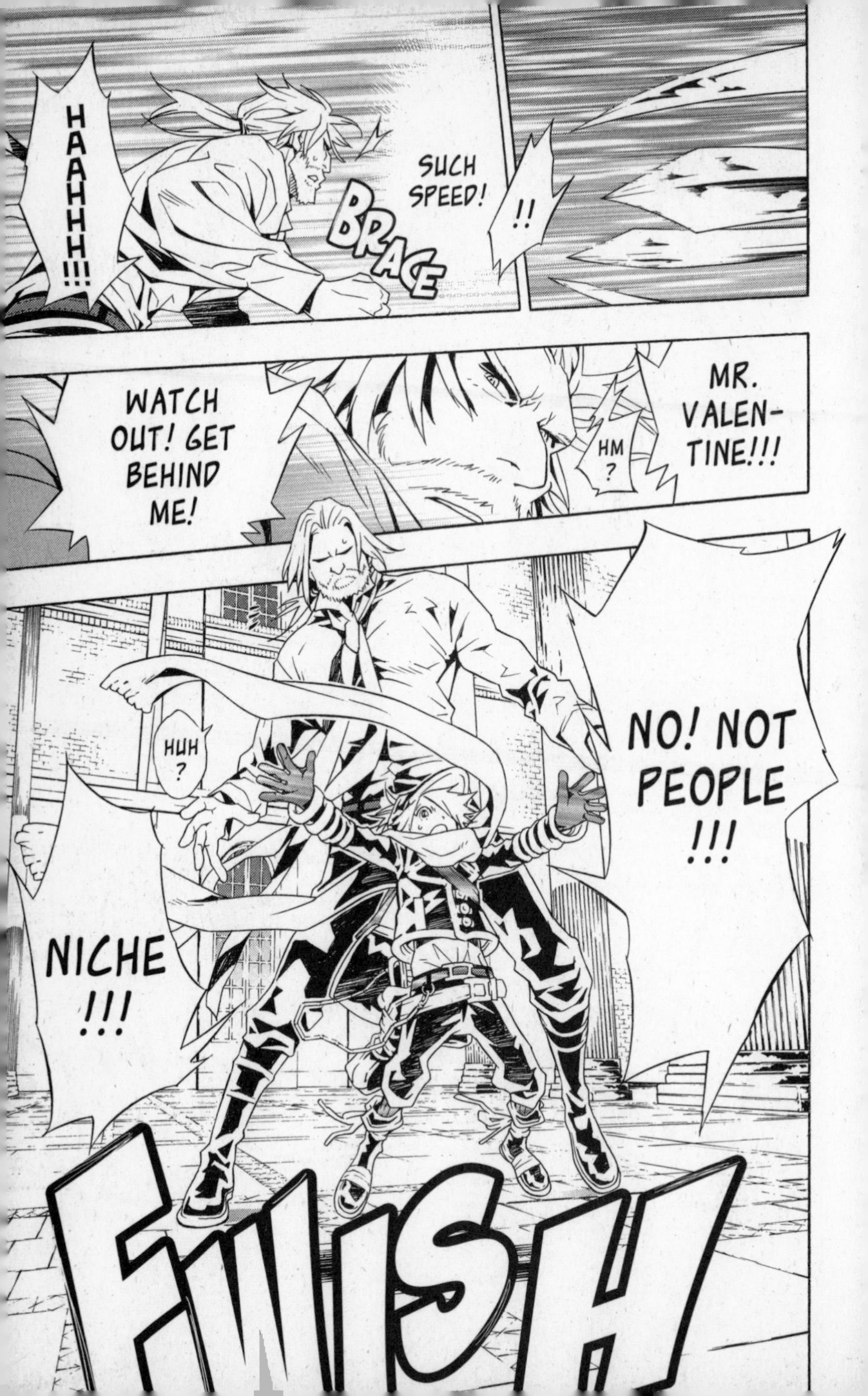
!!
SUCH SPEED!
BRACE
HAAHHHH!!!
MR. VALEN-TINE!!!
HM?
WATCH OUT! GET BEHIND ME!
NO! NOT PEOPLE!!!
HUH?
NICHE!!!
FWISH!

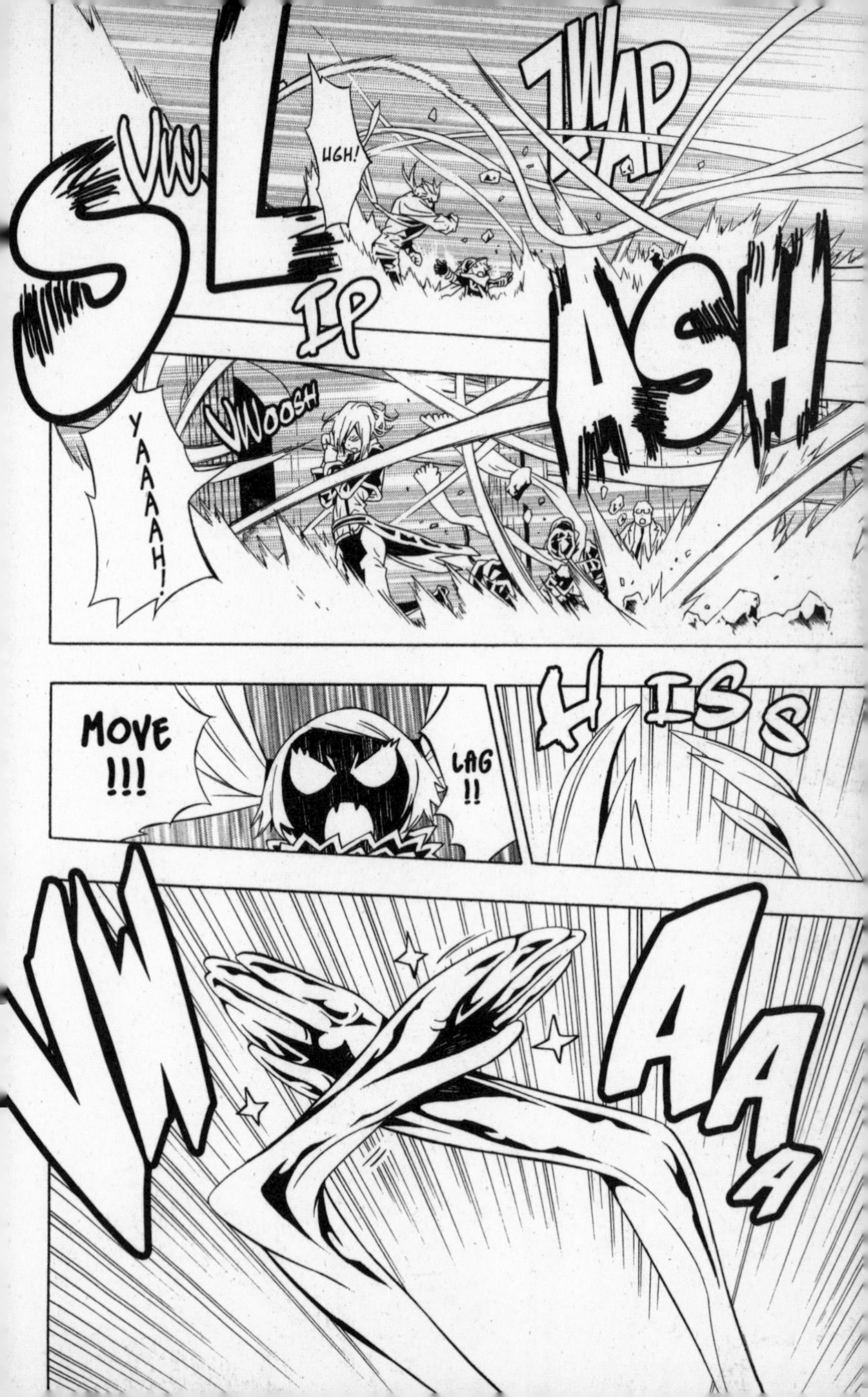
TWAP
UGH!
VWOOSH
YAAAAAH!
HISS
LAG !!
MOVE !!!

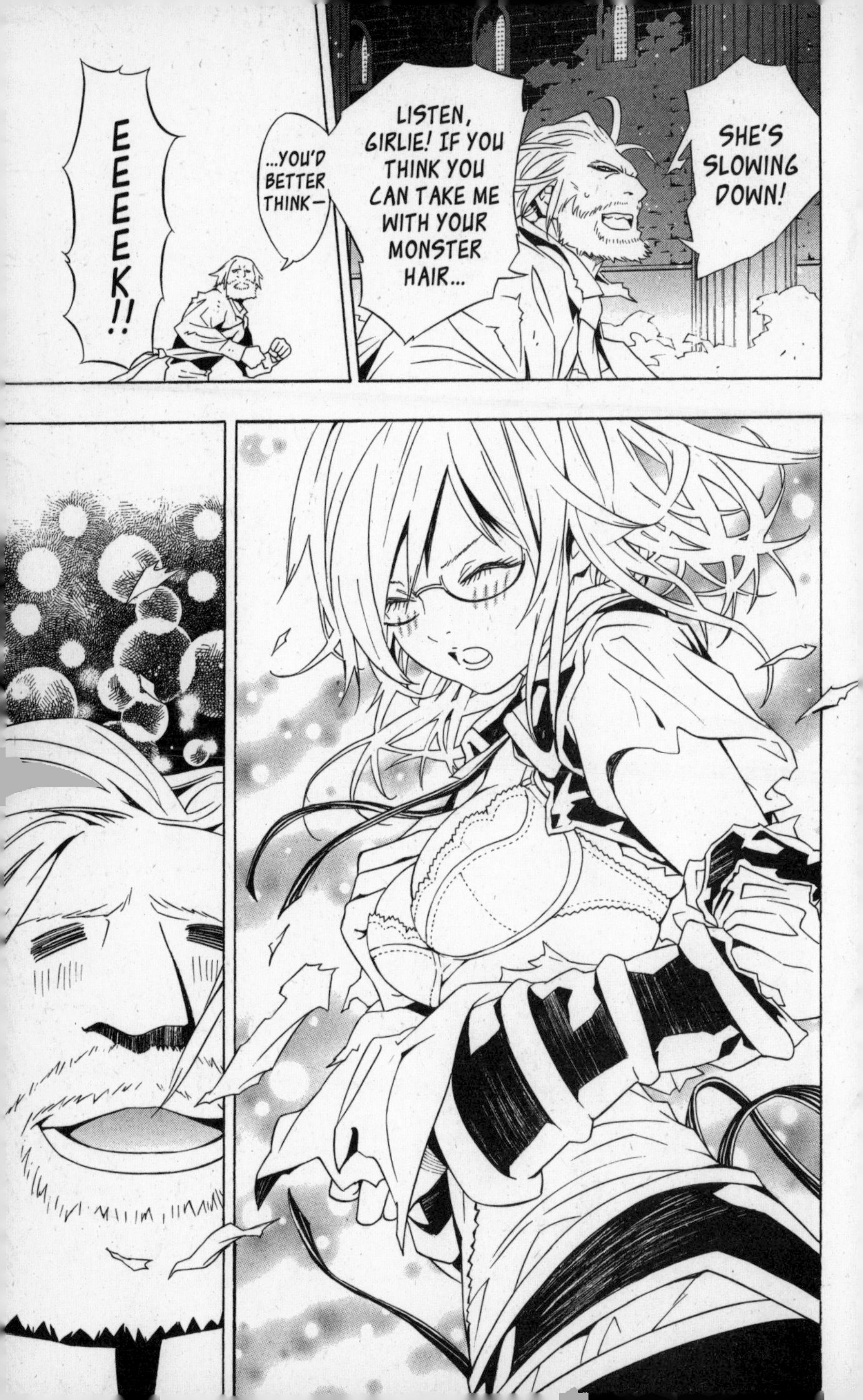
SHE'S SLOWING DOWN!
LISTEN, GIRLIE! IF YOU THINK YOU CAN TAKE ME WITH YOUR MONSTER HAIR...
...YOU'D BETTER THINK—
EEEEEK!!

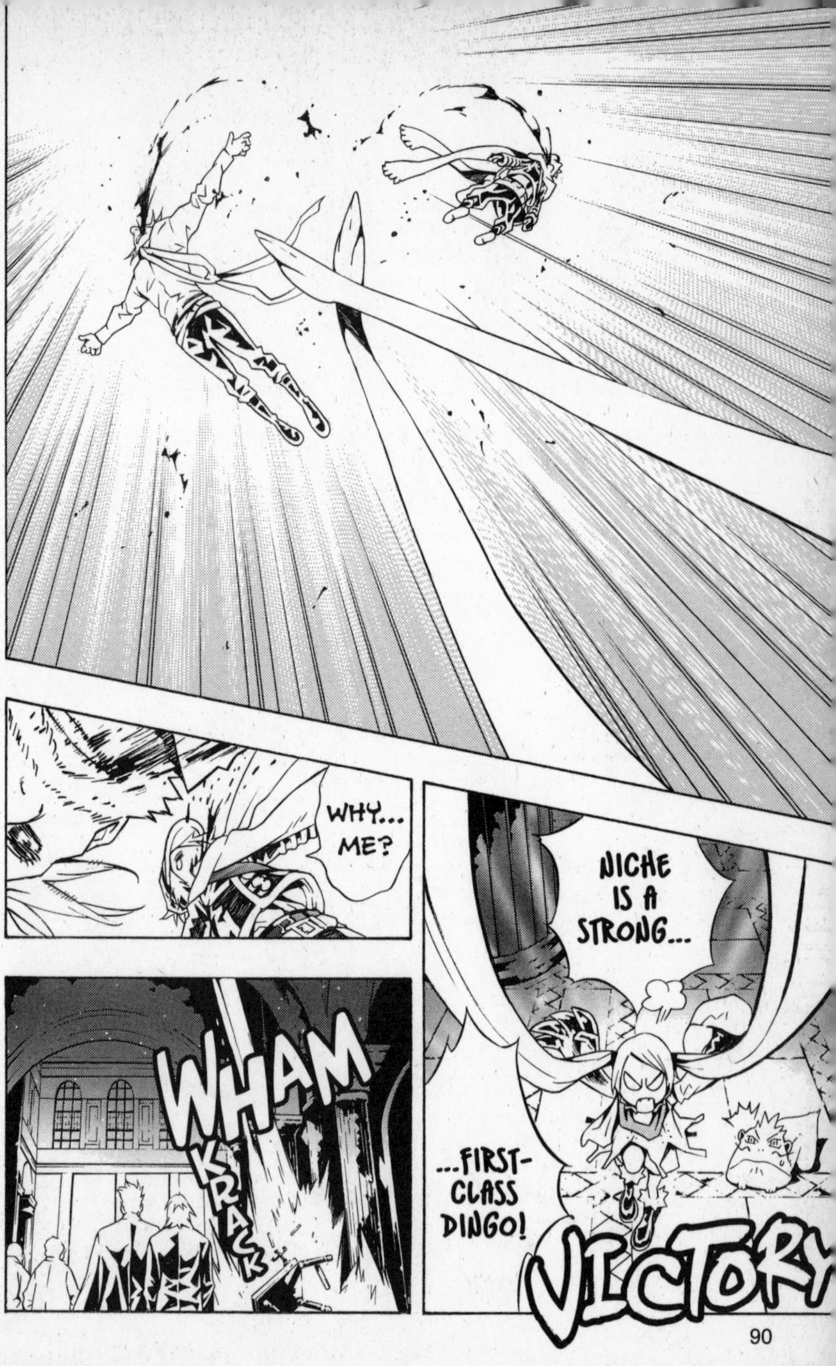
NICHE IS A STRONG...
...FIRST-CLASS DINGO!
VICTORY
WHY... ME?
WHAM
KRACK

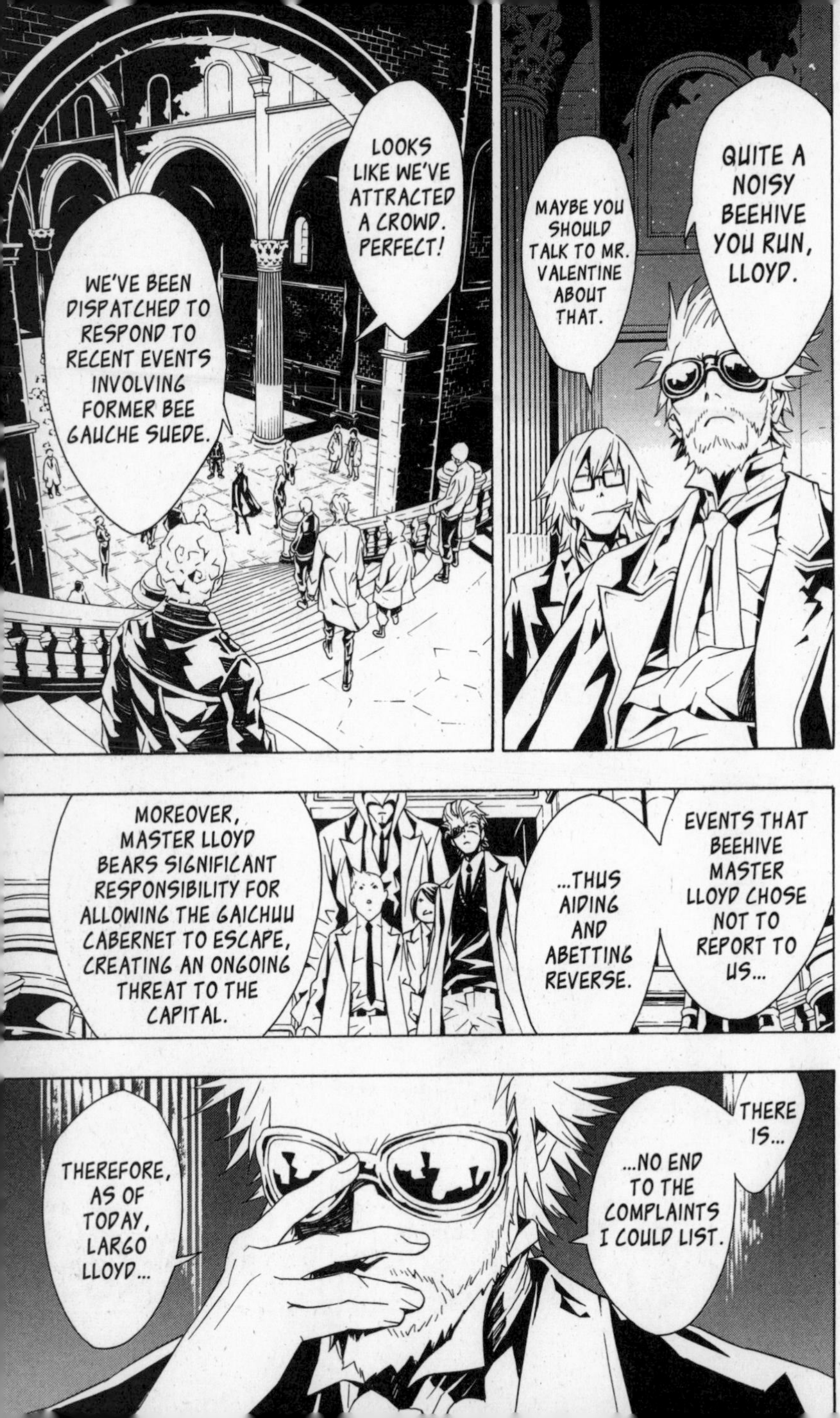
QUITE A NOISY BEEHIVE YOU RUN, LLOYD.
MAYBE YOU SHOULD TALK TO MR. VALENTINE ABOUT THAT.
LOOKS LIKE WE'VE ATTRACTED A CROWD. PERFECT!
WE'VE BEEN DISPATCHED TO RESPOND TO RECENT EVENTS INVOLVING FORMER BEE GAUCHE SUEDE.
EVENTS THAT BEEHIVE MASTER LLOYD CHOSE NOT TO REPORT TO US...
...THUS AIDING AND ABETTING REVERSE.
MOREOVER, MASTER LLOYD BEARS SIGNIFICANT RESPONSIBILITY FOR ALLOWING THE GAICHUU CABERNET TO ESCAPE, CREATING AN ONGOING THREAT TO THE CAPITAL.
THERE IS...
...NO END TO THE COMPLAINTS I COULD LIST.
THEREFORE, AS OF TODAY, LARGO LLOYD...

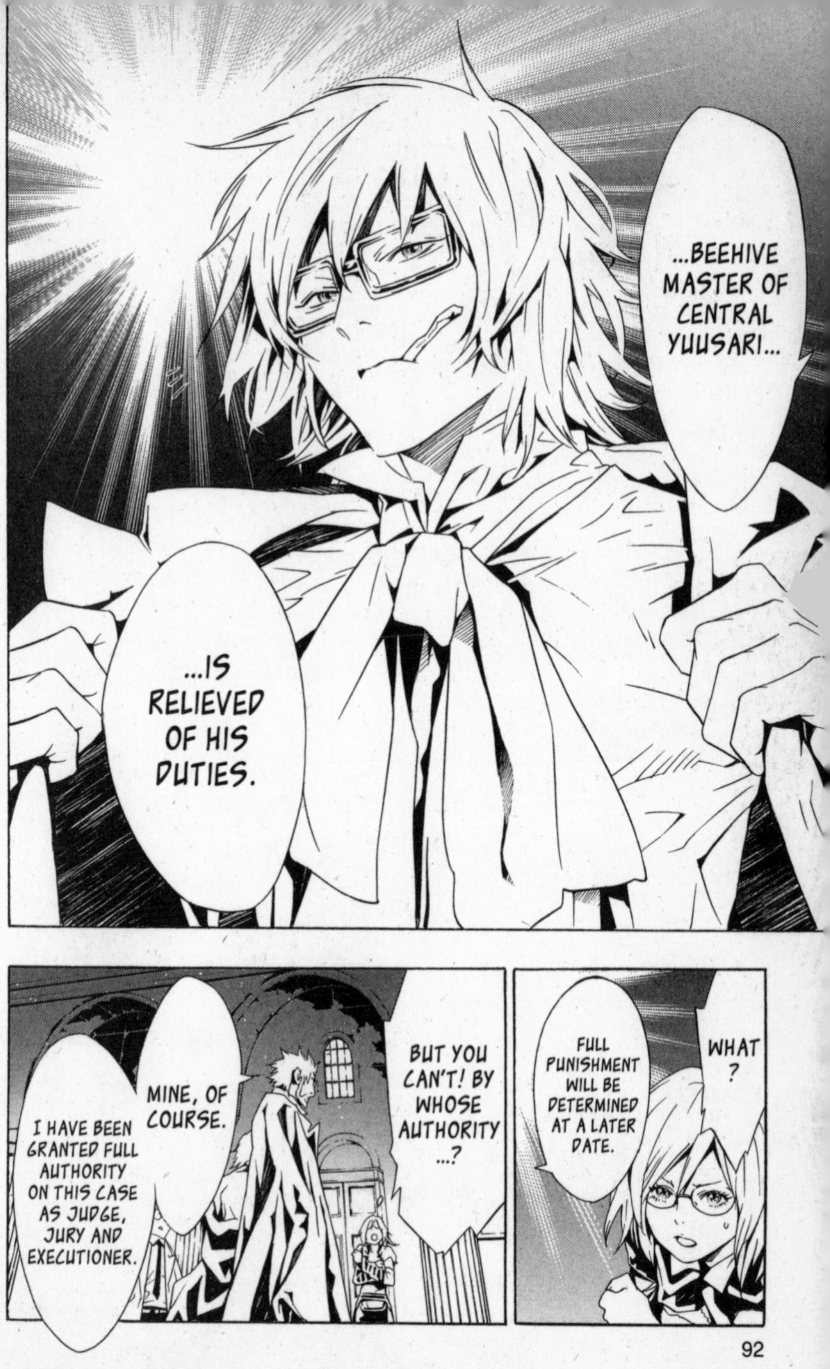
...BEEHIVE MASTER OF CENTRAL YUUSARI...
...IS RELIEVED OF HIS DUTIES.
WHAT?
FULL PUNISHMENT WILL BE DETERMINED AT A LATER DATE.
BUT YOU CAN'T! BY WHOSE AUTHORITY ...?
MINE, OF COURSE.
I HAVE BEEN GRANTED FULL AUTHORITY ON THIS CASE AS JUDGE, JURY AND EXECUTIONER.

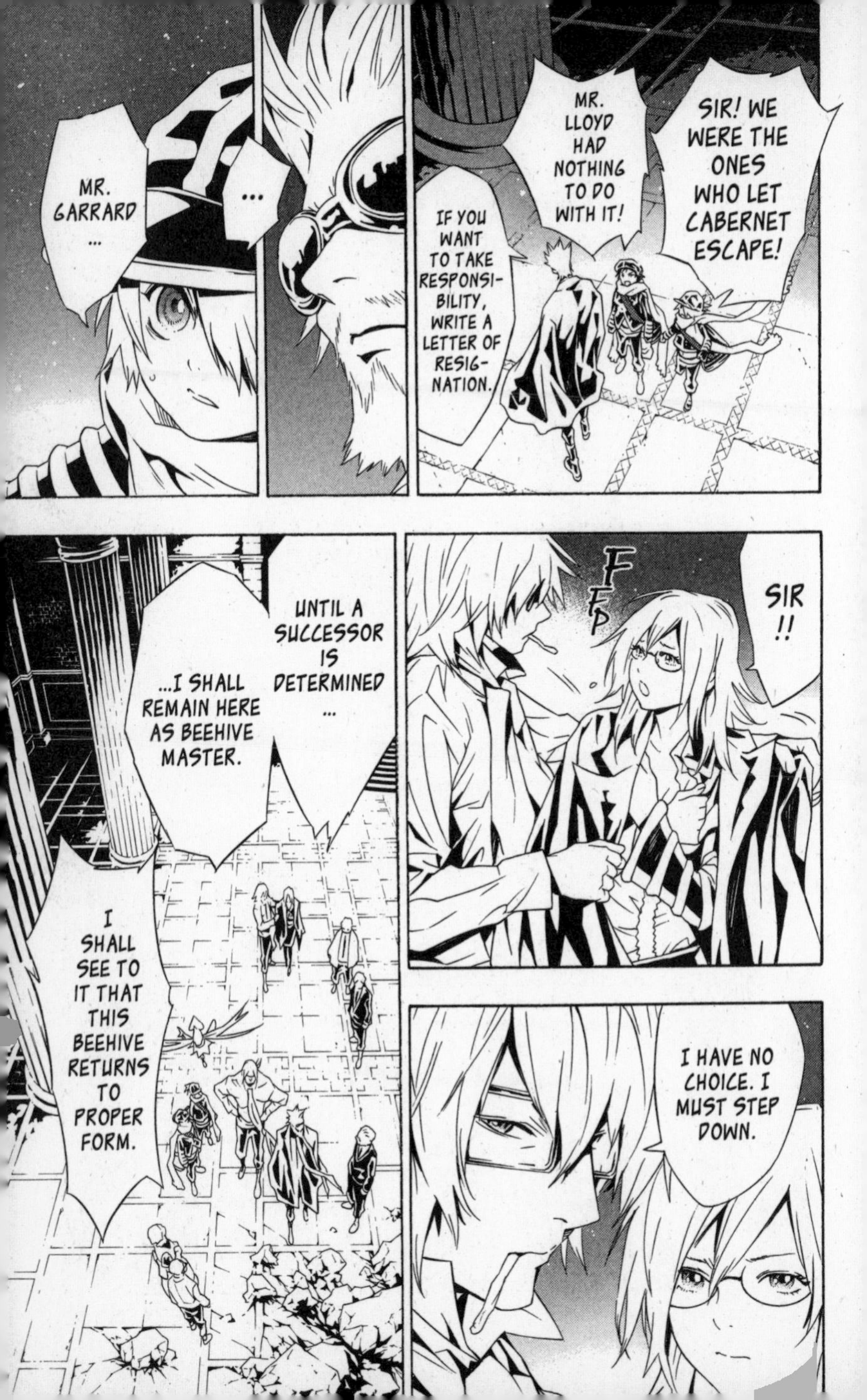
SIR! WE WERE THE ONES WHO LET CABERNET ESCAPE!
MR. LLOYD HAD NOTHING TO DO WITH IT!
IF YOU WANT TO TAKE RESPONSIBILITY, WRITE A LETTER OF RESIGNATION.
...
MR. GARRARD ...
SIR !!
FFP
I HAVE NO CHOICE. I MUST STEP DOWN.
UNTIL A SUCCESSOR IS DETERMINED ...
...I SHALL REMAIN HERE AS BEEHIVE MASTER.
I SHALL SEE TO IT THAT THIS BEEHIVE RETURNS TO PROPER FORM.

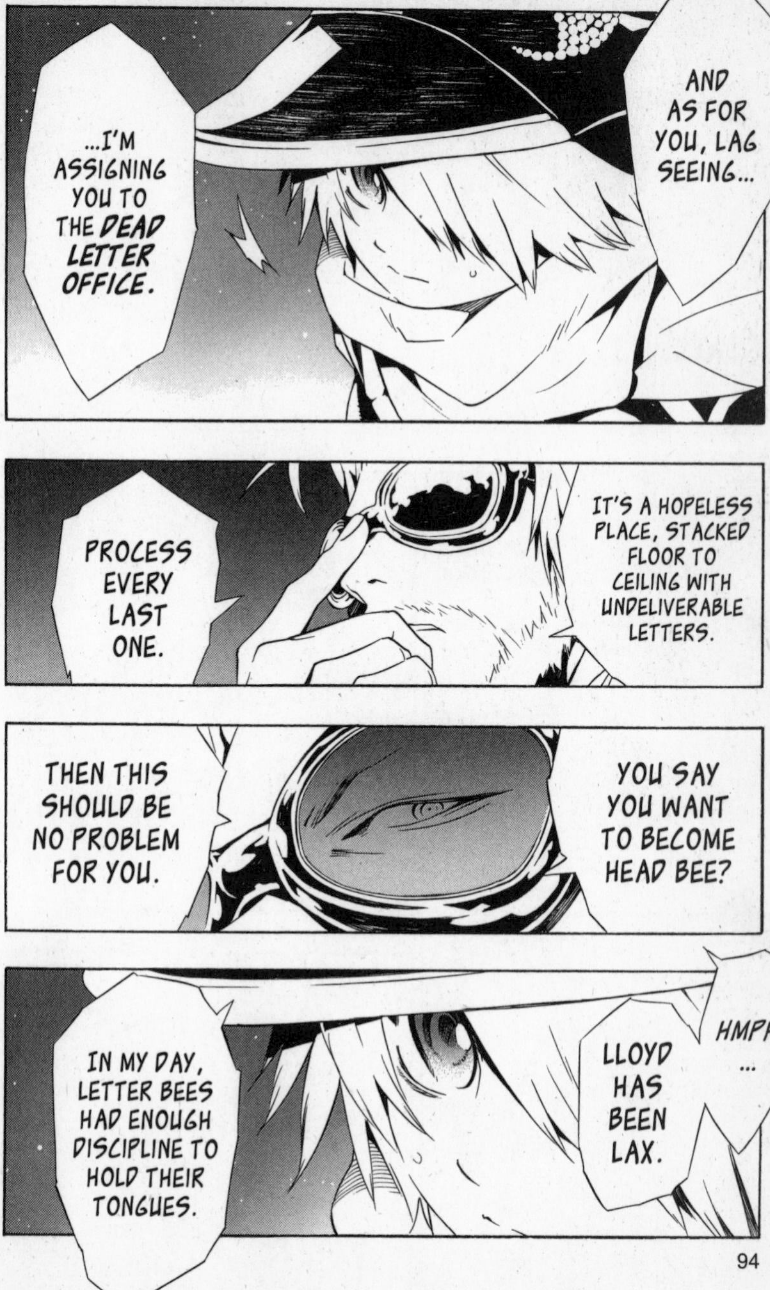
AND AS FOR YOU, LAG SEEING...
...I'M ASSIGNING YOU TO THE DEAD LETTER OFFICE.
IT'S A HOPELESS PLACE, STACKED FLOOR TO CEILING WITH UNDELIVERABLE LETTERS.
PROCESS EVERY LAST ONE.
YOU SAY YOU WANT TO BECOME HEAD BEE?
THEN THIS SHOULD BE NO PROBLEM FOR YOU.
HMPH...
LLOYD HAS BEEN LAX.
IN MY DAY, LETTER BEES HAD ENOUGH DISCIPLINE TO HOLD THEIR TONGUES.

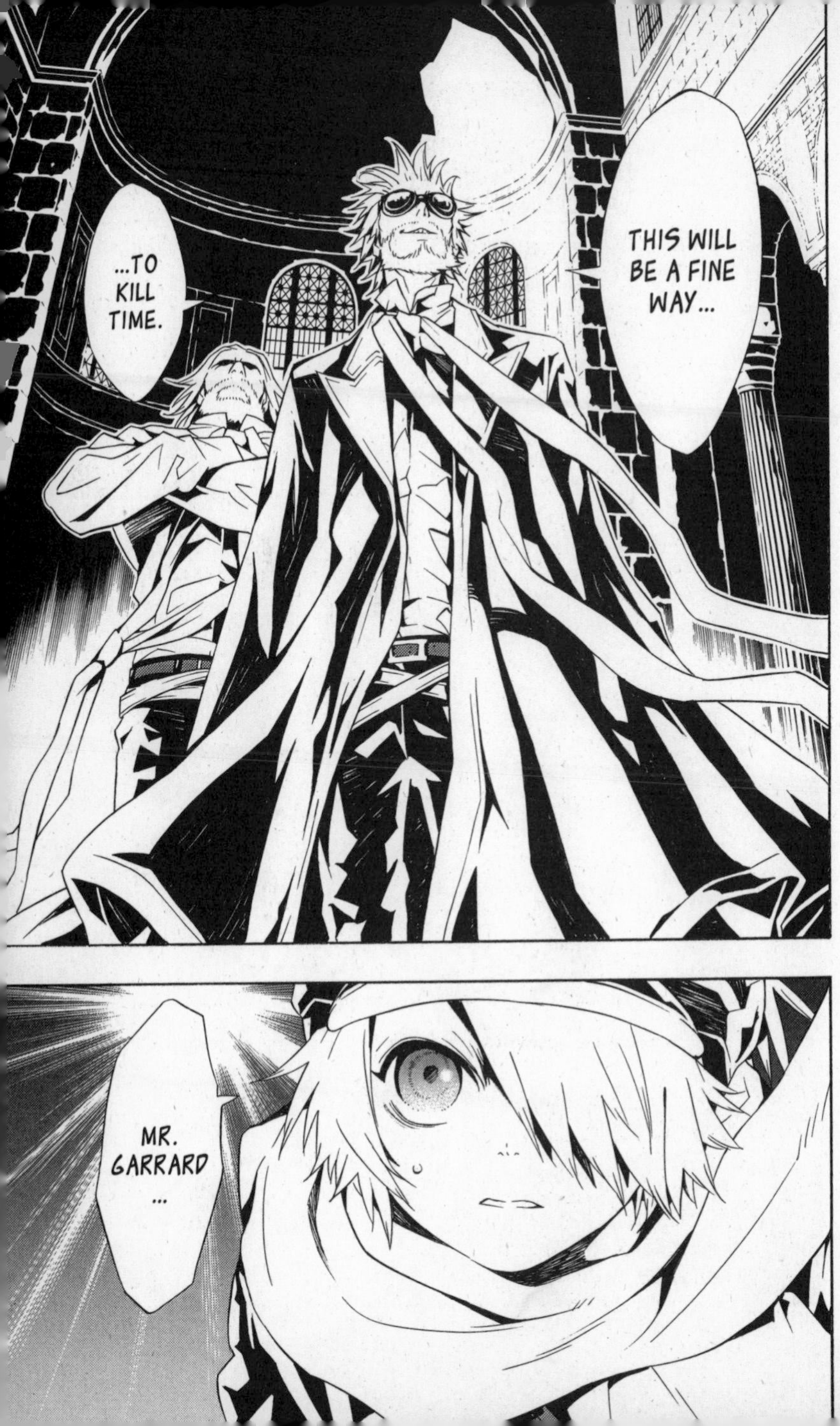
THIS WILL BE A FINE WAY...
...TO KILL TIME.
MR. GARRARD ...

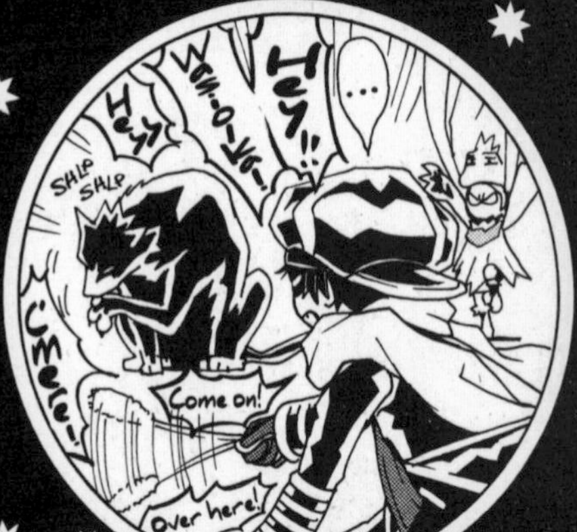
...
Hey!!
Hey
SHLP SHLP
C'mere!
Come on!
Over here!

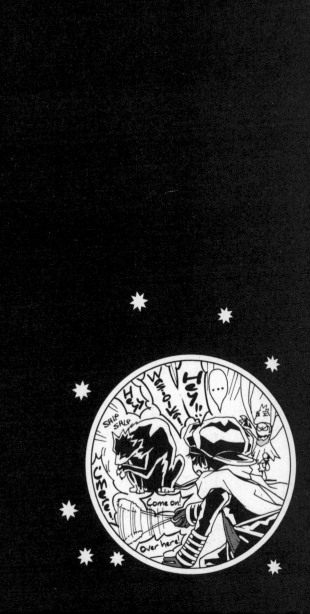

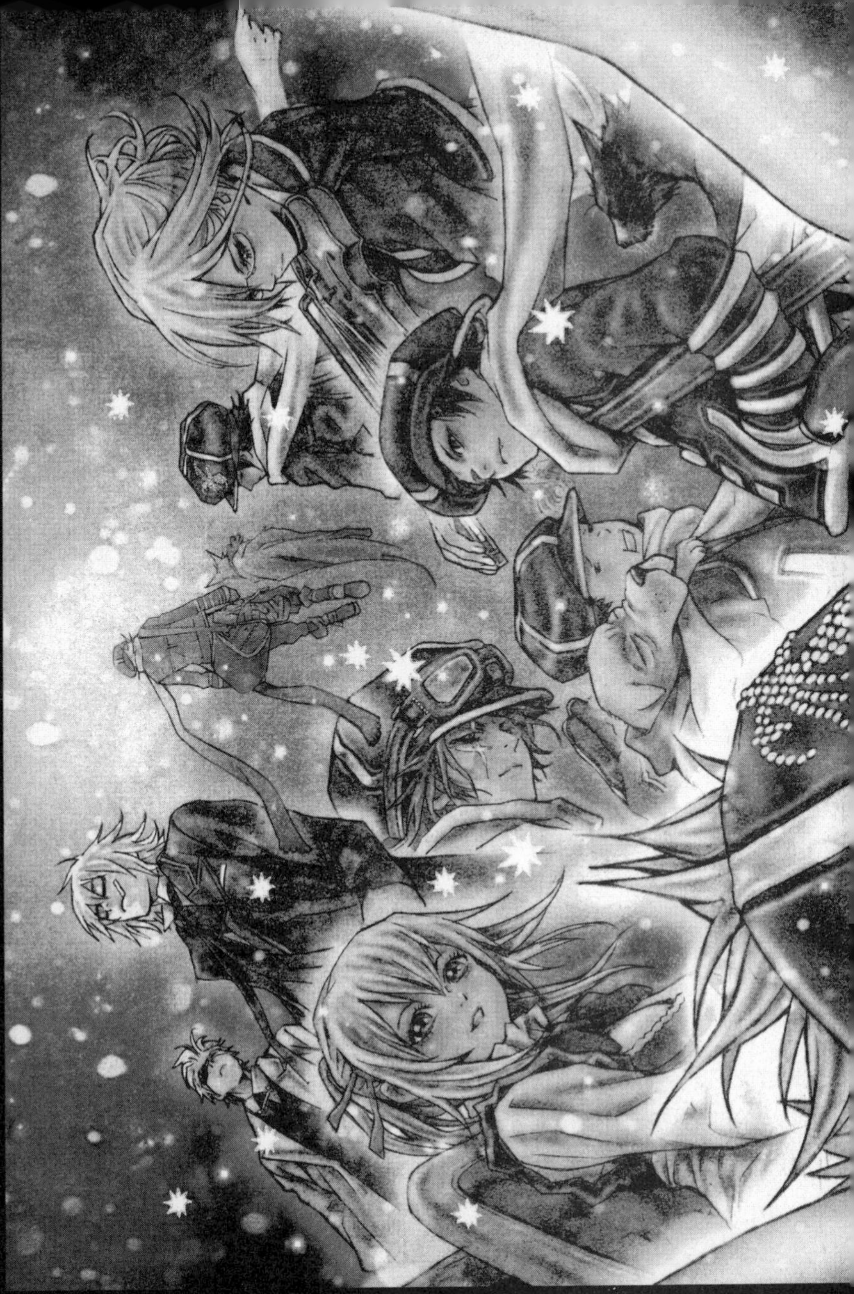

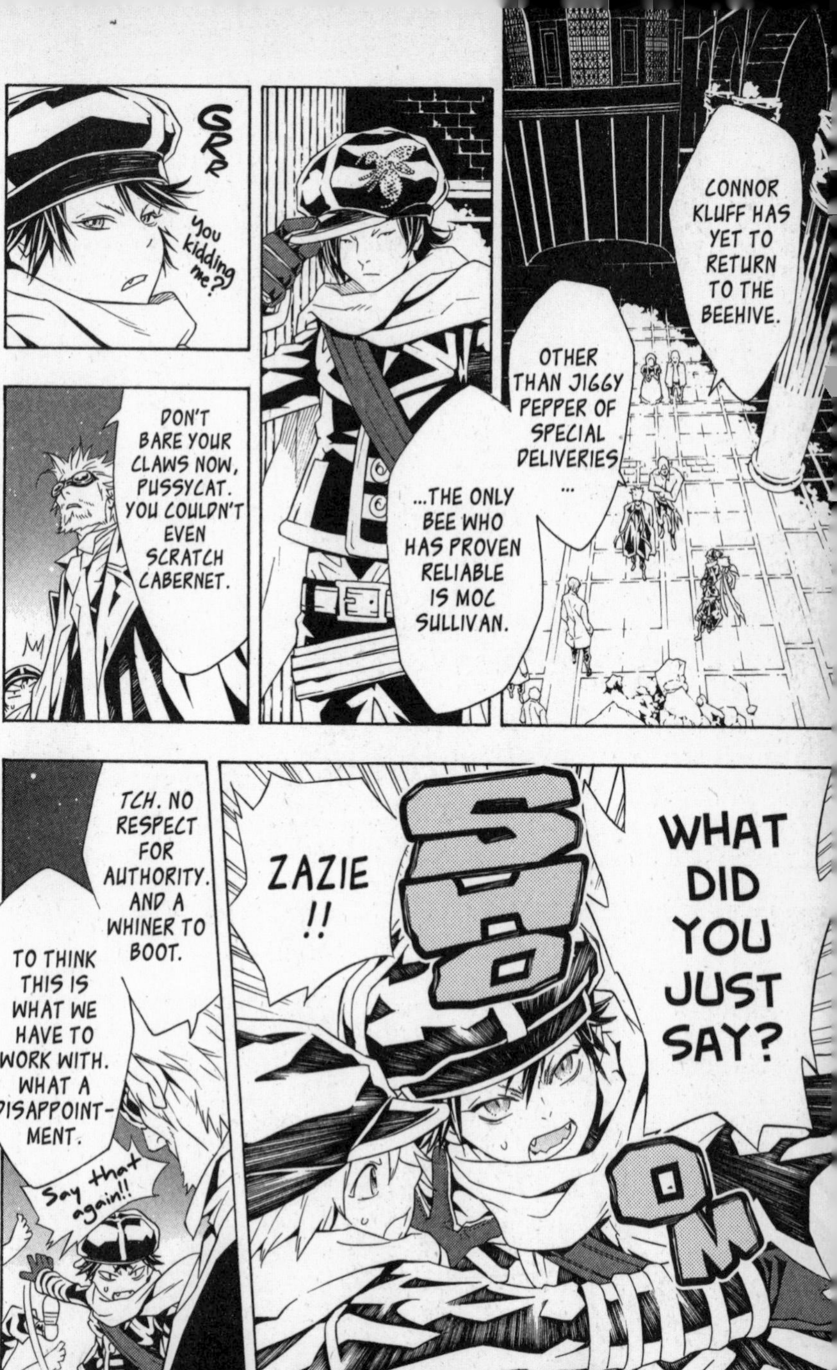
CONNOR KLUFF HAS YET TO RETURN TO THE BEEHIVE.
OTHER THAN JIGGY PEPPER OF SPECIAL DELIVERIES...
...THE ONLY BEE WHO HAS PROVEN RELIABLE IS MOC SULLIVAN.
GRR
You kidding me?
DON'T BARE YOUR CLAWS NOW, PUSSYCAT. YOU COULDN'T EVEN SCRATCH CABERNET.
WHAT DID YOU JUST SAY?
ZAZIE!!
TCH. NO RESPECT FOR AUTHORITY. AND A WHINER TO BOOT.
TO THINK THIS IS WHAT WE HAVE TO WORK WITH. WHAT A DISAPPOINTMENT.
Say that again!!

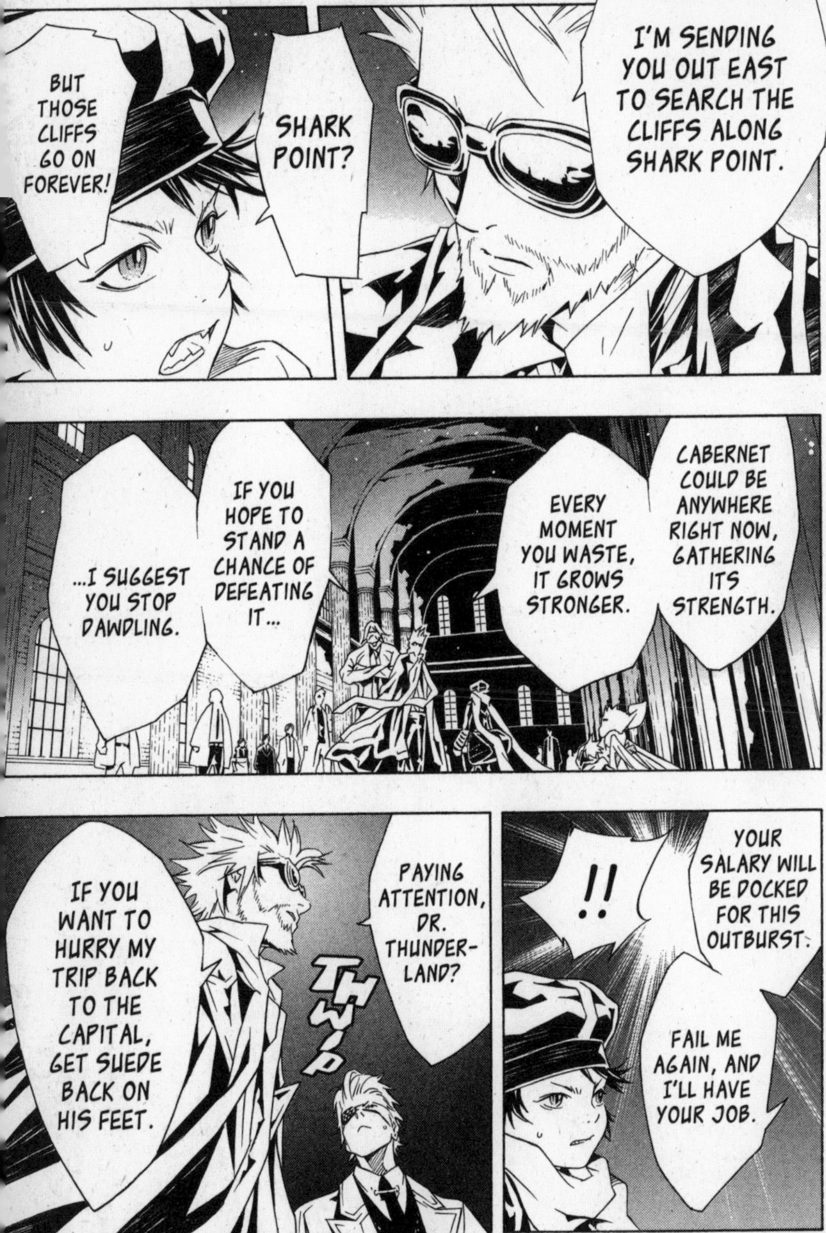
I'M SENDING YOU OUT EAST TO SEARCH THE CLIFFS ALONG SHARK POINT.
SHARK POINT?
BUT THOSE CLIFFS GO ON FOREVER!
CABERNET COULD BE ANYWHERE RIGHT NOW, GATHERING ITS STRENGTH.
EVERY MOMENT YOU WASTE, IT GROWS STRONGER.
IF YOU HOPE TO STAND A CHANCE OF DEFEATING IT...
...I SUGGEST YOU STOP DAWDLING.
YOUR SALARY WILL BE DOCKED FOR THIS OUTBURST.
!!
FAIL ME AGAIN, AND I'LL HAVE YOUR JOB.
PAYING ATTENTION, DR. THUNDER-LAND?
THWIP
IF YOU WANT TO HURRY MY TRIP BACK TO THE CAPITAL, GET SUEDE BACK ON HIS FEET.

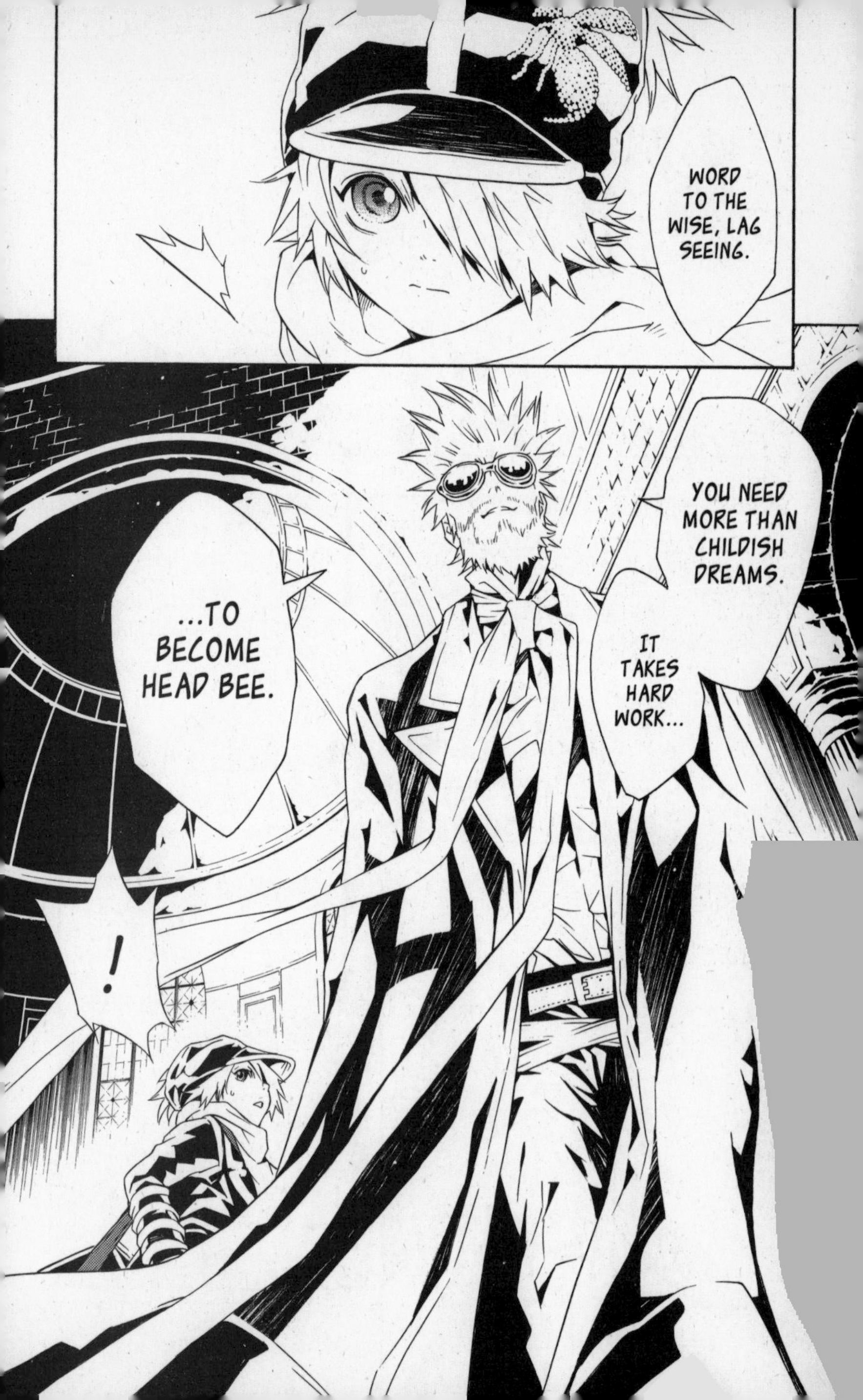
WORD TO THE WISE, LAG SEEING.
YOU NEED MORE THAN CHILDISH DREAMS.
IT TAKES HARD WORK...
...TO BECOME HEAD BEE.
!

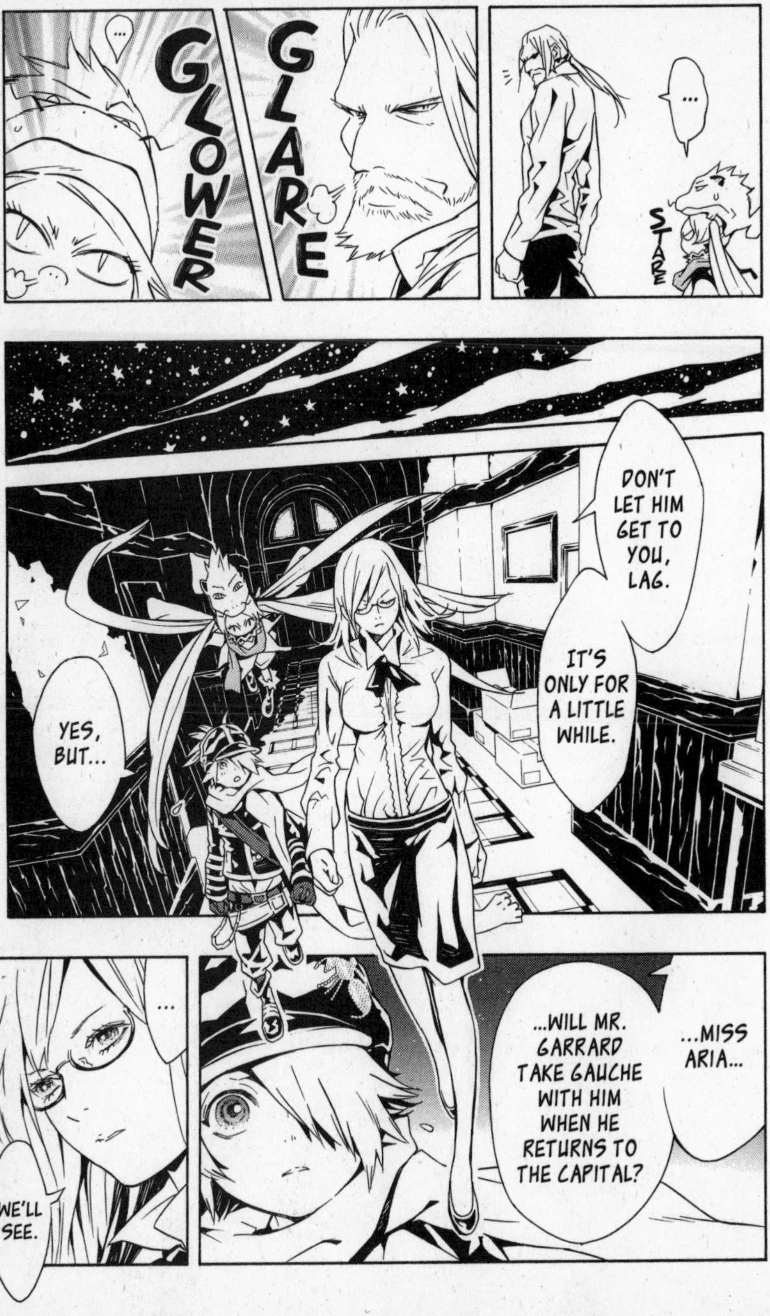
...
STARE
GLARE
...
GLOWER
DON'T LET HIM GET TO YOU, LAG.
IT'S ONLY FOR A LITTLE WHILE.
YES, BUT...
...MISS ARIA...
...WILL MR. GARRARD TAKE GAUCHE WITH HIM WHEN HE RETURNS TO THE CAPITAL?
...
WE'LL SEE.

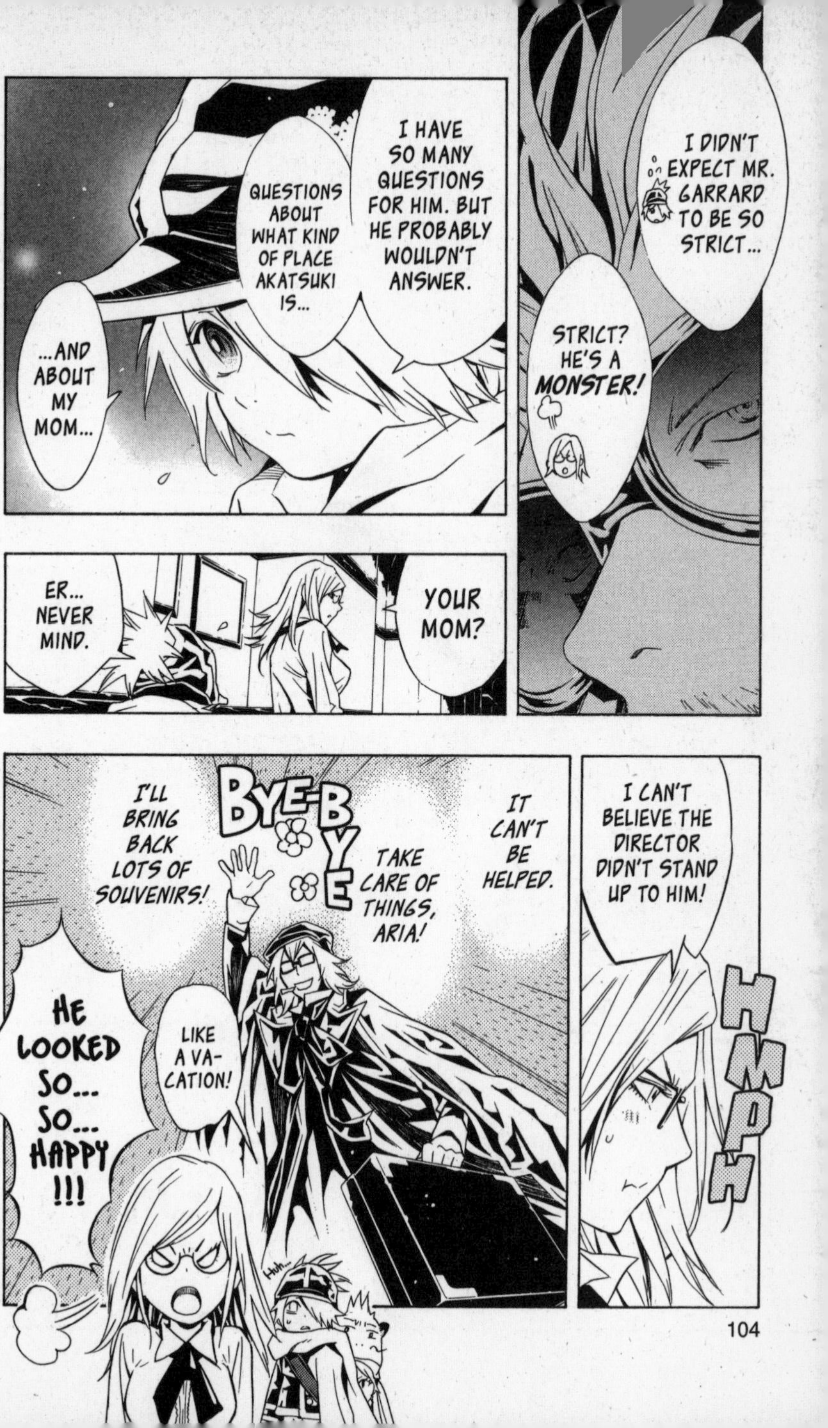
I DIDN'T EXPECT MR. GARRARD TO BE SO STRICT...
STRICT? HE'S A MONSTER!
I HAVE SO MANY QUESTIONS FOR HIM. BUT HE PROBABLY WOULDN'T ANSWER.
QUESTIONS ABOUT WHAT KIND OF PLACE AKATSUKI IS...
...AND ABOUT MY MOM...
YOUR MOM?
ER... NEVER MIND.
I CAN'T BELIEVE THE DIRECTOR DIDN'T STAND UP TO HIM!
HMPH
IT CAN'T BE HELPED.
TAKE CARE OF THINGS, ARIA!
BYE-BYE
I'LL BRING BACK LOTS OF SOUVENIRS!
LIKE A VA-CATION!
HE LOOKED SO... SO... HAPPY!!!
Huh...

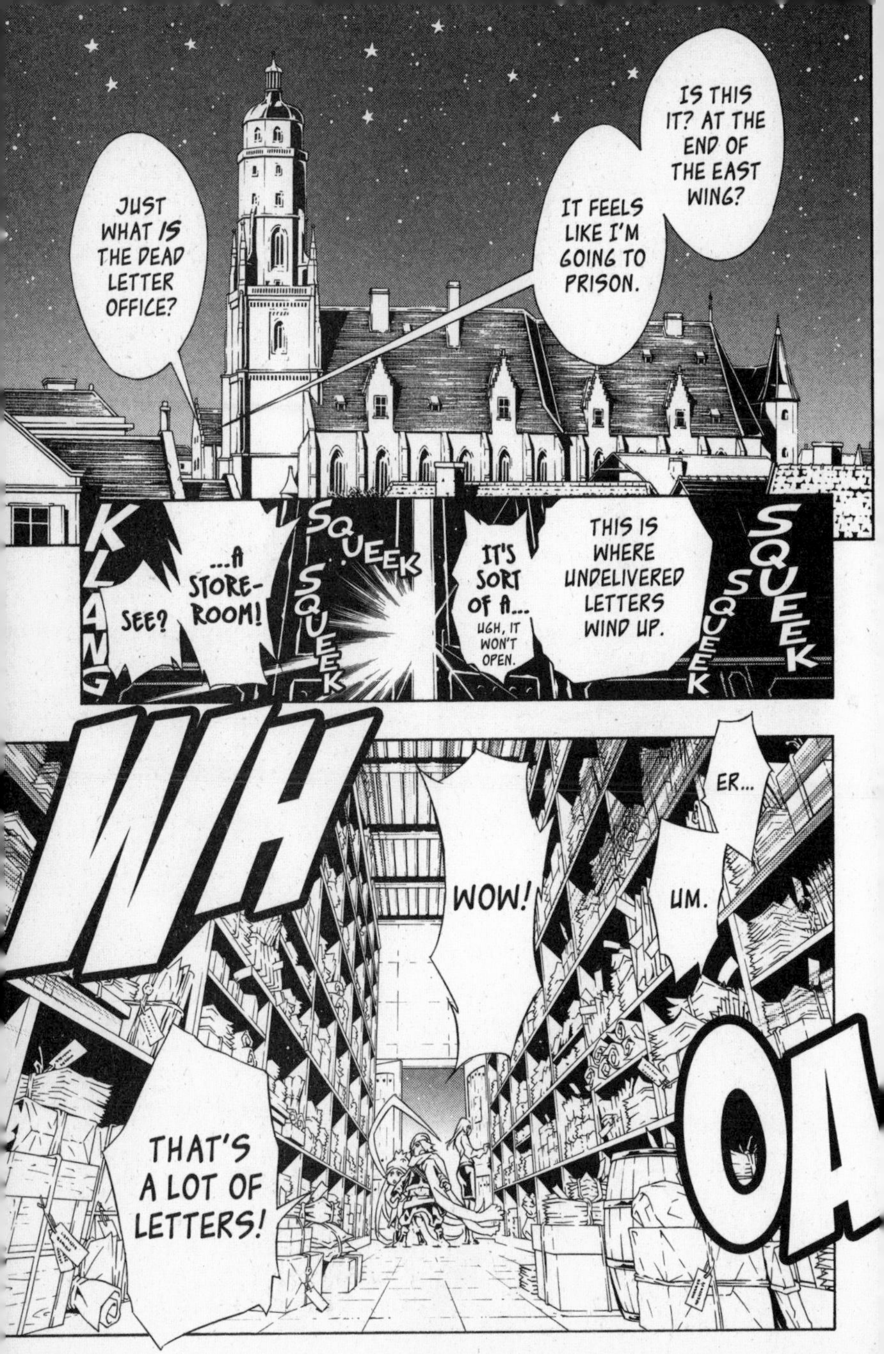
IS THIS IT? AT THE END OF THE EAST WING?
IT FEELS LIKE I'M GOING TO PRISON.
JUST WHAT *IS* THE DEAD LETTER OFFICE?
SQUEEK
SQUEEK
THIS IS WHERE UNDELIVERED LETTERS WIND UP.
IT'S SORT OF A...
UGH, IT WON'T OPEN.
SQUEEK
SQUEEK
...A STOREROOM!
SEE?
KLANG
ER...
UM.
OA
WOW!
WH
THAT'S A LOT OF LETTERS!

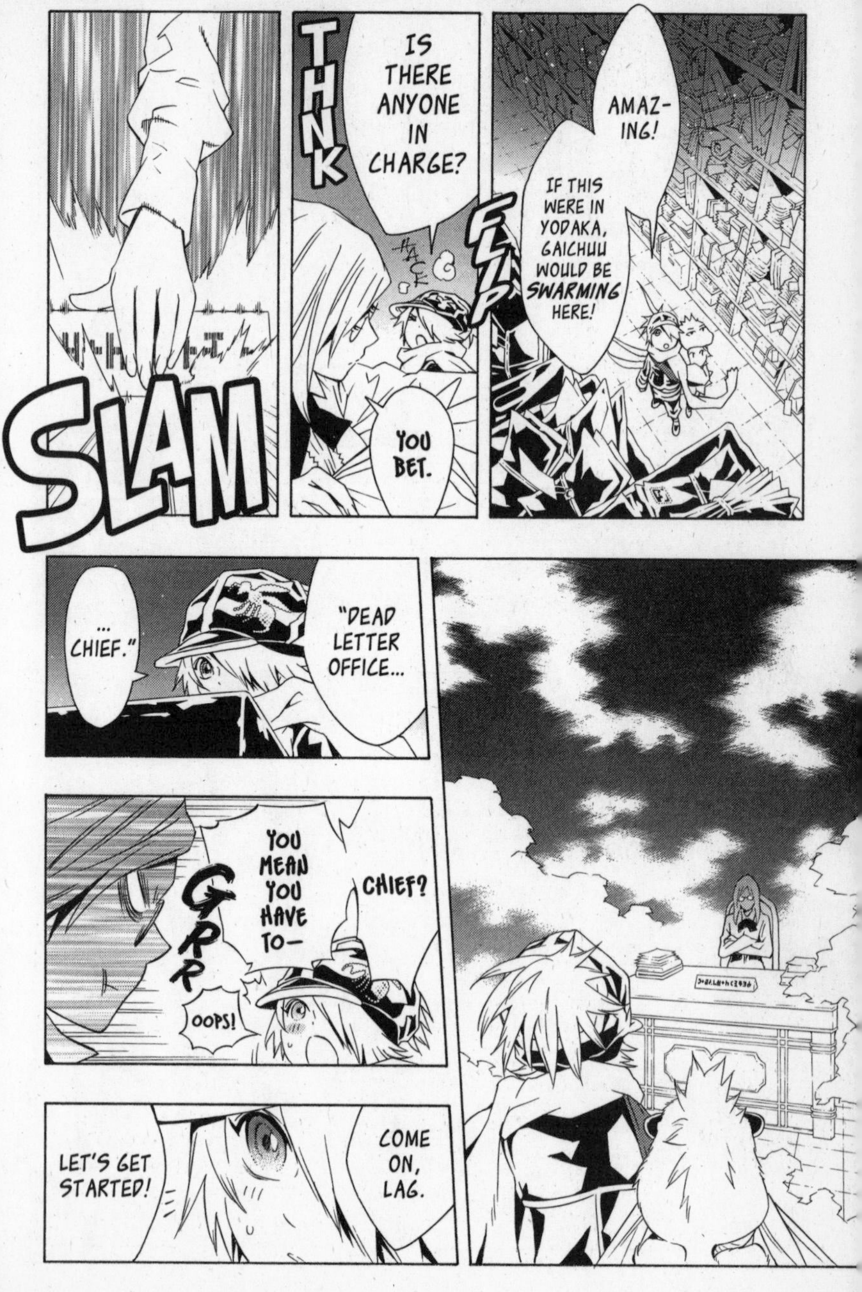
AMAZ-ING!
IF THIS WERE IN YODAKA, GAICHUU WOULD BE SWARMING HERE!
FLIP
THNK
IS THERE ANYONE IN CHARGE?
YOU BET.
SLAM
"DEAD LETTER OFFICE...
... CHIEF."
CHIEF?
YOU MEAN YOU HAVE TO—
GRR
OOPS!
COME ON, LAG.
LET'S GET STARTED!

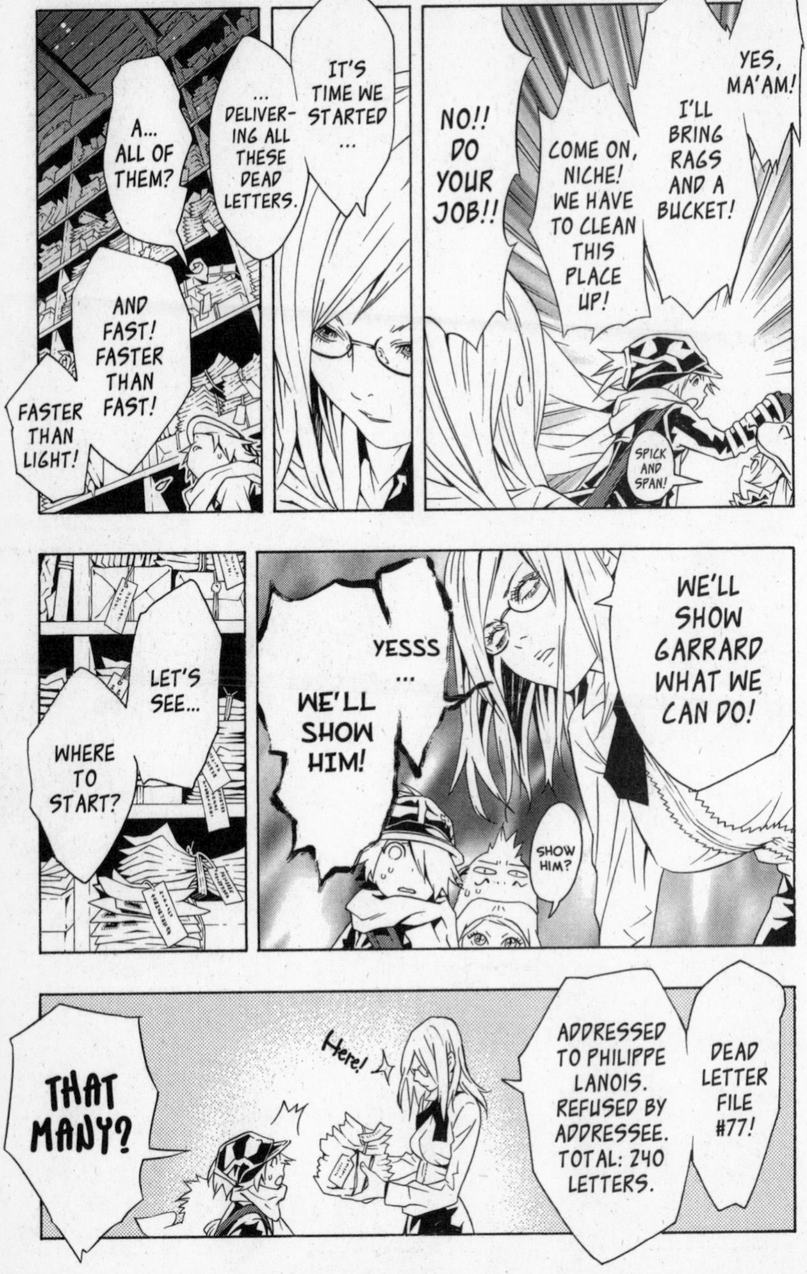
YES, MA'AM!
I'LL BRING RAGS AND A BUCKET!
COME ON, NICHE! WE HAVE TO CLEAN THIS PLACE UP!
NO!! DO YOUR JOB!!
SPICK AND SPAN!
IT'S TIME WE STARTED ...
... DELIVERING ALL THESE DEAD LETTERS.
A... ALL OF THEM?
AND FAST! FASTER THAN FAST!
FASTER THAN LIGHT!
WE'LL SHOW GARRARD WHAT WE CAN DO!
YESSS ...
WE'LL SHOW HIM!
SHOW HIM?
LET'S SEE...
WHERE TO START?
DEAD LETTER FILE #77!
ADDRESSED TO PHILIPPE LANOIS. REFUSED BY ADDRESSEE. TOTAL: 240 LETTERS.
Here!
THAT MANY?

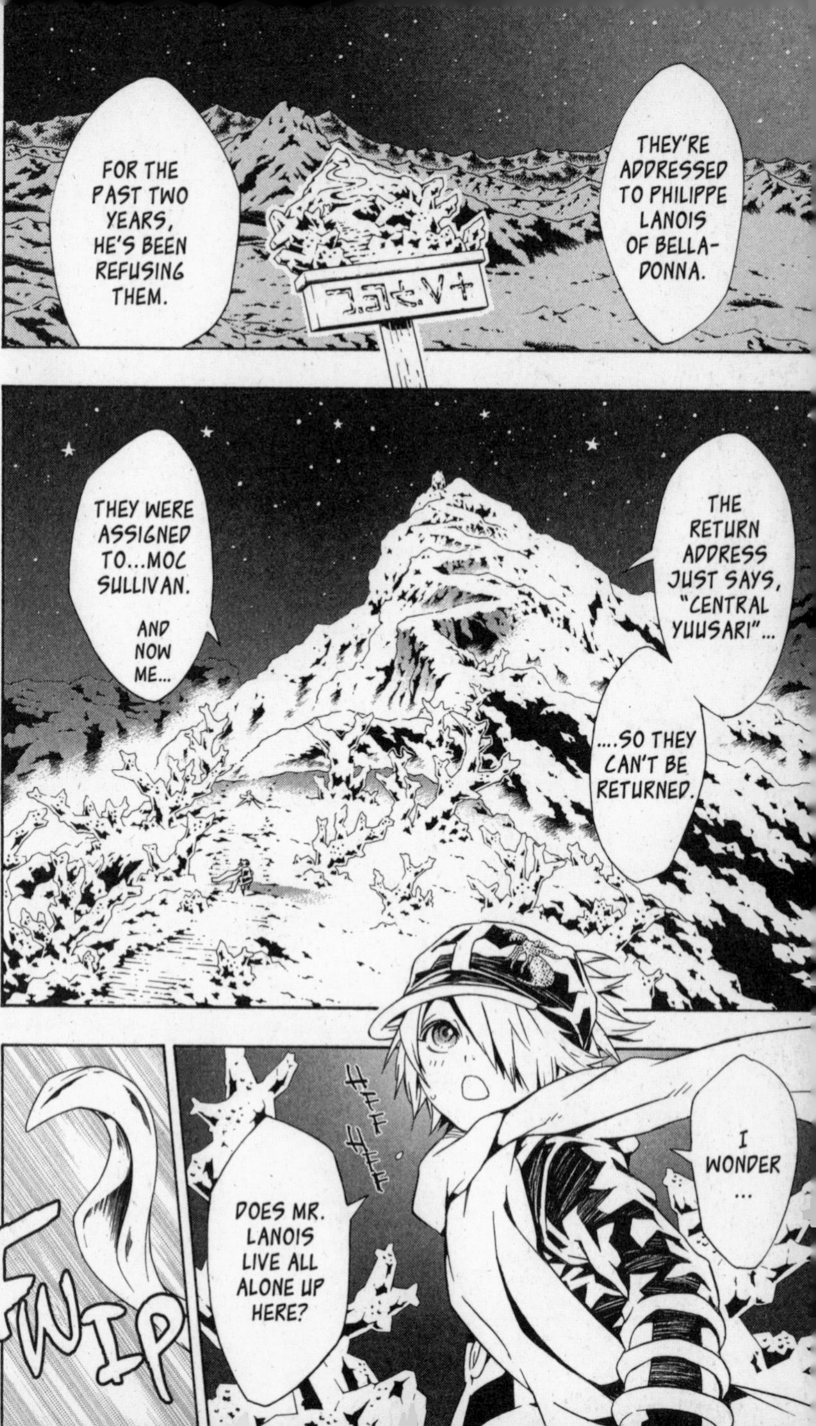
THEY'RE ADDRESSED TO PHILIPPE LANOIS OF BELLA-DONNA.
FOR THE PAST TWO YEARS, HE'S BEEN REFUSING THEM.
THE RETURN ADDRESS JUST SAYS, "CENTRAL YUUSARI"...
...SO THEY CAN'T BE RETURNED.
THEY WERE ASSIGNED TO...MOC SULLIVAN.
AND NOW ME...
I WONDER...
DOES MR. LANOIS LIVE ALL ALONE UP HERE?
HEFF HEFF
FWIP

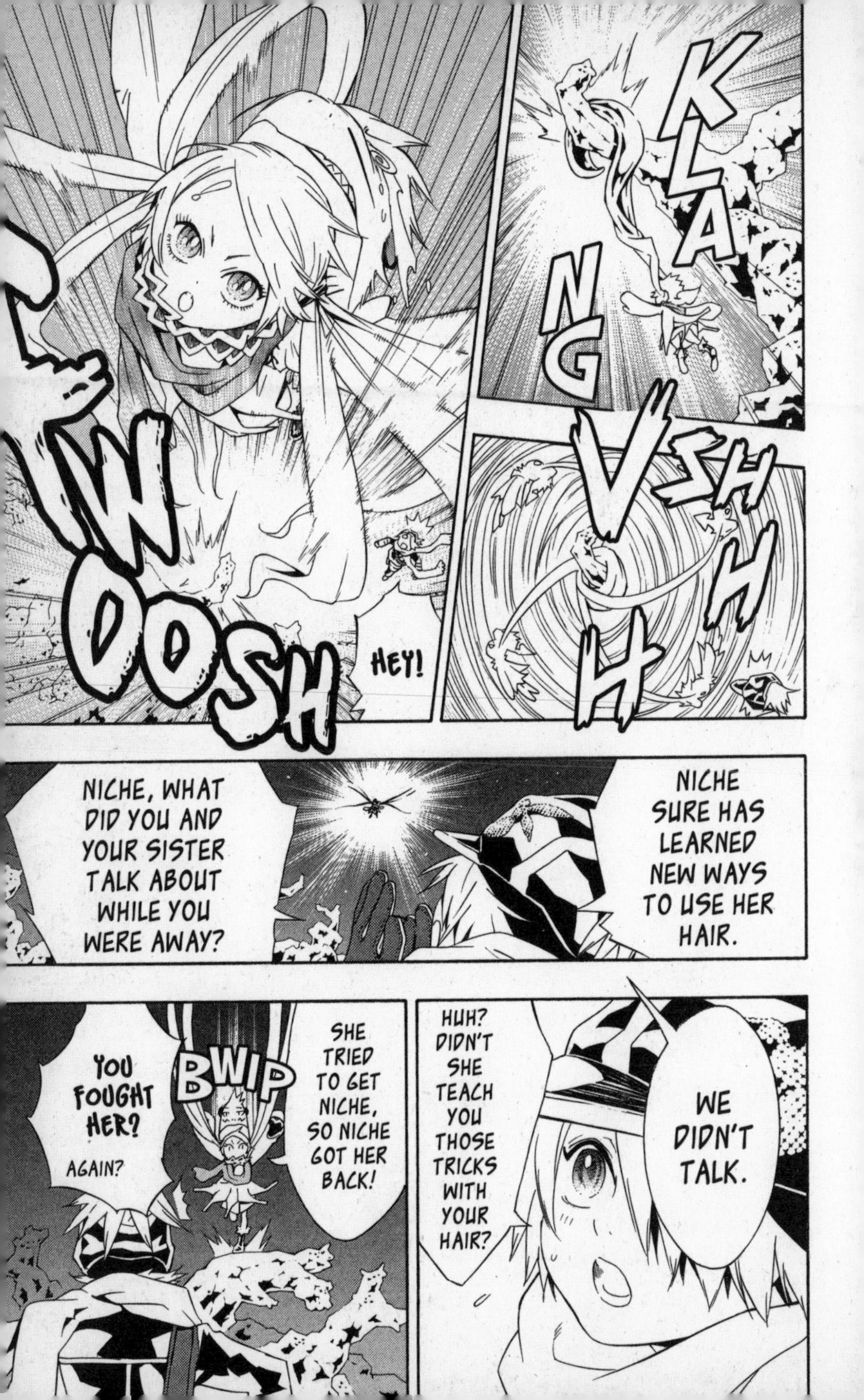
KLANG
VSHHH
WOOSH
HEY!
NICHE SURE HAS LEARNED NEW WAYS TO USE HER HAIR.
NICHE, WHAT DID YOU AND YOUR SISTER TALK ABOUT WHILE YOU WERE AWAY?
WE DIDN'T TALK.
HUH? DIDN'T SHE TEACH YOU THOSE TRICKS WITH YOUR HAIR?
SHE TRIED TO GET NICHE, SO NICHE GOT HER BACK!
BWIP
YOU FOUGHT HER?
AGAIN?

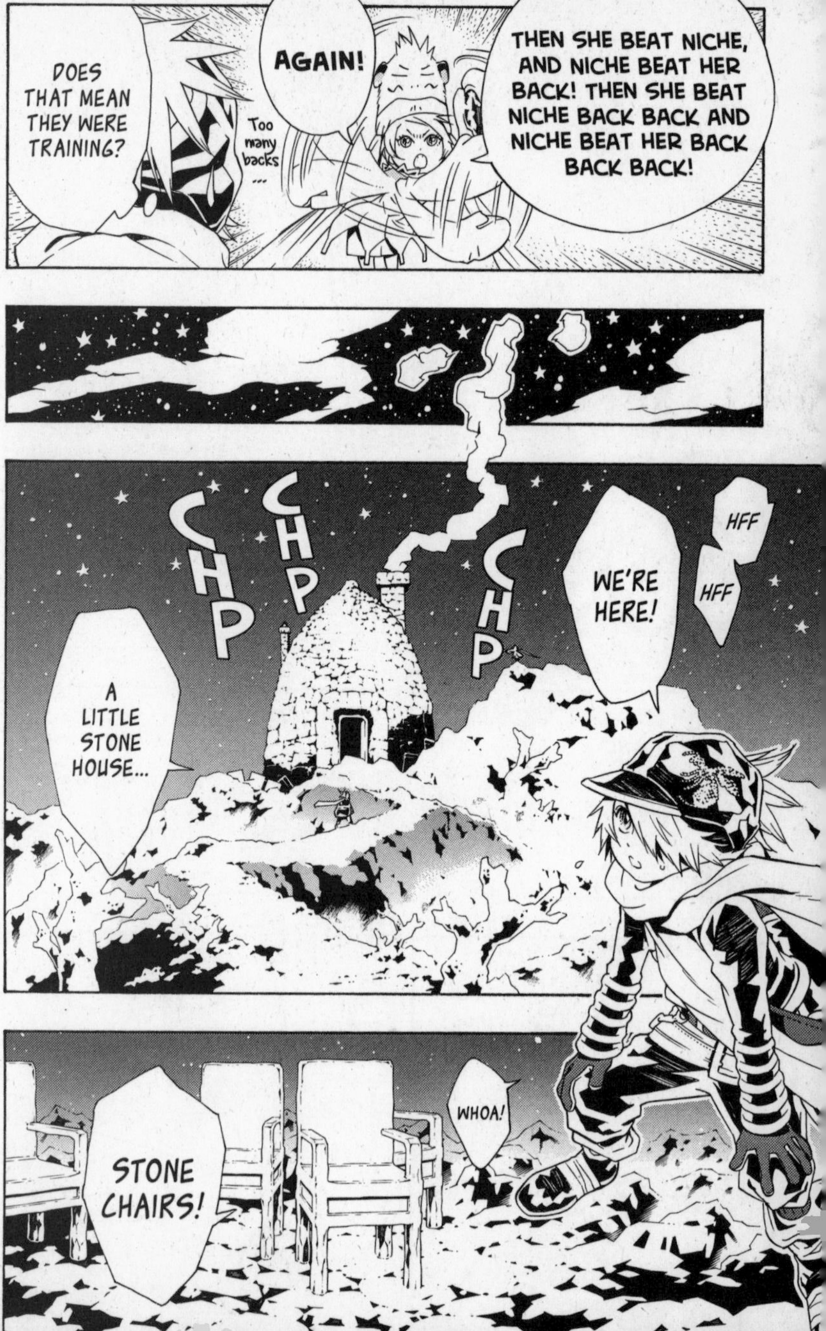
THEN SHE BEAT NICHE, AND NICHE BEAT HER BACK! THEN SHE BEAT NICHE BACK BACK AND NICHE BEAT HER BACK BACK BACK!
AGAIN!
Too many backs...
DOES THAT MEAN THEY WERE TRAINING?
HFF
HFF
WE'RE HERE!
CHP
CHP
CHP
A LITTLE STONE HOUSE...
WHOA!
STONE CHAIRS!

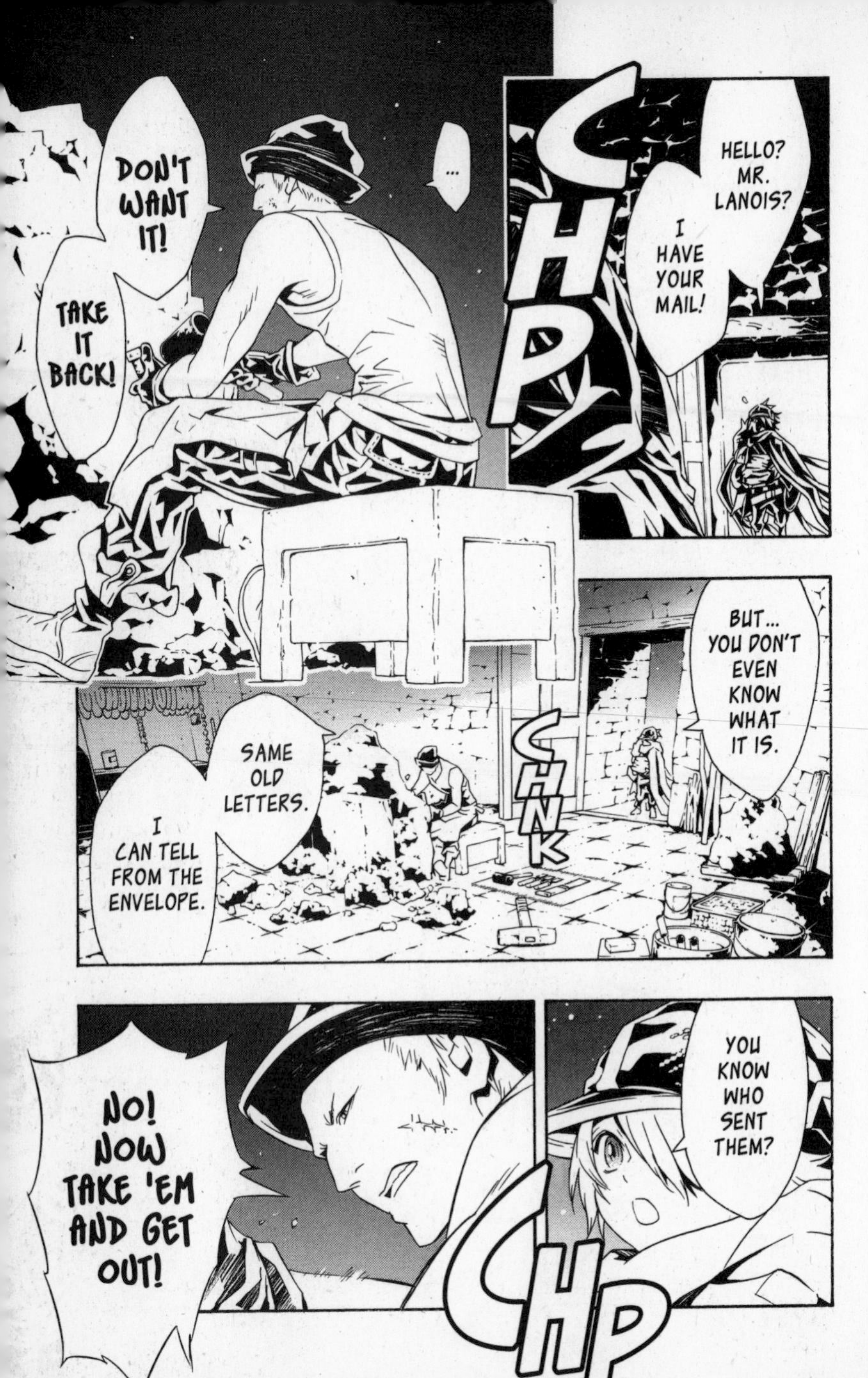
CHP
HELLO? MR. LANOIS?
I HAVE YOUR MAIL!
...
DON'T WANT IT!
TAKE IT BACK!
BUT... YOU DON'T EVEN KNOW WHAT IT IS.
CHNK
SAME OLD LETTERS.
I CAN TELL FROM THE ENVELOPE.
YOU KNOW WHO SENT THEM?
CHP
NO! NOW TAKE 'EM AND GET OUT!

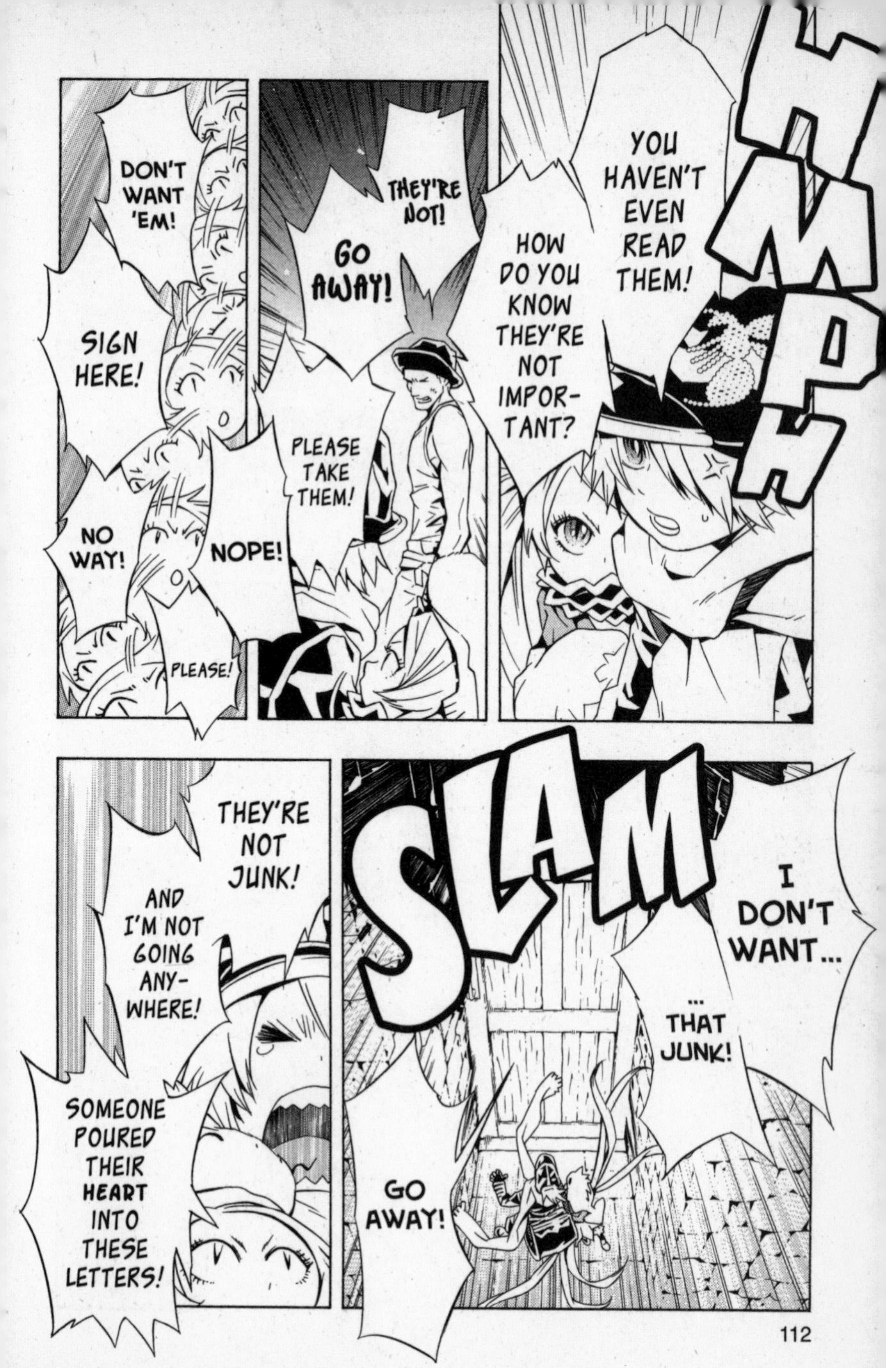
HMPH
YOU HAVEN'T EVEN READ THEM!
HOW DO YOU KNOW THEY'RE NOT IMPOR-TANT?
THEY'RE NOT!
GO AWAY!
PLEASE TAKE THEM!
DON'T WANT 'EM!
SIGN HERE!
NOPE!
NO WAY!
PLEASE!
SLAM
I DON'T WANT...
... THAT JUNK!
GO AWAY!
THEY'RE NOT JUNK!
AND I'M NOT GOING ANY-WHERE!
SOMEONE POURED THEIR HEART INTO THESE LETTERS!

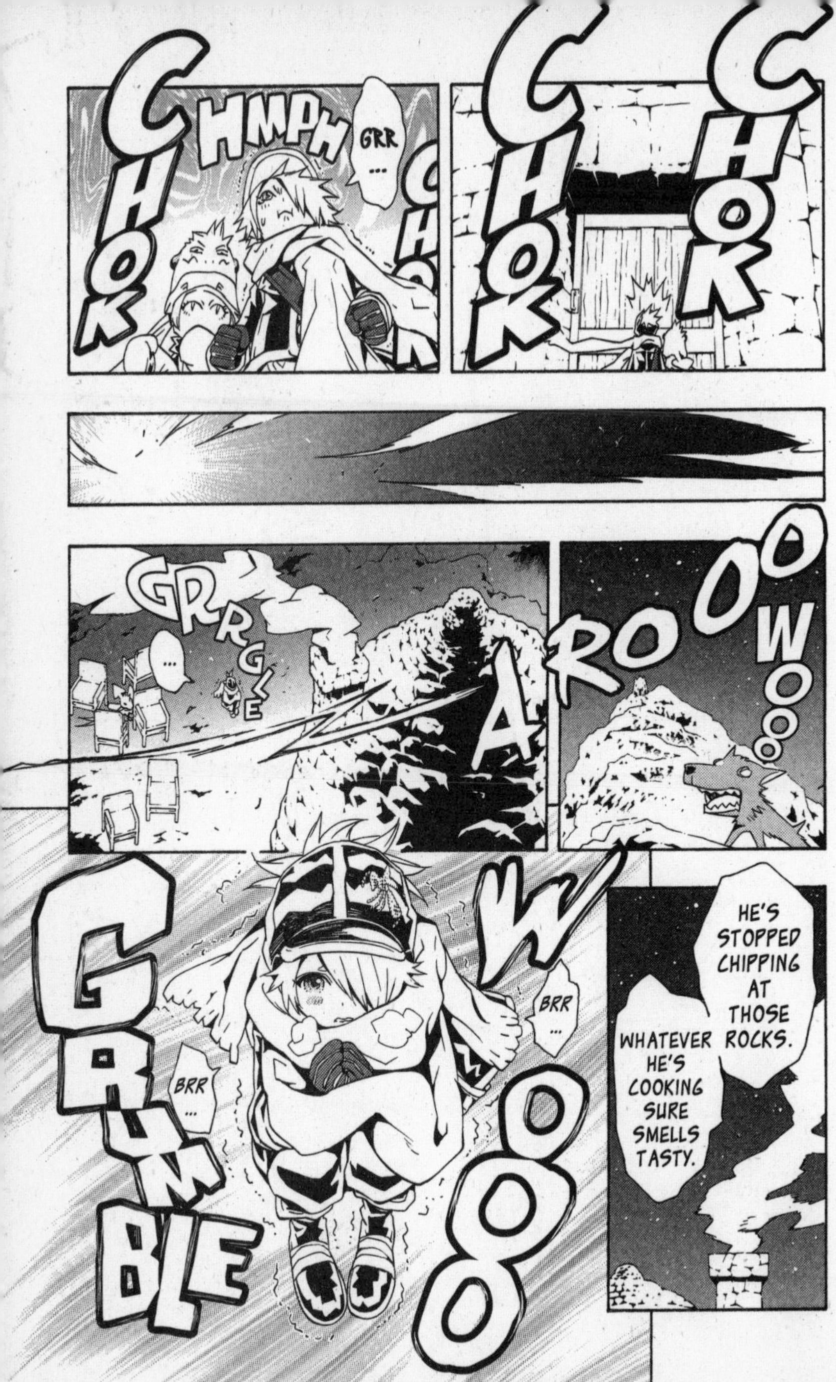
CHOK
CHOK
CHOK
CHMPH
GRR ...
CHOK
AROOOOWOOOO
GRRRGLE
...
HE'S STOPPED CHIPPING AT THOSE ROCKS.
WHATEVER HE'S COOKING SURE SMELLS TASTY.
BRR ...
BRR ...
GRUMBLE
WOOOO

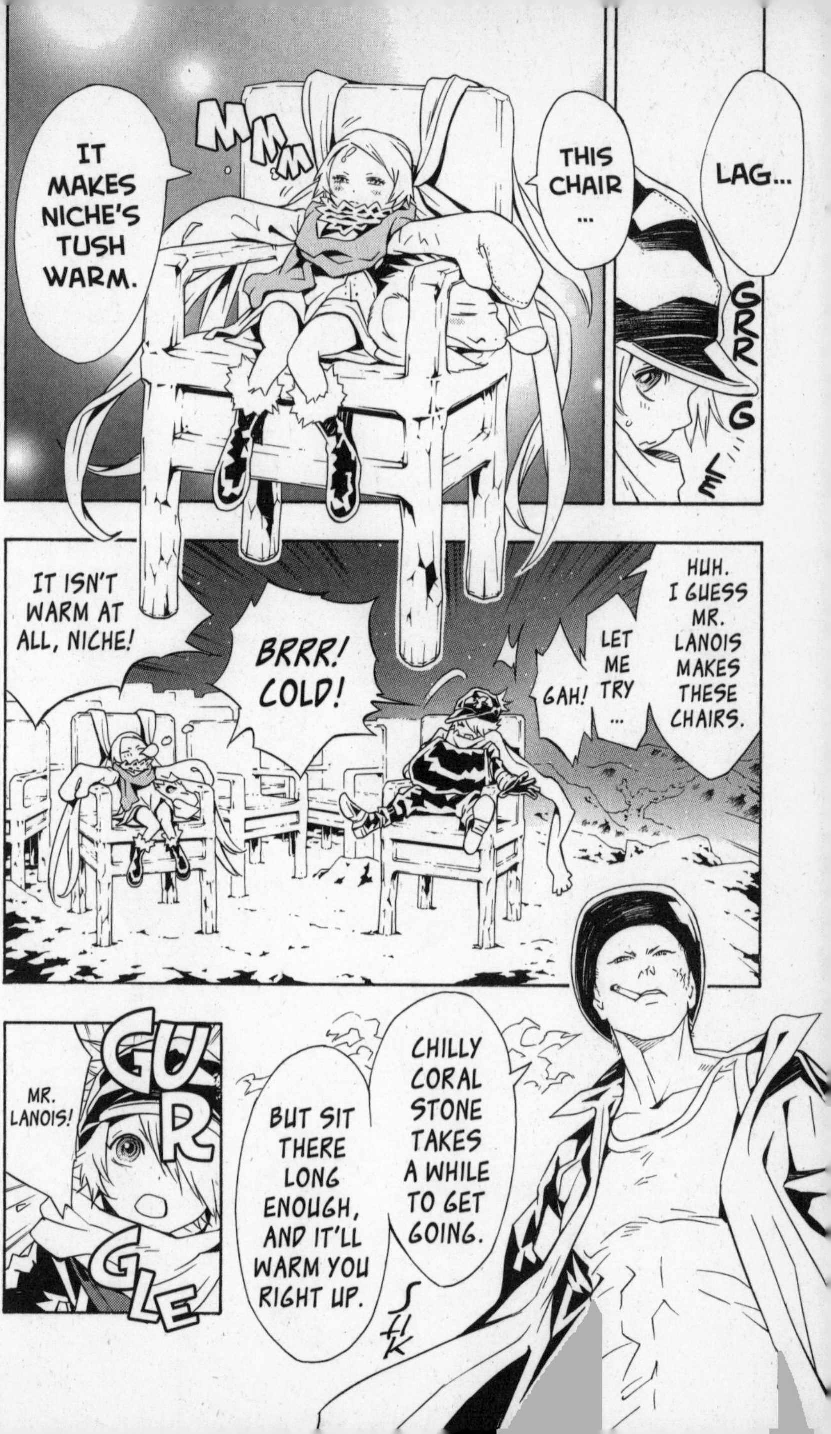
LAG...
GRRGLE
THIS CHAIR ...
MMM
IT MAKES NICHE'S TUSH WARM.
HUH. I GUESS MR. LANOIS MAKES THESE CHAIRS.
LET ME TRY ...
GAH!
BRRR! COLD!
IT ISN'T WARM AT ALL, NICHE!
CHILLY CORAL STONE TAKES A WHILE TO GET GOING.
BUT SIT THERE LONG ENOUGH, AND IT'LL WARM YOU RIGHT UP.
SHK
GURGLE
MR. LANOIS!

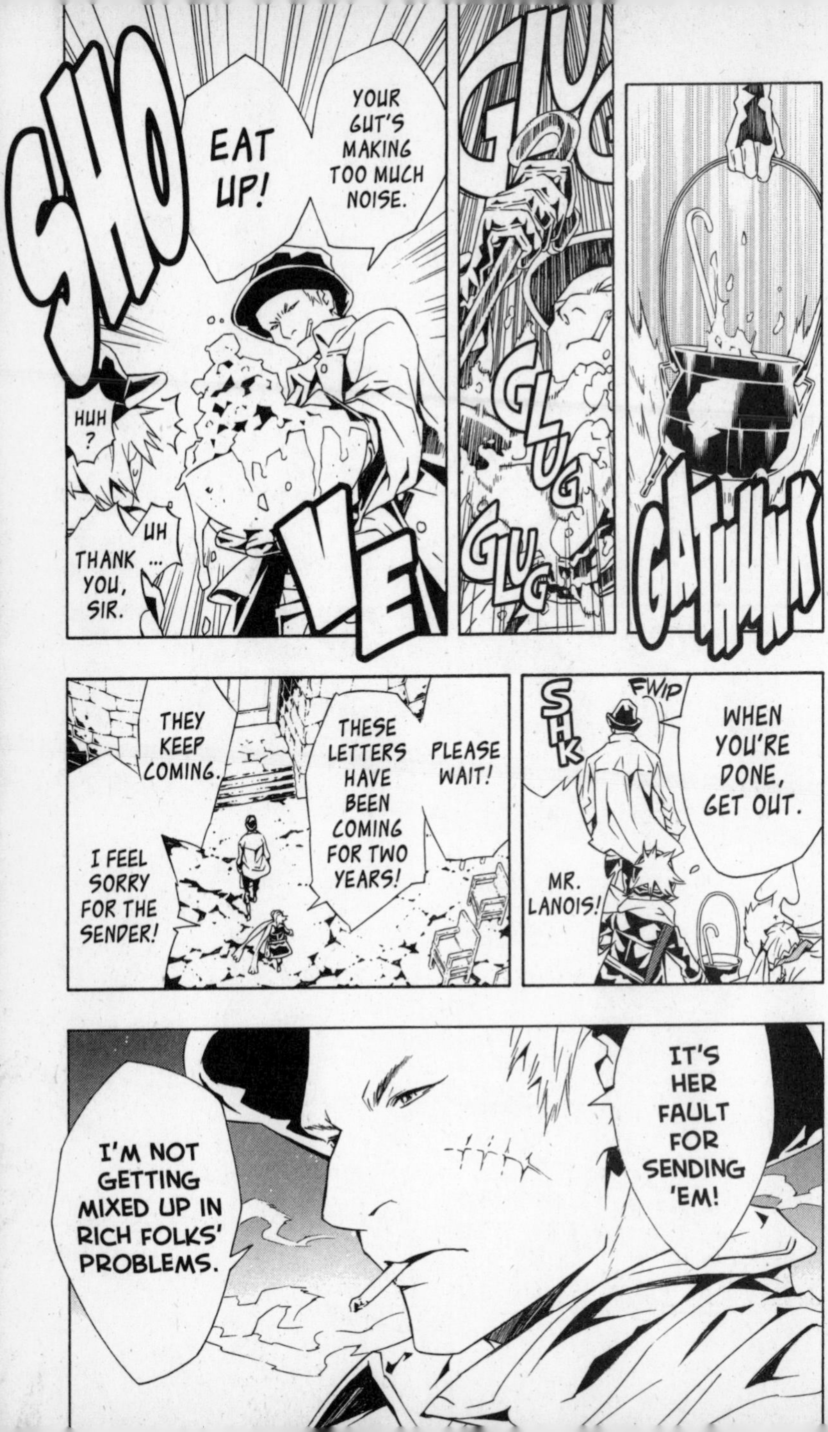
GATHUNK
GLUG
GLUG
GLUG
YOUR GUT'S MAKING TOO MUCH NOISE.
EAT UP!
SHOVE
HUH?
UH...
THANK YOU, SIR.
FWIP
WHEN YOU'RE DONE, GET OUT.
SHK
MR. LANOIS!
PLEASE WAIT!
THESE LETTERS HAVE BEEN COMING FOR TWO YEARS!
THEY KEEP COMING.
I FEEL SORRY FOR THE SENDER!
IT'S HER FAULT FOR SENDING 'EM!
I'M NOT GETTING MIXED UP IN RICH FOLKS' PROBLEMS.

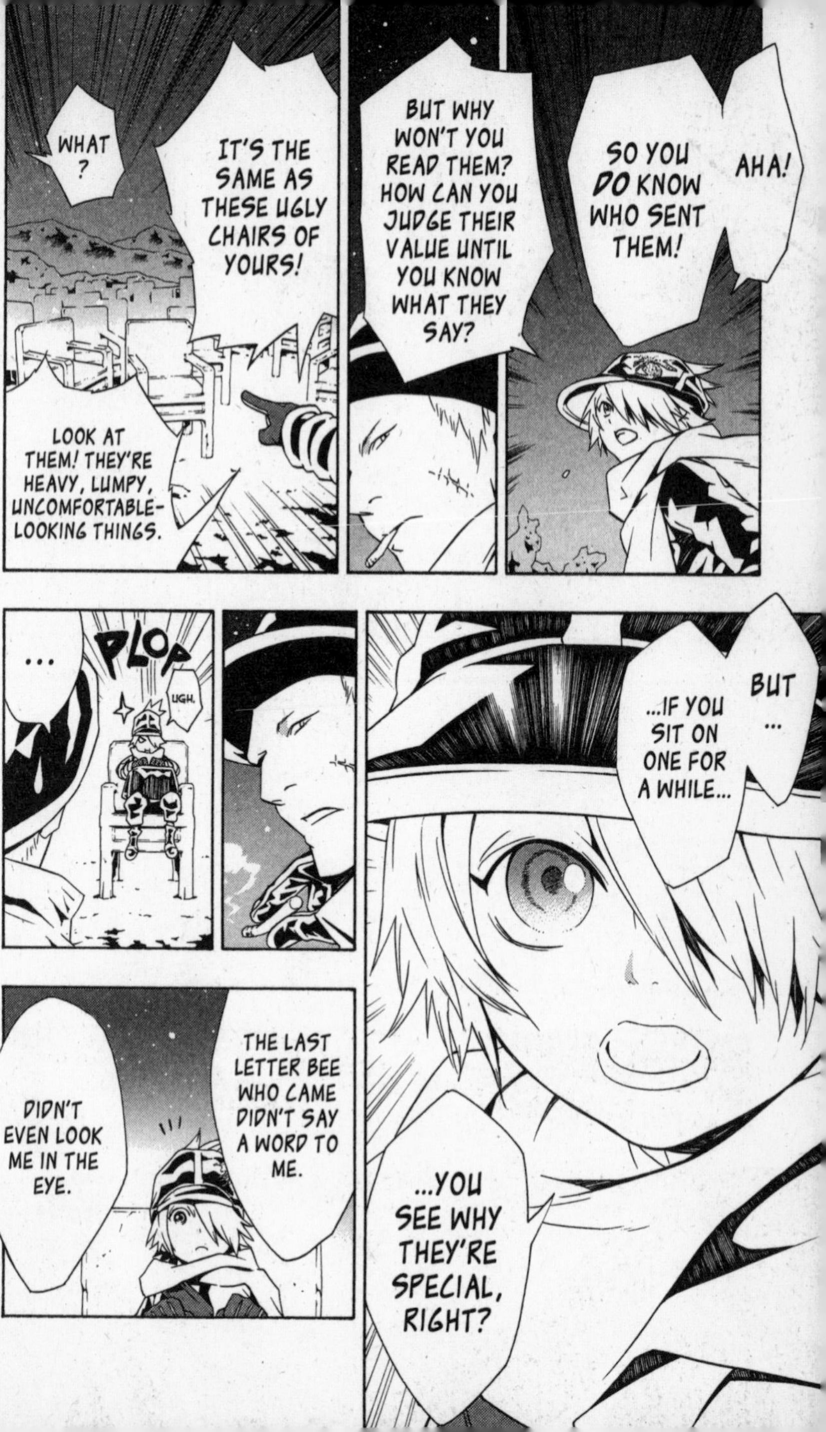
AHA!
SO YOU DO KNOW WHO SENT THEM!
BUT WHY WON'T YOU READ THEM? HOW CAN YOU JUDGE THEIR VALUE UNTIL YOU KNOW WHAT THEY SAY?
IT'S THE SAME AS THESE UGLY CHAIRS OF YOURS!
WHAT?
LOOK AT THEM! THEY'RE HEAVY, LUMPY, UNCOMFORTABLE-LOOKING THINGS.
BUT...
...IF YOU SIT ON ONE FOR A WHILE...
...YOU SEE WHY THEY'RE SPECIAL, RIGHT?
PLOP
UGH.
...
THE LAST LETTER BEE WHO CAME DIDN'T SAY A WORD TO ME.
DIDN'T EVEN LOOK ME IN THE EYE.

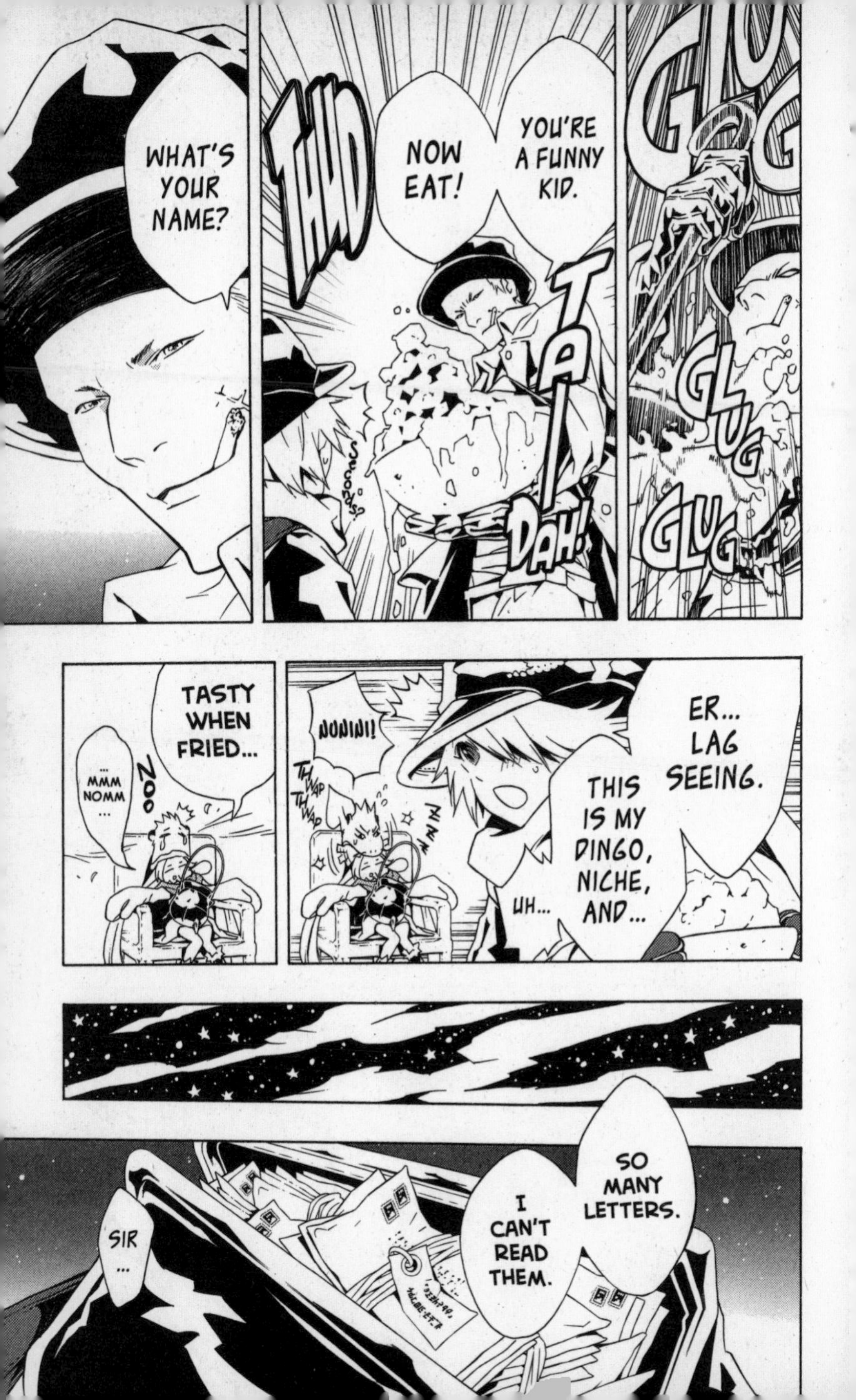
GLUG
GLUG
GLUG
YOU'RE A FUNNY KID.
NOW EAT!
THUD
TA-DAH!
SECONDS?
WHAT'S YOUR NAME?
ER... LAG SEEING.
THIS IS MY DINGO, NICHE, AND...
UH...
NUNINI!
THWAP THWAP
TASTY WHEN FRIED...
ZOO
... MMM NOMM ...
SO MANY LETTERS.
I CAN'T READ THEM.
SIR ...

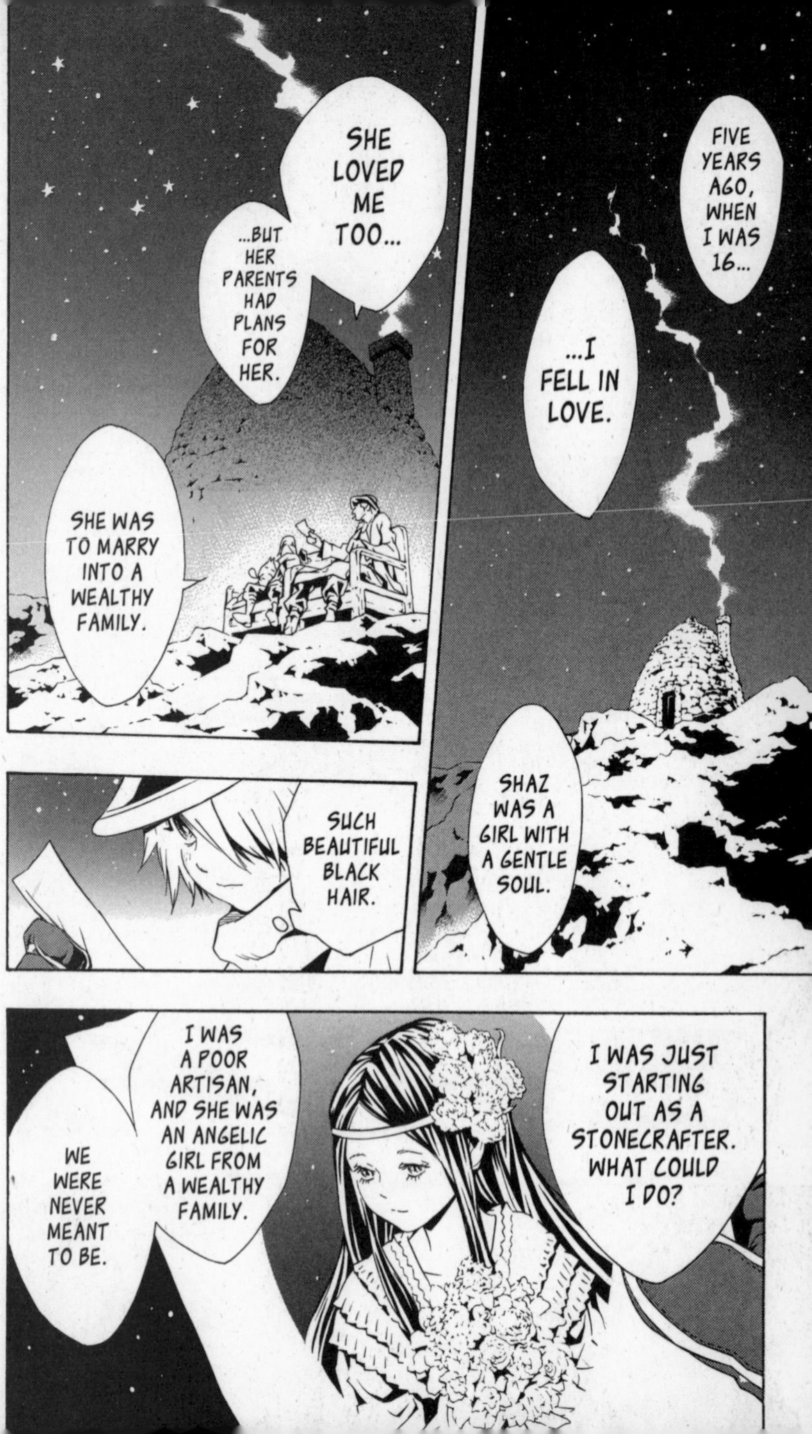
FIVE YEARS AGO, WHEN I WAS 16...
...I FELL IN LOVE.
SHAZ WAS A GIRL WITH A GENTLE SOUL.
SHE LOVED ME TOO...
...BUT HER PARENTS HAD PLANS FOR HER.
SHE WAS TO MARRY INTO A WEALTHY FAMILY.
SUCH BEAUTIFUL BLACK HAIR.
I WAS JUST STARTING OUT AS A STONECRAFTER. WHAT COULD I DO?
I WAS A POOR ARTISAN, AND SHE WAS AN ANGELIC GIRL FROM A WEALTHY FAMILY.
WE WERE NEVER MEANT TO BE.

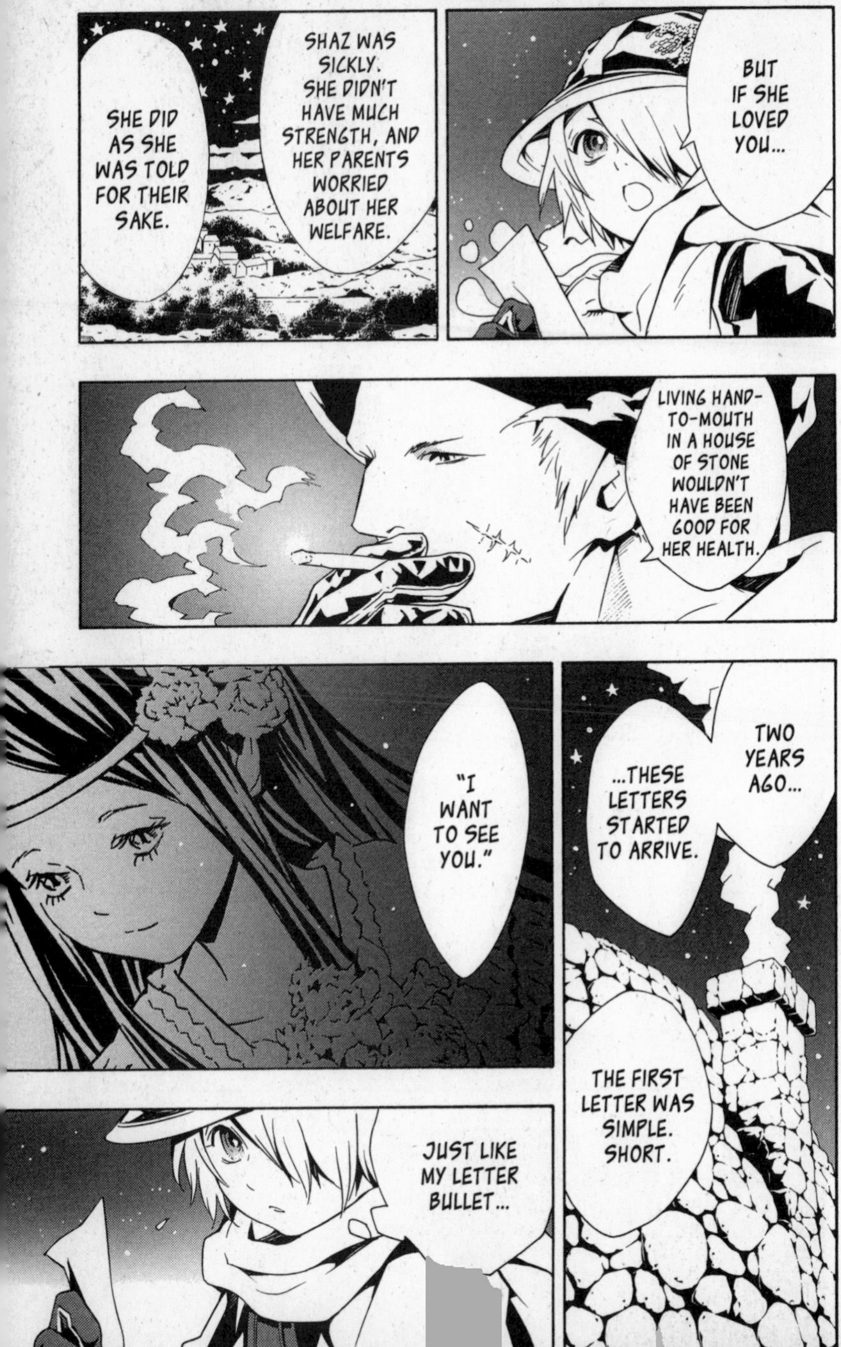
BUT IF SHE LOVED YOU...
SHAZ WAS SICKLY. SHE DIDN'T HAVE MUCH STRENGTH, AND HER PARENTS WORRIED ABOUT HER WELFARE.
SHE DID AS SHE WAS TOLD FOR THEIR SAKE.
LIVING HAND-TO-MOUTH IN A HOUSE OF STONE WOULDN'T HAVE BEEN GOOD FOR HER HEALTH.
TWO YEARS AGO...
...THESE LETTERS STARTED TO ARRIVE.
THE FIRST LETTER WAS SIMPLE. SHORT.
"I WANT TO SEE YOU."
JUST LIKE MY LETTER BULLET...

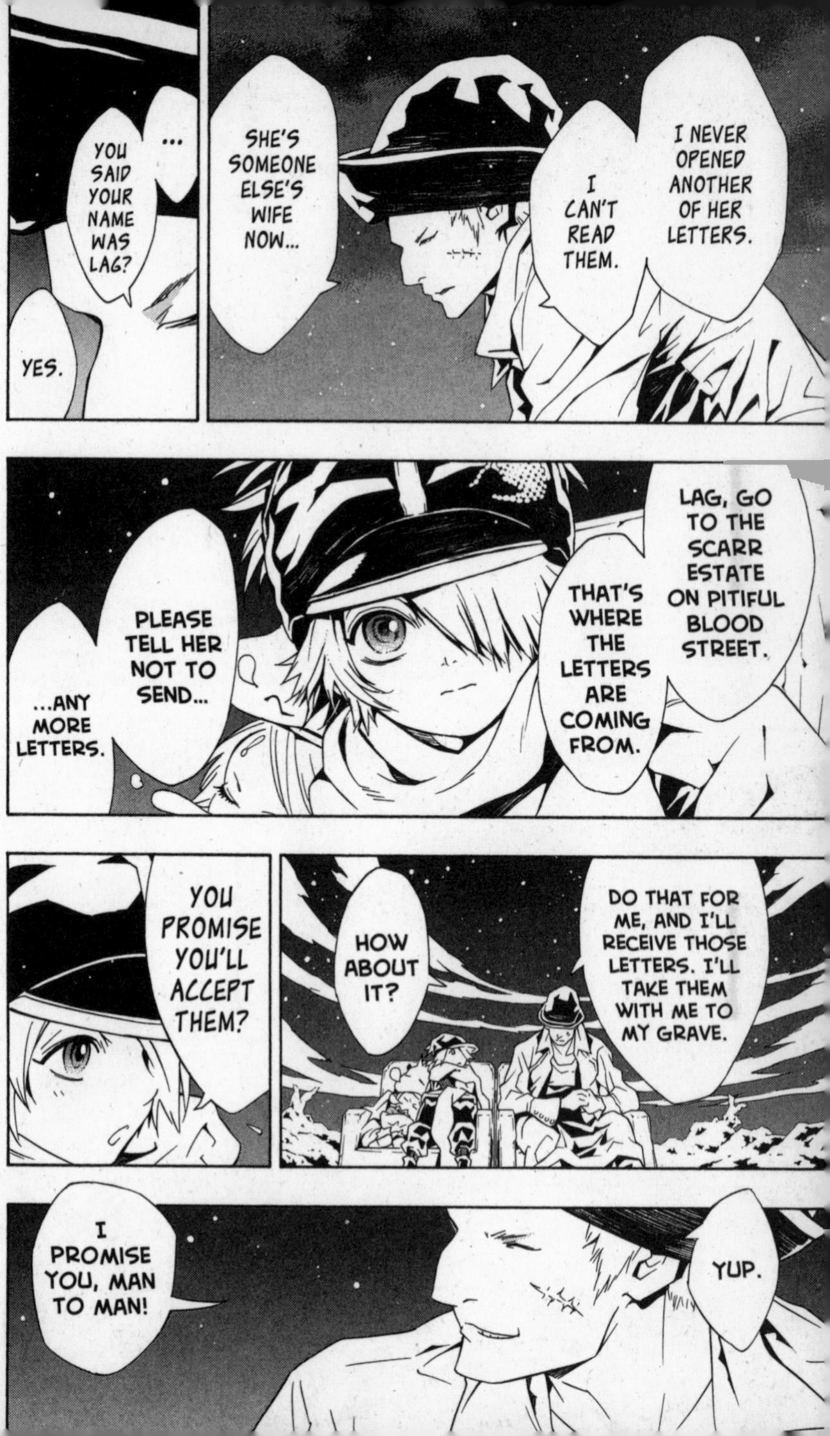
I NEVER OPENED ANOTHER OF HER LETTERS.
I CAN'T READ THEM.
SHE'S SOMEONE ELSE'S WIFE NOW...
...
YOU SAID YOUR NAME WAS LAG?
YES.
LAG, GO TO THE SCARR ESTATE ON PITIFUL BLOOD STREET.
THAT'S WHERE THE LETTERS ARE COMING FROM.
PLEASE TELL HER NOT TO SEND...
...ANY MORE LETTERS.
DO THAT FOR ME, AND I'LL RECEIVE THOSE LETTERS. I'LL TAKE THEM WITH ME TO MY GRAVE.
HOW ABOUT IT?
YOU PROMISE YOU'LL ACCEPT THEM?
YUP.
I PROMISE YOU, MAN TO MAN!

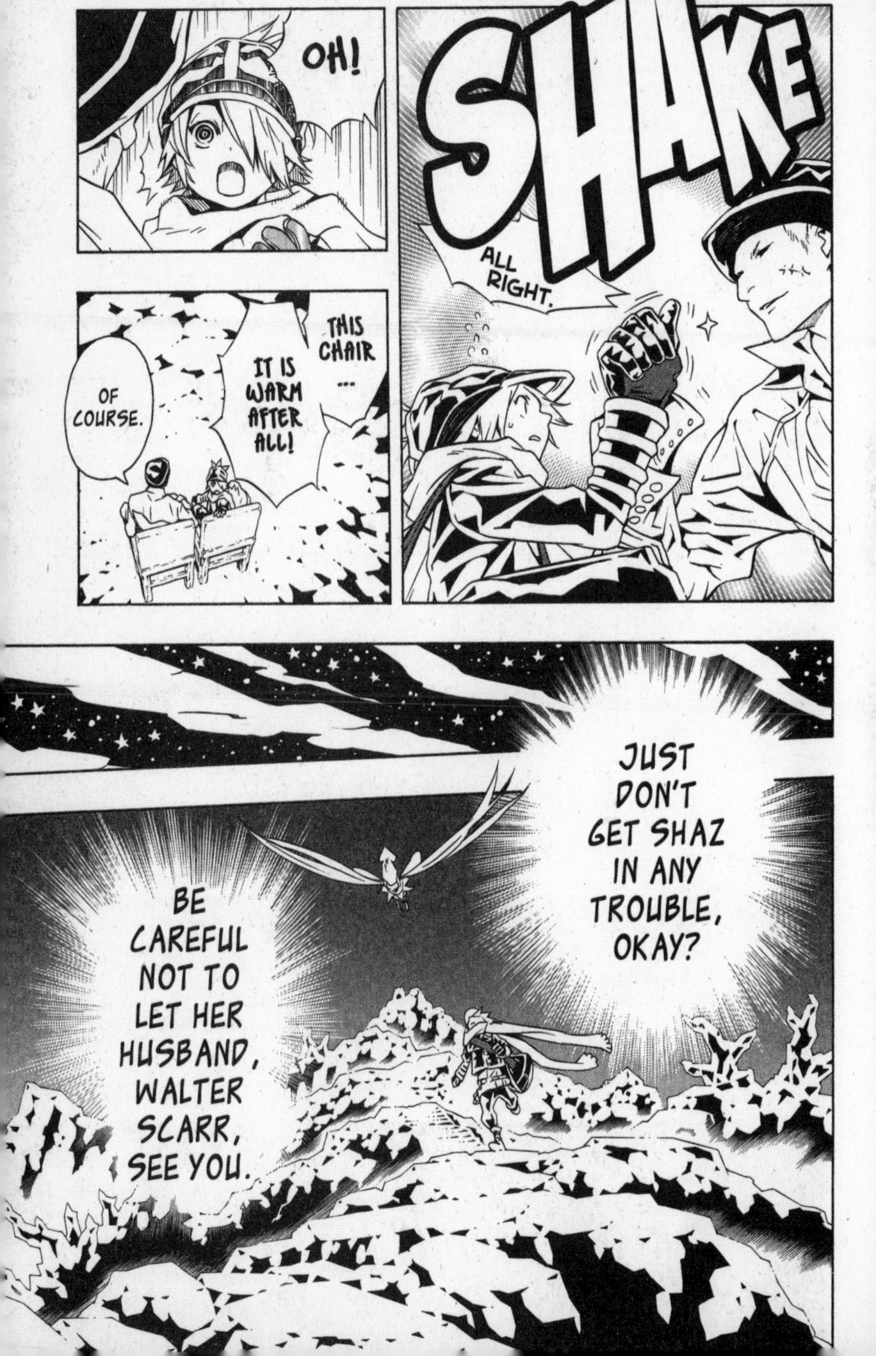
SHAKE
ALL RIGHT.
OH!
THIS CHAIR ...
IT IS WARM AFTER ALL!
OF COURSE.
JUST DON'T GET SHAZ IN ANY TROUBLE, OKAY?
BE CAREFUL NOT TO LET HER HUSBAND, WALTER SCARR, SEE YOU.

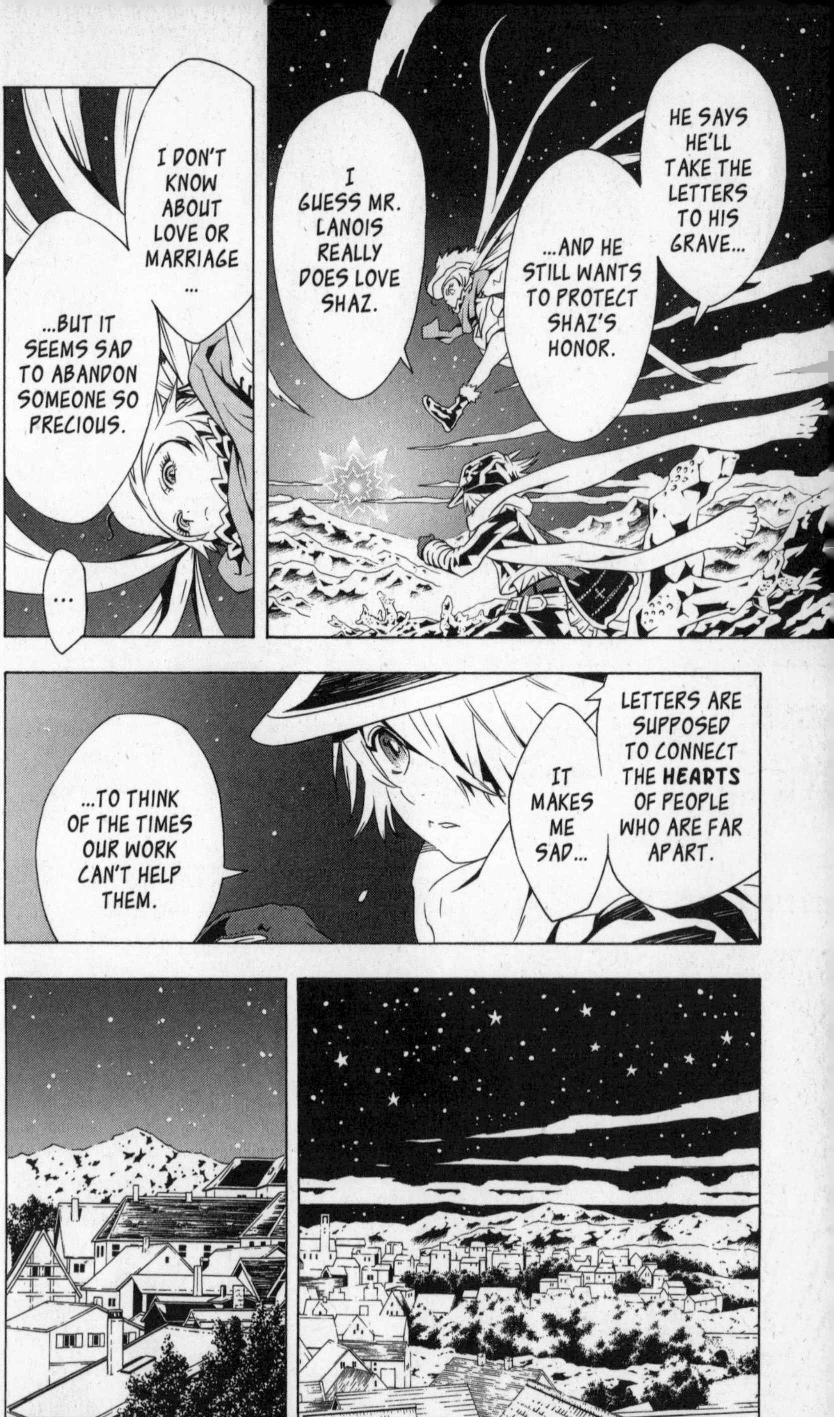
HE SAYS HE'LL TAKE THE LETTERS TO HIS GRAVE...
...AND HE STILL WANTS TO PROTECT SHAZ'S HONOR.
I GUESS MR. LANOIS REALLY DOES LOVE SHAZ.
I DON'T KNOW ABOUT LOVE OR MARRIAGE ...
...BUT IT SEEMS SAD TO ABANDON SOMEONE SO PRECIOUS.
...
LETTERS ARE SUPPOSED TO CONNECT THE **HEARTS** OF PEOPLE WHO ARE FAR APART.
IT MAKES ME SAD...
...TO THINK OF THE TIMES OUR WORK CAN'T HELP THEM.

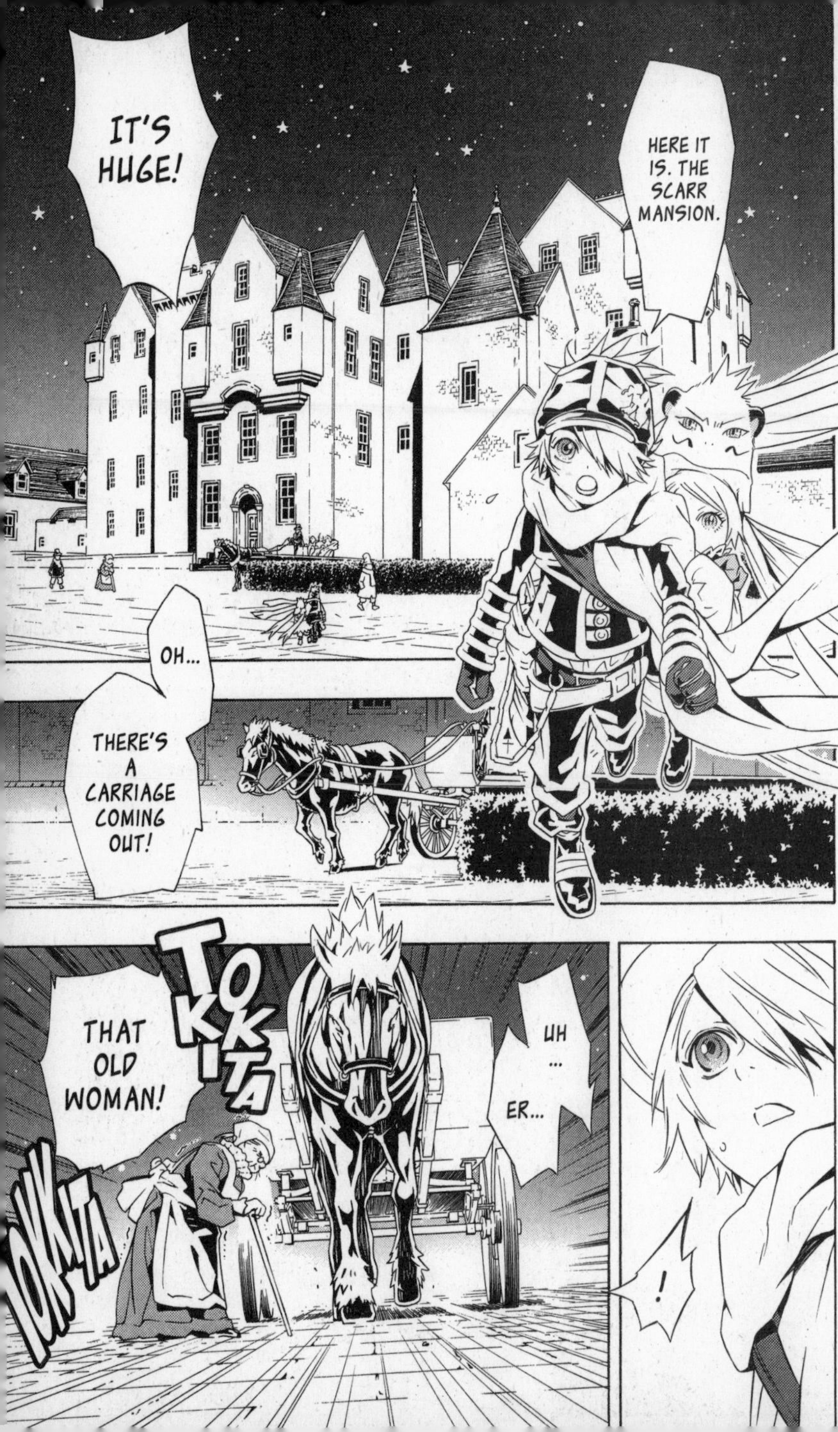
HERE IT IS. THE SCARR MANSION.
IT'S HUGE!
OH...
THERE'S A CARRIAGE COMING OUT!
!
UH ... ER...
TOKITA
THAT OLD WOMAN!
TOKKITA

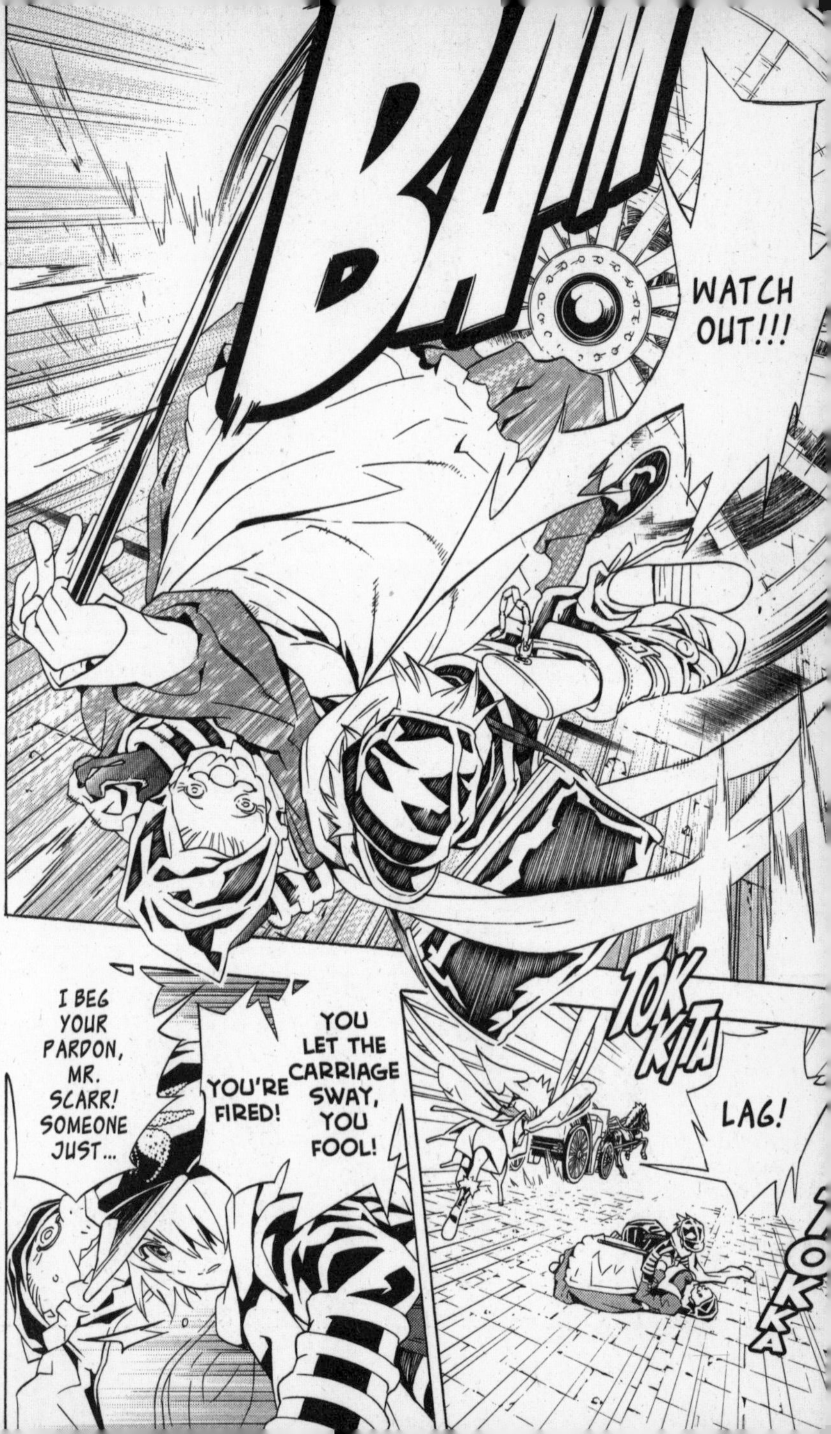
BAM
WATCH OUT!!!
LAG!
YOU LET THE CARRIAGE SWAY, YOU FOOL!
YOU'RE FIRED!
I BEG YOUR PARDON, MR. SCARR! SOMEONE JUST...

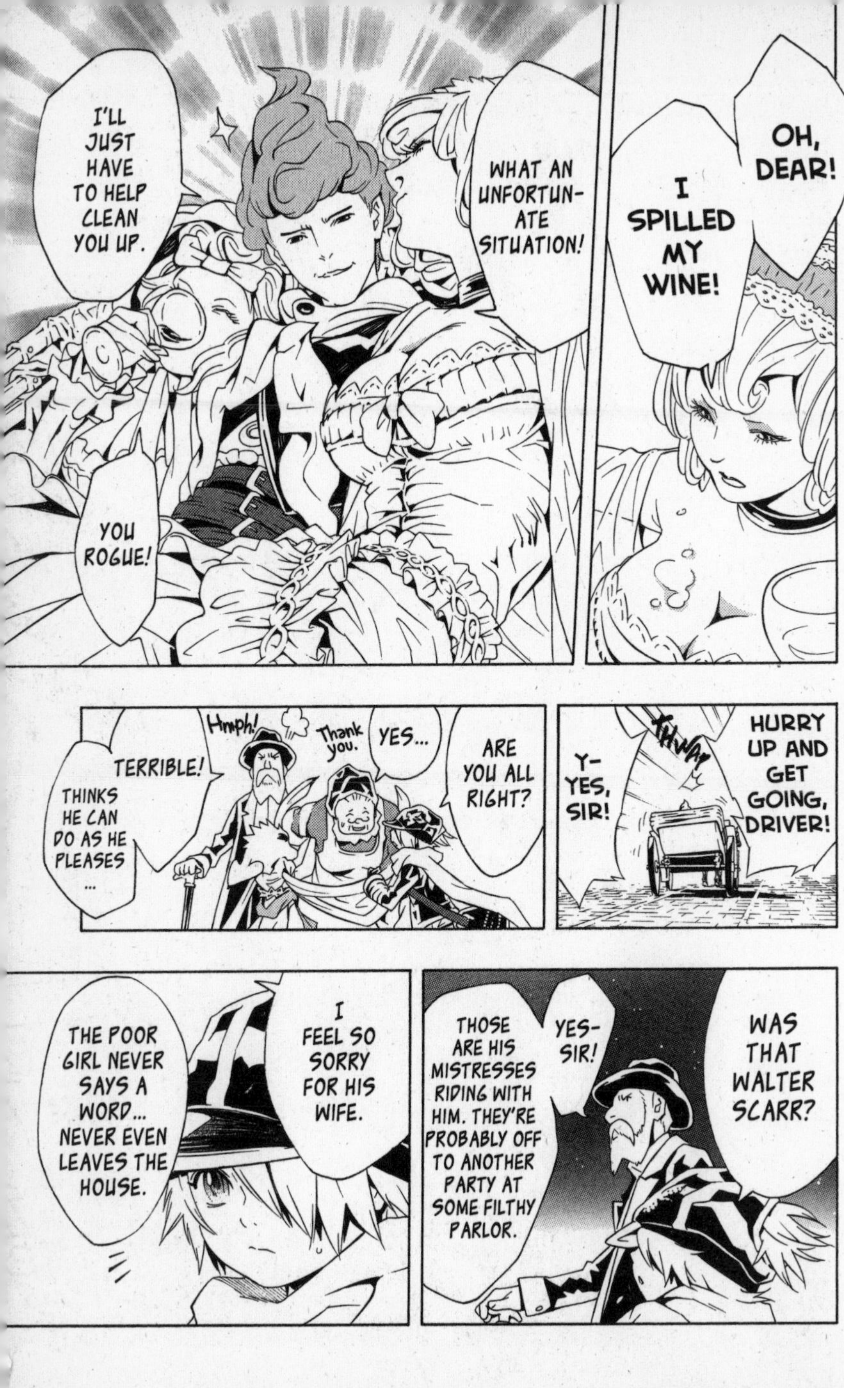
OH, DEAR!
I SPILLED MY WINE!
WHAT AN UNFORTUNATE SITUATION!
I'LL JUST HAVE TO HELP CLEAN YOU UP.
YOU ROGUE!
HURRY UP AND GET GOING, DRIVER!
THWAP
Y-YES, SIR!
ARE YOU ALL RIGHT?
YES...
Thank you.
Hmph!
TERRIBLE!
THINKS HE CAN DO AS HE PLEASES ...
WAS THAT WALTER SCARR?
YES-SIR!
THOSE ARE HIS MISTRESSES RIDING WITH HIM. THEY'RE PROBABLY OFF TO ANOTHER PARTY AT SOME FILTHY PARLOR.
I FEEL SO SORRY FOR HIS WIFE.
THE POOR GIRL NEVER SAYS A WORD... NEVER EVEN LEAVES THE HOUSE.

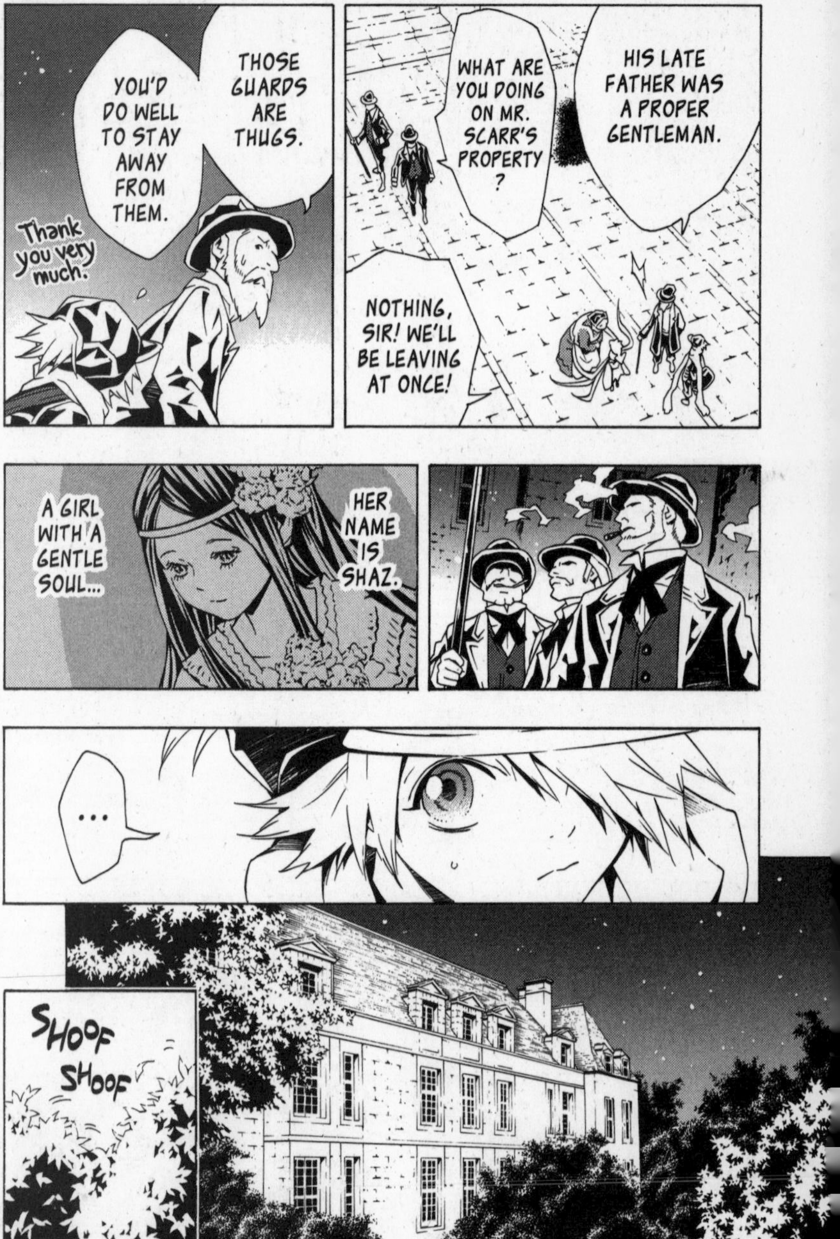
HIS LATE FATHER WAS A PROPER GENTLEMAN.
WHAT ARE YOU DOING ON MR. SCARR'S PROPERTY?
NOTHING, SIR! WE'LL BE LEAVING AT ONCE!
THOSE GUARDS ARE THUGS.
YOU'D DO WELL TO STAY AWAY FROM THEM.
Thank you very much.
HER NAME IS SHAZ.
A GIRL WITH A GENTLE SOUL...
...
SHOOF
SHOOF

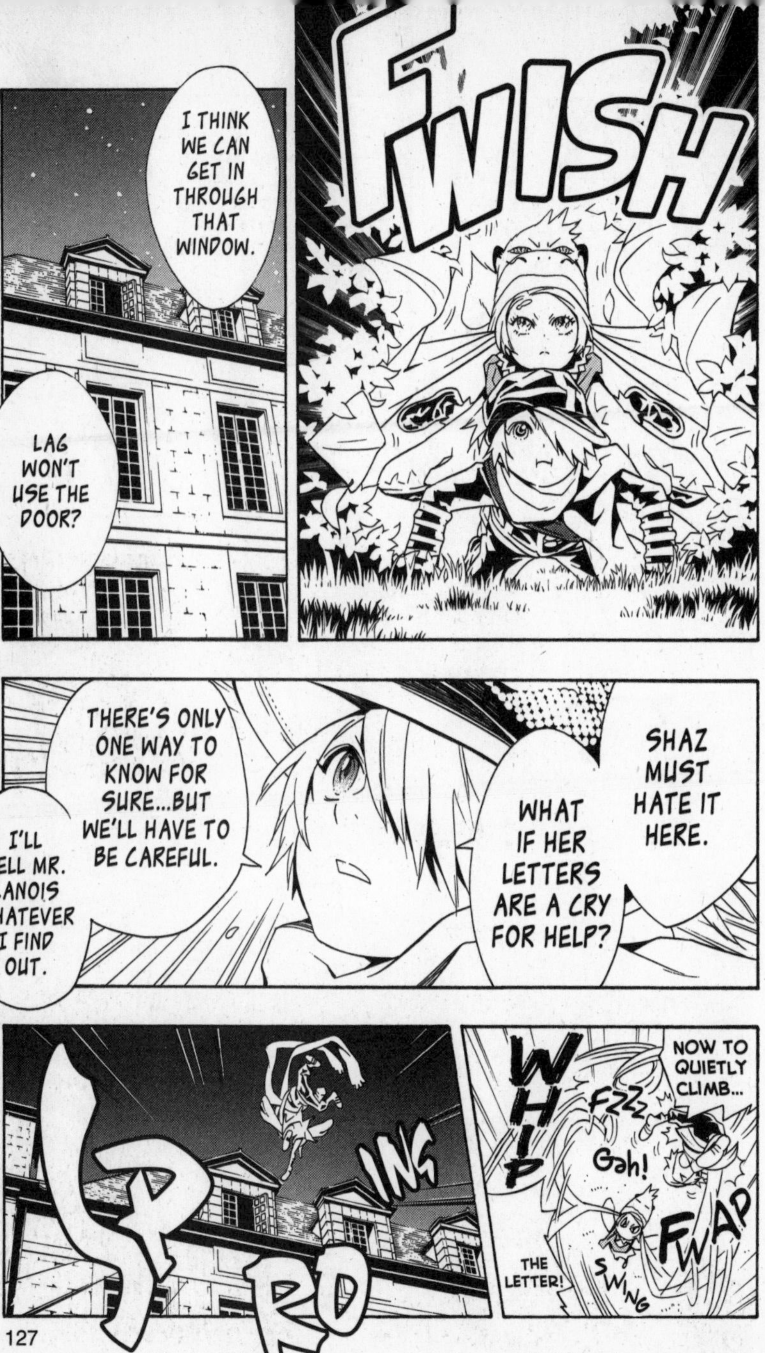
FWISH
I THINK WE CAN GET IN THROUGH THAT WINDOW.
LAG WON'T USE THE DOOR?
SHAZ MUST HATE IT HERE.
WHAT IF HER LETTERS ARE A CRY FOR HELP?
THERE'S ONLY ONE WAY TO KNOW FOR SURE...BUT WE'LL HAVE TO BE CAREFUL.
I'LL TELL MR. LANOIS WHATEVER I FIND OUT.
NOW TO QUIETLY CLIMB...
WHIP
FZZZ
Gah!
FWAP
THE LETTER!
SWING
SPROING

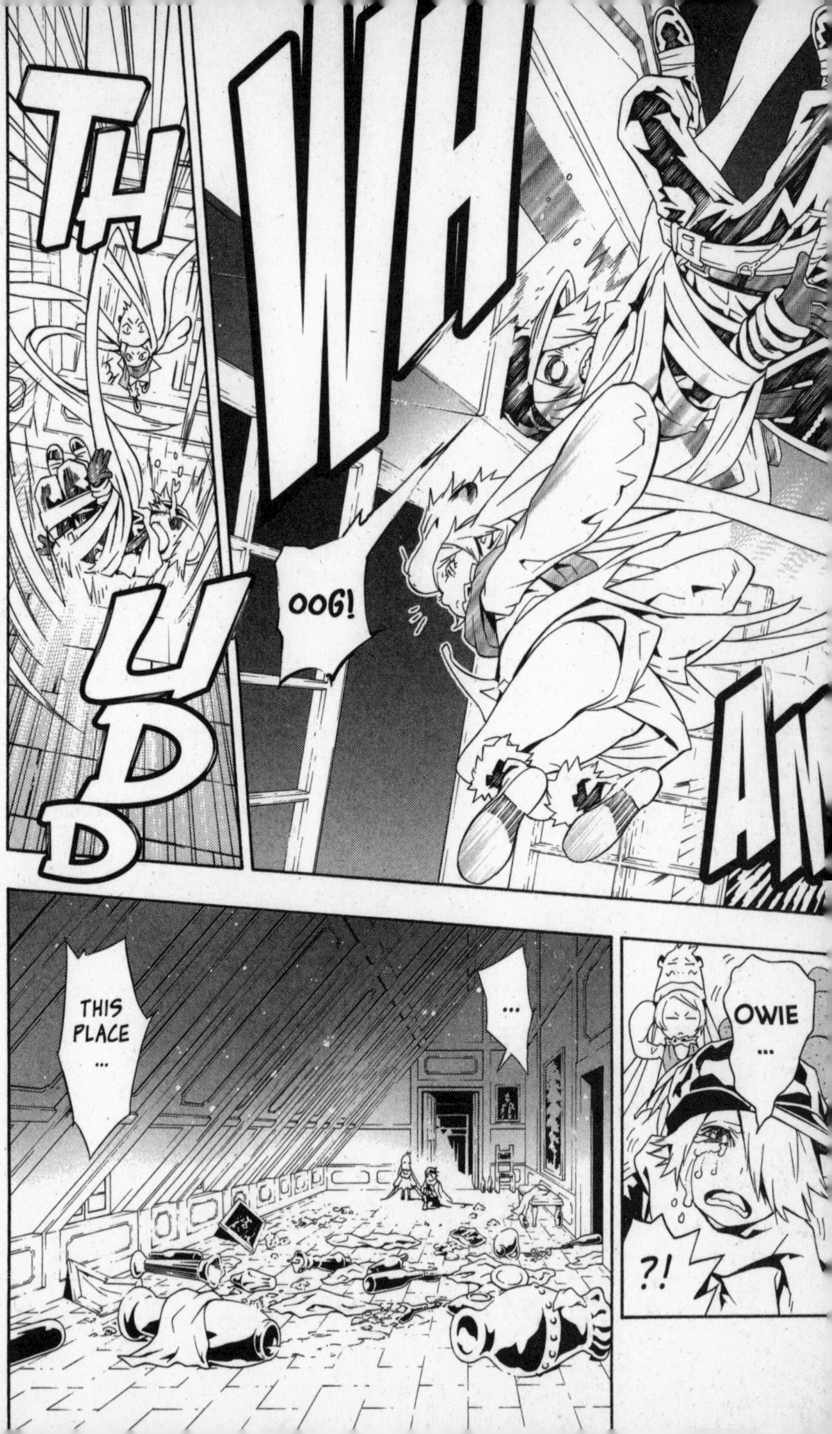
WH
AM
OOG!
TH
UDD
OWIE ...
?!
...
THIS PLACE ...

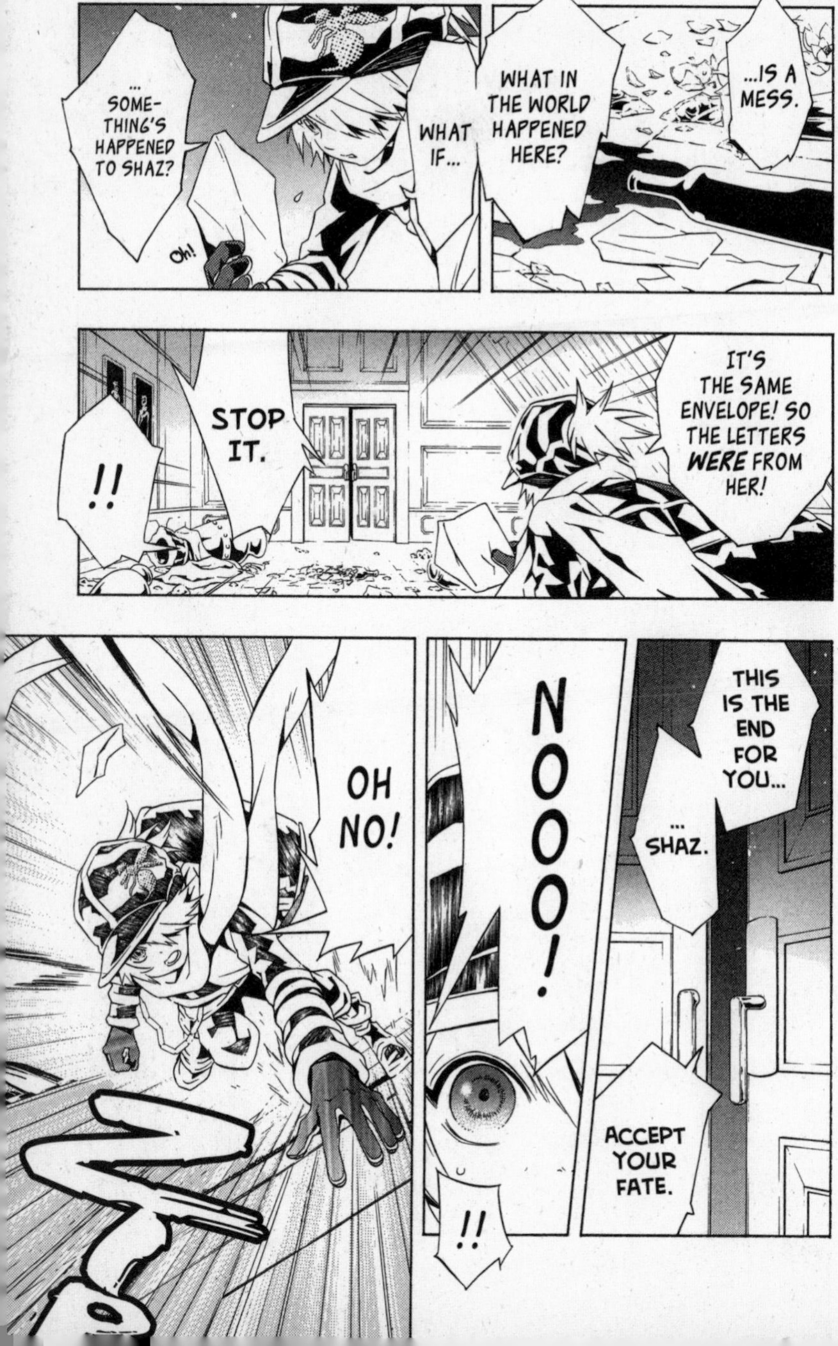
...IS A MESS.
WHAT IN THE WORLD HAPPENED HERE?
WHAT IF...
... SOME-THING'S HAPPENED TO SHAZ?
Oh!
IT'S THE SAME ENVELOPE! SO THE LETTERS *WERE* FROM HER!
STOP IT.
!!
THIS IS THE END FOR YOU...
... SHAZ.
ACCEPT YOUR FATE.
NOOOO!
!!
OH NO!

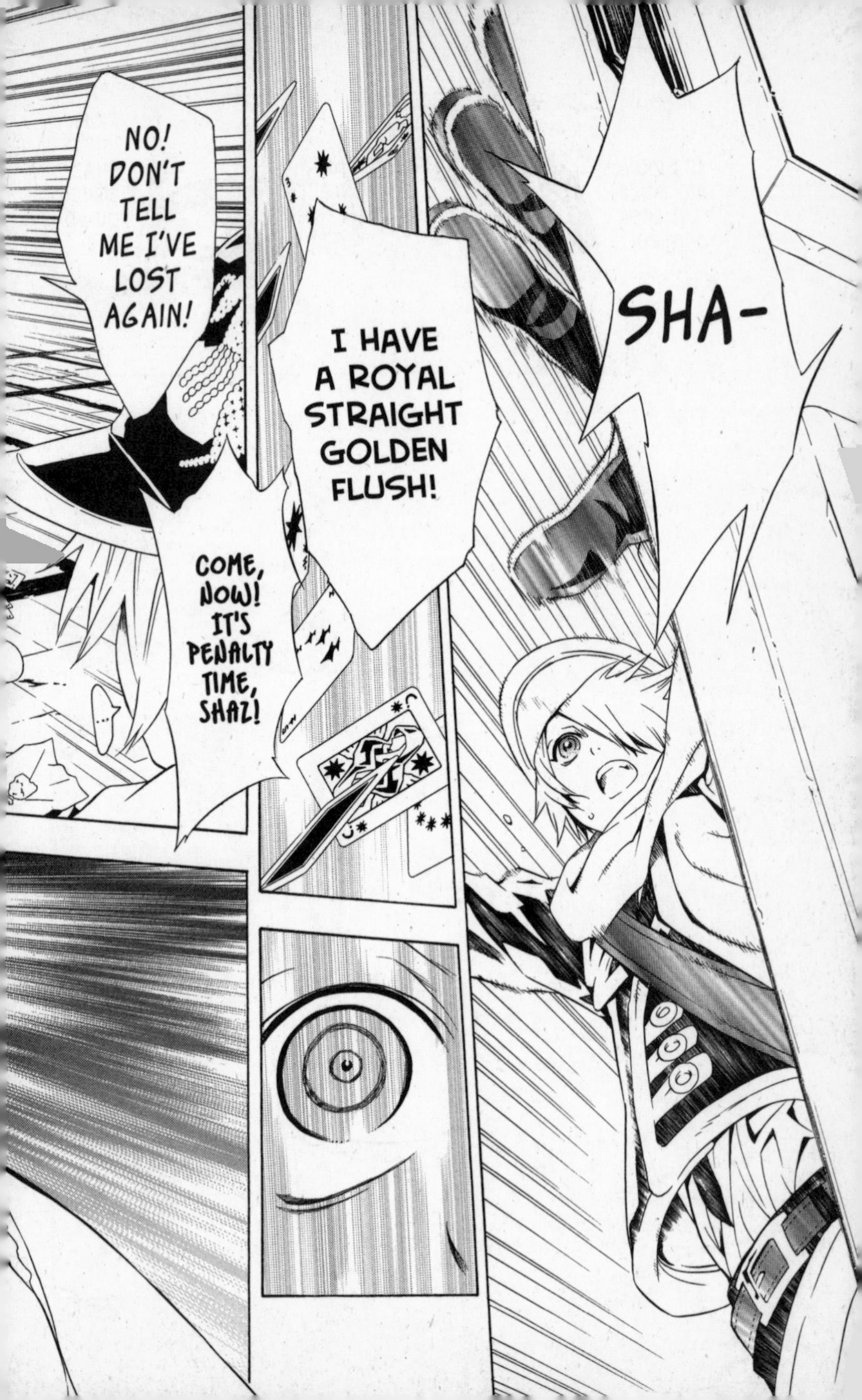
SHA-
I HAVE A ROYAL STRAIGHT GOLDEN FLUSH!
NO! DON'T TELL ME I'VE LOST AGAIN!
COME, NOW! IT'S PENALTY TIME, SHAZ!

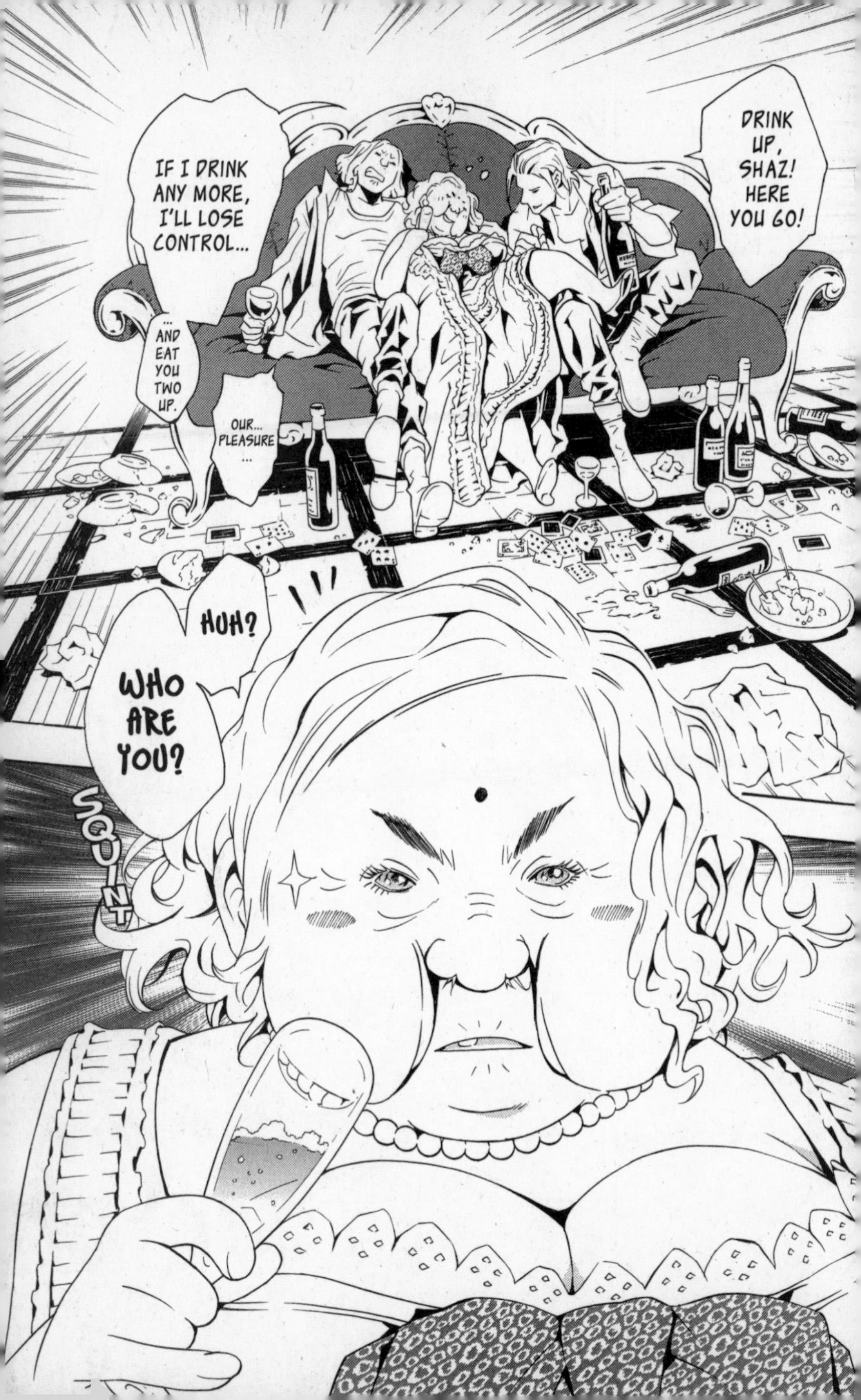
DRINK UP, SHAZ! HERE YOU GO!
IF I DRINK ANY MORE, I'LL LOSE CONTROL...
...AND EAT YOU TWO UP.
OUR... PLEASURE...
HUH?
WHO ARE YOU?
SQUINT

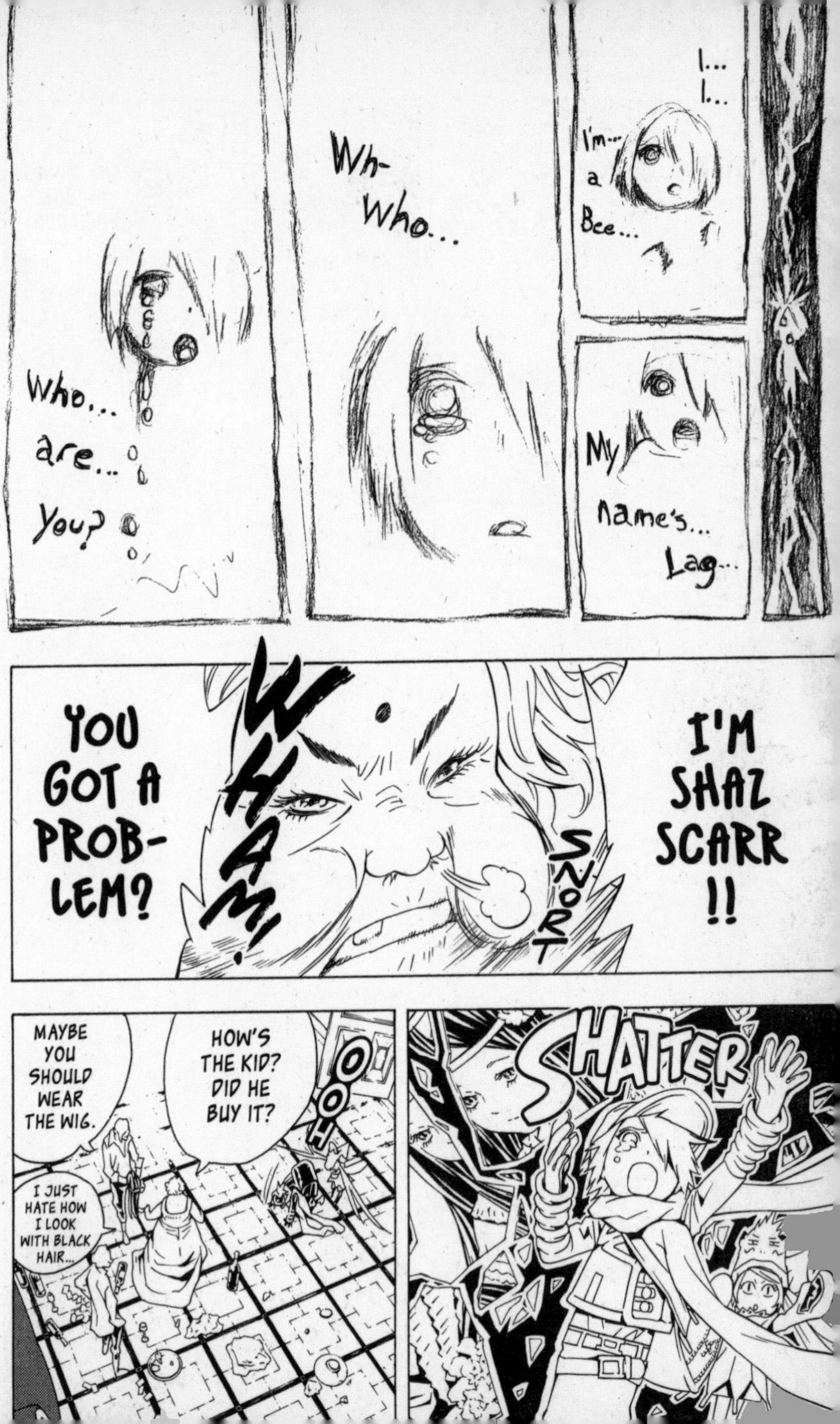
I... I...
I'm... a Bee...
My name's... Lag...
Wh- Who...
Who... are... you?
I'M SHAZ SCARR!!
SNORT
WHAM!
YOU GOT A PROBLEM?
SHATTER
OOOH
HOW'S THE KID? DID HE BUY IT?
MAYBE YOU SHOULD WEAR THE WIG.
I JUST HATE HOW I LOOK WITH BLACK HAIR...

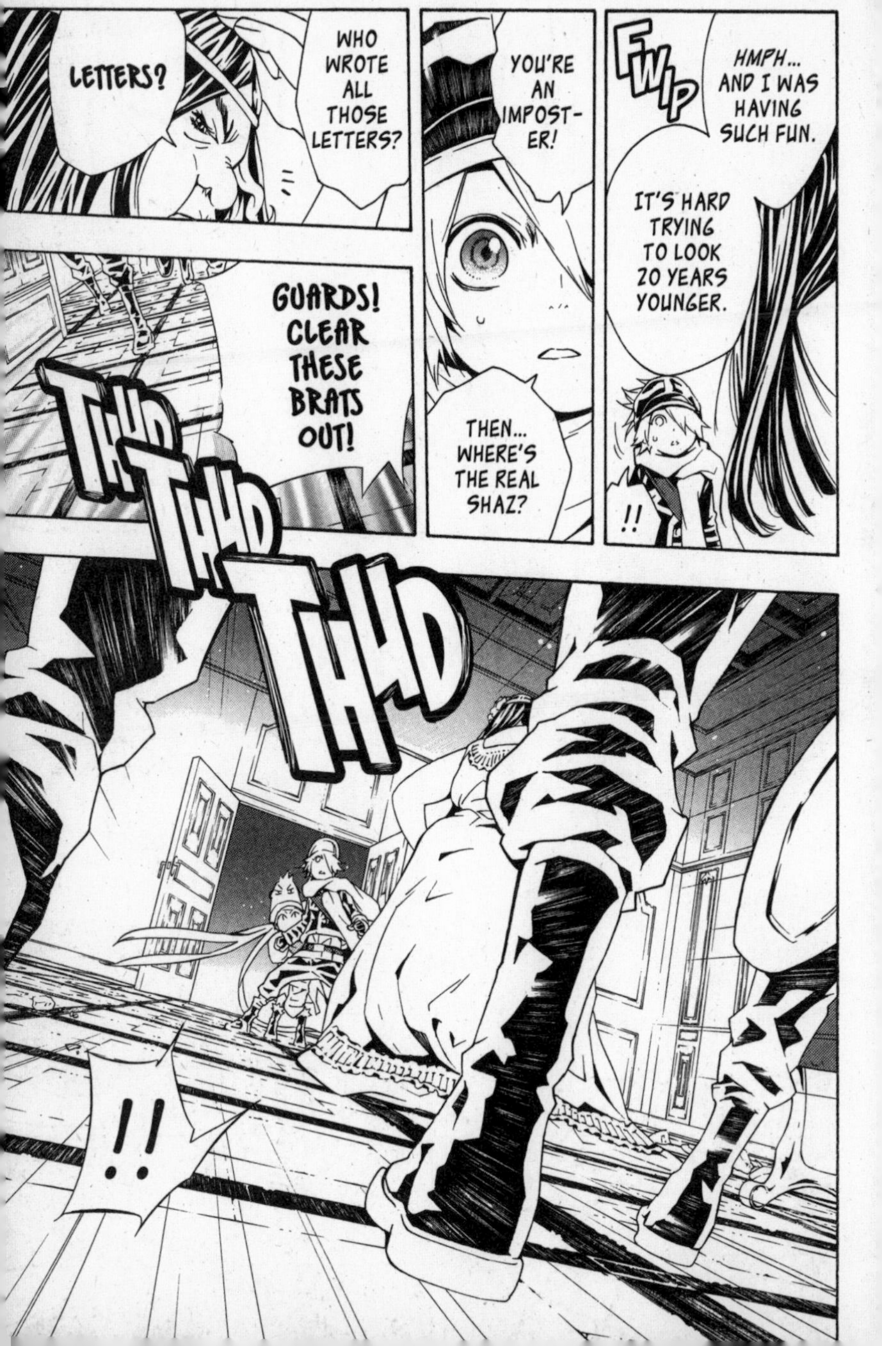
HMPH... AND I WAS HAVING SUCH FUN.
FWIP
IT'S HARD TRYING TO LOOK 20 YEARS YOUNGER.
!!
YOU'RE AN IMPOST-ER!
THEN... WHERE'S THE REAL SHAZ?
WHO WROTE ALL THOSE LETTERS?
LETTERS?
GUARDS! CLEAR THESE BRATS OUT!
THUD THUD THUD
!!

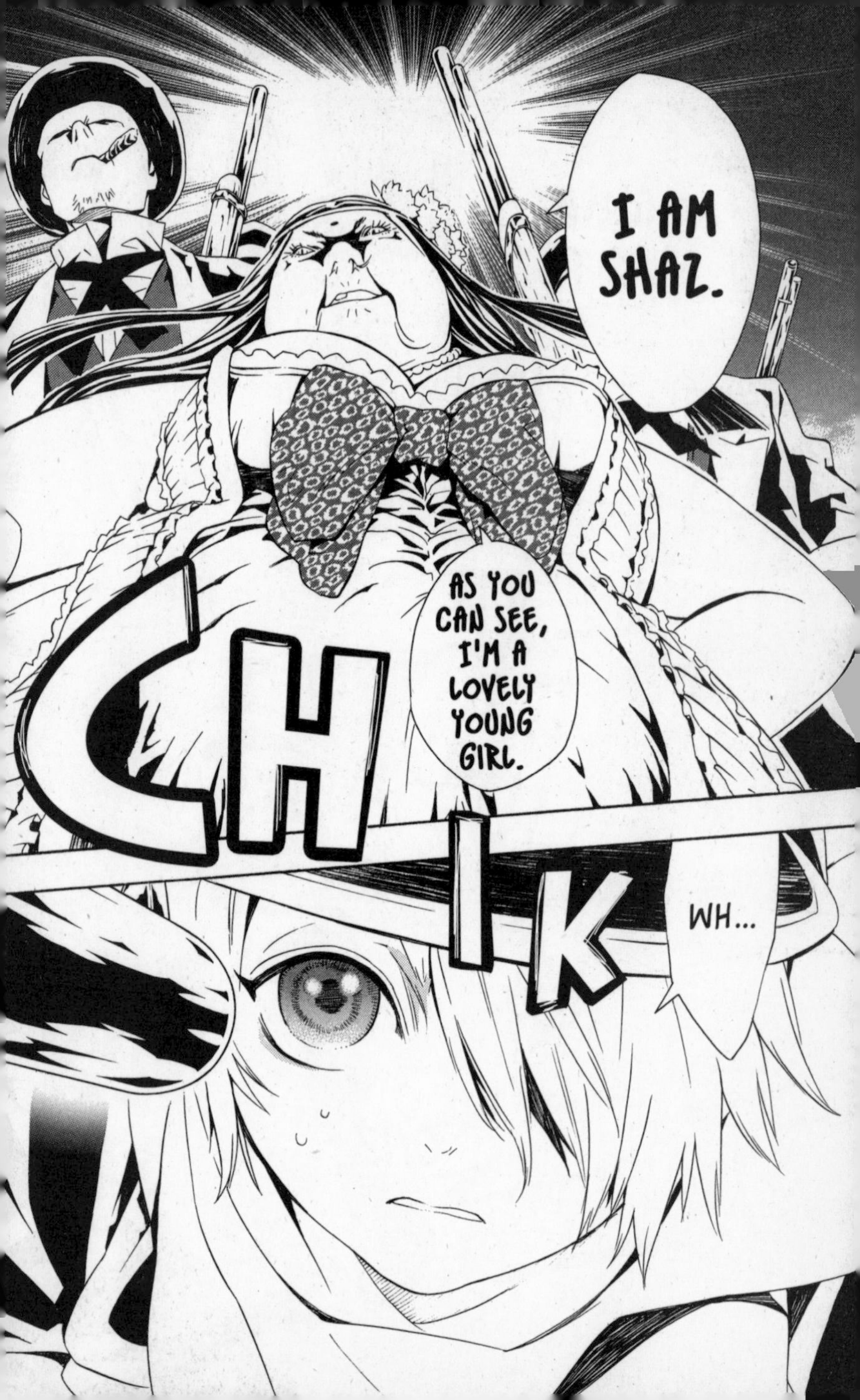
I AM SHAZ.
AS YOU CAN SEE, I'M A LOVELY YOUNG GIRL.
CHIK
WH...

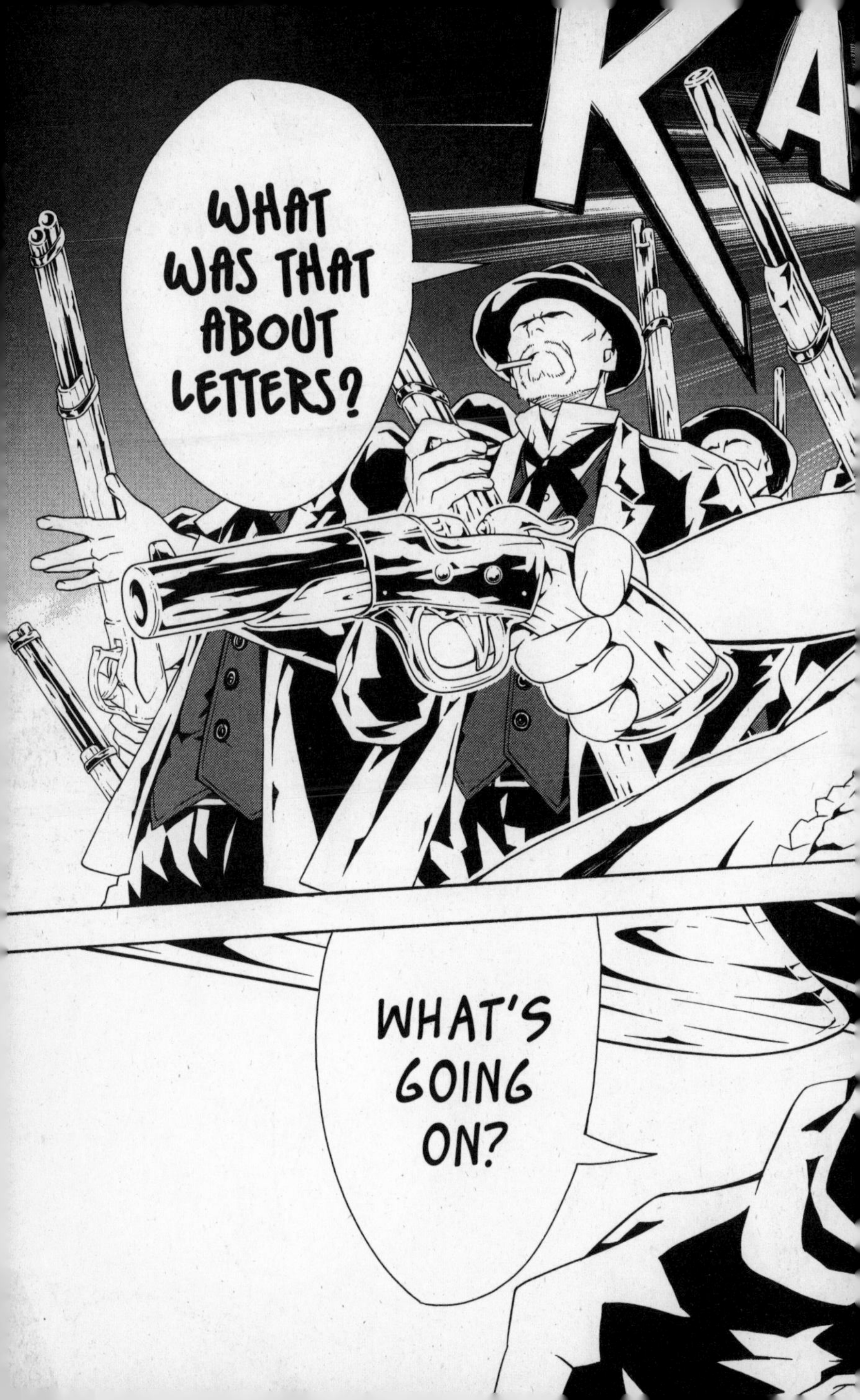
KA
WHAT WAS THAT ABOUT LETTERS?
WHAT'S GOING ON?

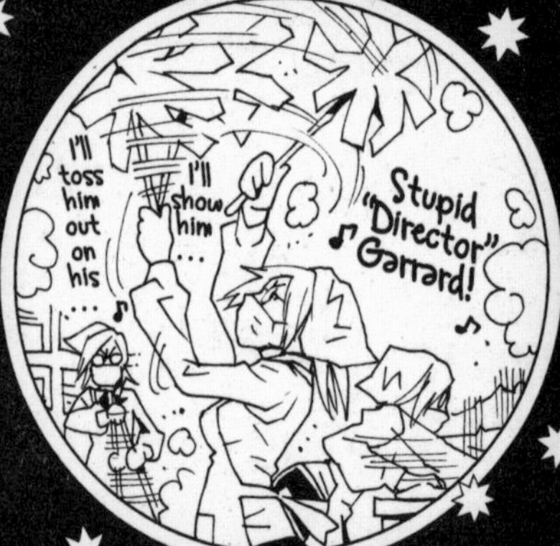
Stupid "Director" Garrard!
I'll show him...
I'll toss him out on his...

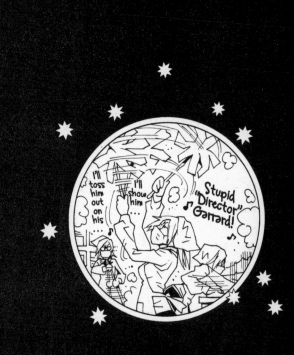

# Chapter 34: Love Like Stone

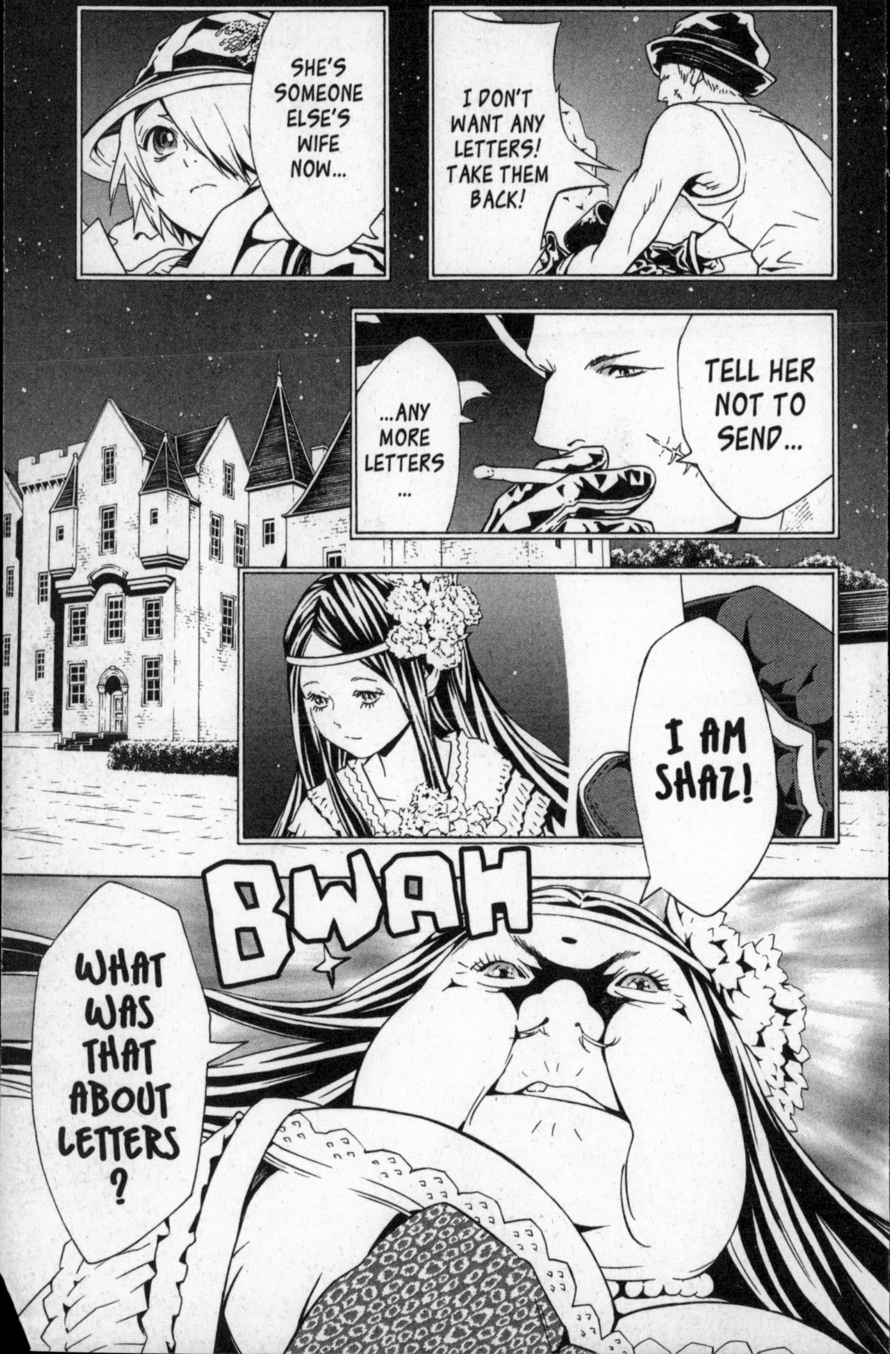
I DON'T WANT ANY LETTERS! TAKE THEM BACK!
SHE'S SOMEONE ELSE'S WIFE NOW...
TELL HER NOT TO SEND...
...ANY MORE LETTERS ...
I AM SHAZ!
BWAH
WHAT WAS THAT ABOUT LETTERS?

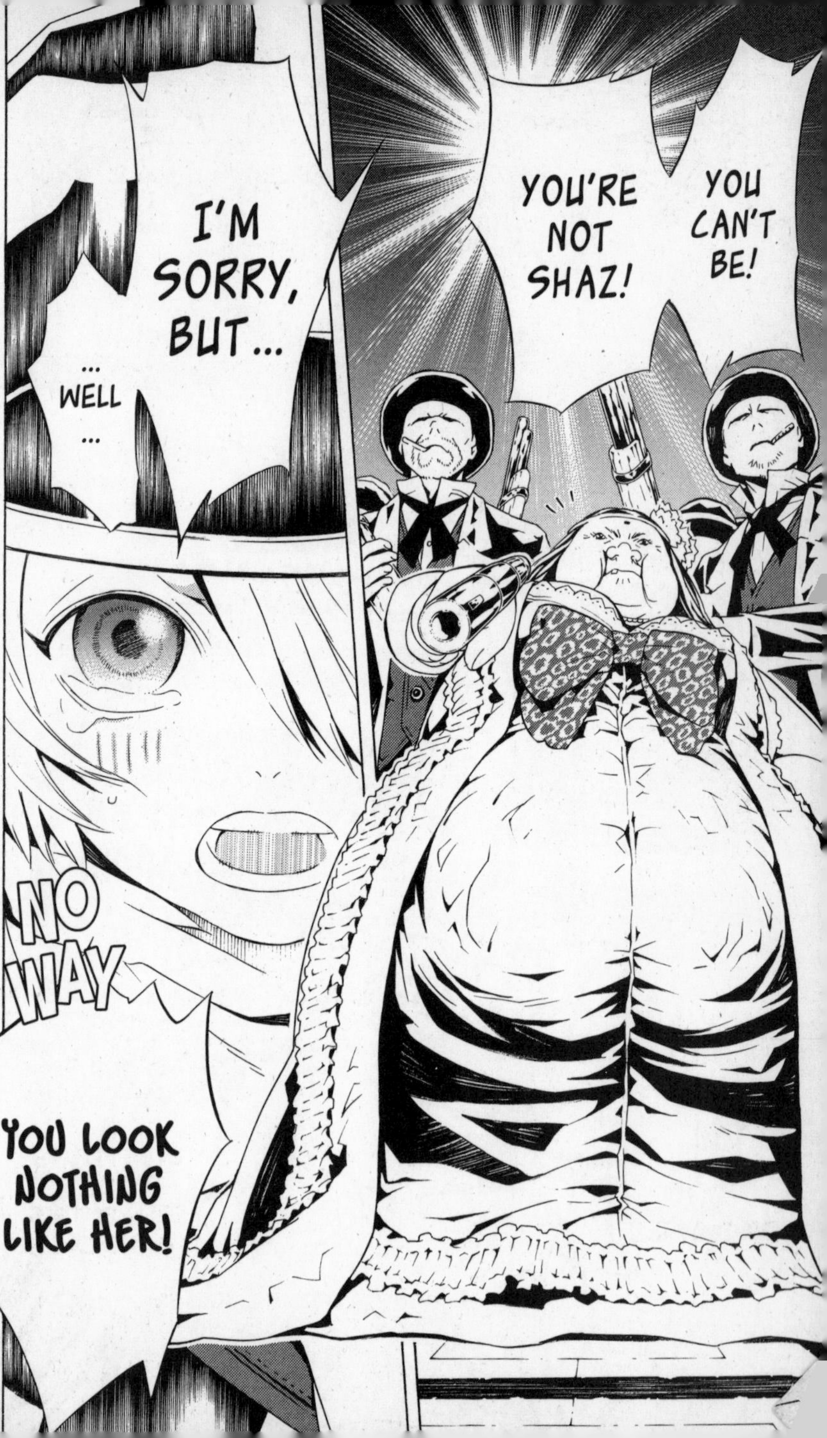
YOU CAN'T BE!
YOU'RE NOT SHAZ!
I'M SORRY, BUT...
... WELL ...
NO WAY
YOU LOOK NOTHING LIKE HER!

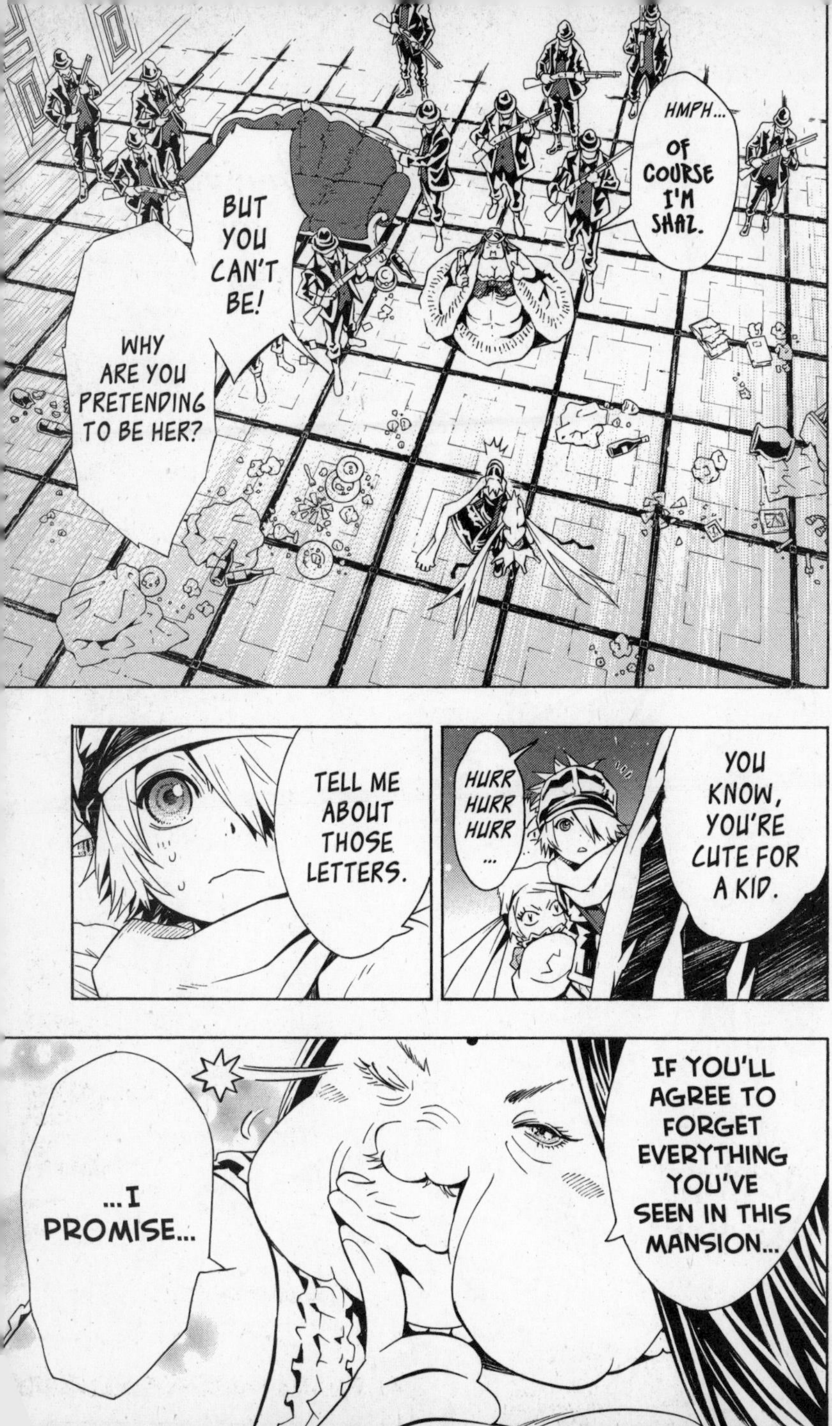
HMPH... OF COURSE I'M SHAZ.
BUT YOU CAN'T BE!
WHY ARE YOU PRETENDING TO BE HER?
YOU KNOW, YOU'RE CUTE FOR A KID.
HURR HURR HURR ...
TELL ME ABOUT THOSE LETTERS.
IF YOU'LL AGREE TO FORGET EVERYTHING YOU'VE SEEN IN THIS MANSION...
...I PROMISE...

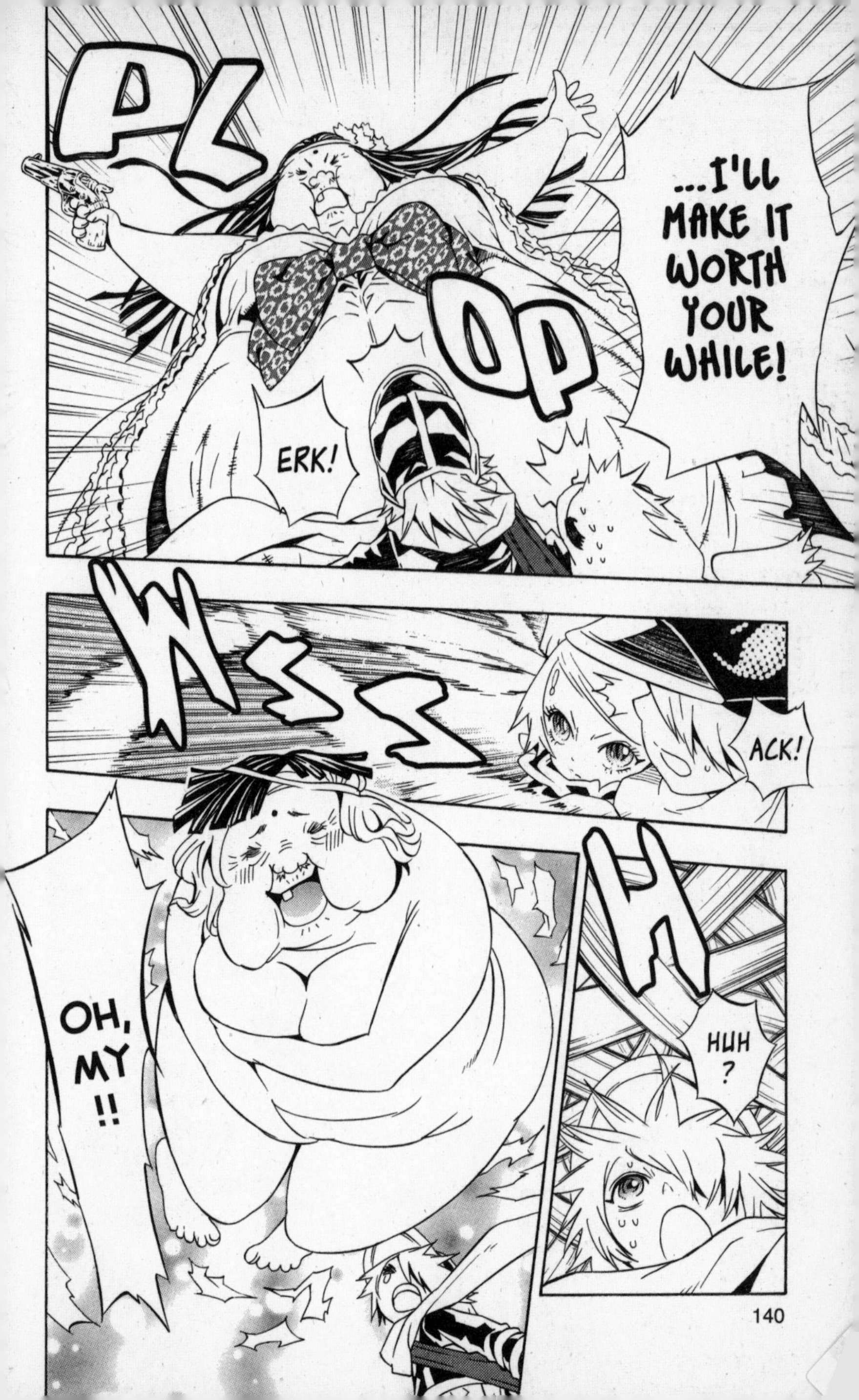
...I'LL MAKE IT WORTH YOUR WHILE!
PLOP
ERK!
ACK!
HUH?
OH, MY!!

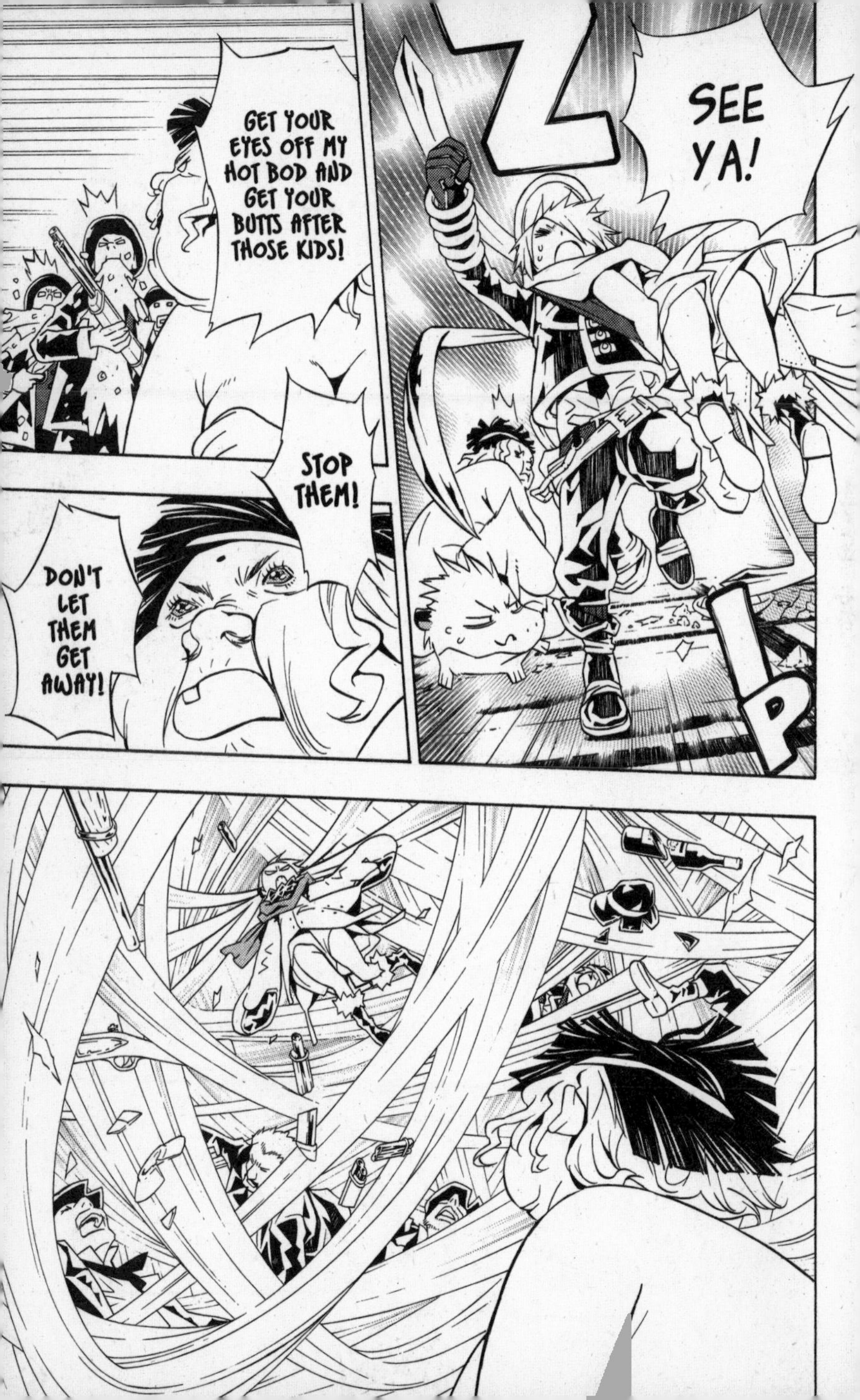

SEE YA!
Z
IP
GET YOUR EYES OFF MY HOT BOD AND GET YOUR BUTTS AFTER THOSE KIDS!
STOP THEM!
DON'T LET THEM GET AWAY!

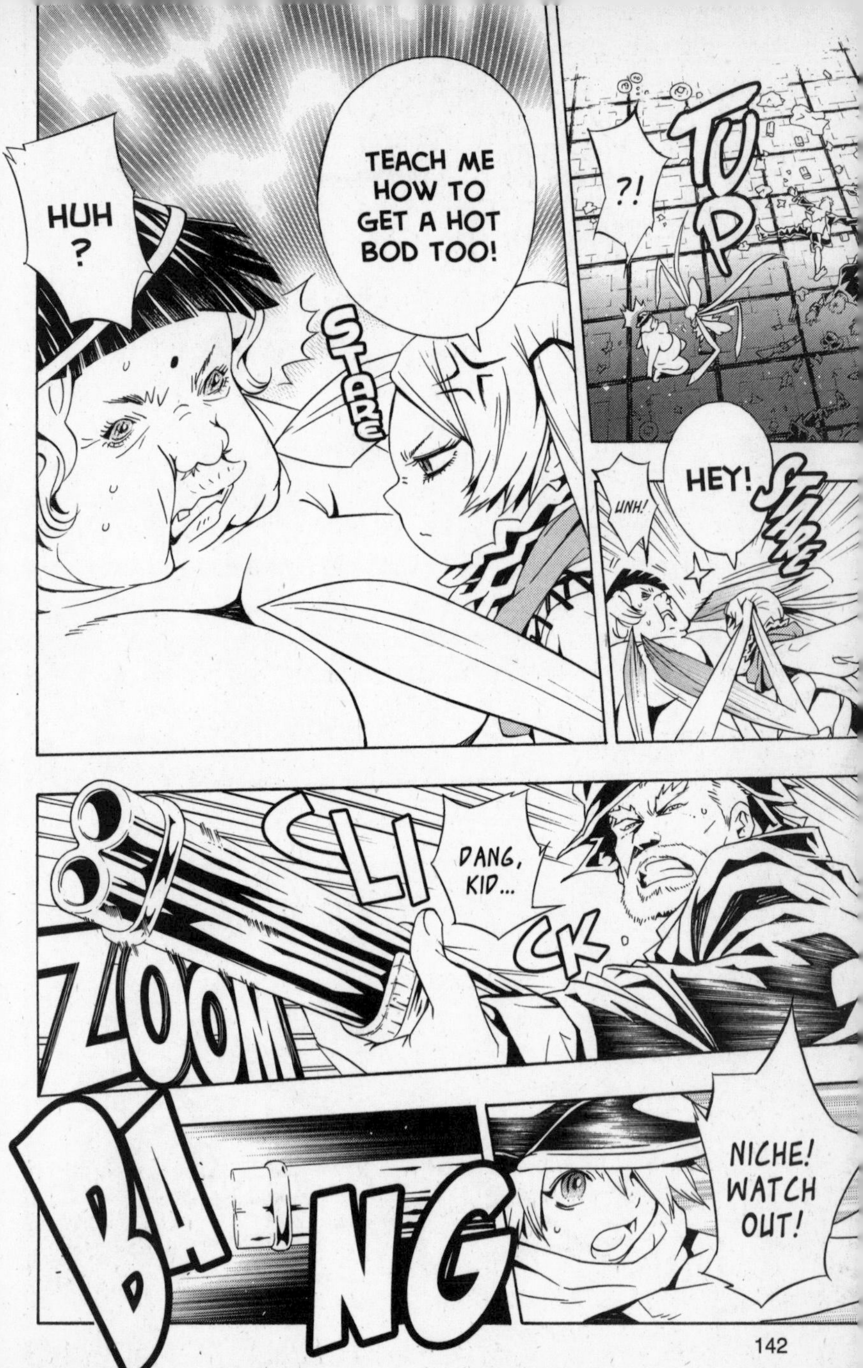
TUP
?!
STARE
HEY!
UNH!
TEACH ME HOW TO GET A HOT BOD TOO!
STARE
HUH ?
DANG, KID...
CLICK
ZOOM
NICHE! WATCH OUT!
BANG

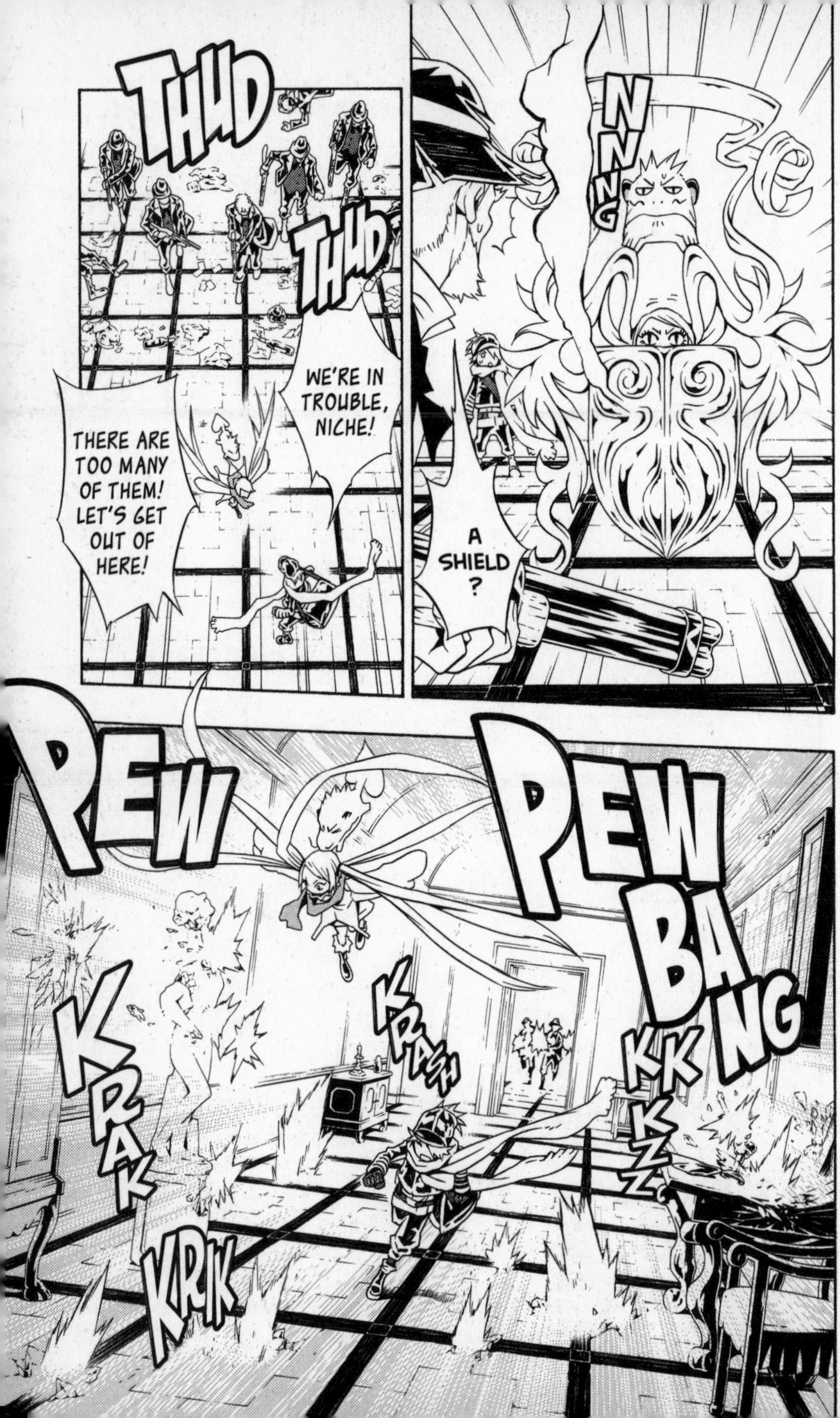
NNNG
A SHIELD?
THUD
THUD
WE'RE IN TROUBLE, NICHE!
THERE ARE TOO MANY OF THEM! LET'S GET OUT OF HERE!
PEW
BANG
KKKZZ
KRASH
PEW
KRAK
KRIK

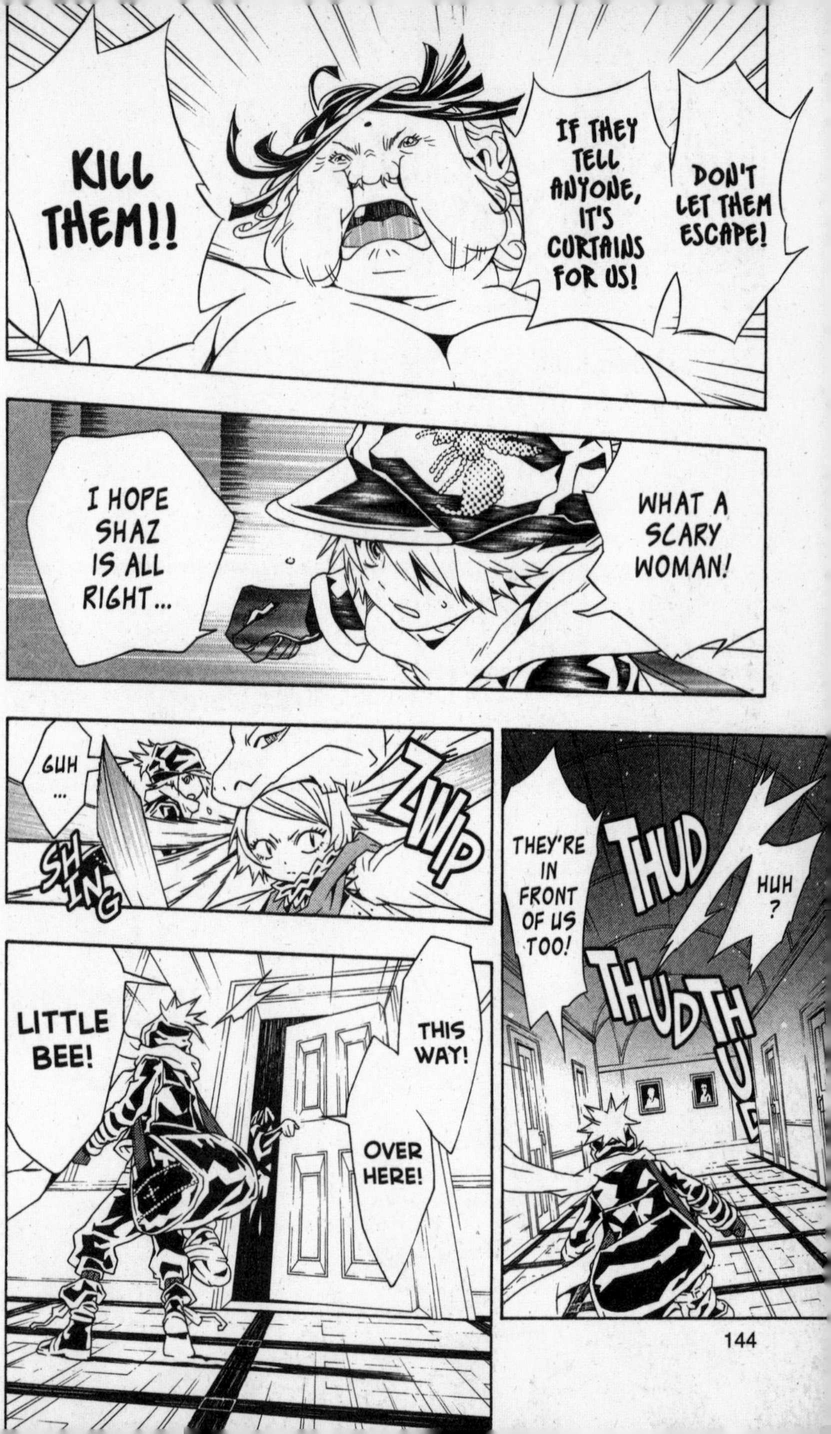
DON'T LET THEM ESCAPE!
IF THEY TELL ANYONE, IT'S CURTAINS FOR US!
KILL THEM!!
WHAT A SCARY WOMAN!
I HOPE SHAZ IS ALL RIGHT...
HUH?
THUD
THEY'RE IN FRONT OF US TOO!
THUD THUD
ZWIP
GUH...
SHING
THIS WAY!
OVER HERE!
LITTLE BEE!

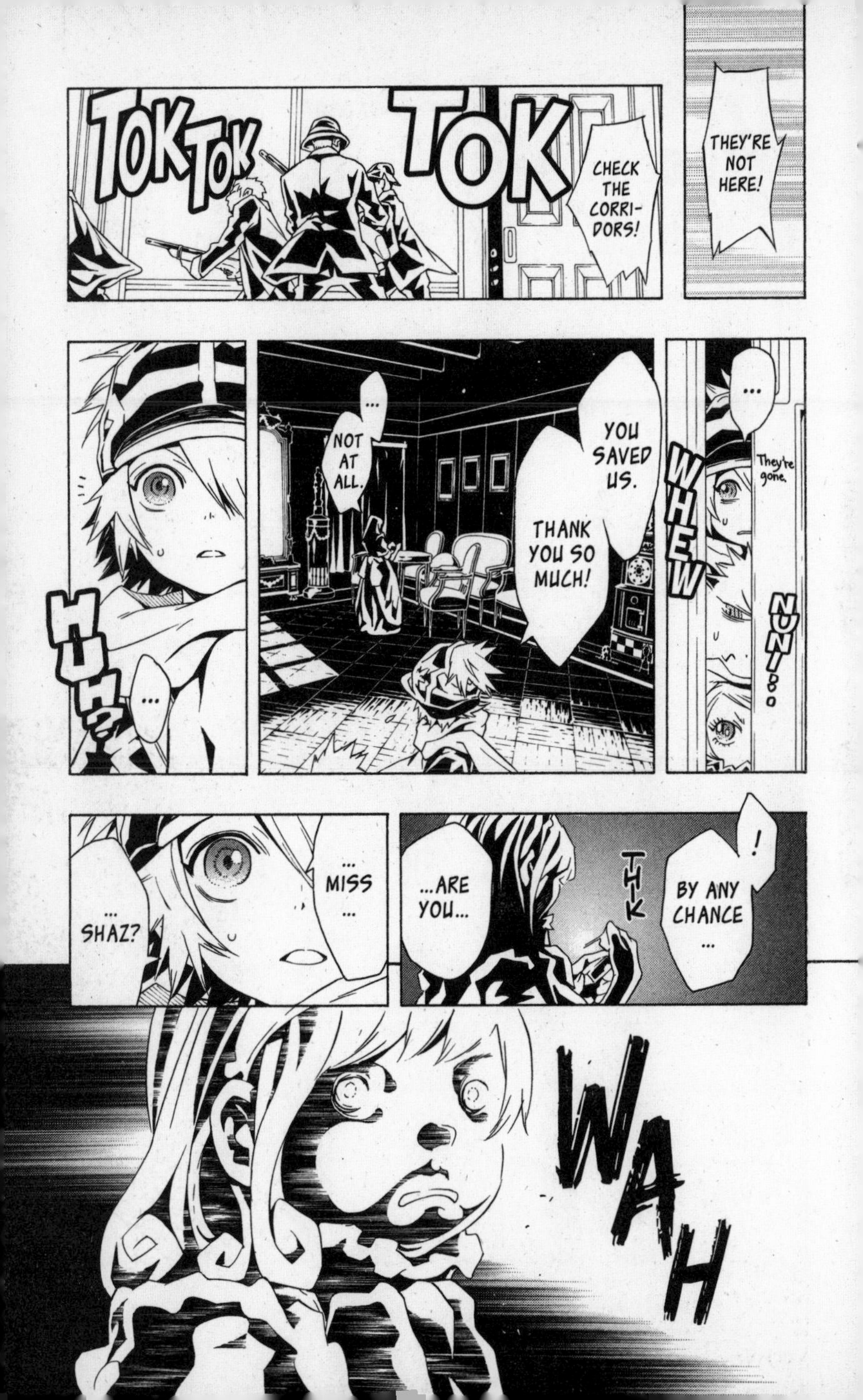
THEY'RE NOT HERE!
CHECK THE CORRI-DORS!
TOK
TOK TOK
...
They're gone.
WHEW
NUNI...
YOU SAVED US.
THANK YOU SO MUCH!
... NOT AT ALL.
HUH?
...
!
BY ANY CHANCE ...
THIK
...ARE YOU...
... MISS ...
... SHAZ?
WAH

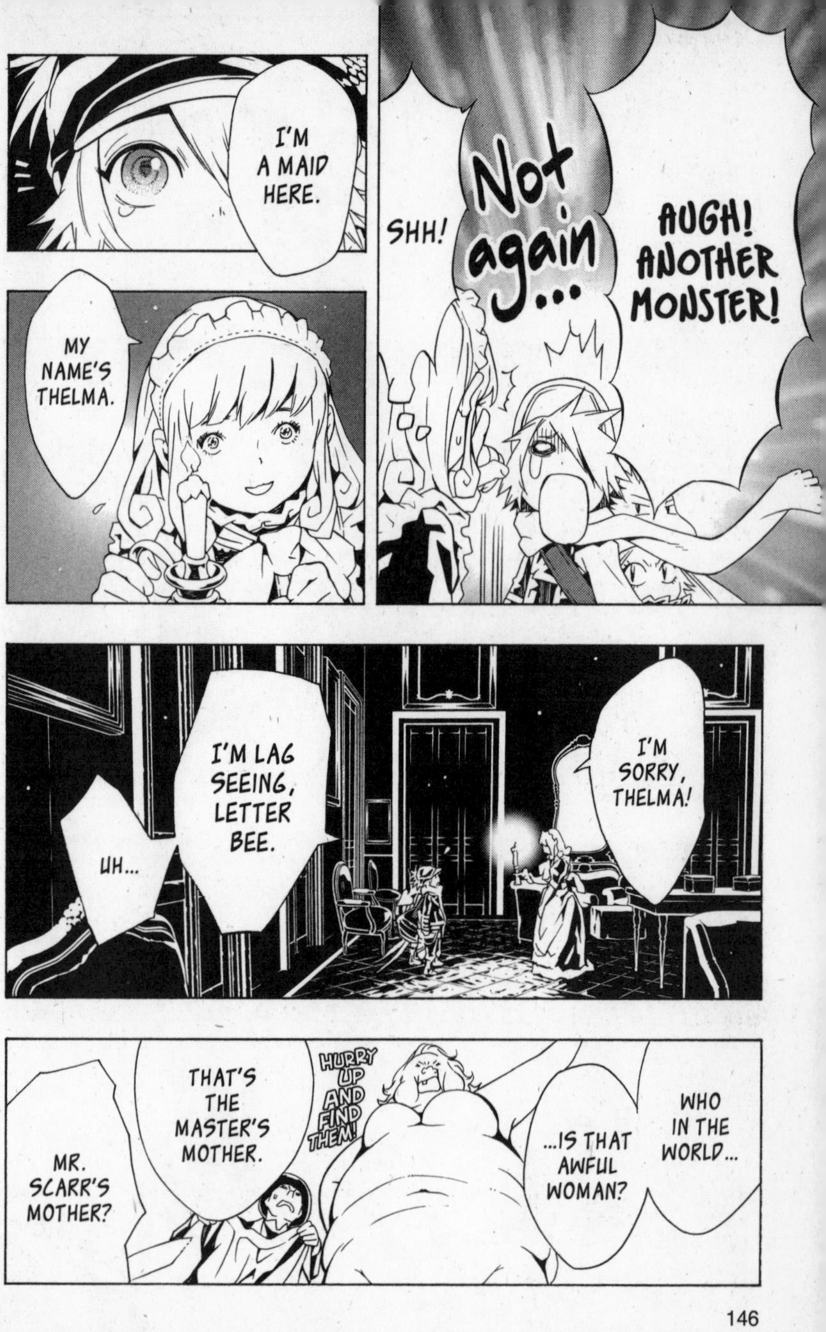
AUGH! ANOTHER MONSTER!
Not again...
SHH!
I'M A MAID HERE.
MY NAME'S THELMA.
I'M SORRY, THELMA!
I'M LAG SEEING, LETTER BEE.
UH...
WHO IN THE WORLD...
...IS THAT AWFUL WOMAN?
HURRY UP AND FIND THEM!
THAT'S THE MASTER'S MOTHER.
MR. SCARR'S MOTHER?

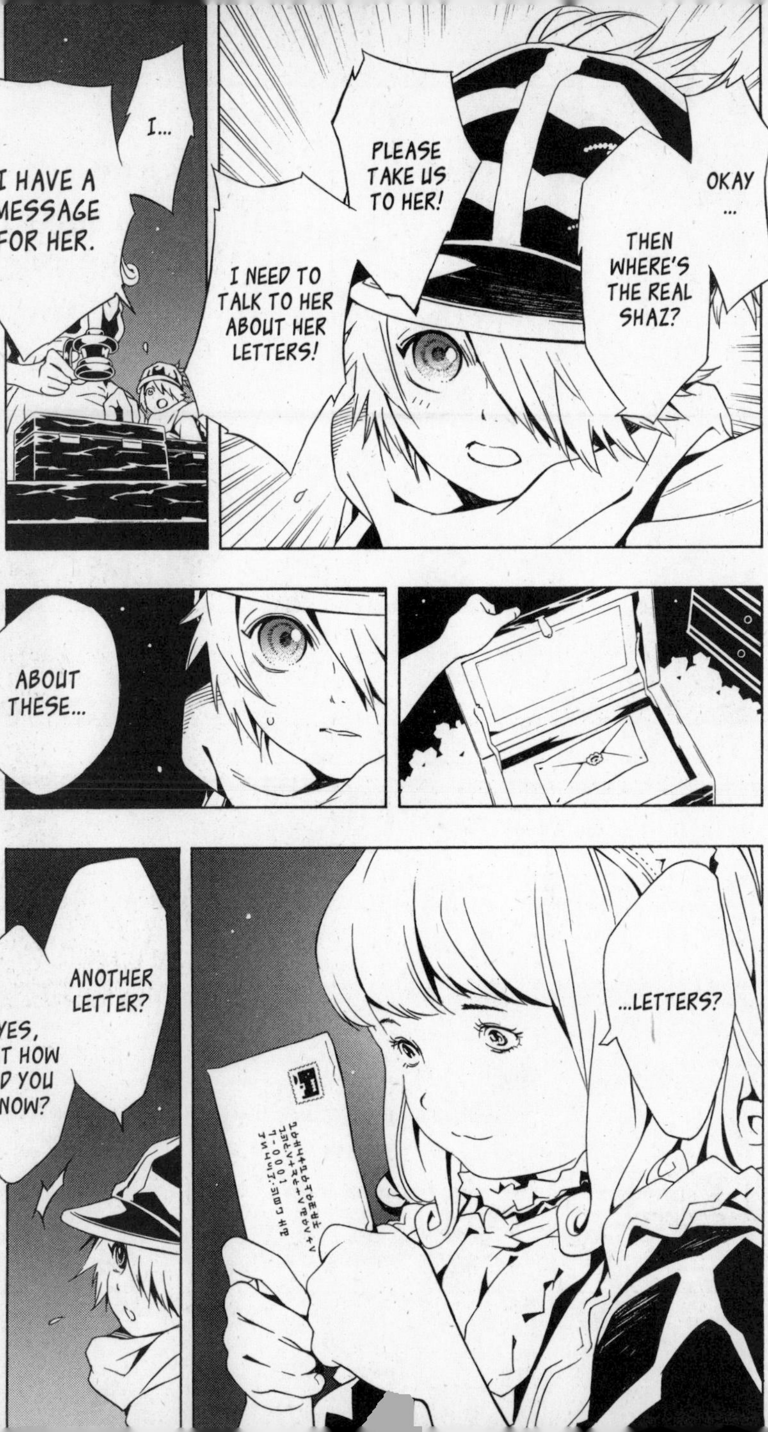
OKAY ...
THEN WHERE'S THE REAL SHAZ?
PLEASE TAKE US TO HER!
I NEED TO TALK TO HER ABOUT HER LETTERS!
I...
I HAVE A MESSAGE FOR HER.
ABOUT THESE...
...LETTERS?
ANOTHER LETTER?
YES, BUT HOW DID YOU KNOW?

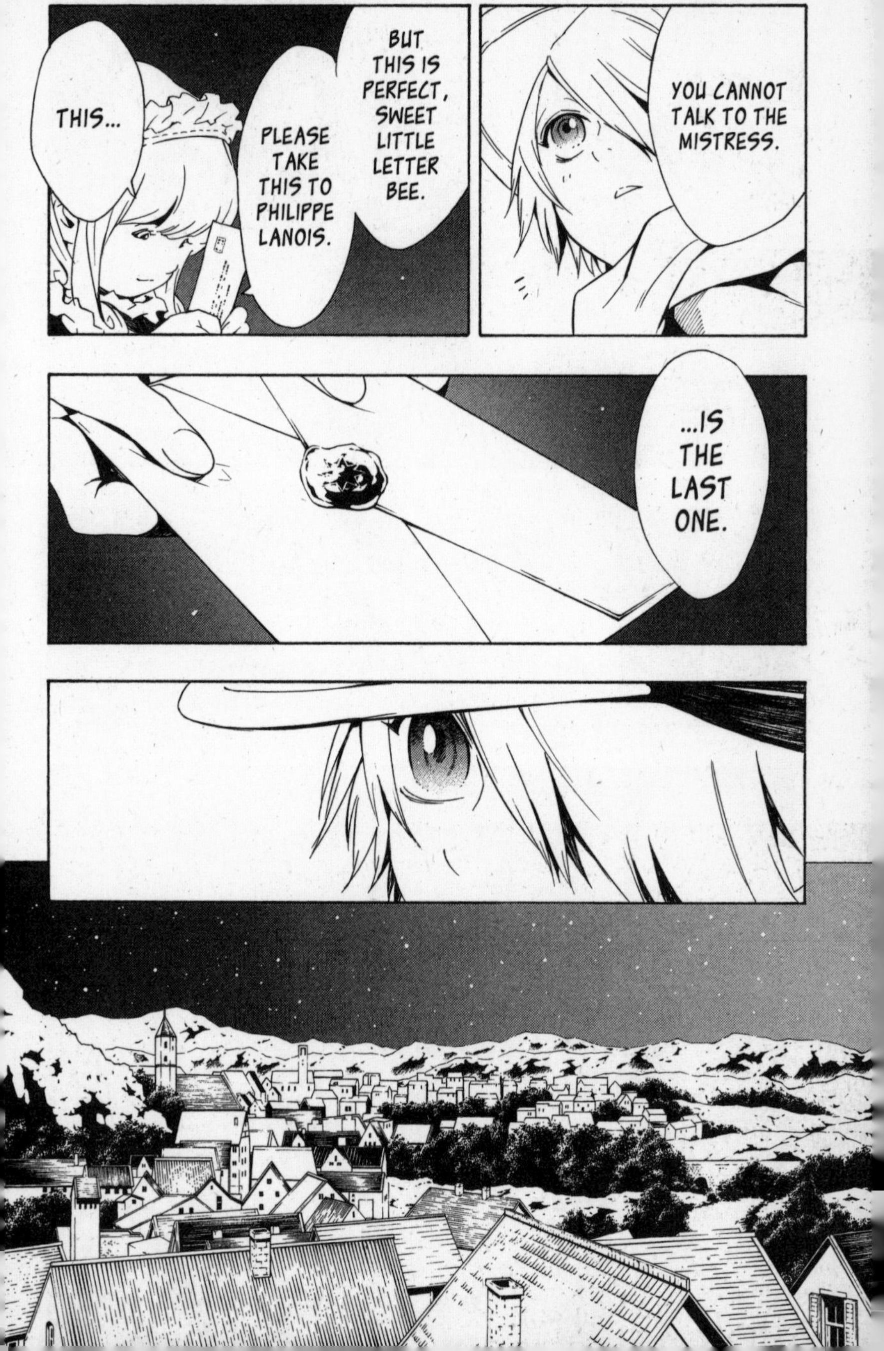
YOU CANNOT TALK TO THE MISTRESS.
BUT THIS IS PERFECT, SWEET LITTLE LETTER BEE.
PLEASE TAKE THIS TO PHILIPPE LANOIS.
THIS...
...IS THE LAST ONE.

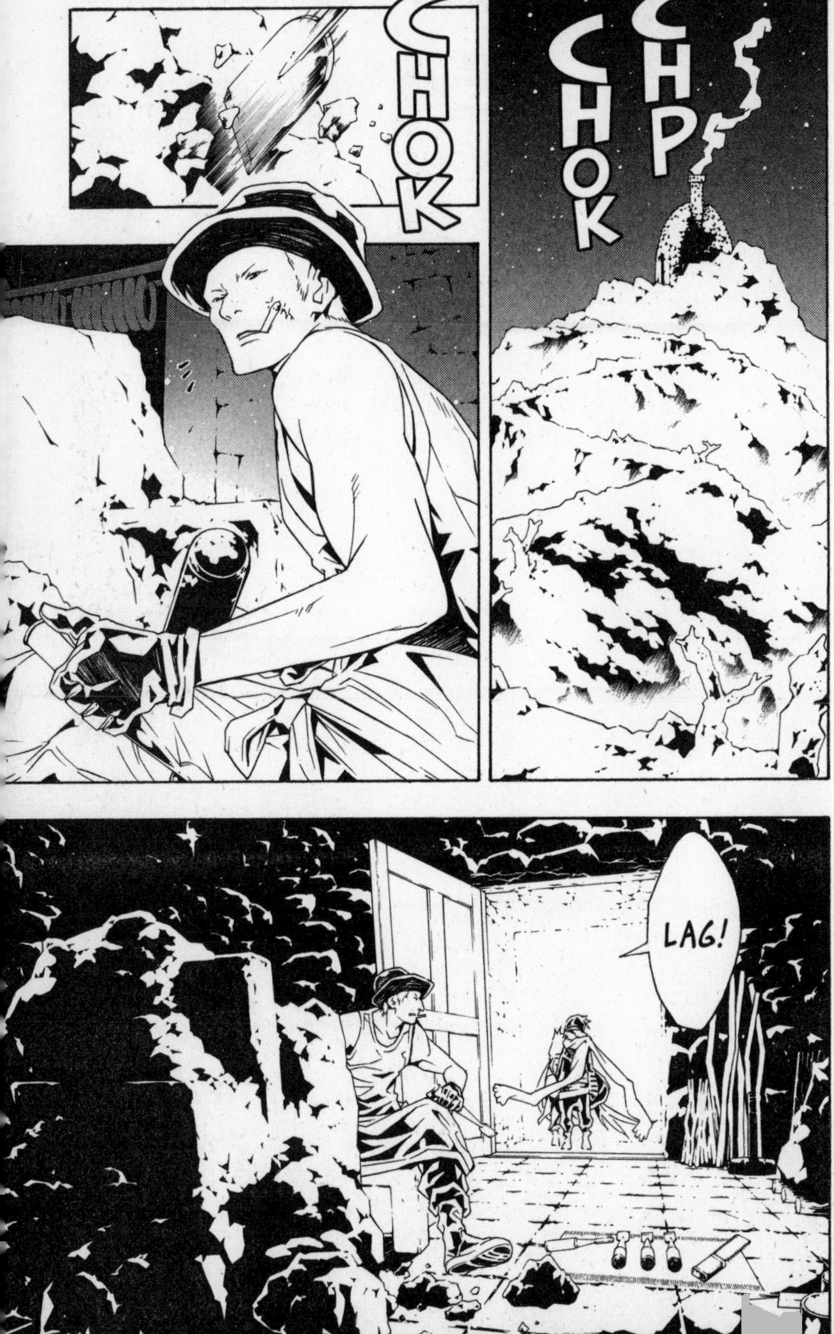
CHP
CHOK
CHOK
LAG!

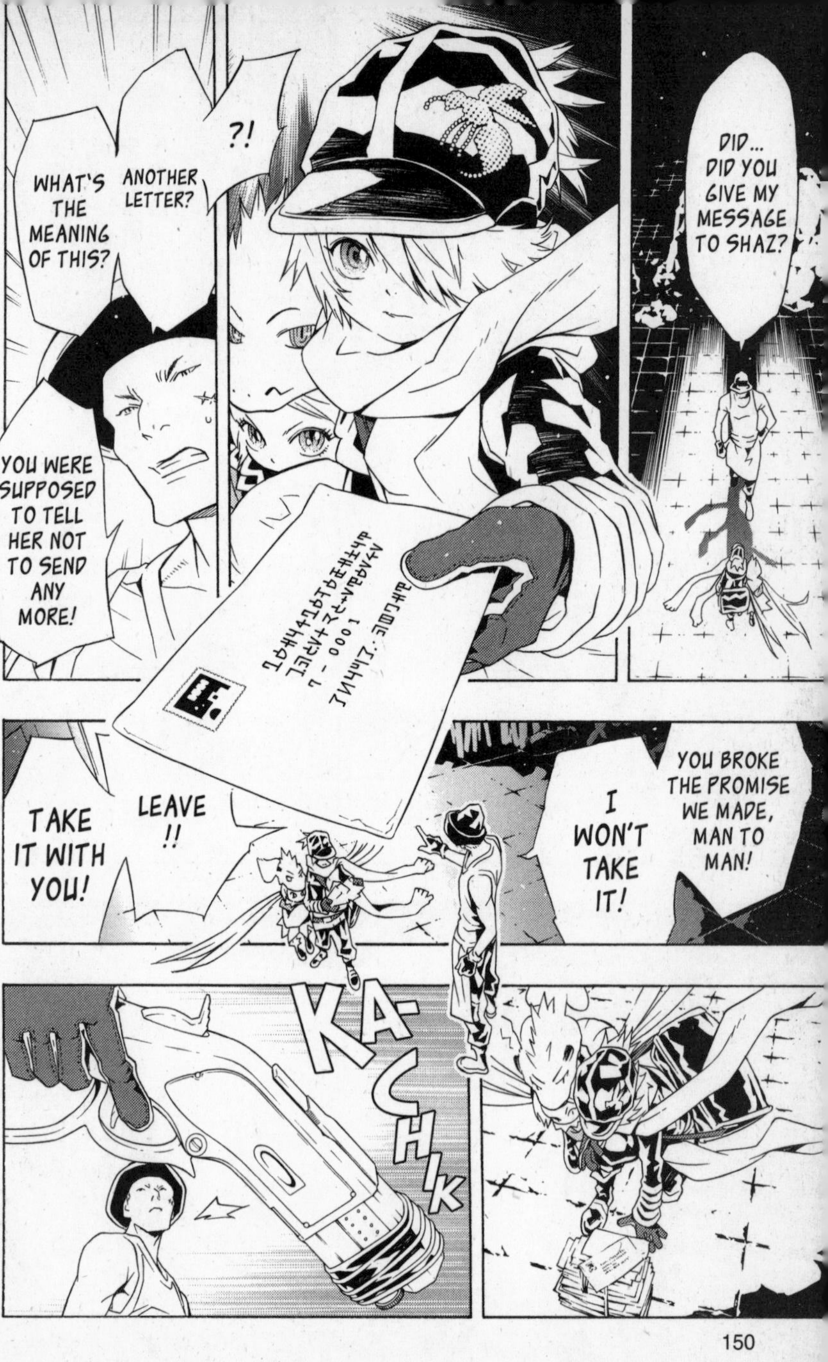
DID... DID YOU GIVE MY MESSAGE TO SHAZ?
?!
ANOTHER LETTER?
WHAT'S THE MEANING OF THIS?
YOU WERE SUPPOSED TO TELL HER NOT TO SEND ANY MORE!
YOU BROKE THE PROMISE WE MADE, MAN TO MAN!
I WON'T TAKE IT!
LEAVE !!
TAKE IT WITH YOU!
KA-CHIK

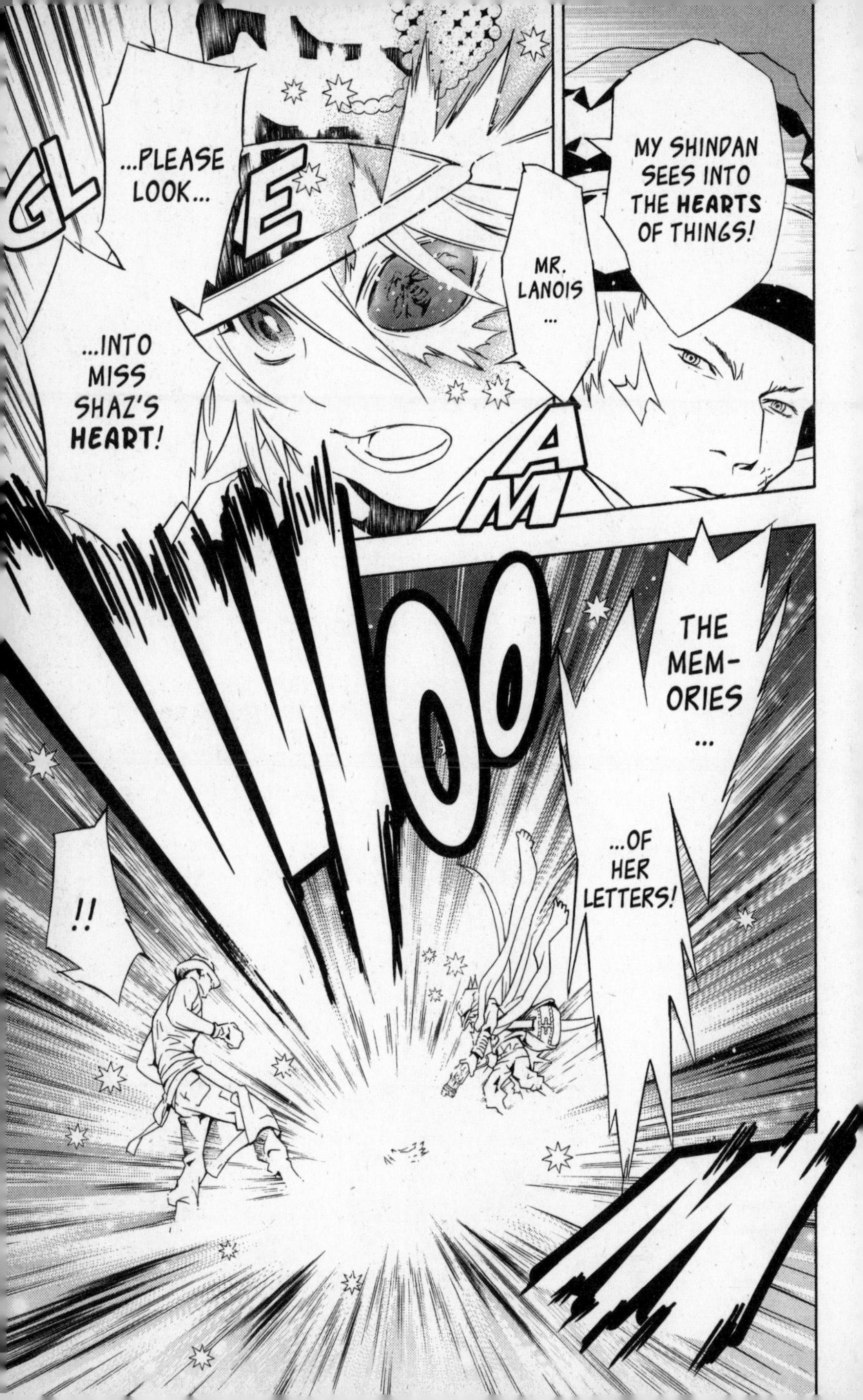
MY SHINDAN SEES INTO THE HEARTS OF THINGS!
MR. LANOIS ...
...PLEASE LOOK...
GLEAM
...INTO MISS SHAZ'S HEART!
THE MEM-ORIES ...
...OF HER LETTERS!
!!
WHOO

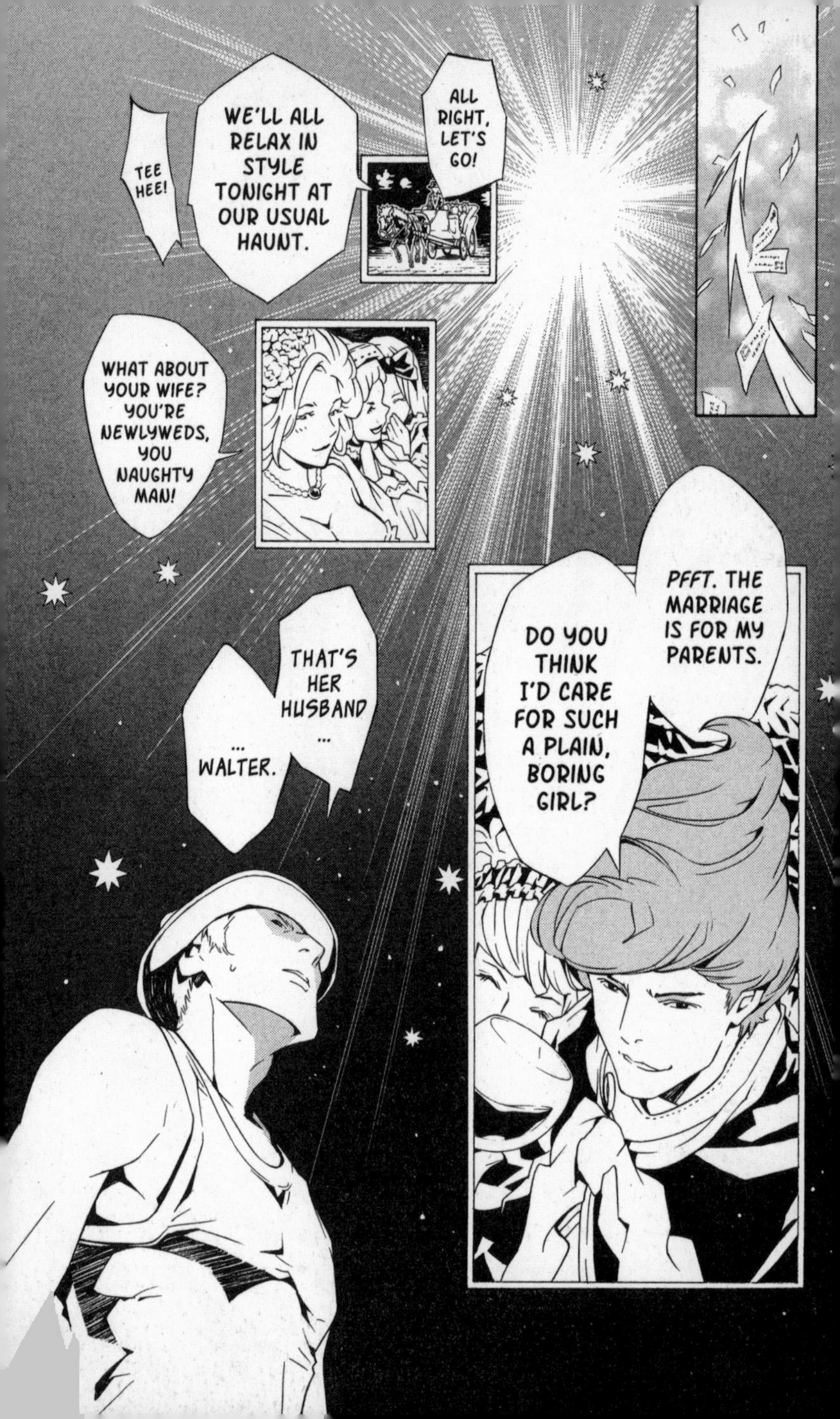
ALL RIGHT, LET'S GO!
WE'LL ALL RELAX IN STYLE TONIGHT AT OUR USUAL HAUNT.
TEE HEE!
WHAT ABOUT YOUR WIFE? YOU'RE NEWLYWEDS, YOU NAUGHTY MAN!
PFFT. THE MARRIAGE IS FOR MY PARENTS.
DO YOU THINK I'D CARE FOR SUCH A PLAIN, BORING GIRL?
THAT'S HER HUSBAND ...
... WALTER.

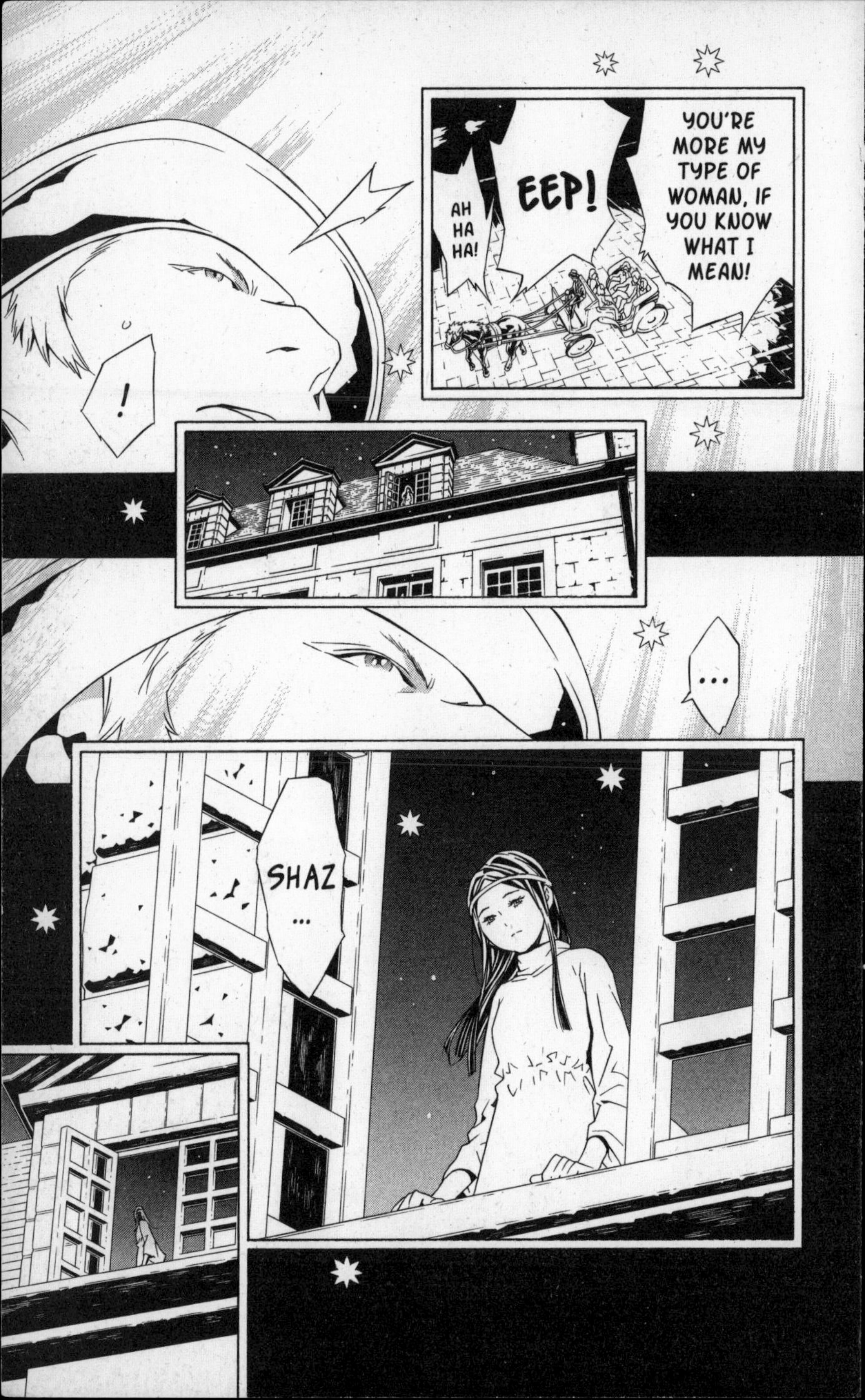
YOU'RE MORE MY TYPE OF WOMAN, IF YOU KNOW WHAT I MEAN!
EEP!
AH HA HA!
!
...
SHAZ ...

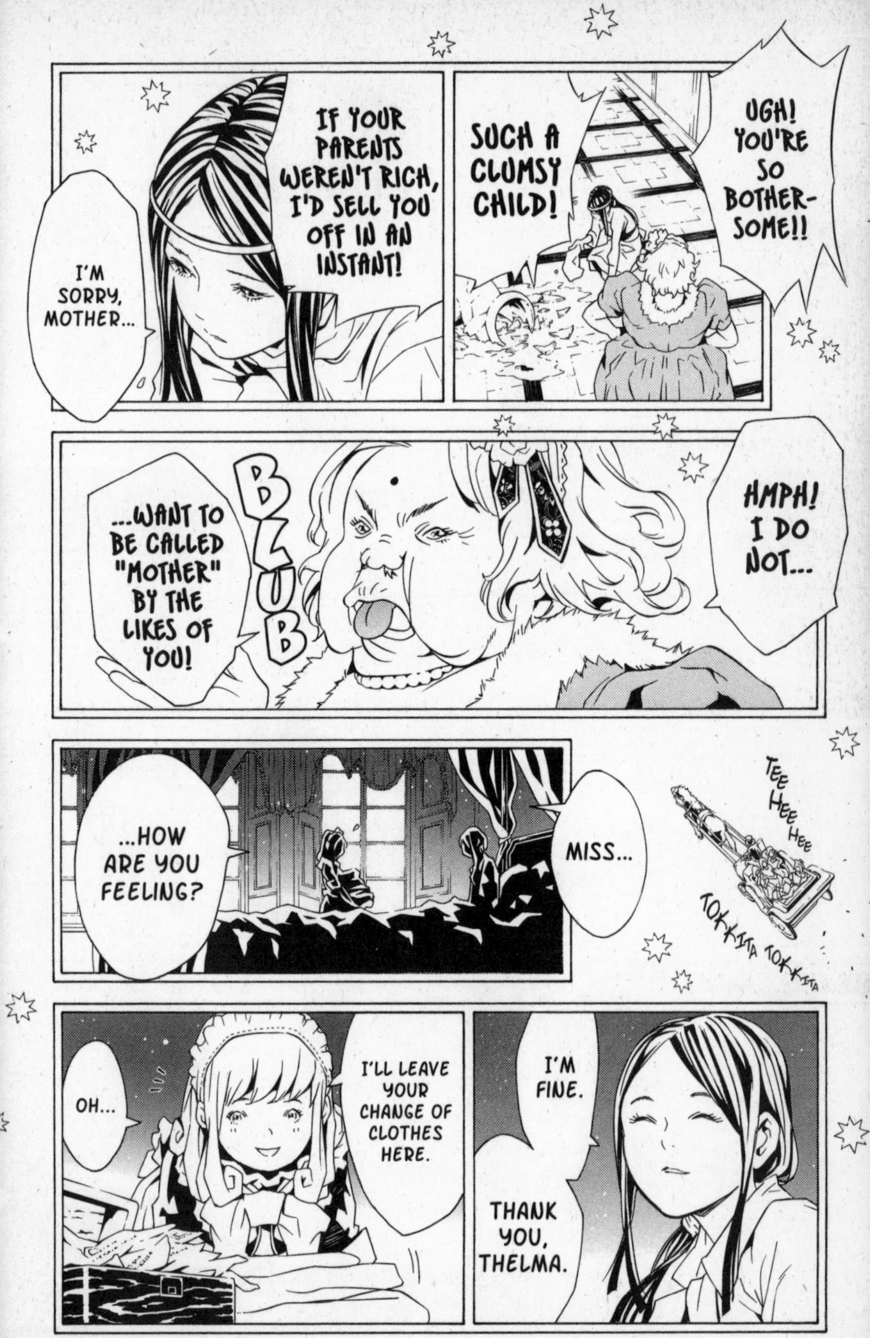
UGH! YOU'RE SO BOTHER-SOME!!
SUCH A CLUMSY CHILD!
IF YOUR PARENTS WEREN'T RICH, I'D SELL YOU OFF IN AN INSTANT!
I'M SORRY, MOTHER...
HMPH! I DO NOT...
BLUB
...WANT TO BE CALLED "MOTHER" BY THE LIKES OF YOU!
TEE HEE HEE
TOK-KITA TOK-KITA
MISS...
...HOW ARE YOU FEELING?
I'M FINE.
THANK YOU, THELMA.
I'LL LEAVE YOUR CHANGE OF CLOTHES HERE.
OH...

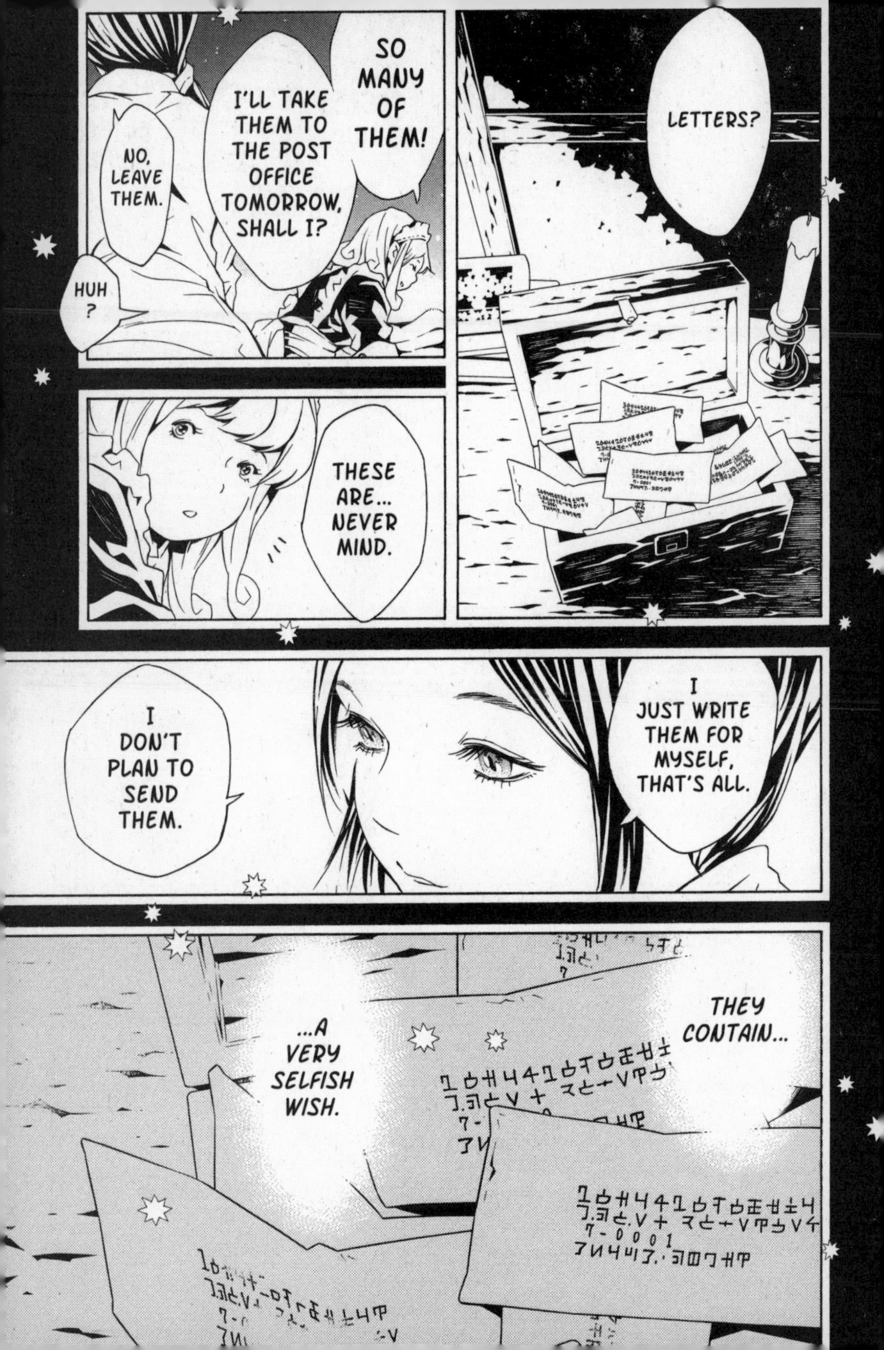
LETTERS?
SO MANY OF THEM!
I'LL TAKE THEM TO THE POST OFFICE TOMORROW, SHALL I?
NO, LEAVE THEM.
HUH?
THESE ARE... NEVER MIND.
I JUST WRITE THEM FOR MYSELF, THAT'S ALL.
I DON'T PLAN TO SEND THEM.
THEY CONTAIN...
...A VERY SELFISH WISH.

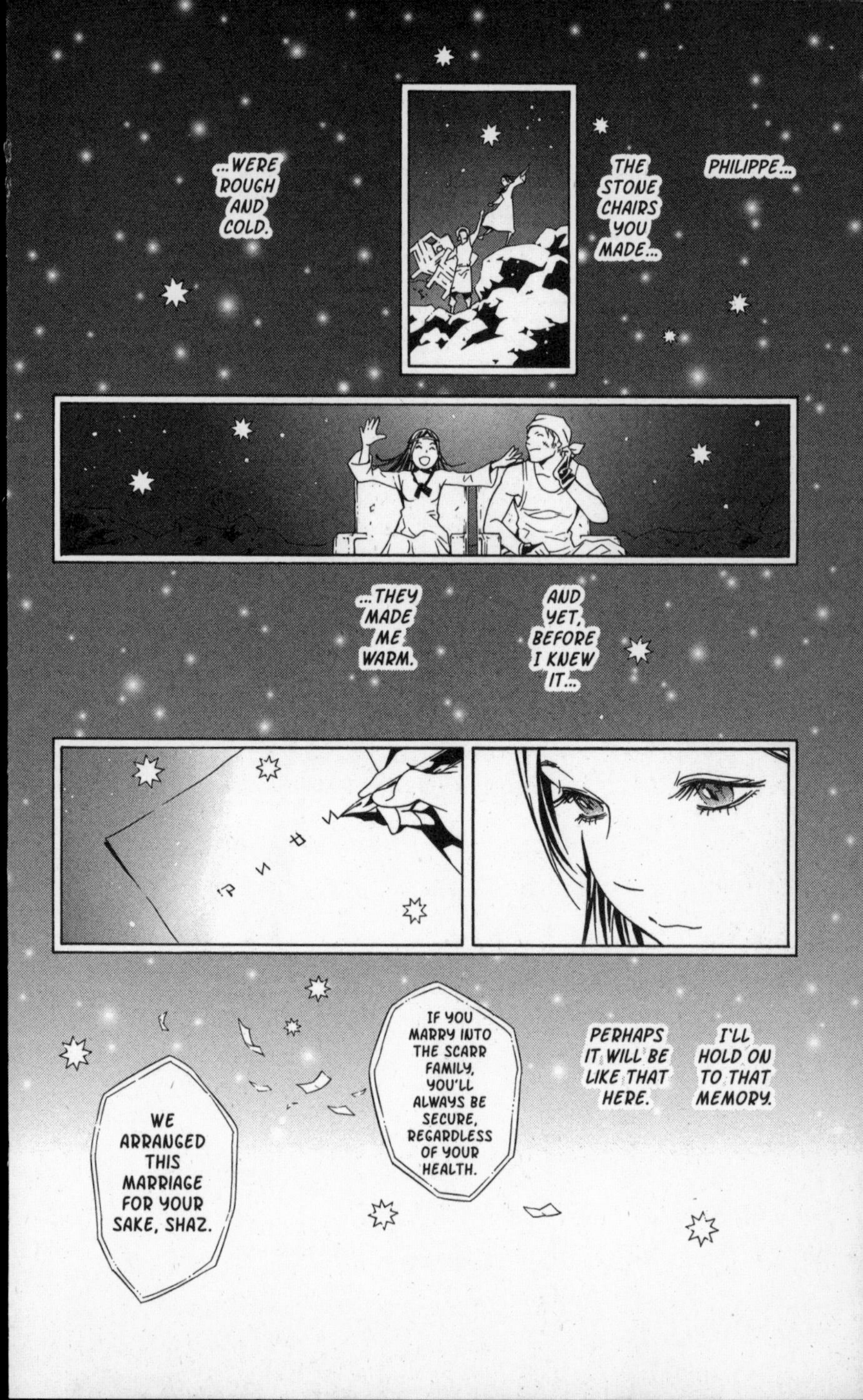
PHILIPPE...
THE STONE CHAIRS YOU MADE...
...WERE ROUGH AND COLD.
AND YET, BEFORE I KNEW IT...
...THEY MADE ME WARM.
I'LL HOLD ON TO THAT MEMORY.
PERHAPS IT WILL BE LIKE THAT HERE.
IF YOU MARRY INTO THE SCARR FAMILY, YOU'LL ALWAYS BE SECURE, REGARDLESS OF YOUR HEALTH.
WE ARRANGED THIS MARRIAGE FOR YOUR SAKE, SHAZ.

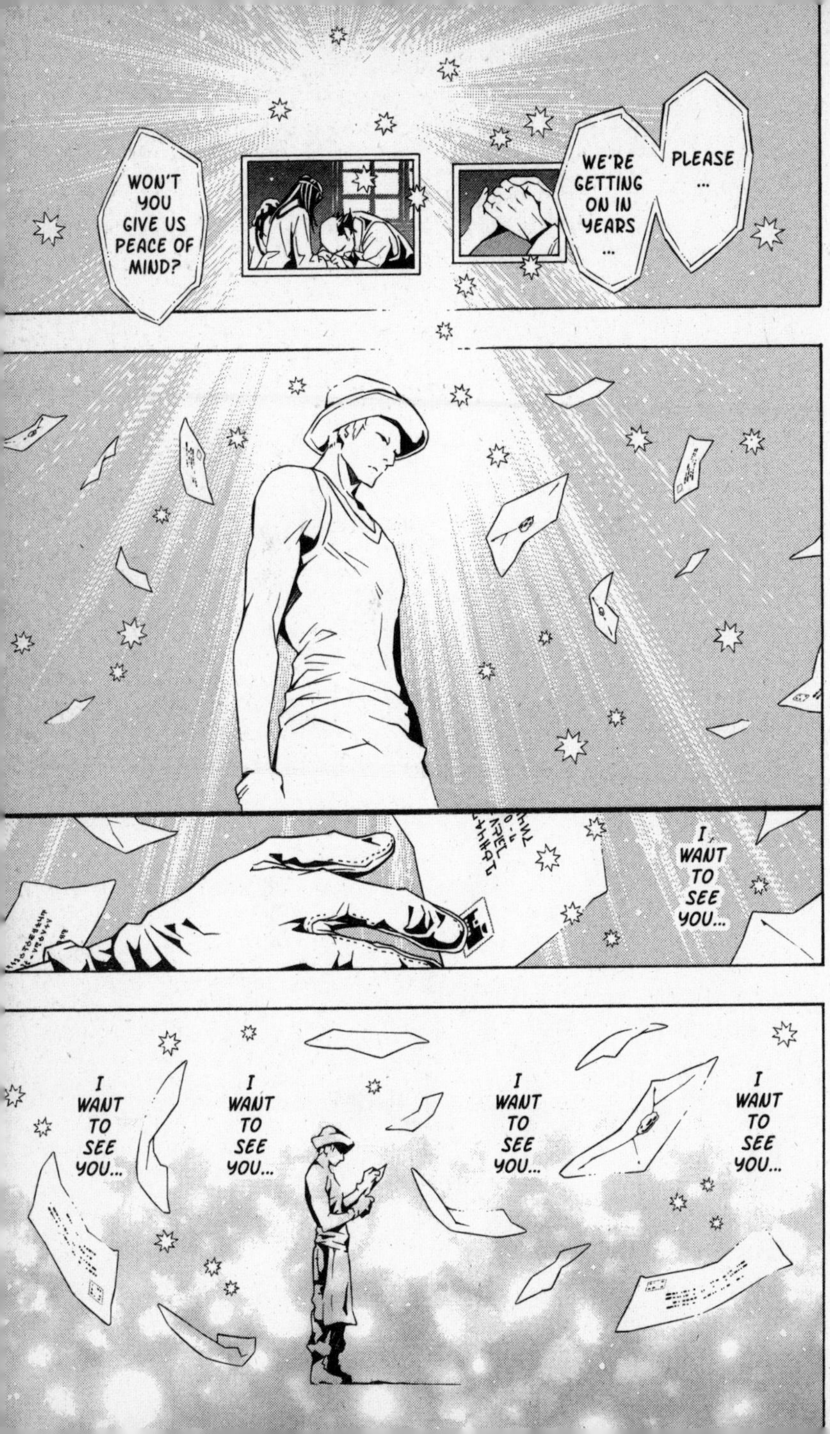
PLEASE ...
WE'RE GETTING ON IN YEARS ...
WON'T YOU GIVE US PEACE OF MIND?
I WANT TO SEE YOU...
I WANT TO SEE YOU...
I WANT TO SEE YOU...
I WANT TO SEE YOU...
I WANT TO SEE YOU...

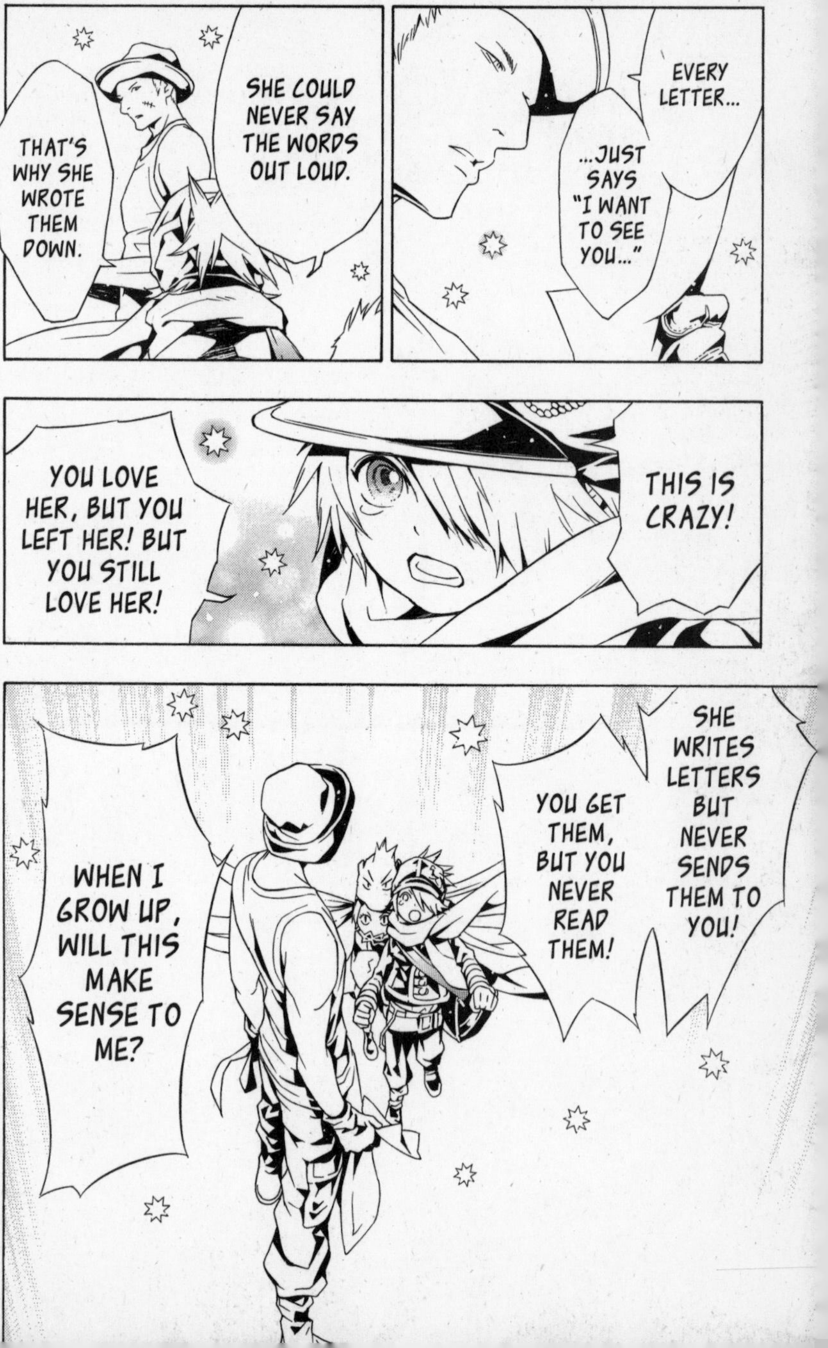
EVERY LETTER...
...JUST SAYS "I WANT TO SEE YOU..."
SHE COULD NEVER SAY THE WORDS OUT LOUD.
THAT'S WHY SHE WROTE THEM DOWN.
THIS IS CRAZY!
YOU LOVE HER, BUT YOU LEFT HER! BUT YOU STILL LOVE HER!
SHE WRITES LETTERS BUT NEVER SENDS THEM TO YOU!
YOU GET THEM, BUT YOU NEVER READ THEM!
WHEN I GROW UP, WILL THIS MAKE SENSE TO ME?

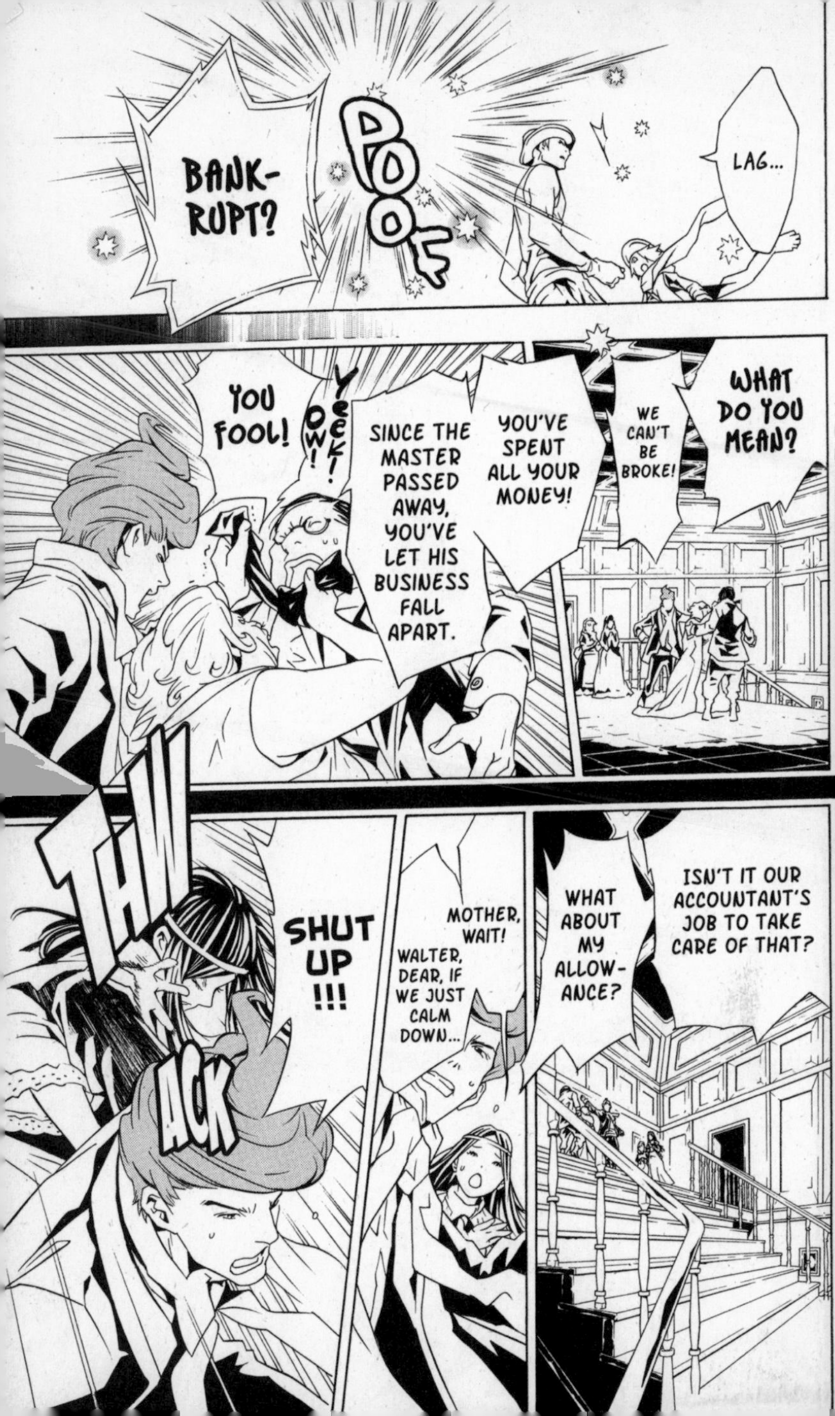
LAG...
POOF
BANKRUPT?
WHAT DO YOU MEAN?
WE CAN'T BE BROKE!
YOU'VE SPENT ALL YOUR MONEY!
SINCE THE MASTER PASSED AWAY, YOU'VE LET HIS BUSINESS FALL APART.
YEEK!
OW!
YOU FOOL!
ISN'T IT OUR ACCOUNTANT'S JOB TO TAKE CARE OF THAT?
WHAT ABOUT MY ALLOWANCE?
MOTHER, WAIT!
WALTER, DEAR, IF WE JUST CALM DOWN...
SHUT UP!!!
THWACK

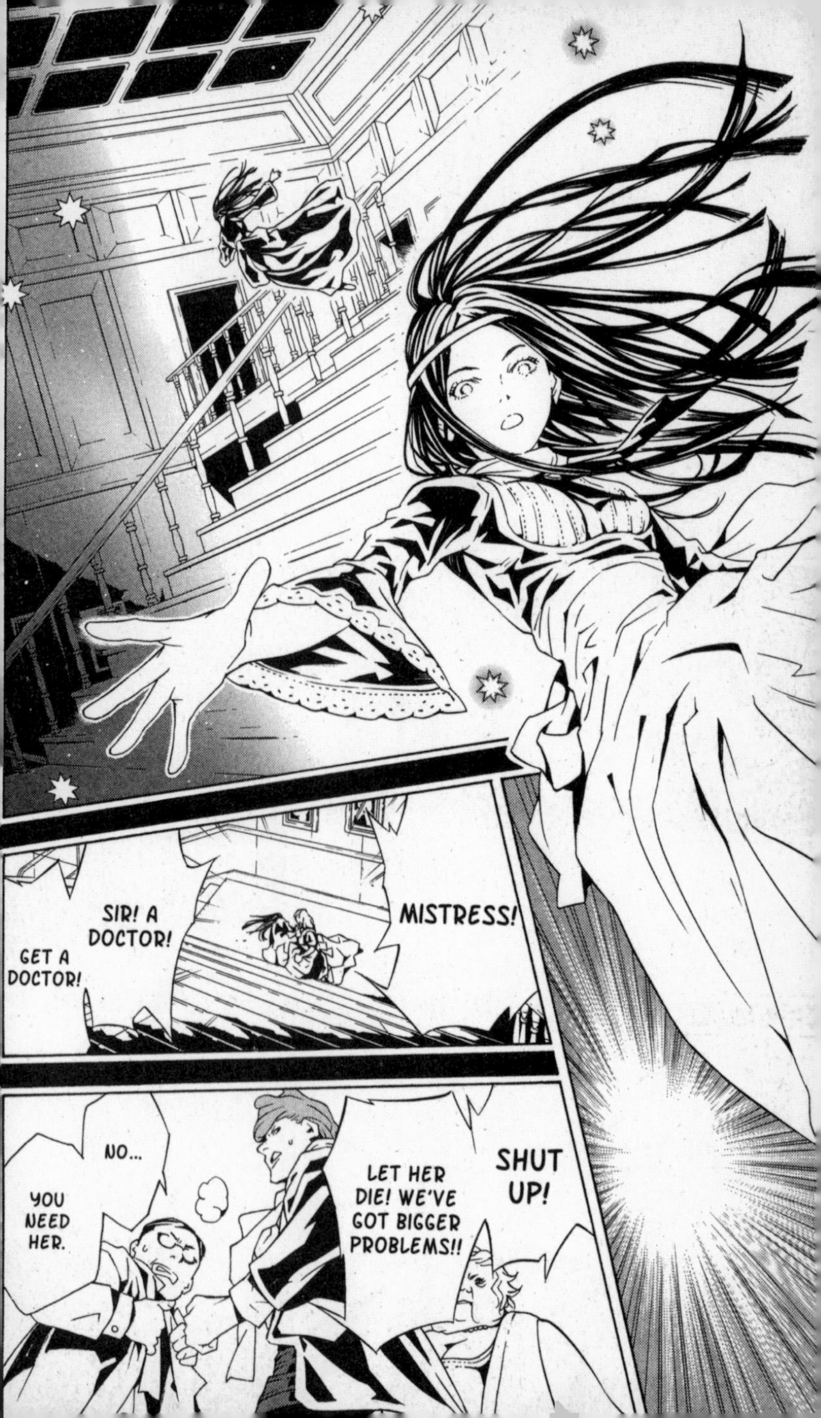
MISTRESS!
SIR! A DOCTOR!
GET A DOCTOR!
SHUT UP!
LET HER DIE! WE'VE GOT BIGGER PROBLEMS!!
NO...
YOU NEED HER.

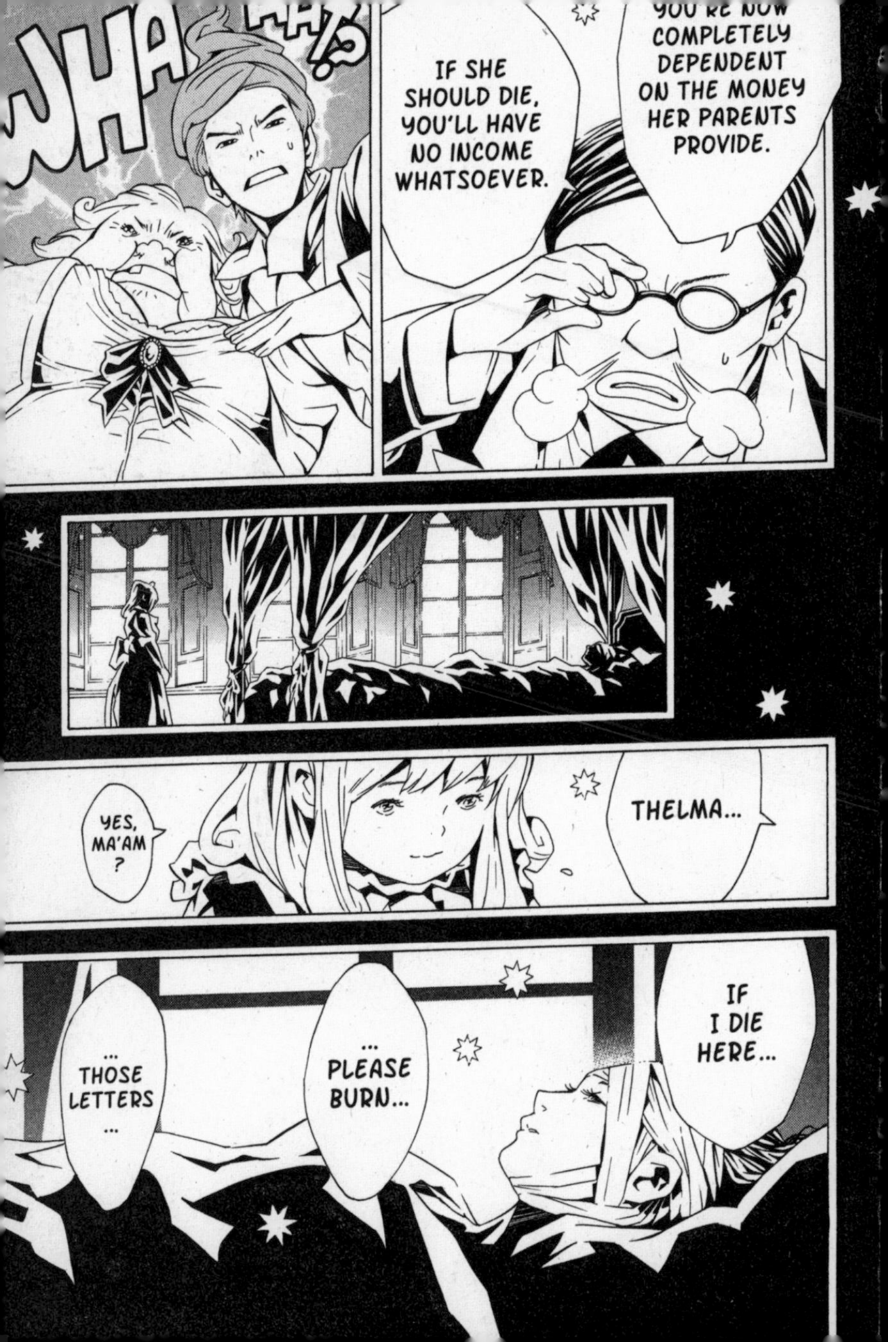
YOU'RE NOW COMPLETELY DEPENDENT ON THE MONEY HER PARENTS PROVIDE.
IF SHE SHOULD DIE, YOU'LL HAVE NO INCOME WHATSOEVER.
WHAT!?
THELMA...
YES, MA'AM?
IF I DIE HERE...
... PLEASE BURN...
... THOSE LETTERS ...

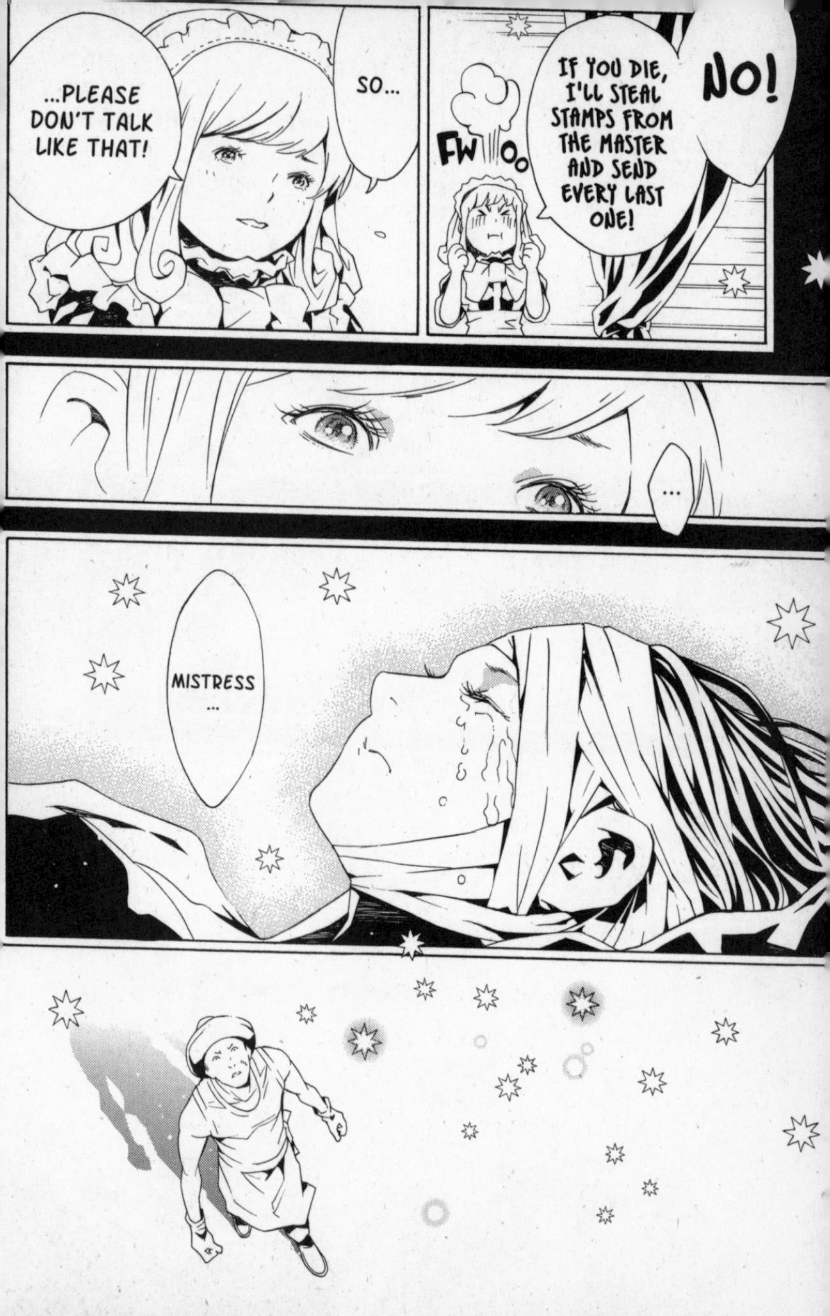
NO!
IF YOU DIE, I'LL STEAL STAMPS FROM THE MASTER AND SEND EVERY LAST ONE!
FWOO
SO...
...PLEASE DON'T TALK LIKE THAT!
...
MISTRESS ...

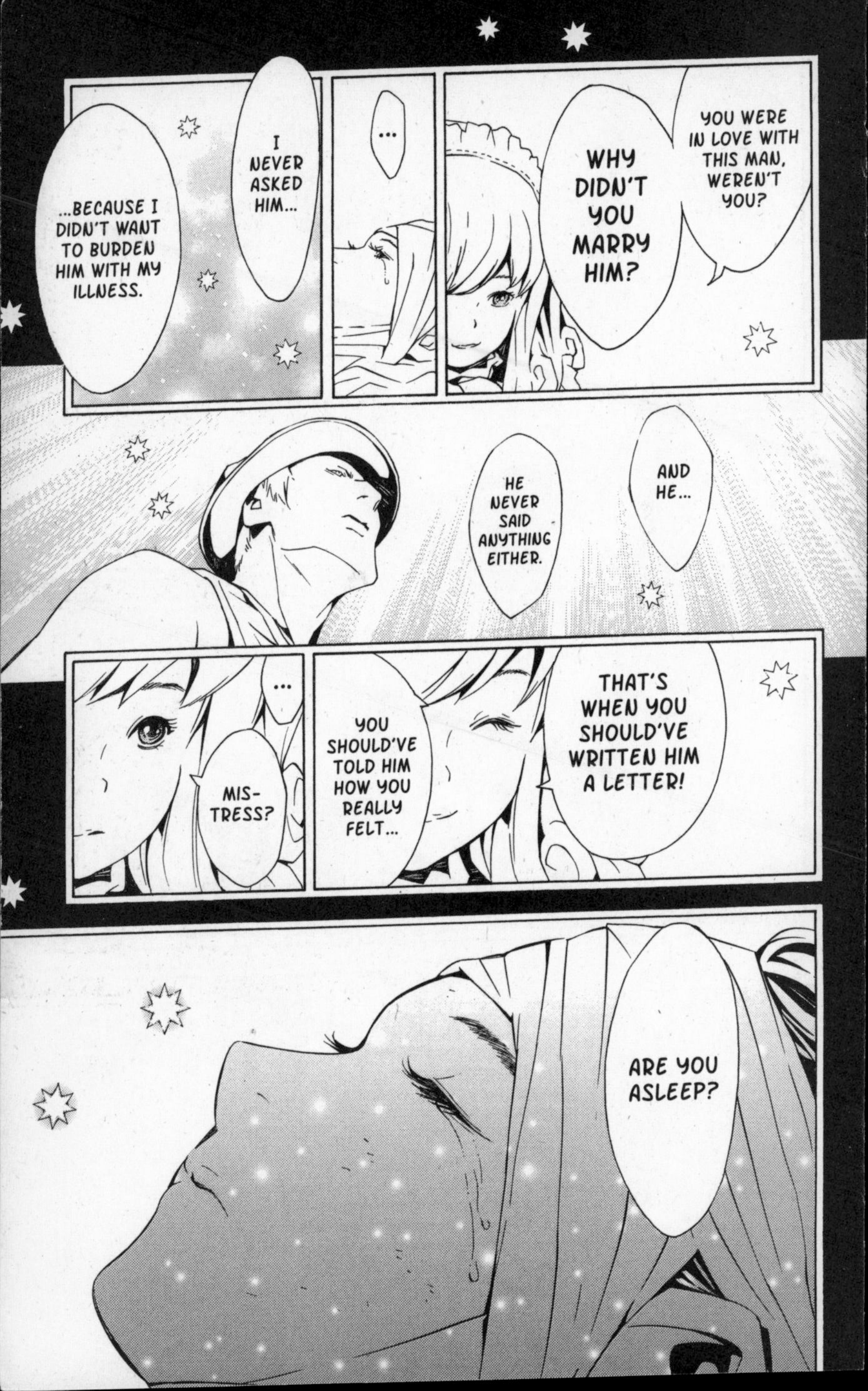
YOU WERE IN LOVE WITH THIS MAN, WEREN'T YOU?
WHY DIDN'T YOU MARRY HIM?
...
I NEVER ASKED HIM...
...BECAUSE I DIDN'T WANT TO BURDEN HIM WITH MY ILLNESS.
AND HE...
HE NEVER SAID ANYTHING EITHER.
THAT'S WHEN YOU SHOULD'VE WRITTEN HIM A LETTER!
YOU SHOULD'VE TOLD HIM HOW YOU REALLY FELT...
...
MIS-TRESS?
ARE YOU ASLEEP?

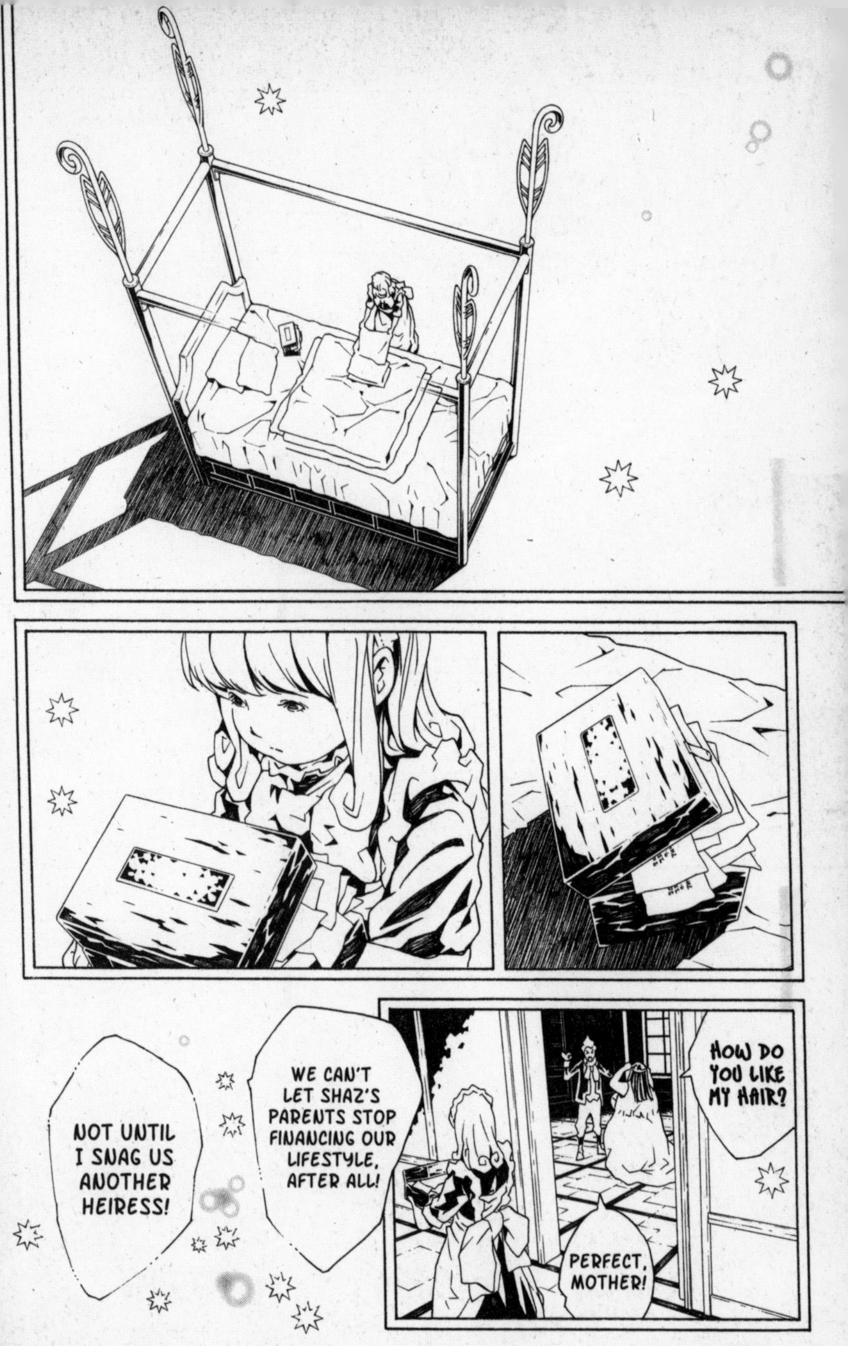

HOW DO YOU LIKE MY HAIR?
PERFECT, MOTHER!
WE CAN'T LET SHAZ'S PARENTS STOP FINANCING OUR LIFESTYLE, AFTER ALL!
NOT UNTIL I SNAG US ANOTHER HEIRESS!

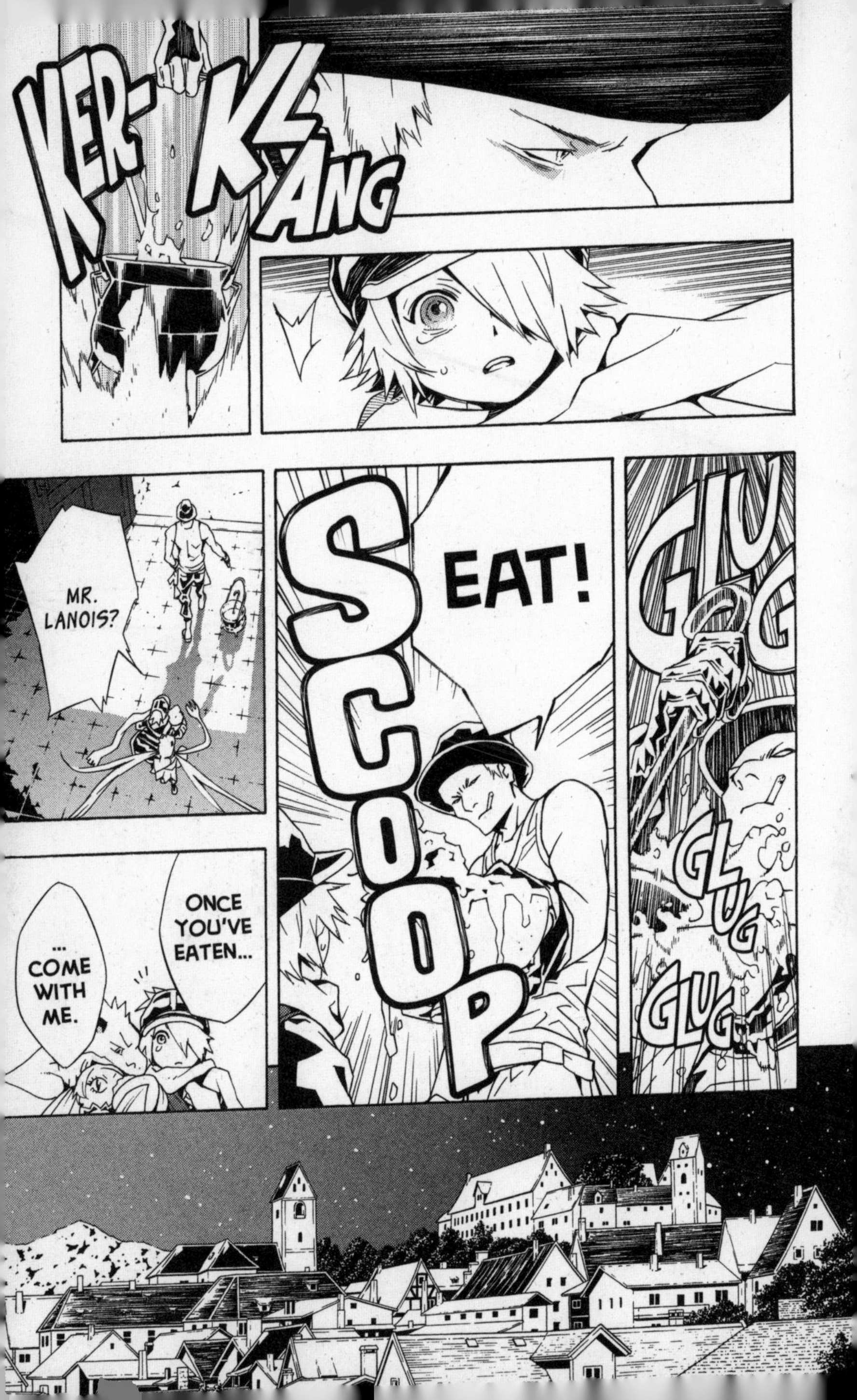
KER-KLANG
GLUG GLUG
GLUG
GLUG
EAT!
SCOOP
MR. LANOIS?
ONCE YOU'VE EATEN...
... COME WITH ME.

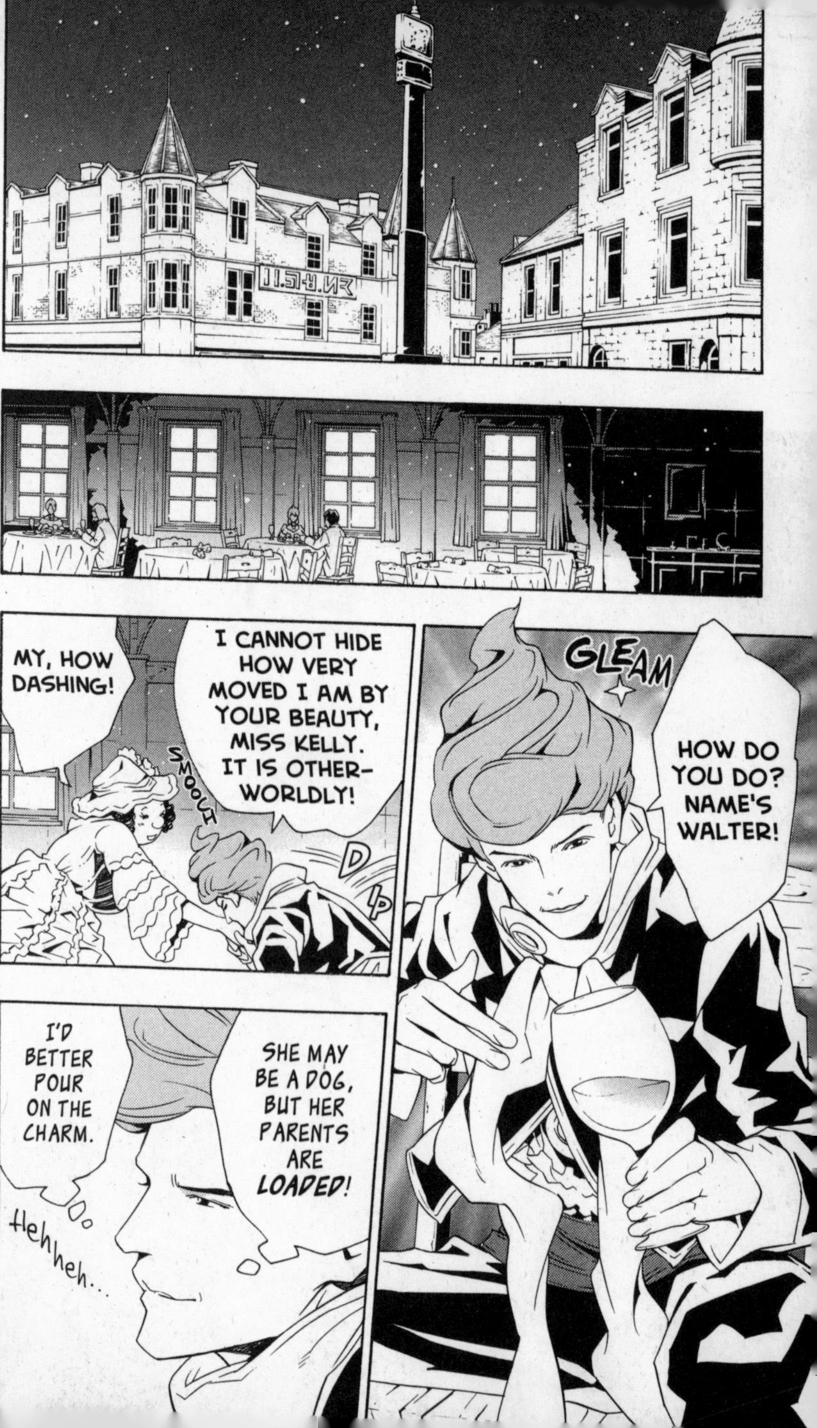
GLEAM
HOW DO YOU DO? NAME'S WALTER!
I CANNOT HIDE HOW VERY MOVED I AM BY YOUR BEAUTY, MISS KELLY. IT IS OTHER-WORLDLY!
MY, HOW DASHING!
SMOOCH
DIP
SHE MAY BE A DOG, BUT HER PARENTS ARE *LOADED*!
I'D BETTER POUR ON THE CHARM.
Hehheh...

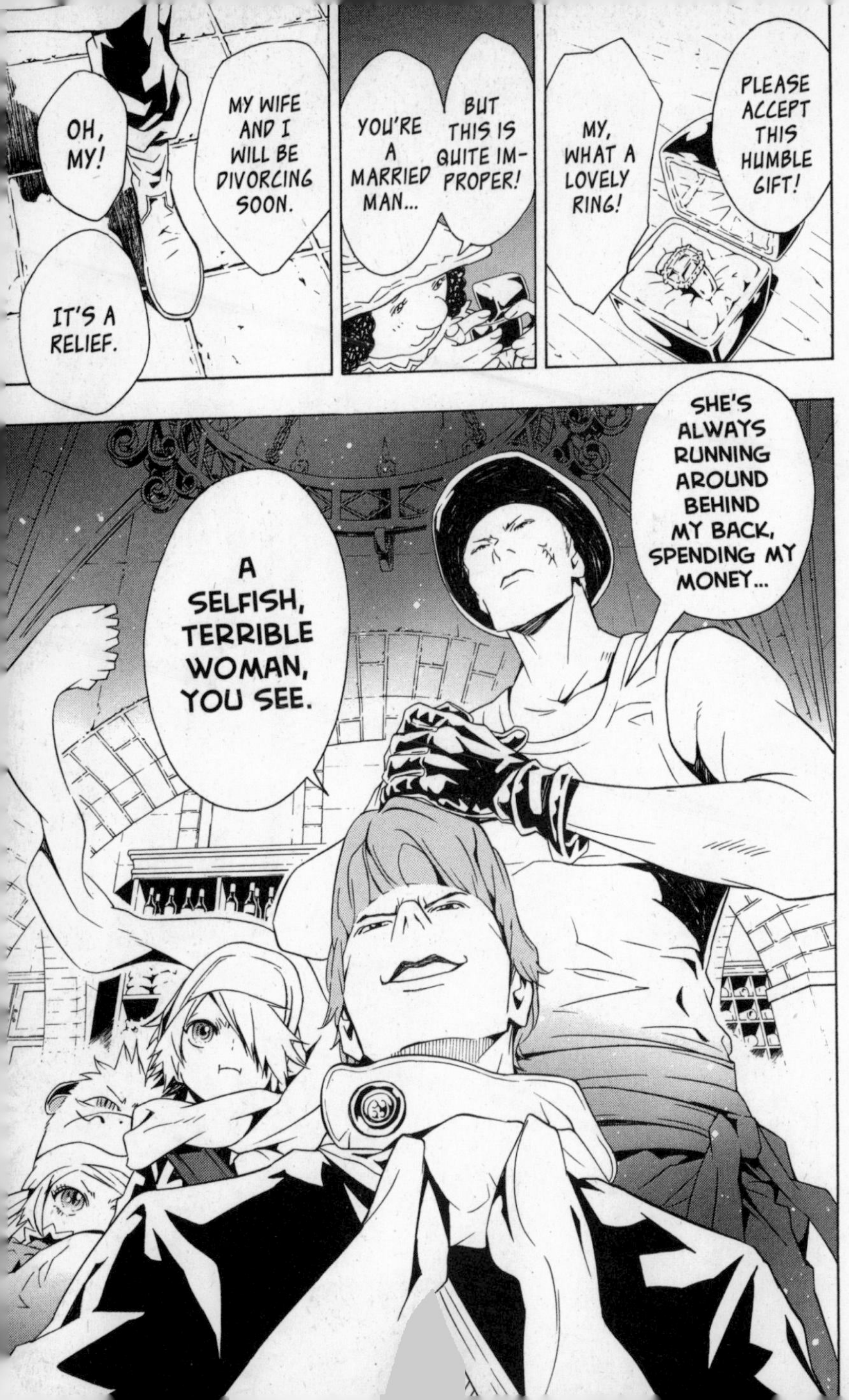
PLEASE ACCEPT THIS HUMBLE GIFT!
MY, WHAT A LOVELY RING!
BUT THIS IS QUITE IM-PROPER!
YOU'RE A MARRIED MAN...
MY WIFE AND I WILL BE DIVORCING SOON.
OH, MY!
IT'S A RELIEF.
SHE'S ALWAYS RUNNING AROUND BEHIND MY BACK, SPENDING MY MONEY...
A SELFISH, TERRIBLE WOMAN, YOU SEE.

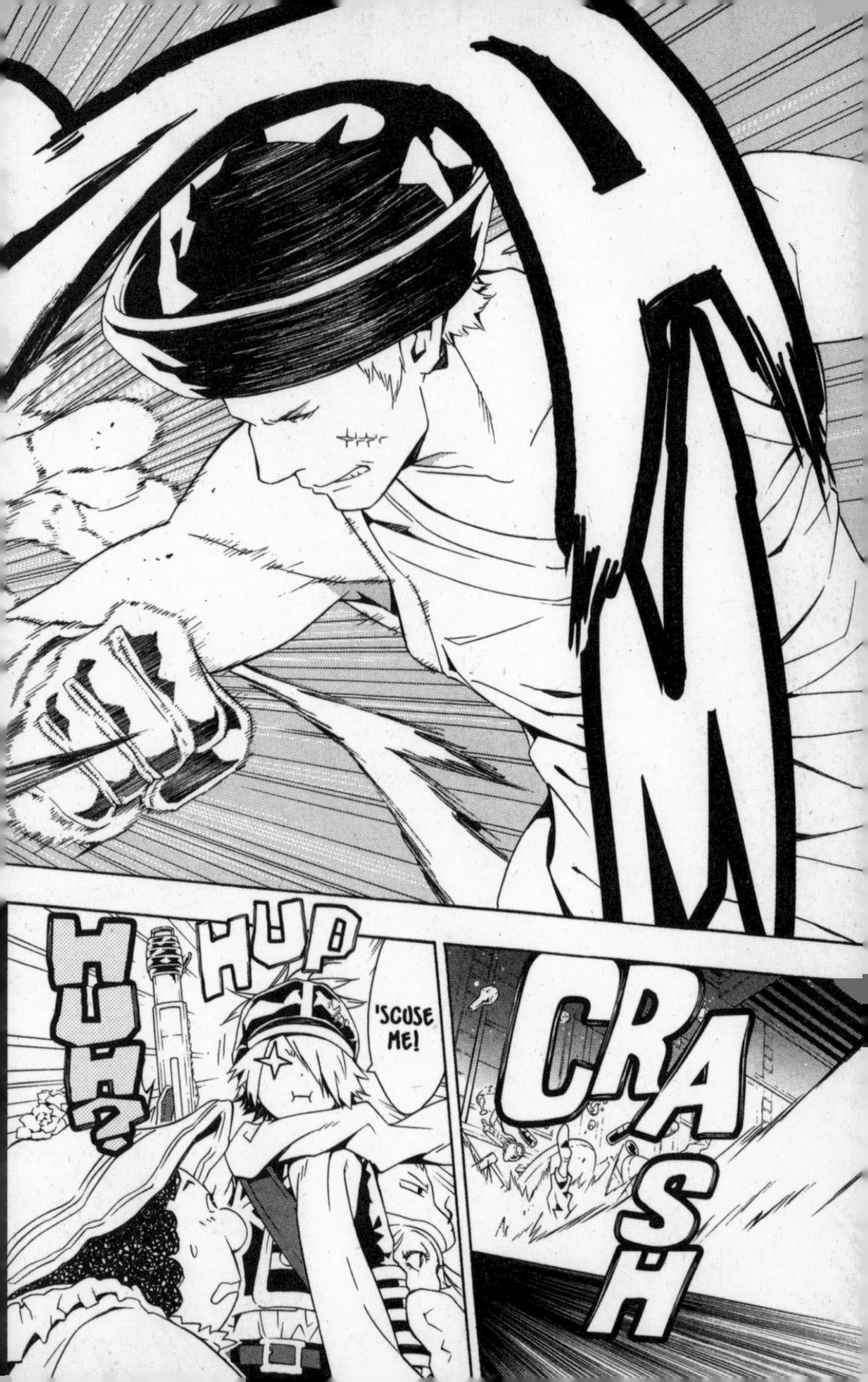
CRASH
HUP
'SCUSE ME!
HUH?

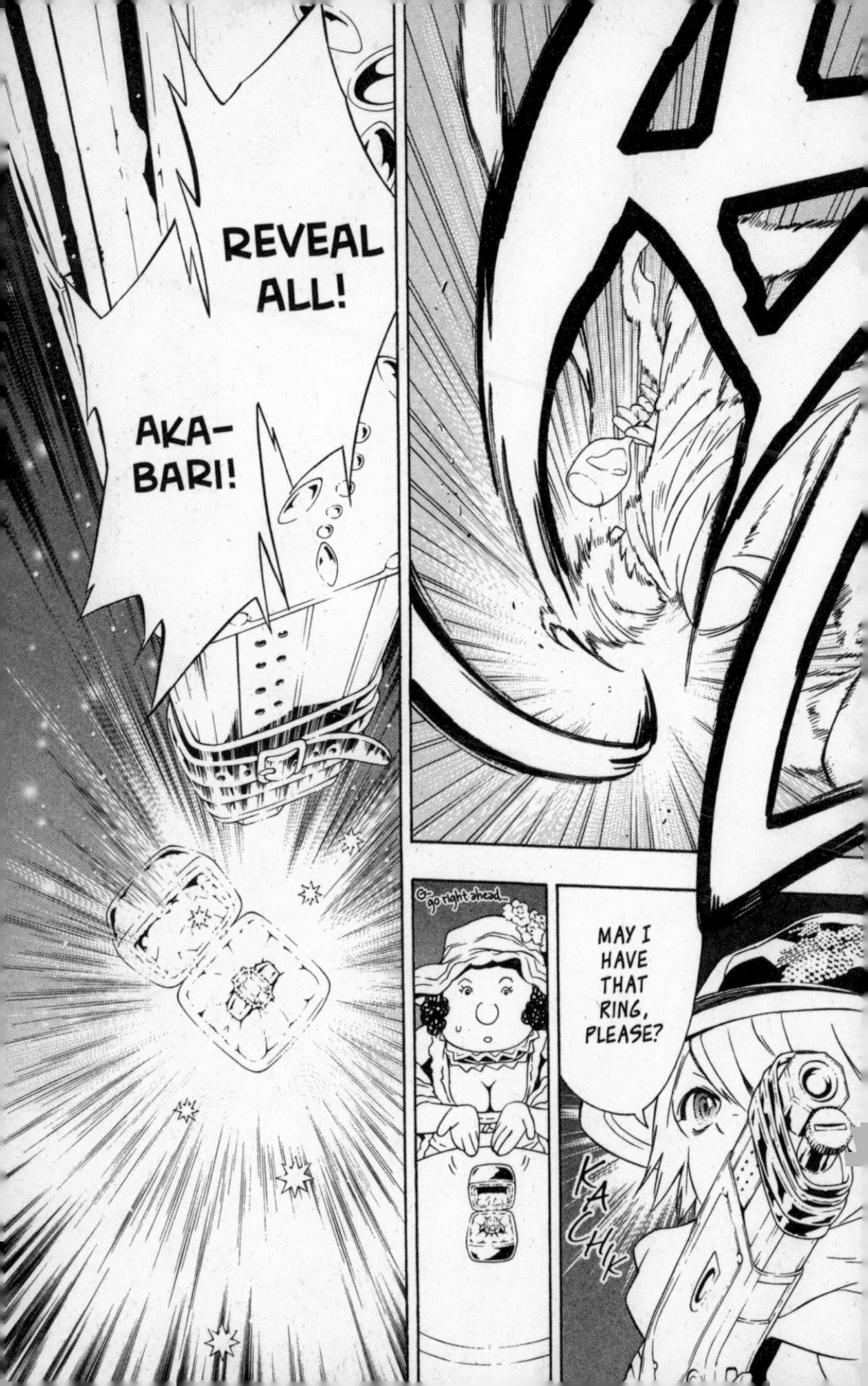
MAY I HAVE THAT RING, PLEASE?
KACHIK
G-go right ahead...
REVEAL ALL!
AKA-BARI!

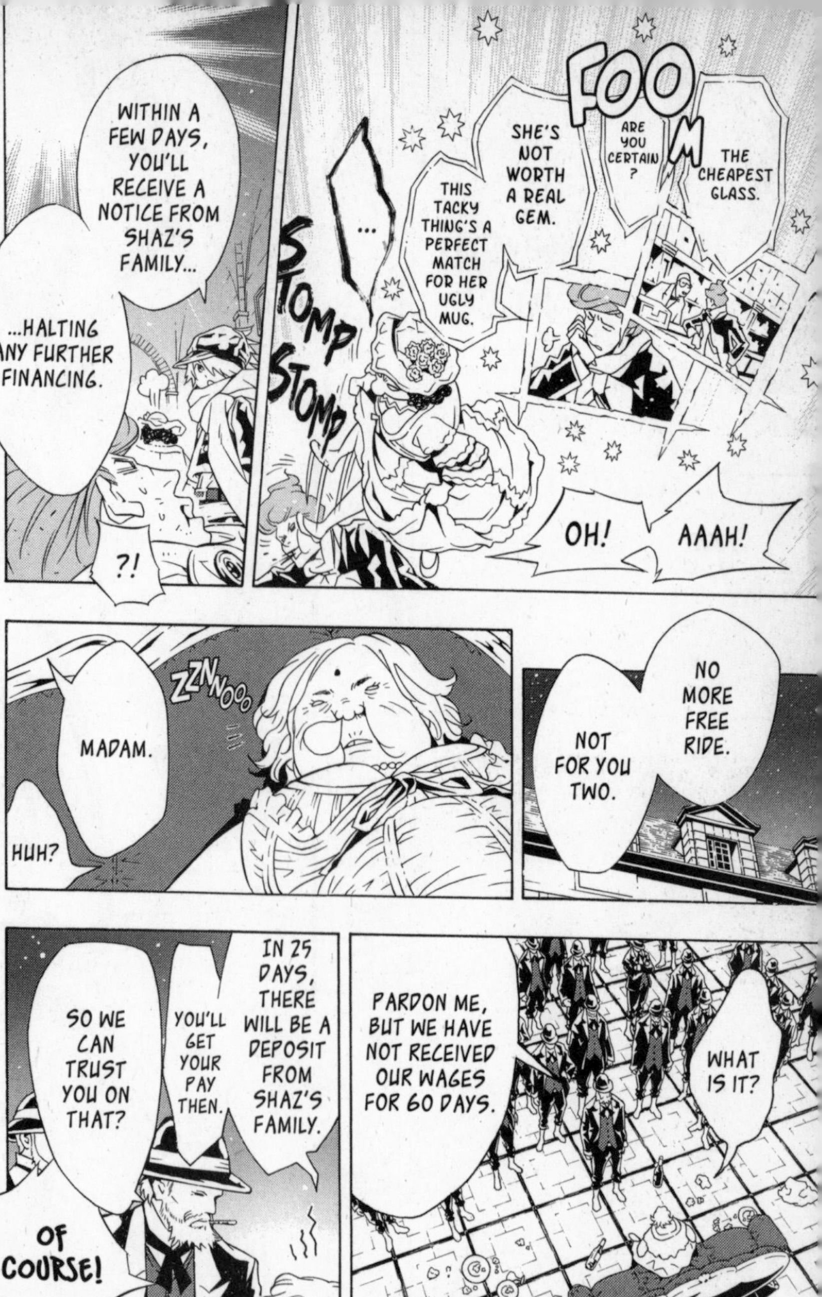
FOOM
THE CHEAPEST GLASS.
ARE YOU CERTAIN?
SHE'S NOT WORTH A REAL GEM.
THIS TACKY THING'S A PERFECT MATCH FOR HER UGLY MUG.
...
STOMP STOMP
AAAH!
OH!
WITHIN A FEW DAYS, YOU'LL RECEIVE A NOTICE FROM SHAZ'S FAMILY...
...HALTING ANY FURTHER FINANCING.
?!
NO MORE FREE RIDE.
NOT FOR YOU TWO.
ZZNNOOO
MADAM.
HUH?
WHAT IS IT?
PARDON ME, BUT WE HAVE NOT RECEIVED OUR WAGES FOR 60 DAYS.
IN 25 DAYS, THERE WILL BE A DEPOSIT FROM SHAZ'S FAMILY.
YOU'LL GET YOUR PAY THEN.
SO WE CAN TRUST YOU ON THAT?
OF COURSE!

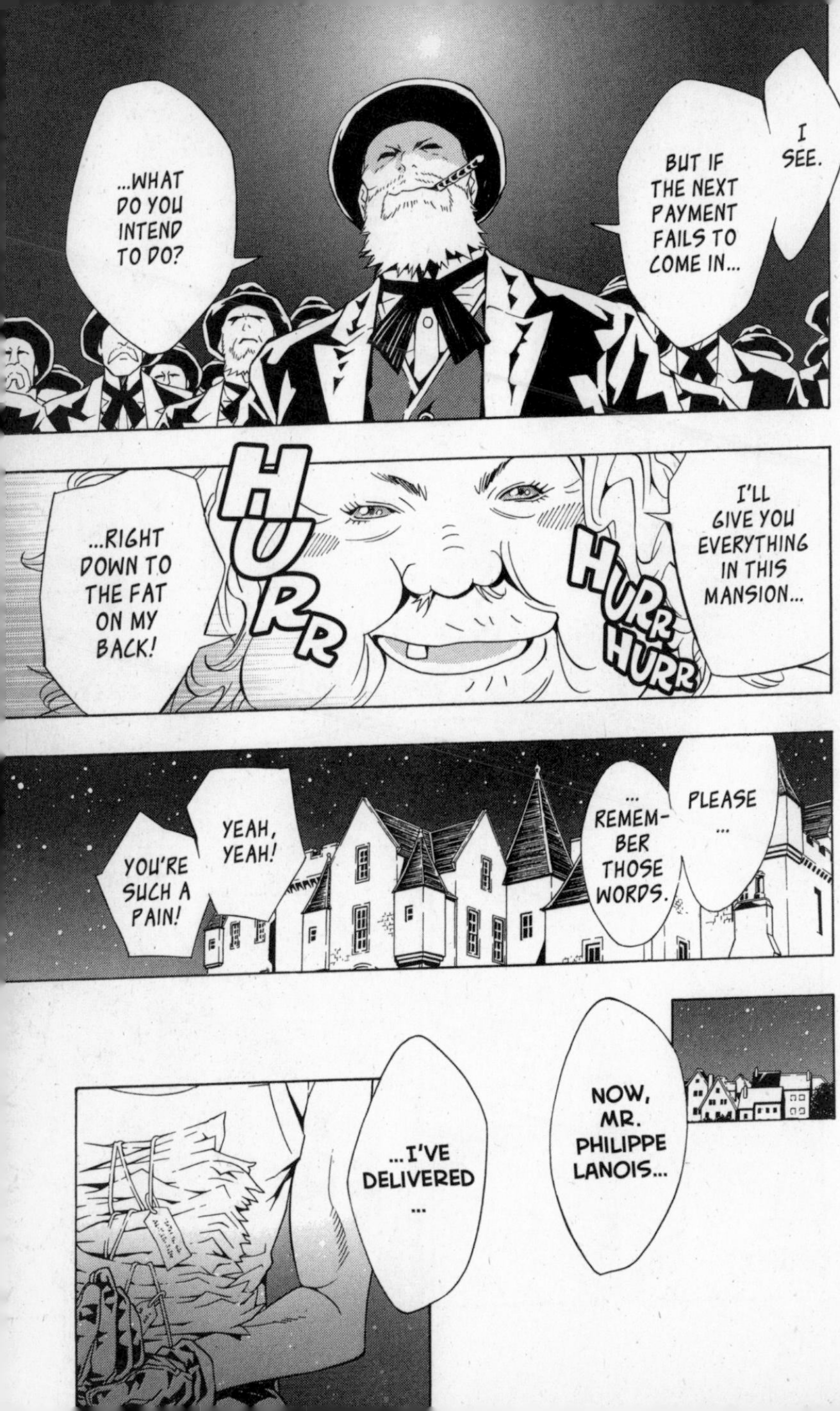
I SEE.
BUT IF THE NEXT PAYMENT FAILS TO COME IN...
...WHAT DO YOU INTEND TO DO?
I'LL GIVE YOU EVERYTHING IN THIS MANSION...
HURR HURR
HURR
...RIGHT DOWN TO THE FAT ON MY BACK!
PLEASE...
...REMEMBER THOSE WORDS.
YEAH, YEAH!
YOU'RE SUCH A PAIN!
NOW, MR. PHILIPPE LANOIS...
...I'VE DELIVERED...

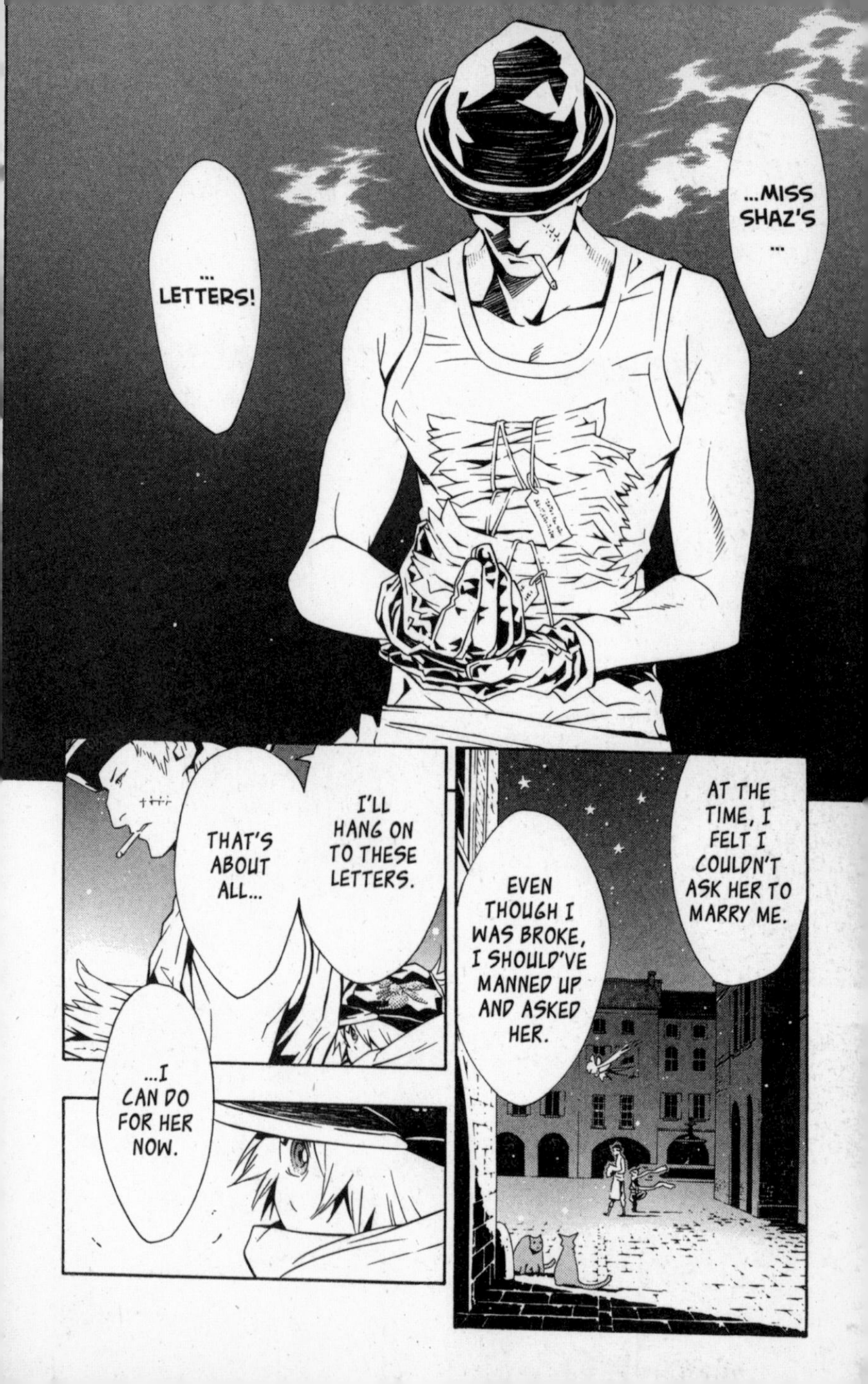
...MISS SHAZ'S ...
... LETTERS!
AT THE TIME, I FELT I COULDN'T ASK HER TO MARRY ME.
EVEN THOUGH I WAS BROKE, I SHOULD'VE MANNED UP AND ASKED HER.
I'LL HANG ON TO THESE LETTERS.
THAT'S ABOUT ALL...
...I CAN DO FOR HER NOW.

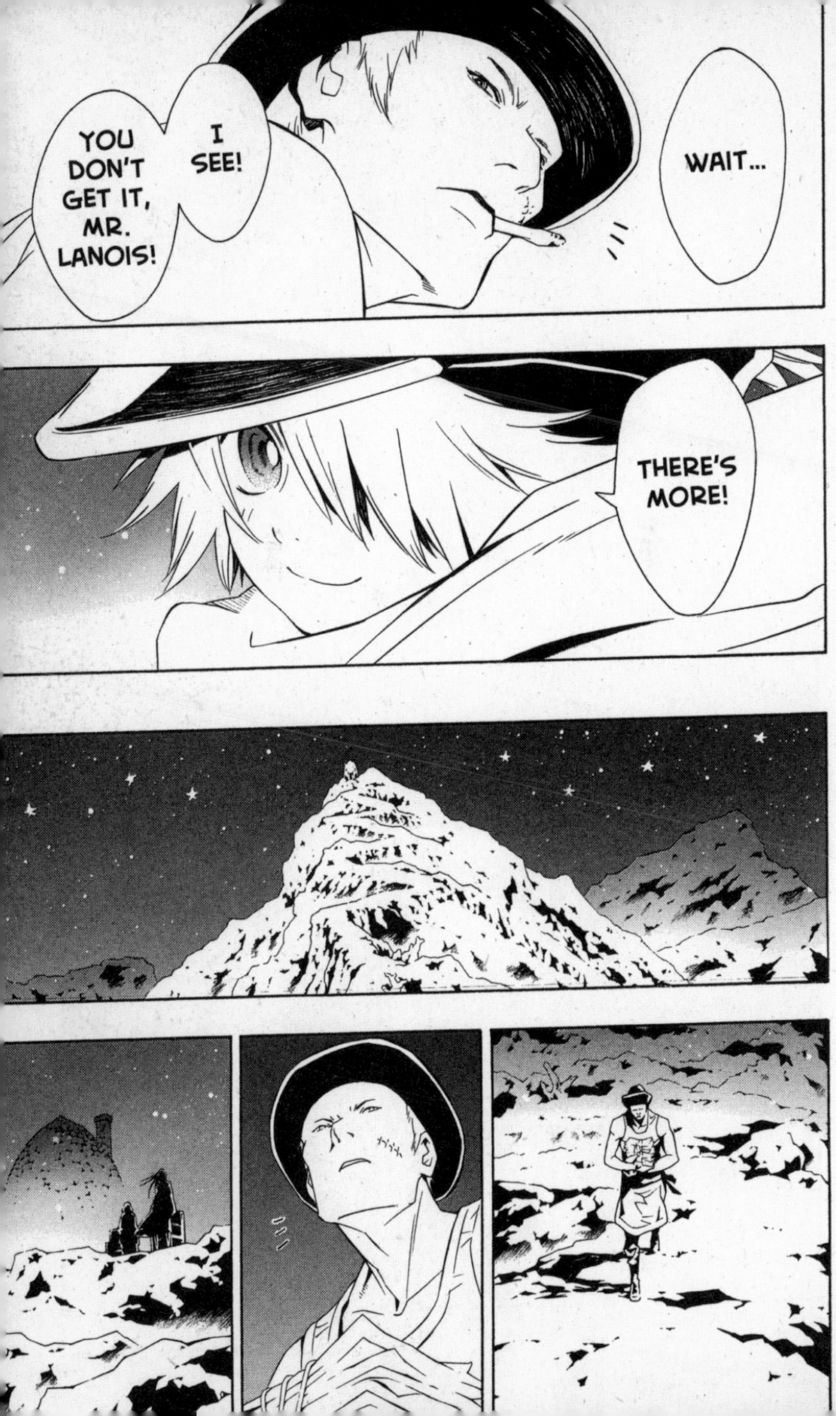
WAIT...
I SEE!
YOU DON'T GET IT, MR. LANOIS!
THERE'S MORE!

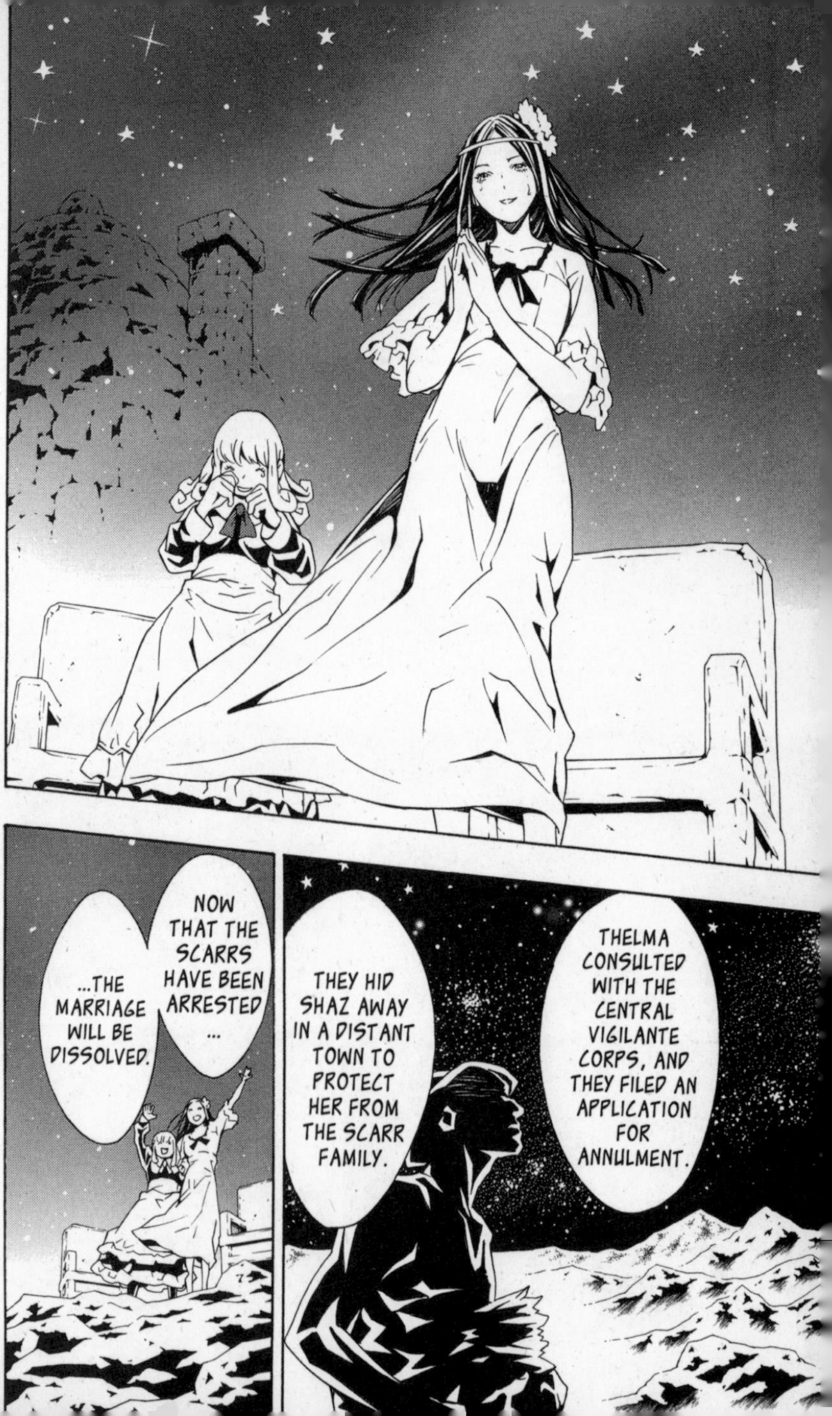
THELMA CONSULTED WITH THE CENTRAL VIGILANTE CORPS, AND THEY FILED AN APPLICATION FOR ANNULMENT.
THEY HID SHAZ AWAY IN A DISTANT TOWN TO PROTECT HER FROM THE SCARR FAMILY.
NOW THAT THE SCARRS HAVE BEEN ARRESTED ...
...THE MARRIAGE WILL BE DISSOLVED.

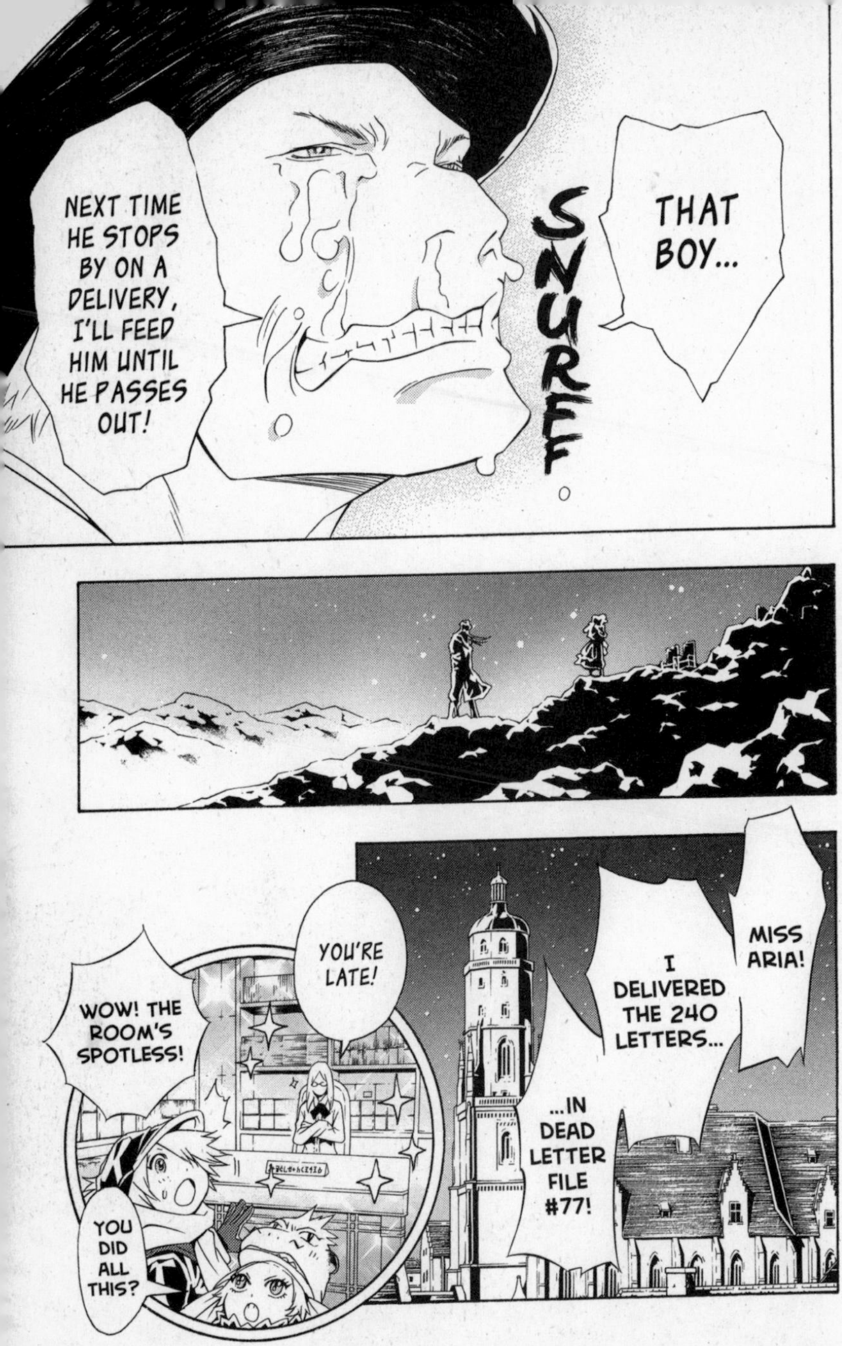
THAT BOY...
SNURFF
NEXT TIME HE STOPS BY ON A DELIVERY, I'LL FEED HIM UNTIL HE PASSES OUT!
MISS ARIA!
I DELIVERED THE 240 LETTERS...
...IN DEAD LETTER FILE #77!
YOU'RE LATE!
WOW! THE ROOM'S SPOTLESS!
YOU DID ALL THIS?

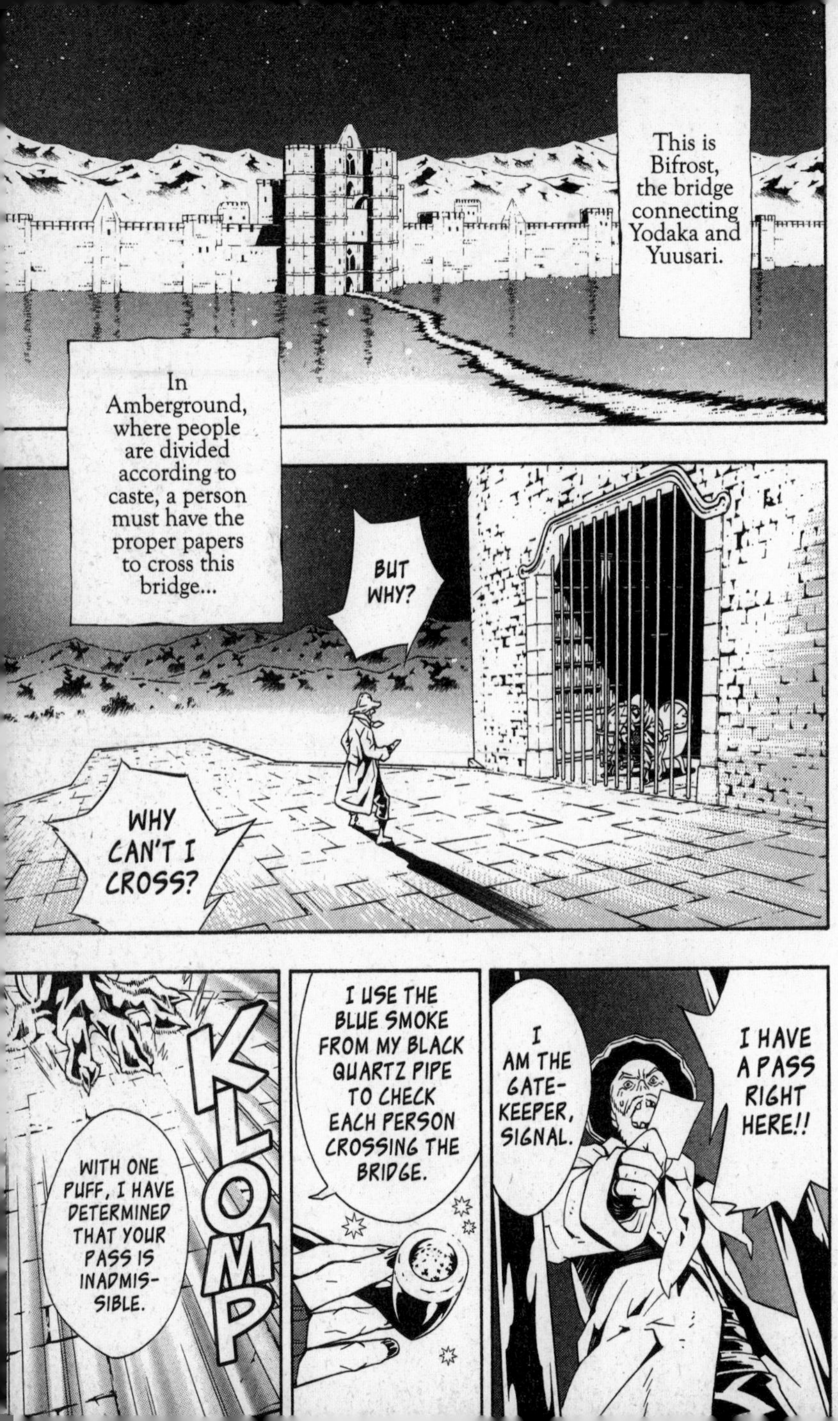
This is Bifrost, the bridge connecting Yodaka and Yuusari.
In Amberground, where people are divided according to caste, a person must have the proper papers to cross this bridge...
BUT WHY?
WHY CAN'T I CROSS?
I HAVE A PASS RIGHT HERE!!
I AM THE GATE-KEEPER, SIGNAL.
I USE THE BLUE SMOKE FROM MY BLACK QUARTZ PIPE TO CHECK EACH PERSON CROSSING THE BRIDGE.
KLOMP
WITH ONE PUFF, I HAVE DETERMINED THAT YOUR PASS IS INADMIS-SIBLE.

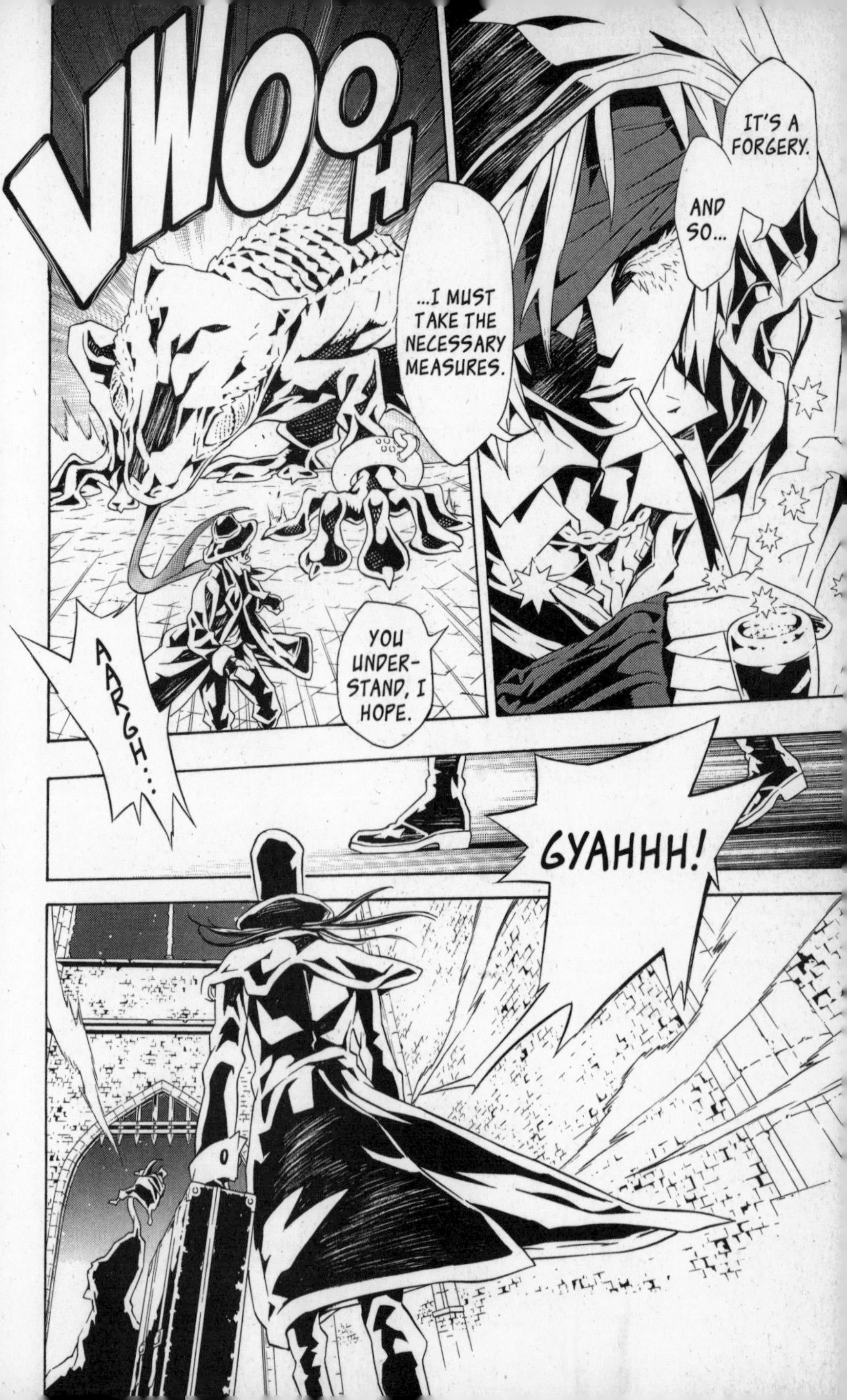
IT'S A FORGERY.
AND SO...
...I MUST TAKE THE NECESSARY MEASURES.
VWOOH
YOU UNDERSTAND, I HOPE.
AARGH...
GYAHHH!

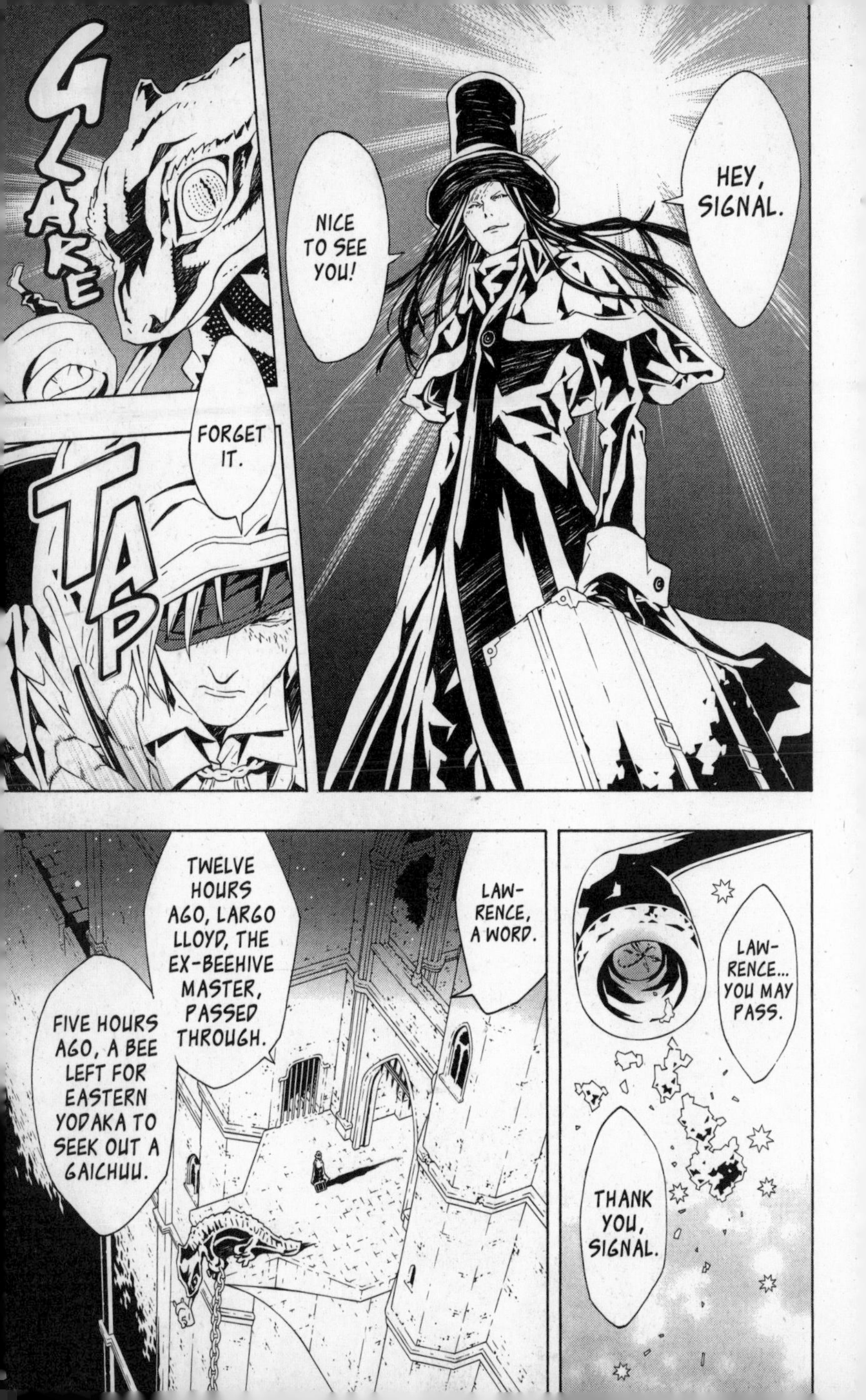
HEY, SIGNAL.
NICE TO SEE YOU!
GLARE
FORGET IT.
TAP
LAW-RENCE... YOU MAY PASS.
THANK YOU, SIGNAL.
LAW-RENCE, A WORD.
TWELVE HOURS AGO, LARGO LLOYD, THE EX-BEEHIVE MASTER, PASSED THROUGH.
FIVE HOURS AGO, A BEE LEFT FOR EASTERN YODAKA TO SEEK OUT A GAICHUU.

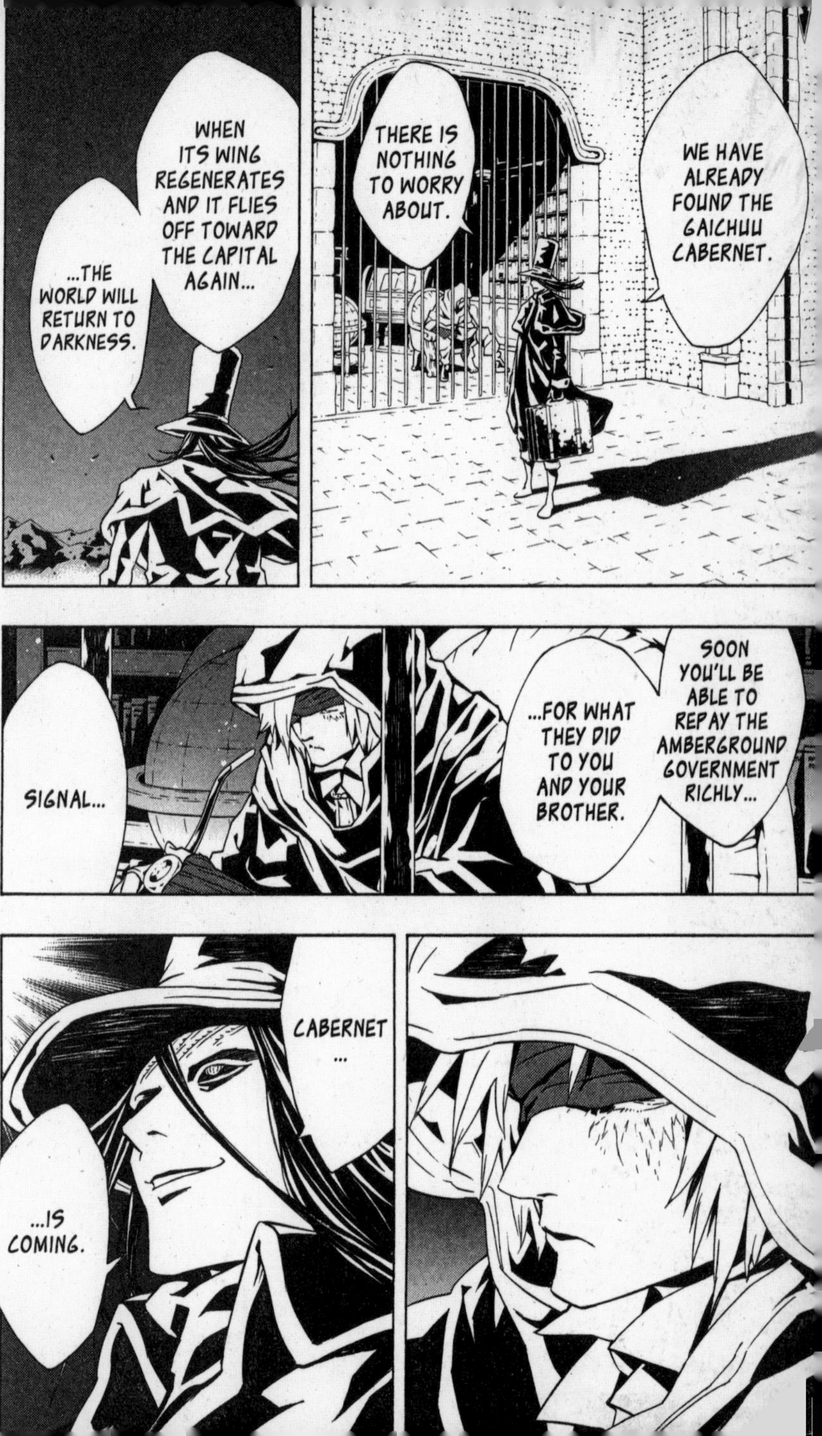
WE HAVE ALREADY FOUND THE GAICHUU CABERNET.
THERE IS NOTHING TO WORRY ABOUT.
WHEN ITS WING REGENERATES AND IT FLIES OFF TOWARD THE CAPITAL AGAIN...
...THE WORLD WILL RETURN TO DARKNESS.
SOON YOU'LL BE ABLE TO REPAY THE AMBERGROUND GOVERNMENT RICHLY...
...FOR WHAT THEY DID TO YOU AND YOUR BROTHER.
SIGNAL...
CABERNET ...
...IS COMING.

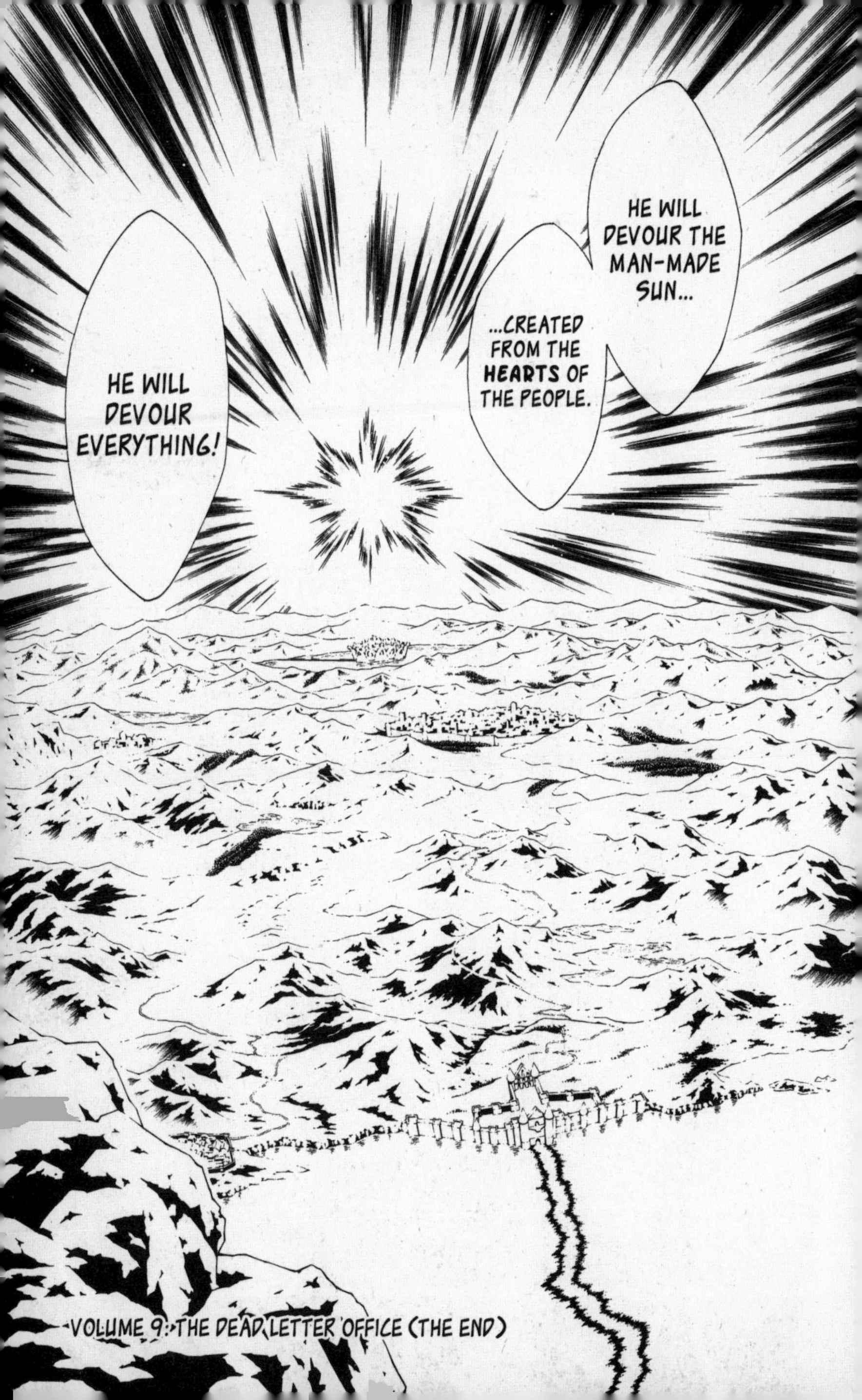
HE WILL DEVOUR THE MAN-MADE SUN...
...CREATED FROM THE **HEARTS** OF THE PEOPLE.
HE WILL DEVOUR EVERYTHING!

VOLUME 9: THE DEAD LETTER OFFICE (THE END)

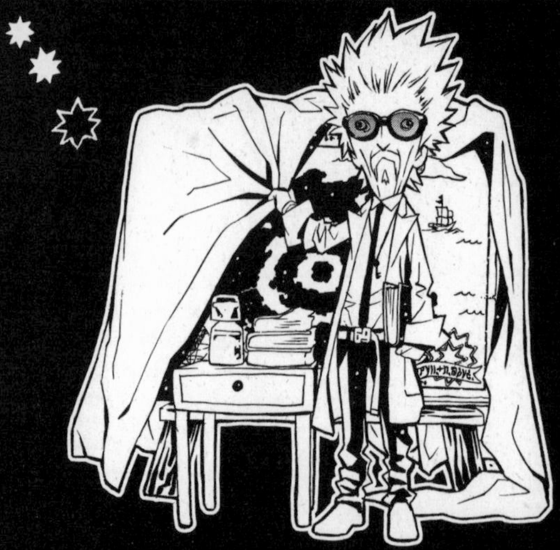

# Dr. Thunderland's Reference Desk

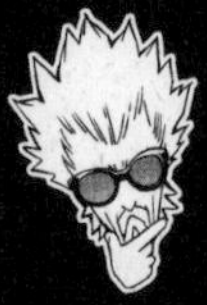

I am Dr. Thunderland.

The Yuusari Beehive—forget it. The world introduced in this volume—forget it. Forget it! Forget it, forget it, forget it!

*Arrgh…*

Heyyyyyyy! Is anybody listening?

When I skimmed this volume, I thought, "There's me! I'm in this one!" I really did.

It was my time. I was so certain.

But no! It turned out to be Garrard! I guess, on reflection, he doesn't look like me at all.

■ HEARTOMETER
The Heartometer is an analog gauge that measures the amount of *heart* a person has left. There are many devices like this in Amberground. Most of them were developed in the capital.

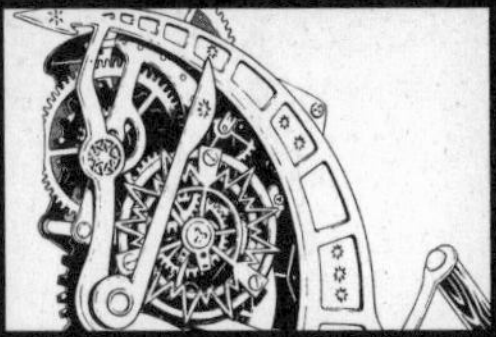

*Hmph!* I'm still angry. That's why I'm not trying to make this interesting.

■ CENTRAL YUUSARI EMPLOYMENT AGENCY
This agency finds jobs and provides consultation and training for those looking for work. It assists many dingos and day laborers. I know, I know...I warned you this would be pretty dry reading, but what can I say? I can't leave my job. Oh, and it looks like Sarah from Honey Waters works there. Sounds like Hunt was made a trainee at the Bioscience Advisory Panel. I guess you just have to have passion. I wonder if I'll be rewarded someday if I hold on to my passion. Pick me, pick me!

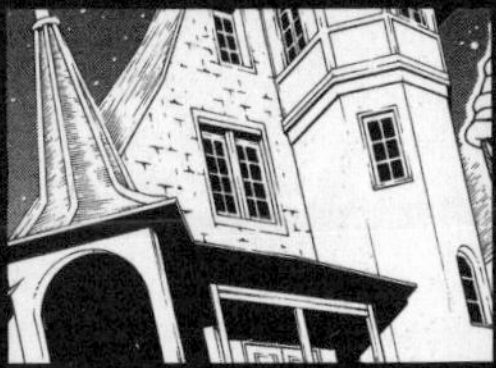

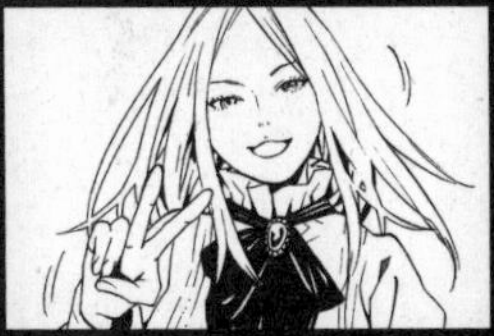

■ GIGANTIC ULTRASONIC WAVE TRANSMITTING DEVICE
I bought one of these. It was for bugs or something. What is it supposed to do? I couldn't tell if it was working or not!

■ CAPITAL INSPECTORS
Hmm...Ex-Bee Garrard and his ex-dingo Hazel. They say they've come from the capital, but, like the Man Who Could Not Become Spirit, it's possible that they've never really been there at all.

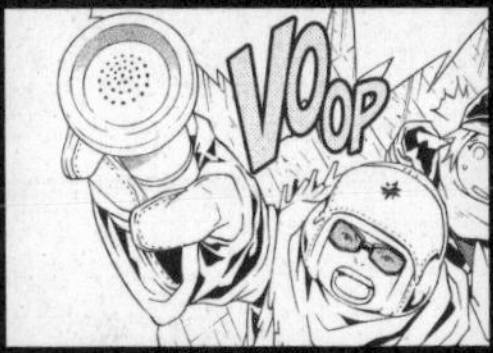
VOOP

Perhaps they have an ulterior motive, perhaps they simply want to cause trouble, but they've taken on the task of reforming their old haunt. To think they'd fire the laid-back Lloyd and demote Aria and Lag! Since then, everyone in the Beehive has been on pins and needles. But when they return to the capital, they'll take Gauche with them. This is a problem.

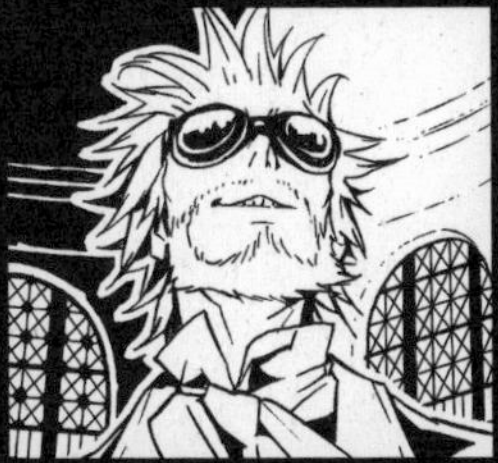

Oh! I have a good idea! Make me the Beehive Director! I promise to put Aria in a skimpy uniform! Hubba hubba! Or would that be an HR violation? Maybe I'm better off working alone.

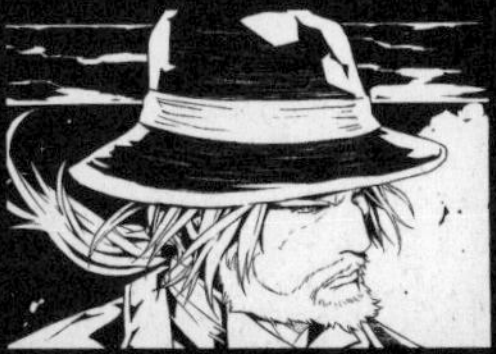

nb: Pedigree / A finishing move made famous by Triple H of the WWE. Double-arm facebuster.

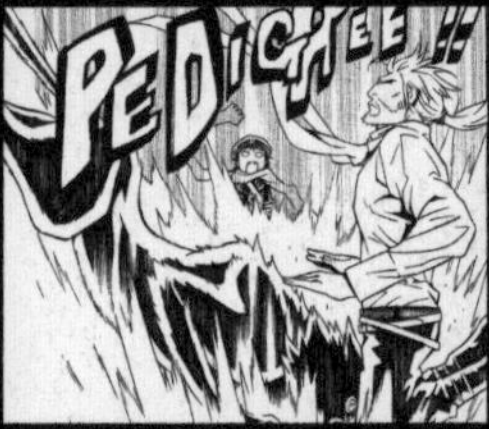
PEDIGREE!!

■ DEAD LETTER OFFICE

There are a lot of dead letters! Bees make deliveries on foot, so there's no guarantee that everything will be delivered safely and on time.

It seems that instead of looking for addressees who have moved, Moc Sullivan has been treating them as cold letters so he can move on quickly to the next delivery. He's a completely different Bee from Lag, who puts his all into delivering each letter. Oh well...it's just a difference in their personalities. It takes all kinds to keep an organization running. But I must say, that woman who disguised herself as Shaz had me shaking in my shoes. The hairs in her nostrils could reach the Milky Way.

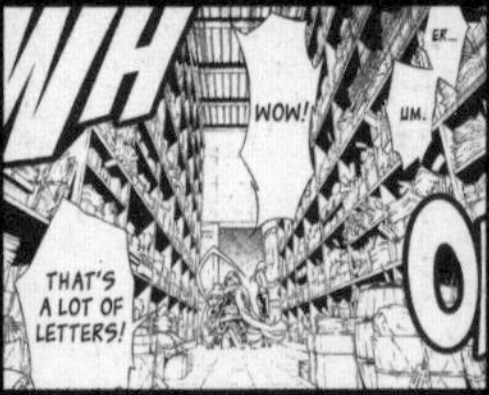
ER...
UM.
WOW!
THAT'S A LOT OF LETTERS!

nb: Belladonna / A perennial that grows in Europe and America. In the language of flowers, it means "silence." It's also the title of an album by musician Daniel Lanois.

nb: Pitiful / 1. pathetic; sorry; pitiable. 2. despicable; shameless.

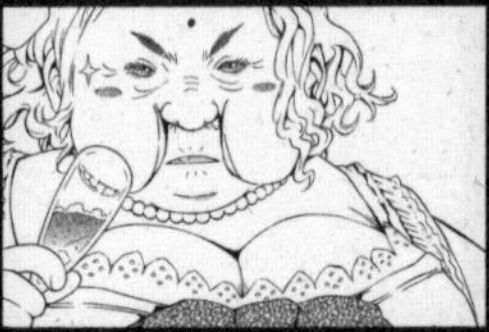

■ MAN-MADE SUN

What?! It's made of *heart*? Are you serious? I...didn't know that... But wait a minute! It could be that Lawrence of Reverse is just saying that! What's going on here? Oh! I've got it! Obviously, I'm the one destined to seize the moment and solve this mystery! Yes, that must be it!

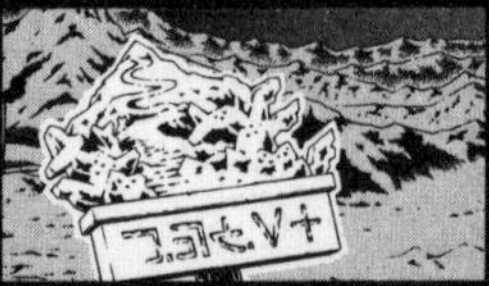

So this is what the author was waiting for! The runway has been far too long, but that's okay! Time for take-off!

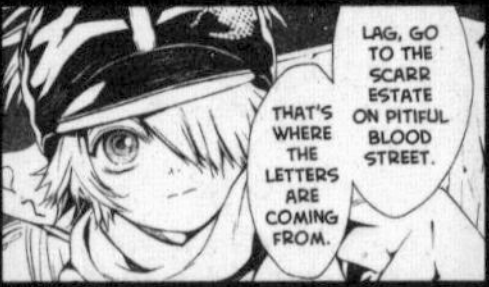
LAG, GO TO THE SCARR ESTATE ON PITIFUL BLOOD STREET.
THAT'S WHERE THE LETTERS ARE COMING FROM.

*Sigh*...I don't know if I can keep up this optimistic front.

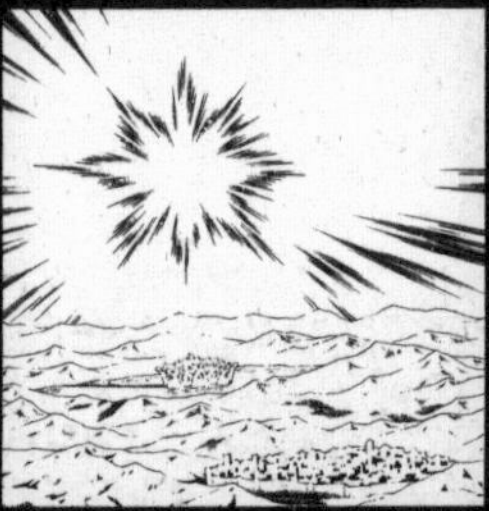

# Route Map

Finally, I am including a map indicating the route followed in this volume, created at Lonely Goatherd Map Station of Central Yuusari.

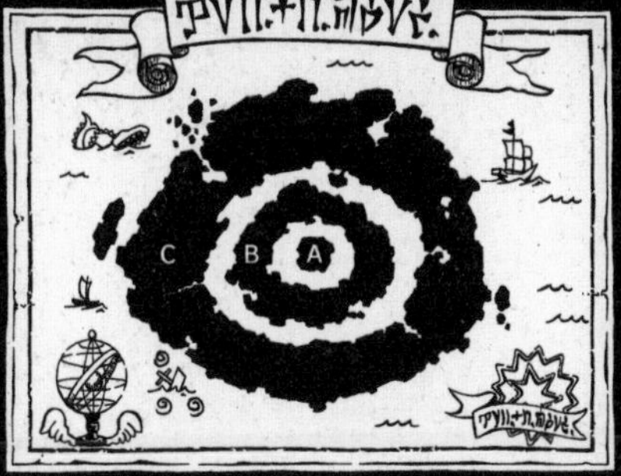

C
B
A


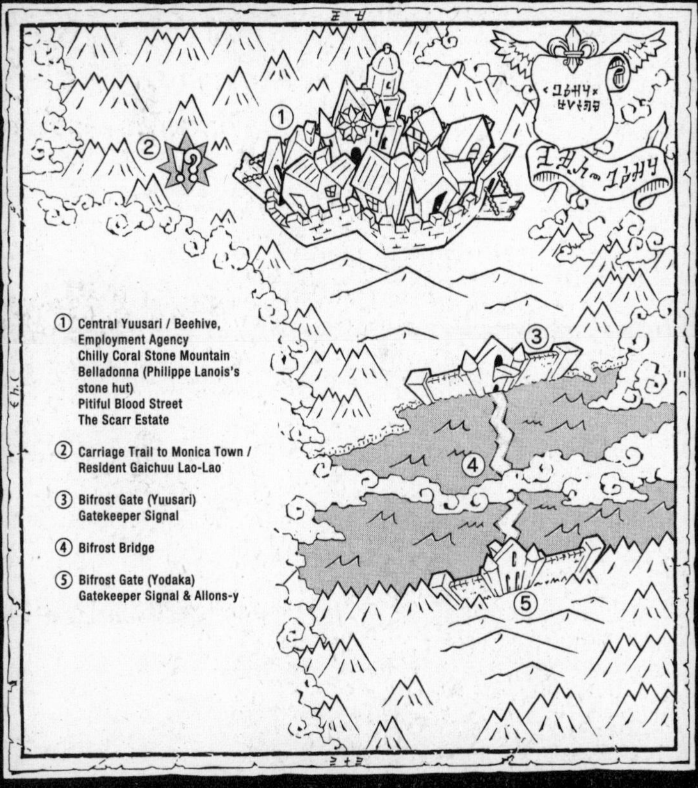

① Central Yuusari / Beehive, Employment Agency
Chilly Coral Stone Mountain
Belladonna (Philippe Lanois's stone hut)
Pitiful Blood Street
The Scarr Estate
② Carriage Trail to Monica Town / Resident Gaichuu Lao-Lao
③ Bifrost Gate (Yuusari)
Gatekeeper Signal
④ Bifrost Bridge
⑤ Bifrost Gate (Yodaka)
Gatekeeper Signal & Allons-y


Listen... I hear tell that in your world, you have something called animation. And I hear there's a story about the Bees. I'm probably the hero, right? Thunderland of today...Thunderland of yesterday...Thunderland all the time! I want to see it!

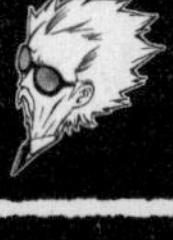

# In the next volume...

The Shining Eye

When Lag falls sick from overwork, Aria takes over his delivery duties.
But will she be able to survive armed with only...a violin? Meanwhile,
Lag's illness takes a strange turn...

**Available August 2012!**

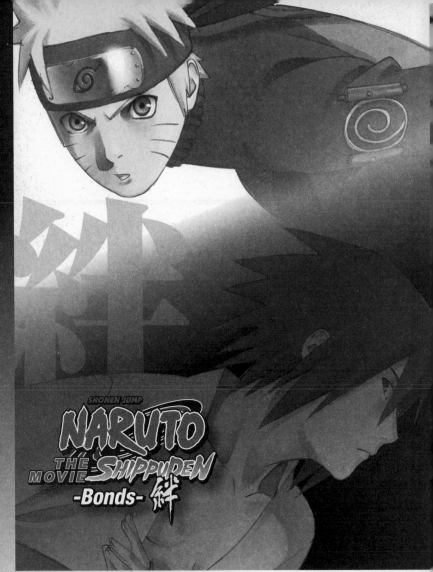

© 2002 MASASHI KISHIMOTO /2007 SHIPPUDEN © NMP 2008

# Now Available on
# DVD and Blu-ray

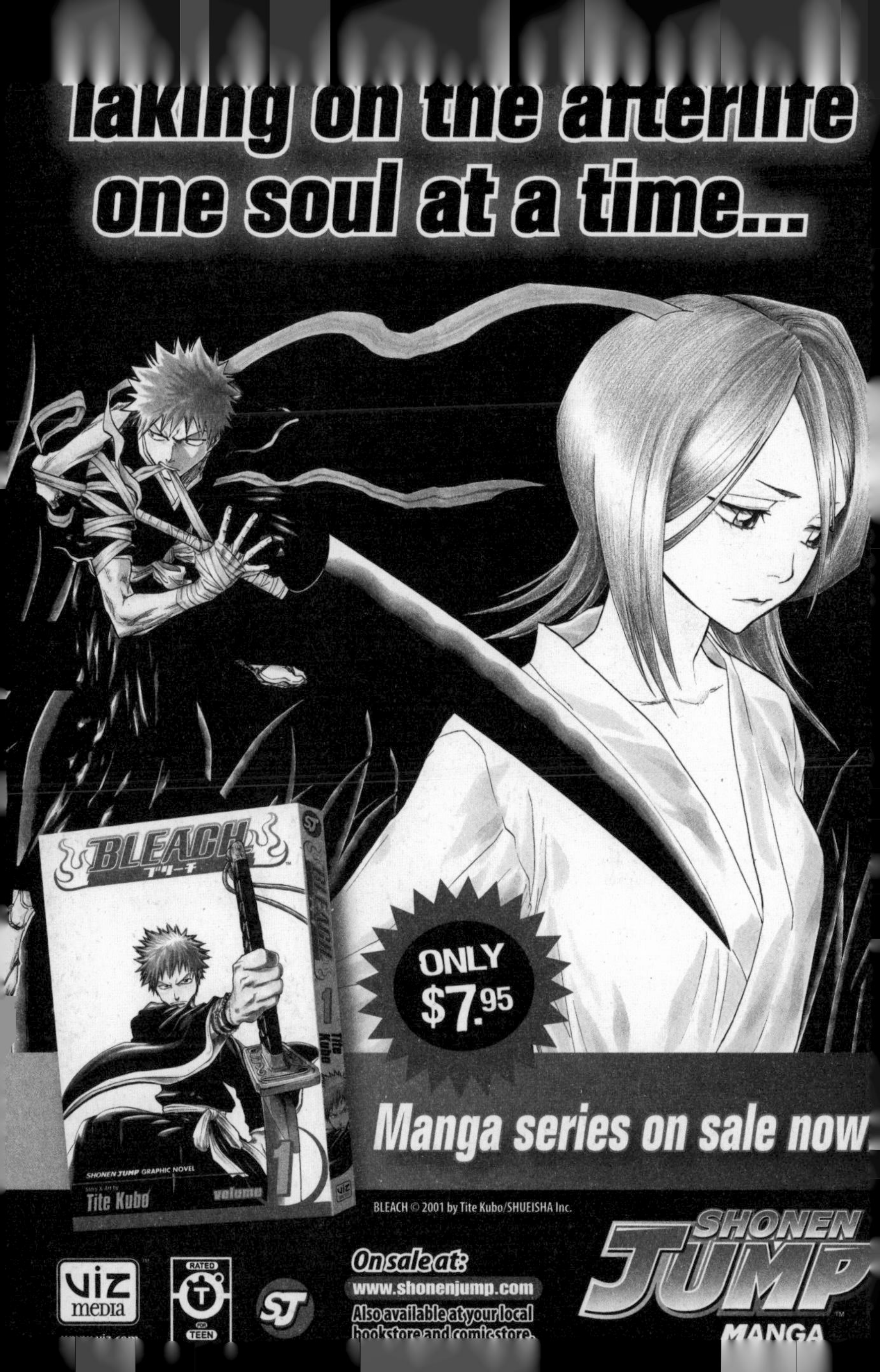

Taking on the afterlife
one soul at a time...
BLEACH
ブリーチ
SHONEN JUMP GRAPHIC NOVEL
Story & Art by
Tite Kubo
volume 1
ONLY
$7.95
Manga series on sale now!
BLEACH © 2001 by Tite Kubo/SHUEISHA Inc.
SHONEN JUMP
MANGA
On sale at:
www.shonenjump.com
Also available at your local
bookstore and comic store.
viz media
RATED T FOR TEEN

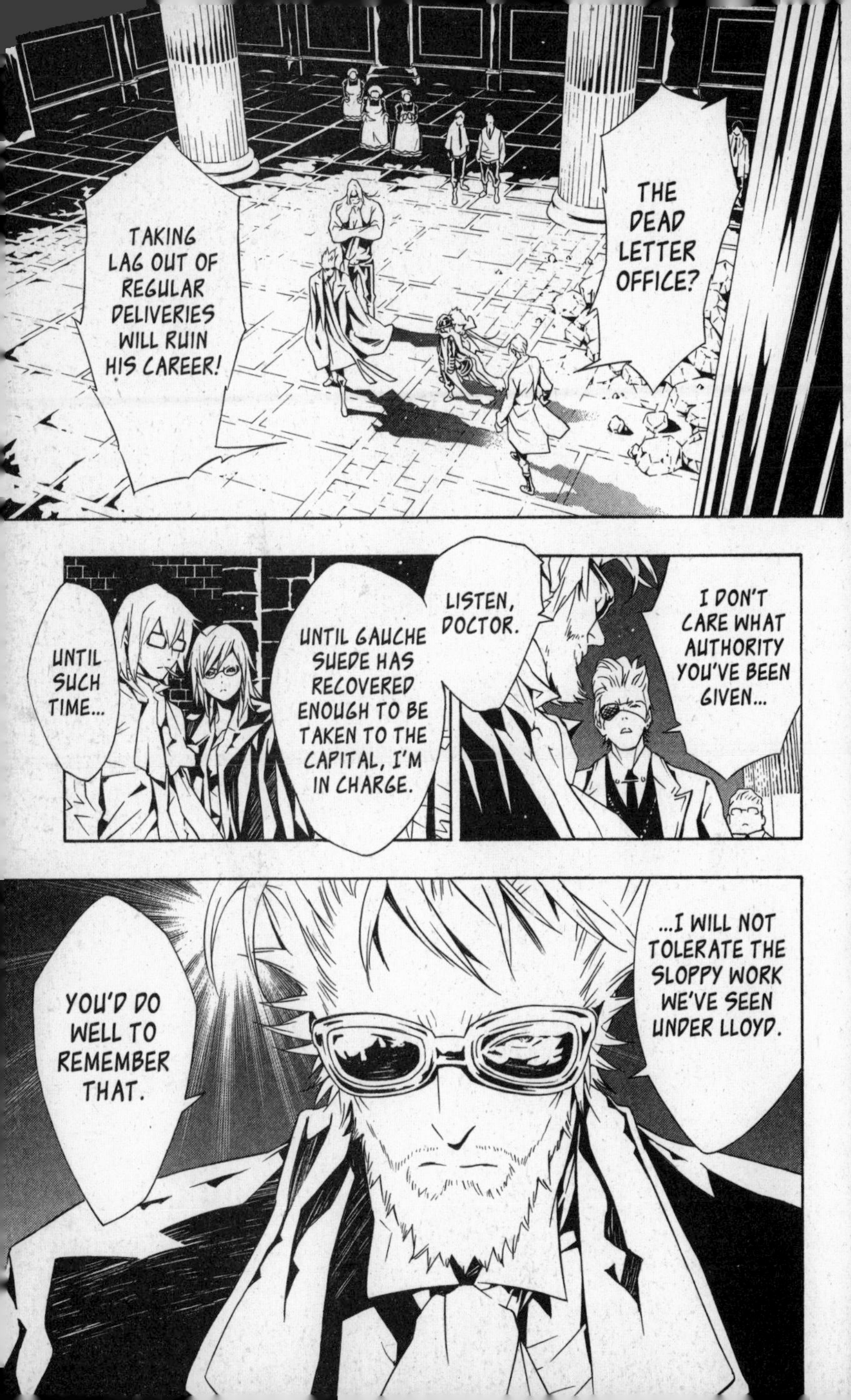
THE DEAD LETTER OFFICE?
TAKING LAG OUT OF REGULAR DELIVERIES WILL RUIN HIS CAREER!
I DON'T CARE WHAT AUTHORITY YOU'VE BEEN GIVEN...
LISTEN, DOCTOR.
UNTIL GAUCHE SUEDE HAS RECOVERED ENOUGH TO BE TAKEN TO THE CAPITAL, I'M IN CHARGE.
UNTIL SUCH TIME...
...I WILL NOT TOLERATE THE SLOPPY WORK WE'VE SEEN UNDER LLOYD.
YOU'D DO WELL TO REMEMBER THAT.

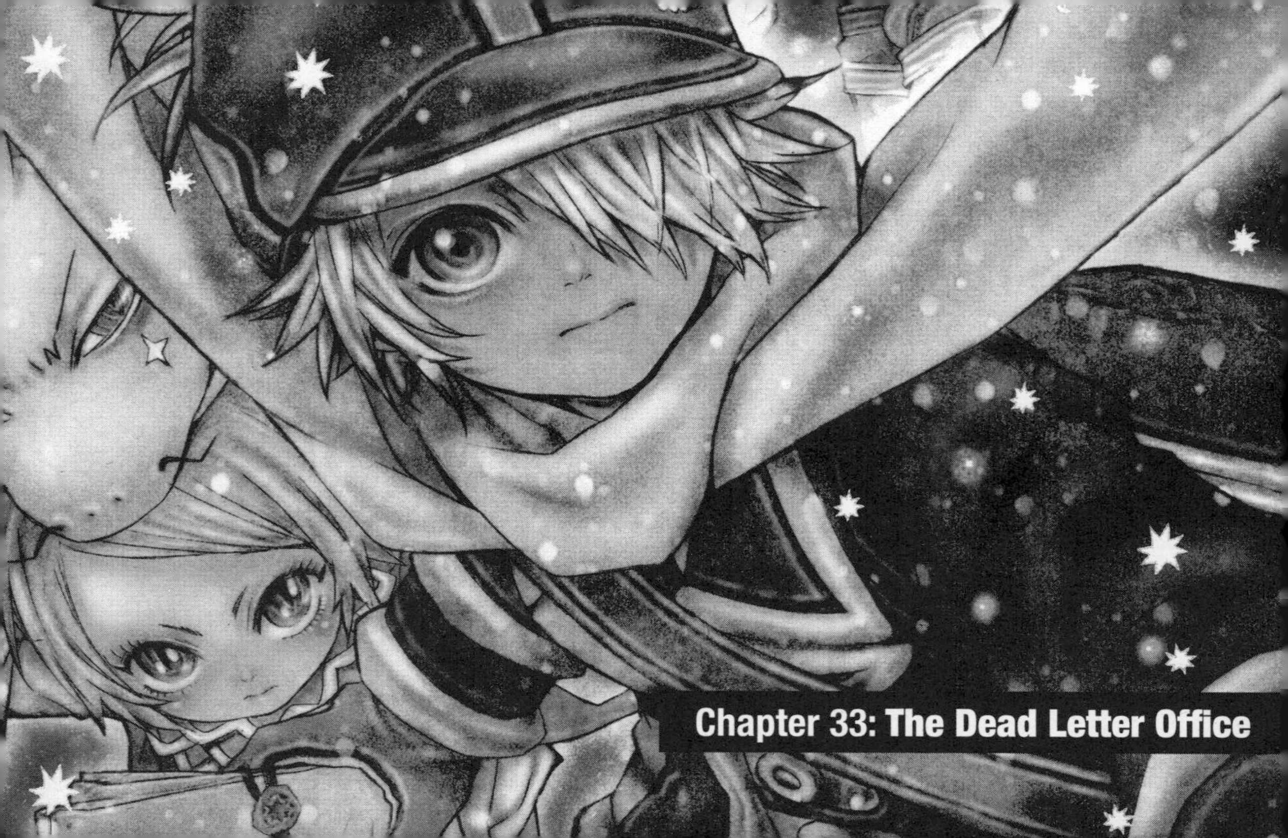
Chapter 33: The Dead Letter Office